Muslims through Discourse

Muslims through Discourse

RELIGION AND RITUAL IN GAYO SOCIETY

John R. Bowen

PRINCETON UNIVERSITY PRESS

PRINCETON, NEW JERSEY

Library of Congress Cataloging-in-Publication Data

Bowen, John Richard, 1951–
Muslims through discourse: religion and ritual
in Gayo Society / John R. Bowen
p. cm.
Contents: Includes bibliographical references and index.
ISBN 0-691-09475-6
ISBN 0-691-02870-2 (pbk.)
1. Gayos (Indonesian people)—Religious life and customs.
2. Islam—Indonesia—Sumatra. 3. Sumatra (Indonesia)—Social life
and customs. I. Title.
BP63.I52S893   1993
297'.09598'1—dc20   92-34217

This book has been composed in Linotron Times Roman

Princeton University Press books are printed on acid-free paper,
and meet the guidelines for permanence and durability of the
Committee on Production Guidelines for Book Longevity of
the Council on Library Resources

Printed in the United States of America

1   3   5   7   9   10   8   6   4   2
(Pbk.)
1   3   5   7   9   10   8   6   4   2

To Pang Gayo

CONTENTS

PART THREE: *Negotiating Public Rituals*

LIST OF ILLUSTRATIONS

ACKNOWLEDGMENTS

THIS BOOK results from the endeavors of my Gayo friends and teachers to instruct me about the Islamic foundations of their lives; much of it, indeed, is but an effort to convey their teachings accurately.

I owe a great deal to several families in Isak, Takèngën, and Jakarta for hospitality, knowledge, and friendship over what is now fifteen years. Most of them appear prominently in this work: Tengku Asaluddin and Ibu Mpun Samsu, Aman and Inën Déwi, Abang and Akan Kerna, Abang and Akan Das, Abang and Akan Gemboyah, and, above all, Abang Evi and his entire family, one of whose children now resides near us in the United States. The Takèngën scholars Tengku Ali Salwany, Tengku Aman Murni, and Tengku Ali Jaidun have on many occasions clarified for me their perceptions of religious issues, as did, in Isak, the late Inën Saidmerah, the late Mpun Bani, Aman and Inën Bani, Abang Jukri, Abang Wahid, Abang Mudë Kursi, and Abang Irmas.

A number of scholarly colleagues have also helped me to formulate the problems addressed here. Steve Caton and David Edwards encouraged me to pursue religion as discourse; Dale Eickelman and Peter Heath, to treat the "periphery" as centrally bearing on questions of Islamic culture. Joe Errington, Barbara Metcalf, and Mary Steedly read the manuscript and gave insightful comments; Martin van Bruinessen and Michael Fischer provided helpful corrections; and at Princeton University Press, Mary Murrell and Carolyn Fox smoothly guided the manuscript through production.

Support for research and writing has come from the National Endowment for the Humanities, the Wenner-Gren Foundation, the Fulbright-Hays program, the Social Science Research Council, the Southeast Asia Council of the Association for Asian Studies, and the Faculty of Arts and Sciences at Washington University. The Lembaga Pengetahuan Ilmiah Indonesia sponsored the original research. Part of Chapter 9 originally appeared in *Man* 27 (1992) and is used here with kind permission of the Royal Anthropological Institute. Material in Chapter 12 first appeared in *American Ethnologist* 19 (1992) and is used here with the editor's permission. Map 1 was drawn by Mary Kennedy; Map 2 is taken from my *Sumatran Politics and Poetics* (1991) by permission of the editors; Map 3 and Diagram 8.1 were drawn by Jimmy Railey.

My wife and children have supported and encouraged me through this project, which has included a trip to the highlands and endless writing thereafter, and, once again, I thank them.

NOTE ON TRANSCRIPTION

IN TRANSCRIBING Gayo speech, I have tried to follow modern Indonesian orthography whenever possible. I use diacritics only to distinguish among mid-central /ë/, mid-high front /é/, and mid-front /è/. The unmarked /e/ indicates a schwa.

I have had to make choices in transcribing Arabic words and their Indonesian or Gayo cognates. Here a choice of transcription carries religious meaning; in Chapter 4, for example, I discuss the range of sounds between the Arabic-sounding /do'ā'/ (prayer; used to emphasize one's own religious purity) and the Gayo-sounding /dowa/ (spell). In most cases, rather than present the reader with two or more spellings for a single term, I have adopted a single standardized spelling for each word. In some instances I use a long vowel marker that fits the Arabic word but that is heard in only some Gayo speech (for example, in the word *hadīth*). In some other cases I have preserved two transcriptions, especially when moving between Gayo and Indonesian texts: for example, *telkin* (Gayo) and *talqīn* (Arabic; Indonesian) for the catechism read to the dead; or *kikah* (Gayo) and *'aqīqa* (Arabic) for the seventh-day naming ritual. See also the Glossary for a list of words found in the text and more information on the method of transcription.

When appropriate (as in the case of spells), I have broken texts into lines in order to highlight their poetic organization; in these texts, a one-space indentation indicates breaks within a line.

PART ONE

A Genealogy of Divergent Understandings

Chapter One

INTRODUCTION

WHEN, in early 1978, I arrived in the Gayo highlands of Sumatra to begin fieldwork, I intended to study social structure and history. I did not plan to investigate local forms of Islam. Although my colleagues working in mainland Southeast Asia had immersed themselves in the study of Theravada Buddhism, and all South Asianists were conversant in matters of caste, those of us engaging in Indonesian studies by and large left the systematic study of Islam out of our curricula. We were looking for local knowledge and for cultural diversity, neither of which would we find, we thought, in a world religion that aimed to regiment society around a universalistic pretense.

I soon learned, however, that Gayo, who had been Muslims since at least the seventeenth century, had developed much of their "local" knowledge about the world by elaborating, transforming, and adapting elements from broader Muslim traditions. They elucidated the powers of place spirits and ancestors using the Muslim idea of sainthood; they explained their abilities to hunt and farm through Muslim narratives about Adam, Eve, and their children; and they explained how healing worked by describing how God, through the prophet Muhammad, had created the universe. Underpinning these specific accounts was a general conception of the relation between the inner, spiritual, world and its outer, material, counterpart—a conception derived from a widespread Sufi Muslim tradition.

But it was not only such mundane activities as farming and healing that engaged Gayo attention. Gayo men and women also fervently argued about how best to carry out basic Islamic rituals. Since the 1930s, a controversy over the details of congregational worship had divided many communities and continued to provoke animated disputes. Perhaps the most energetic debates concerned the reciting of Qur'ānic verses for the benefit of a deceased man or woman. In 1948 a provincial assembly of scholars had tried to settle these quarrels, but they continued, unquelled, thereafter. Gayo also divided on how to sacrifice an animal during the month of pilgrimage or on the occasion of a birth, and what practical effects the sacrifice might have. In short, the elements of Muslim tradition that were most universal were also matters of intense local concern and debate.

On returning from Indonesia, and while writing a dissertation on social structure, I began to look for evidence of similar issues in other Muslim societies in Indonesia and elsewhere. Surely, I thought, the lively debates over prayer, recitation, and sacrifice in the Gayo highlands could hardly be unique to that area, nor was it likely that only the Gayo would have reworked Muslim narratives and speculative writings into exegeses of local, practical activities. Yet I found few treatments of these issues in the anthropological literature on Indonesia.

I first encountered this odd absence of data when writing a study of the *talqīn*, a catechism read to the deceased after burial (Bowen 1984). The appropriateness of the talqīn was a major issue for the Gayo and for other Indonesian Muslims. The disputes, to be discussed at length in Chapter 11, pitted those who thought that reminding the dead of the tenets of their faith spared them from harsh beatings by vengeful angels against those who believed that talking to the dead had no place in religion and distracted people from their duties toward the living.

The controversy implicated the legitimacy of all communication with ancestral spirits and had been widely discussed for decades in Indonesian periodicals and books. Yet no archipelagic ethnographies took up these disputes, and but a few even mentioned the practice. This omission was doubly surprising, as death ritual was of such central importance to Indonesians and had been a favorite topic for anthropological research in the region, from Hertz's (1960) seminal essay to such fine recent ethnographies (on non-Muslim peoples) as Metcalf's (1982) study of the Berawan, and Volkman's (1985) of the Toraja. It appeared that anthropologists and other scholars working in Indonesia steered away from such otherwise analytically central rituals when they were performed by Muslims.[1]

Indeed, until recently scholars studying Muslim societies and cultures throughout Asia and the Middle East followed two largely separate paths, depending on whether they were primarily interested in local culture or in religious texts. Scholars concerned with local forms of culture looked for what was quintessentially characteristic of a particular people or region—the rites, myths, or ideas that made them distinctive, rather than those they shared with other Muslims. This research strategy was in keeping with anthropology's general project of illuminating the diverse particulars of cultural life, and, specifically, of treating religion as a local cultural system (Geertz 1966). For North Africa, for example, a particularly brilliant suc-

---

[1] The talqīn is mentioned in Clifford Geertz's *Religion of Java* (1960:71), a work whose scope makes it of enduring value. Geertz's article on the funeral and social change (1959) concerns not the debates over Islamic ritual form, but the difficulties of reconciling rural solidarities (and Islamic ritual patterns) with new political ideologies. Detailed descriptions of the talqīn can be found in older accounts of other Muslim societies, such as Lane on Egypt (1860), Snouck Hurgronje on Mecca (1931), and Westermark on Morocco (1926); these descriptions do not, however, encompass local ideas and debates about these and other ritual practices.

cession of studies appeared in the 1970s. In these works ethnographers illuminated the ideas of divine grace, personal obligation, and the marabout that animated Sufi lodges, courtroom practice, and market exchange (Eickelman 1976; Geertz, Geertz, and Rosen 1979; Gilsenan 1973).

Particular cultures, thus clarified, could then be juxtaposed to show the variability and mutability of religious ideas across the Muslim world, as in Clifford Geertz's (1968) comparison of the very different forms taken by Islamic mysticism in Java and Morocco. In these studies the features of cultural life that distinguished between cultures and regions were placed in the forefront; the features of religious life that were more broadly distributed across Muslim societies remained in the background.[2] Rituals of regular worship, acts of prayer or sacrifice, or vernacular texts on law or history were by and large left to those specialists interested in the high culture, or "great tradition," of Islam.[3]

But if anthropologists by and large focused on the locally distinctive at the expense of the religiously shared, Islamicists focused on texts and their interpretation at the expense of everyday religious understandings and practices. The major topics and questions within the field of Islamic studies or Orientalism—the pre-Islamic sources of Islamic ideas, the development of scriptural sciences, the nature of Islamic jurisprudence—concerned above all how to properly understand the major texts of the religious tradition: the Qur'ān, the hadīth (reports of the prophet Muhammad's words and deeds), and the commentaries on each. The approach was generally critical and philological—where did the text, its terms, and its ideas come from?—rather than ethnographic and semiotic—how did (and do) people understand, debate, and apply the text?[4] It also presumed that there was a conceptual and normative core to Islam (containing, of course, several schools and positions) that, adequately understood, could stand for the religion as a whole.

---

[2] On the neglect of everyday Islamic ritual in earlier work see Antoun (1976:163), Eickelman (1989a:258), and el-Zein (1977). James Siegel's study of religious change in Aceh (1969) is a notable exception.

[3] The contrast of a "little tradition" of village folk-culture and a "great tradition" of elite urban-culture was developed by Robert Redfield (1956), although it has roots in Max Weber's work and in the general post-Romantic anthropological preference for the particularistic over the world-civilizational (see Stocking 1989). For reflections on how Redfield's framework opened up world civilizations to anthropology, and how it may have limited the extent of that opening, see, on Hinduism, Singer (1964); on Christianity, Brandes (1989); on Islam, Antoun (1989) and Eickelman (1982).

[4] For reassessments of this tradition from the standpoint of the history of religions see the essays in Martin (1985). Andrew Rippin (1988) draws on reader-response literary theory in his sophisticated critique of older tafsīr scholarship; his analysis joins William Cantwell Smith's plea for understanding how scripture becomes meaningful to the faithful rather than what it means as a system of ideas (1963).

More recent work in Islamic studies has transformed the field. Scholars working from the perspective of comparative religious studies have brought a sophisticated hermeneutics to bear on their scriptural interpretation; many have also carried out fieldwork and therefore appreciate the diversity of everyday Muslim lives.[5] Yet even the best of this work retains a focus on a core, normative, Islamic tradition. The discourse of comparative religious studies assumes that one may compare sets of shared ideas, images, and norms taken from each of several religious systems. It thus places in the background precisely what anthropology highlights: the processes by which Islamic ideas and practices have taken on locally specified social and cultural meanings.[6] Let us return to the example of funerals: Anthropologists have tended to analyze funerals as texts about a local culture, and thus generally slight Islamic funerals for their apparent derivation from nonlocal texts. By contrast, religious scholars have tended to investigate the general features of Muslim conceptions of, or practices surrounding, death, and thus generally neglect the local diversity of ideas and practices.[7]

The idea of an Islamic core has lent a normative and cultural priority to the Middle East vis-à-vis the rest of Muslim world.[8] Thus Marshall Hodgson's influential concept of "Islamicate culture" (1974) includes features of Arabic and Persian societies, such as architecture, calligraphy, and the caliphate, but not the cultural products of Islamic West Africa or Malaysia (see Burke 1979; Eickelman 1982). From this perspective history runs outward from the Middle East. The very coherence of a recent history of Islamic societies (Lapidus 1988), for example, is based on the notion that a Middle Eastern paradigm of social, religious, and state institutions was "transferred" to all Islamic societies (1988:xxi) and that all such societies are today "based upon the constellation of lineage, tribal, religious, and political institutions first evident in the ancient cities of Mesopotamia in the third millenium B.C." (1988:879), a notion that becomes exceedingly shopworn by the time the author reaches the societies of modern Southeast Asia.

Perhaps a lingering awe at the textual expertise of Islamicists drives some anthropologists to continue citing general accounts or normative texts

---

[5] See the articles in Martin (1985) and in Rippin, ed. (1988), and the comparative work on oral aspects of scripture by William Graham (1987). Frederick Denny's study of Qur'ān recitation (1988) is based on Islamicist training and fieldwork in Indonesia.

[6] See in this regard the critique of Graham's analysis of the ritual core of Islam (1983) by the anthropologists Tapper and Tapper (1987), who in their own analysis concentrate entirely on local meanings and practice.

[7] See, for example, Denny's description of a set of prescribed, universally accepted practices (1985b:314–21), or Smith and Haddad's (1981) exposition of Muslim scholars' views on death and the afterlife.

[8] One must immediately note the exception of Annemarie Schimmel, whose work has highlighted the Islamic religious and cultural forms of South Asia (1975, 1985).

as authoritative statements on what Islam essentially is, deterring them from investigating the diverse religious ideas of the people with whom they work. Such has been particularly the case in studies of gender in Islam, where at least two recent writers (Combs-Schilling 1989; Delaney 1991:283–91) have assumed an inevitable, timeless, and uncontested alliance between monotheism and patriarchy, despite recent studies of the diversity of gender ideas in Islamic scripture, history, and contemporary Muslim lives (Boddy 1989; Malti-Douglas 1991; Mernissi 1991; Tapper and Tapper 1987).

A more recent generation of scholars, working in several disciplines and usually across disciplinary lines, have challenged this older de facto distinction of local practices and normative texts. Indeed, their work has focused precisely on the dynamic tension between local ideas and processes on the one hand, and "the transcendental prescriptions as understood by those involved" (Roff 1987:47) on the other. The central tenet of this recent work has been that the tension between local and universal is itself a central part of many Muslims' lives. On the one hand, Muslims who claim to be creating a purely Islamic, supralocal social world are doing so through the media of historically specific languages, idioms, and institutions.[9] On the other hand, elaborations of "local" perspectives within a historically Muslim environment inevitably draw on broader Muslim traditions to create their own culture of autonomy.[10] One treats Muslim tradition as distinct local "islams" only at the risk of overlooking both the historic connections across different Muslim societies and many Muslims' strong sense of an external, normative reference point for their ideas and practices (see Asad 1986; Boddy 1989; Eickelman 1989a:261–62; Fischer and Abedi 1990).

The point of departure for many of these historians, anthropologists, and textual scholars has been the social life of religious discourse: how written texts and oral traditions are produced, read, and reread. Their efforts have begun to close the gap between the decontextualized reading of normative texts on the one hand, and an ethnographic approach that paid little attention to the social life of texts on the other. The newer discourse-centered approach has been particularly important in analyzing modern Islamic processes of cultural reproduction. In studying Islamic law, scholars have ex-

---

[9] On the importance of this point for understanding Islamic social movements see the study on Egypt by Gilles Kepel (1985); Barbara Metcalf's history of the Deobandi movement in India (1982); Gladney's analysis of successive "tides" of Islam in China (1991); and the essays in Burke and Lapidus (1988). The general point was made repeatedly by Max Weber, of course, and is just as valid for other world-religions.

[10] As has been demonstrated by many studies of Islam on Java, for example, from Clifford Geertz's early work (1960) to more recent ethnographies by Robert Hefner (1985) and Mark Woodward (1989).

amined how scriptural traditions have been interpreted and conveyed in various court settings (Messick 1986; Rosen 1988); in studying village life, they have analyzed how sermons and lessons delivered at Friday worship have been carefully directed at critical social issues (Antoun 1989; Gaffney 1987); in studying theological writings, they have looked at the processes of translation, interpretation, and transformation of texts across societal boundaries (Eickelman 1989; Fischer and Abedi 1990; Metcalf 1990).

Some of this work has exploded the confines of "the religious": one recent study (Fischer and Abedi 1990) explores posters, videocassettes, schools, pilgrimages, and mosque worship on three continents.[11] Most recent work has, however, regarded the institutions that produce religious discourse in the strict sense—the religious court, the mosque, or the religious school. The great success of these studies has been in tracing the first-stage processes of scriptural interpretation by religious "culture brokers." In these settings, questions of the nature and limits of religion itself come less to the fore than do issues of how to move between sacred texts and a variety of practical legal, moral, and social applications.[12]

The Gayo case, as examined here, presents a somewhat different analytical problem. I set out to examine how the Gayo, a largely agrarian people, couch a wide variety of practices, from healing and rice ritual to sacrifice and prayer, in Islamic terms. I also analyze the changing conditions of discussion and reflection on those practices, conditions that include the rise of religious reformism and the formation of a public sphere of religious discourse. This approach highlights the development of controversies over just what Islam is or ought to be, and the diverging responses Gayo have made to these issues. My focus is on the field of debate and discussion in which participants construct discursive linkages to texts, phrases, and ideas held to be part of the universal tradition of Islam. I am interested less in the overall cultural style (Geertz 1968) than I am in the *dīn* (religion) that emerges from the arguments.[13]

I use the term *discourse* in full recognition of its range of meanings in recent anthropology, from the microlevel production of texts (Urban 1991) to the social and political meanings of performances (Brenneis and Myers 1984), and including the Foucauldian sense of a large-scale discursive field

---

[11] Of course, this "explosion" is indebted to the foundational works by Clifford Geertz on religious culture (1960, 1966, 1968).

[12] A different approach, still within the boundaries of religion in the narrow sense, is taken by Loeffler in his study (1988) of the variety of opinions in an Iranian village on questions of salvation, suffering, and fate.

[13] The pun is lifted from Roff (1988:41). Similar emphases on Muslim debate and discourse are to be found in Asad (1986), Eickelman (1989b), Fischer and Abedi (1990), Gilsenan (1982), Mardin (1989), and, among writers in the French ethnological tradition, Berque (1980).

(Foucault 1972; see Mardin 1989). Common to all these uses is an emphasis on social pragmatics. By highlighting discourse I wish to draw on this entire web of meanings and to emphasize three features of Gayo religion and ritual (a phrase I use loosely to designate a topic for study, not a culturally closed field). These features are the centrality of speech events; the cultural importance of commentary on those events; and the heterogeneous, "dispersive" quality (Foucault 1972) of religious discourse.

Gayo religion and ritual is highly *discursive*, in the everyday sense of that term, in that it consists in large part of a set of speech events in which men and women communicate with God, spirits, and, at least indirectly, each other. To underscore speech is not to diminish the importance of bodily movements and mental activity. Anthropologists from Mauss (1950) to Bourdieu (1977) have explored how people learn bodily orientations that then become deeply ingrained ways of acting, and such is the case for the postures of worship discussed in Chapter 13. Yet in their own accounts of religious practice Gayo emphasize language as the critical element that defines an event as, for instance, worship, recitation, or sacrifice. In this respect they share a general Muslim emphasis on the mastery of sacred language (Fischer and Abedi 1990; Graham 1987) and also an Indonesia-wide emphasis on ritual speaking and (oral and written) narratives (Kuipers 1990; Sweeney 1987).

These speech events are also discursive practices, and the approach taken here draws on the long line of anthropologists studying "practical religion," from Malinowski (1935) and Evans-Pritchard (1937) to Tambiah (1970), and including those Islamic specialists whose focus is the nexus of texts, interests, and social action (Eickelman 1989b; Fischer and Abedi 1990; Gladney 1991; Lambek 1990; Metcalf 1990). The challenge to older Islamicist research lies here, in asserting that texts are to be studied in their living contexts and not as abstracted windows into belief or as essential statements of religious truth. Studying religion through discursive practices does not deny the importance of semantic and experiential qualities of religion (Geertz 1968:90–117), but it looks for those qualities in specific events of speaking, commenting, and reflecting, rather than in the general qualities of symbols and meanings. In this respect the present volume expands on a theme developed in an earlier study (Bowen 1991) of the history of Gayo public cultural forms.

The debate that opens the next chapter illustrates how Gayo move back and forth across distinct levels of discourse: speech, commentary on speech, and arguments about when commentary is appropriate. These evaluative commentaries are part of religious life, not outside it (see Geertz 1973:170–89). Gayo transmit much of their cultural knowledge in the form of commentary on specific speech events. Historical narratives about place spirits, prophets, or the creation of the cosmos may be told as exegeses of spells or prayers. Speculations about the divine, about the powers of angels, or about the efficacy of healing often occur in situations of practical, didactic immediacy.

The social reproduction of Gayo Muslim knowledge is thus embedded in the practice of *commentary* or exegesis. Here I find apposite Talal Asad's conception of Islam as a "discursive tradition that includes and relates itself to the founding texts of the Qur'an and the Hadith" (1986:14). Asad usefully distinguishes between "theological discourse," discourse about religion, and "liturgical utterances," the ways of speaking employed in praying, sacrificing, or preaching (1983:243). For Asad, if the latter induces religious dispositions in the worshiper, the former attempts to place those dispositions in an encompassing, intelligible framework. It is theological discourse that construes diverse speech events as Islamic by linking them to the broader Muslim traditions.

This distinction allows us to recognize that events that do not establish distinctly religious "moods and motivations" (Geertz 1966:8) may nonetheless be construed in a religious framework and thus become the objects of theological discourse. The Gayo man who utters an invulnerability spell is not creating a religious disposition, but is preparing to fight someone. However, he (or someone else) will explain how such a spell works by invoking the ontological and historical connections between humans, God, and the iron contained in bullets or daggers, and this exegesis makes the spell part of a religious-and-ritual domain for him (though not for all others).

Social actors thus constitute domains of religion when, by engaging in theological discourse, commentary, and exegesis, they link local events to authoritative Islamic texts. For Gayo (and many other) Muslims these texts are not limited to the Qur'ān and hadīth. I shall, therefore, modify Asad's definition to include, as part of the discursive tradition, linkages drawn to such other foundations of Islamic knowledge as oral traditions of prophetic history and systems of cosmological speculation.

Finally, Gayo discourses are *dispersive* in that they cannot be resolved into a single set of symbols or ideas. The divergent ways of talking about religion in the highlands are structured by specific social histories (of education, politics, economics, and scholarship). The analytical category of discourse obviates the need to resolve this diversity into a univocal ethnographic reality where "Nuer say" or "Balinese believe."[14]

The heterogeneity of discourse is most prominently developed as a theme in Michel Foucault's archaeology of knowledge. I take from Foucault's

---

[14] It also differs from the notion of a single religious field made up of complementary ritual complexes, an idea that has been attractive to anthropologists working in Buddhist societies (Holmberg 1989; Ortner 1978; Tambiah 1970:337–50). This contrast in analytical styles suggests that comparative studies of religions and societies may need to adopt analytical frameworks explicitly oriented toward local modes of integration and dispersal.

writings the insight that what may appear to be the unifying categories of a discursive field—categories such as "madness" or "biology" (1972:40–49), or, in this study, "religion"—in fact receive divergent interpretations and thus determine "spaces of dissension" (1972:152). From this perspective there is no unifying schema or field that synoptically captures divergent discourses—no visually unifying chart such as that into which Bourdieu (1977:157) resolves different practices, no encompassing division into great and little traditions.

The title *Muslims through Discourse* is thus intended to resonate multiply: to underscore the discursive texture of Gayo religious practice, commentary, and debate, as well as the constituting process by which Gayo have constructed and reconstructed religious discourses.

The organization of the book reflects my attempts to tack among the intermingled, diverse socioreligious perspectives I found in the highlands. Part 1 is about the development of divergent ideas and practices; a genealogy of the dispersive character of highlands religious discourse. Chapter 2 opens with an argument between two Gayo men about religious practices, in which general concerns about propriety, knowledge, and authority revolve around certain specific speech events. I then discuss the linkages between these speech events and broader divergences in the local political economy of meaning, among them how farming, trade, and politics have motivated positions taken on what *appear* to be more narrowly religious issues.

Chapter 3 places the discourse of Gayo scholars in a local historical context. This contextualizing is not neutral with respect to local disputes, however. In presenting the history of twentieth-century ideas and institutions as background for the remaining chapters, I am employing a narrative form that is most characteristic of Gayo who hold normative and scholarly views of Islam. Gayo scholars tend to view history in terms of recent progress in education, literacy, and social reform. Other Gayo have quite different historical perspectives. Healers or rice ritual specialists, for example, explain what they do in terms of initial events of cosmic creation that gave all humans access to divine powers. For them, the essential historical background is not the recent development of religious learning but the ancient creation of the world.

Part 1 thus tilts the book toward scholarly perspectives on religion, and Part 2 reverses the tilt by starting from the practical powers of speech. Part 2 is grounded in village activities and only secondarily considers their possible scholarly antecedents or reflexes. I focus on ritual practitioners in the multivillage community of Isak, where I had the longest residence in the highlands. Thus in Chapters 4–9 I analyze a particular model for ritual and religious activities in Isak, one centered on communications and transactions between humans and powerful spiritual agents.

In worship, spells, ritual meals, and sacrifice, Gayo men and women are principally engaged in speaking and exchanging with various kinds of spirits in order to improve human health and welfare. In Chapter 4 I examine diverse discourses about the power of speech, and in Chapter 5 I explore Gayo exegeses of powerful speech events. In particular, I consider the ideas of world creation that inform Gayo ritual practitioners and that resonate with Sufi writings in the archipelago and elsewhere. Chapters 6 and 7 then examine how Gayo have elaborated those ideas into practices of healing. Gayo healers exhort and sometimes exorcise spirits that have been sent by other humans. The Gayo discourse of sorcery and retribution allows healers to do combat with each other without "going public." They are thus able to come to grips with deep-seated fears and angers in a society whose public life is relatively egalitarian, inhibits everyday open conflict, and is informed by a shame-driven sense of the self.

Chapters 8 and 9 turn from healing to agriculture. I begin with the public and private discursive practices involved in rice farming, and then present Gayo exegeses of human relations with the productive world of farming and hunting. Gayo have drawn on Muslim oral traditions about the earliest humans (Adam, Eve, Cain, and Abel) to explain how people can derive nourishment from grain and enjoy success in the hunt.

Isak ideas and practices are not isolated from reform-minded developments elsewhere, and challenges by modernist Muslim scholars in the 1980s led Isak ritual practitioners to reconsider, and sometimes reshape, their activities. The modernist emphasis on conforming to the historical example provided by the prophet Muhammad often runs counter to the Isak focus on achieving practical ends through speaking with spirits. The ensuing challenges, debates, and ritual reformulations are most salient and public with respect to events that all Gayo Muslims see as part of a shared religious repertoire: observing Islamic holidays, burying the dead, worshiping God.

Part 3 traces the tension between two models of religious and ritual practice with respect to that repertoire: one model highlights communication and exchange; the other stresses the importance of conforming to scripture-based norms. Chapter 10 concerns the ritual meals (*kenduri*) that provide both a social location and a cultural model for a wide range of observances and activities. I consider divergent interpretations of two rituals: the name-giving ritual for the infant and the celebration of the Prophet's birthday. In Chapter 11, on death, I examine the moral and emotional import of speaking to the dead and reciting verses for their welfare, as well as modernists' objections to these practices.

Chapters 12 and 13 make more visible the texture of religious and ritual life in the main highlands town of Takèngën, where public rituals approximate modernists' views on how they should be performed. Chapter 12 treats the Feast of Sacrifice in village and town settings; Chapter 13, the ritual of worship and the range of personal and political meanings attached to it. I mention only briefly other activities and institutions that are important in town life, including disputes over inheritance and divorce settlements that involve informal and formal adjudication (Bowen 1988); religious schools; and popular religious media, from Qur'ān study groups to religious poetry.

In the final chapter I expand on two themes explored through the course of the book. One concerns the divergent ideas about language and truth that are associated with different religious and ritual practices. Older views regard speech as a token in a scheme of transactions, attributing to it a certain degree of objective efficacy regardless of actors' intentions. Some Muslim scholars have developed this view into a theory of the opacity of forms to intent. Modernists, by contrast, underscore the transparent view provided by scriptural language of an original intent. Representation, rather than efficacy, is their linguistic norm.

The second theme regards the creation of a public sphere of Islam in the colonial period and its subsequent relation to the Indonesian state. This theme has parallels elsewhere, especially in South Asia (Freitag 1988; Metcalf 1982) and Malaysia (Roff 1967). Debates over issues of language and piety generated a new field of religion defined by scriptural scholarship. Although Dutch colonial policy contributed to the emergence of new forms of socioreligious order, the major historical impetus for the development of a public Islamic sphere came from religious and nationalist movements. The new definition of religion excluded many older practices, and efforts to eliminate these practices, only partially successful, have led ritual practitioners to reposition them in more private settings. Some Gayo have maintained older forms in large part by concealing their more objectionable elements and avoiding explicit, public exegesis. Mid-twentieth-century Gayo religious life thus depends on certain critical moves away from the limelight, toward more "offstage" venues (Scott 1990).

The forms of religion and ritual in Gayo villages grew out of a particular history of political developments and religious adaptations. The Gayo highlands lie in the central portions of Aceh province at the tip of Sumatra (see Map 1.1). Northern Gayoland, the region around Lake Tawar and the Isak region just to the south, had about 180,000 people in 1987, most of them living in the vicinity of Takèngën. Before the Dutch conquest of the area in 1904 and the development of a town society in the 1920s, however, virtually all Gayo lived in small villages of thirty to sixty households each. Most villages consisted of two or more kin-based groupings. Each

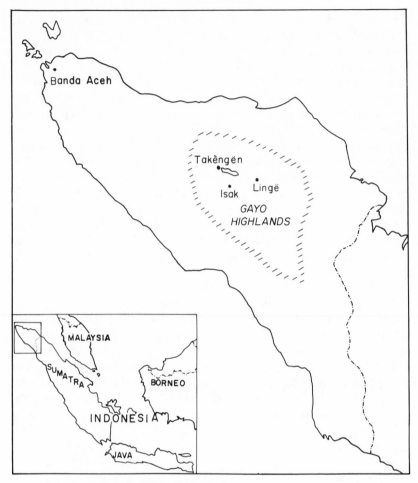

1.1 Aceh Province Showing the Gayo Highlands

was headed by a ruler, the *rëjë*, and had its own religious official, the *imëm*.

Precolonial Gayo villages were scattered across the four plateau regions created by the meandering Bukit Barisan mountain range. Each region developed its own ties to a distinct coastal area and its own set of distinctive speech patterns, cultural styles, and variations on Gayo social organization. Within each region there emerged multiple centers of power. Around 1900, six rulers claimed the status of domain lord (*kejurun*). Four of these domain lords controlled areas of northern Gayoland: Rëjë Lingë in the Isak district, and Rëjë Bukit, Syiah Utama, and Rëjë Ciq Bëbësën in the Lake district.

(The two remaining lords ruled in the eastern and southern parts of the highlands.) The actual power of the domain lord varied greatly from one district to the next and over time, but everywhere it was quite limited: he had no retinue, no army, no court. Other communities and rulers routinely challenged any claims to authority he might make. The five-village community of Isak, for example, considered itself free of the Lingë lord's direct control. Isak itself was split between two political blocs, each of which claimed preeminence (Bowen 1991:30–59).

Most disputes between Gayo villages were resolved by formal speech exchanges between rulers or their spokesmen. If that process proved unsatisfactory, the parties might seek arbitration from the domain lord or proceed to a relatively measured form of warfare. But in most cases villages settled disputes among themselves based on elaborate codes of conduct embodied in short, authoritative maxims (Bowen 1991:139–68). The relatively egalitarian political texture was complemented by a stress on the value of bilateral kinship ties and on self-restraint and shame. The category of shame, *kemèl*, is still cited by Gayo men and women in villages and towns as the norm that keeps social life orderly and enjoyable and prevents arguments from exploding publicly.

Although there is little written material available about Gayo history before about 1870, the Gayo probably were incorporated into the kingdom of Aceh in the seventeenth century and were converted to Islam as part of that political incorporation (Bowen 1991:15–16). Gayo accounts of the process of Islamization also place it in the distant past, often ascribing the coming of Islam to the highlands to historical figures from the seventeenth century.

The Gayo were gradually drawn into the Aceh-Dutch war after the outbreak of fighting in 1873. A series of Dutch expeditions culminated in the massacre of the residents of several villages in 1904. Colonial rule increased the authority of the domain lords, giving them powers of taxation and punishment, and creating a hierarchical administration in each district (Bowen 1991:68–92). These changes profoundly affected social and religious life in the highlands. In Isak, the domain lord for the region, the Kejurun Lingë, moved from his base in Lingë to Isak and, supported by the Dutch, began to assert newfound authority in everyday affairs, including religious affairs. The resentments generated by these new claims to authority gave religious modernism a highly political, anticolonial cast. In Takèngën, nationalists and religious modernists worked together in building new, covertly anticolonial schools; in promoting modern, Indonesia-wide forms of dress, language, literature, and music; and in opposing the increasingly authoritarian pretenses of the domain lords (Bowen 1991:93–102).

After independence in 1945, a coalition of nationalists and pro-Republic religious leaders governed the highlands (Bowen 1991:106–14). This coalition was sundered when, in 1953, a provincewide rebellion broke out. Under the rubric Darul Islam (Ar. Dar al-Islam, the Abode of Islam), the rebellion lasted until 1962 and deepened the cleavage between those who saw Islam as their primary loyalty and those who argued that the Republic had to avoid any trappings of a theocracy. The massacres of 1965–1966, and the efforts by the New Order government thereafter to domesticate the religious parties, have muted dissent but not repaired the rifts (Bowen 1991:119–22).

I have carried out research in the highlands, using the Gayo language, since 1978. From March 1978 to March 1980, I lived in Isak and frequently visited friends in Takèngën. I then spent an additional three months in Takèngën and elsewhere in the highlands. From July 1980 to May 1982 I continued to live in Indonesia, engaged in other research but associating frequently with Gayo friends in Takèngën and in the cities of Banda Aceh, Medan, and Jakarta. I returned to the highlands in 1983, 1985, and 1989, for a total of about six additional months.

Although I have had extensive discussions with both men and women on religious (and many other) topics, the most detailed treatments in this volume are based on talks with men. This gender bias has at least two sources. One regards my fieldwork. I was free to discuss a wide range of topics with women, especially older women, some of whom became close friends (and whose knowledge about birth, initiation rituals, and rice farming is indicated here), but I could not spend long evenings talking about esoteric topics with individual women as I could and did with male friends. The second regards the gendered quality of public religious discourse. Specialized knowledge of religion in the narrow sense, and especially public discourse using that knowledge, was more the province of men than of women. Many women become religious teachers—and in a study of religious schooling their activities would be central—but on doctrinal matters, few women in Isak or Takèngën were publicly involved.

This study also makes rather little use of archival material. Although I have engaged in archival and historical research on the highlands, colonial-era materials are fairly uninformative on highlands religion and ritual. In an earlier work (Bowen 1991) concerned with the history of political and poetic forms, I was able to draw on the rich collection of materials assembled by C. Snouck Hurgronje, the Islamicist and advisor to the Netherlands government on East Indies religious affairs. Snouck Hurgronje's immediate concern was to describe Gayo society and politics prefatory to a likely invasion. He never entered the highlands, working instead with informants who, despite their religious knowledge, may not have had the desire or the capacity to delve too deeply into esoteric matters. In the end, despite Snouck Hurgronje's interest in things Islamic (which he tended to see through a Middle Eastern, normative lens), he provides only brief accounts of Gayo religious affairs. (For the lowlands Acehnese, by contrast, he saw Islam as an element of the resistance to Dutch rule and gave it extensive treatment [Snouck Hurgronje 1906].) My understandings of developments in religious knowledge earlier in this century are thus largely based on conversations with older Gayo men and women.

Chapter Two

RELIGIOUS DISPUTES IN TAKÈNGËN

ALIMIN, ASYIN, AND I had been working away for several hours on a July day in 1989. Seated at Alimin's small tailor kiosk in a residential part of the highlands town of Takèngën, we were trying to read and interpret a book of Gayo-language poetry written in Arabic script and published in Cairo in 1938. Alimin's father had composed many of the poems, and Asyin had sung some of them. The poets admonished their listeners to change their religious ways in accord with modernist teachings, a project with which Alimin, a quiet, intense man in his late forties, whole-heartedly concurred.[1]

"These poems were *da'wa* [call, missionary work]," declared Alimin, jabbing at the page we had just completed. "The people who wrote them knew where they stood; they were not afraid to be forthright. You didn't find them approving of *tahlīl* [mortuary recitations] or *telkin* [< Ar. talqīn, a catechism read to the deceased after burial]." Alimin, along with many other modernists, held that all efforts to benefit the dead through recitations, catechisms, or ritual meals deny the finality of death and the autonomous judgment of God. His comment was a sharp dig at Asyin, whose own compositions were designed as entertainment, definitely not as da'wa. In a poem that he had sung publicly several days before our discussion, Asyin urges people to "say prayers, *tasbīh* [praises to God] or telkin, according to your own convictions." Alimin felt that, by tolerating these improper practices, Asyin was promoting them.

Asyin, in his late sixties but with the impetuosity many singers carry well into their seventies, rose right to the bait. He began to speak quickly, waving his hands up and down in excitement. "Religion should bring people together; there is no room for fighting in religion. We should rise above conflicts. Take the *bismillāh* ["in the name of God," a phrase, sometimes referred to as the *basmala*, uttered in worship, scriptural recitation, and before such mundane activities as eating or leaving the house]. At the main mosque, now, sometimes it is recited aloud [following the modernist preference] and sometimes silently [following the older practice], and people follow the worship leader whatever he does."

"Ah," responded Alimin quickly, "but that is an optional [*sunna*] matter,

---

[1] I recorded the following conversation in my notebook as it took place, then wrote it out in detail very soon thereafter.

and it really does not matter which you do. It is different with matters of principle. There you have to think the matter out for yourself; you use reason rather than following earlier teachings [taqlīd]. *Taqlīd* means: 'whatever father did, I'll just follow.' That is forbidden in religion. The [issue of the] catechism is just such a matter of principle. In 1948 there was a meeting of religious scholars from throughout Aceh; they issued a resolution that forbade the catechism, staging meals for the dead, and other practices."

"But," countered Asyin, "that resolution also said that such disputed matters [*khilafiyah*] must never be raised again, and that whoever does so is working against religion." "No; you're dead wrong," retorted Alimin. Each then told the other several times to be quiet and listen, after which Alimin regained the floor. "The resolution only said that such matters should not be brought up in Friday sermons. It is fine to discuss them in schools or study sessions or with friends. Once you have explained to people what the proof of a point is in the Qur'ān and hadīth, then however they choose is all right." "Yes; that's the point," retorted Asyin: "*'lakum dīnukum waliyadīn'* ["to you your religion (dīn) and to me my religion" (Qur'ān 109:6)]. You let people choose."

"But only after they have been told what really is in the Qur'ān and hadīth," Alimin answered. "And those who are willing to listen, whose hearts are open, they change their ways. But there are others who refuse to change. They say that a practice has become part of local norms [*ëdët*], even when you show them that there are more scriptural proofs for changing—twelve against six, for example. It is clear in such cases: you should choose the [position backed by the] twelve."

"It is not just a claim about ëdët," said Asyin. "They have their own proofs too, and they say that it is twelve to six for them. For the catechism there is a reliable report [*hadīth sahīh*] that the prophet said you should 'teach a person from the cradle to the grave.' So people recite the words of the call to prayer into their newborn child's ear, and they say the catechism to the dead, even though neither infant nor corpse understands." Alimin clearly thought such behavior ridiculous, but he had calmed somewhat and answered: "This hadīth has to be further interpreted [*itafsīri*]. It has become just a saying. It cannot be taken at face value, because it just does not make sense to teach an infant or a corpse. You have to reason for yourself, not just follow others."

Alimin and Asyin continued their debate until a customer arrived to pick up his pants, but they had argued before and would again. Like Muslims elsewhere, Gayo are continually negotiating among themselves about how to properly understand scripture vis-à-vis local religious practices. Do the Qur'ān and the hadīth reveal a single, unique religious norm to be discerned by counting the proofs offered by either side ("twelve against six"),

as Alimin so fervently argued? Or does Islam encompass variant, equally legitimate forms of religious practice, as Asyin declared? Is scripture to be
taken at face value, or judged according to common sense? Are the interpretations held by knowledgeable scholars of the past to be given special
weight? The disputes are often about religious speech: speaking aloud the
bismillāh, "teaching the dead" through the telkin, elaborating on scripture
through poetry. Even the acceptability of *talking* about these issues of reli-
gion-charged speech is at issue: Should individuals dispute these matters, or
should specialists resolve them once and for all?

Sumatrans (and other Muslims) have debated these and other questions
for centuries. Early conversions of Sumatrans to Islam were the result not
of conquest, but of the activities of Muslim teachers, probably including
Sufi missionaries (Johns 1961, 1984). Conversion of local rulers most
likely began in the late thirteenth century. When Marco Polo visited several
states on the north coast of Aceh in 1292, only one ruler had converted to
Islam. The other coastal rulers professed allegiance to "the Great Khan,"
while the people in the mountains were said to "live like beasts" (Polo
1958:252–57). Local chroniclers portrayed the early conversions as the
ruler's miraculous attainment of scriptural knowledge, usually after a visit
by a religious teacher from Mecca (Jones 1979).

By at least the late sixteenth century, Islamic scholars in Aceh were engaged in fierce debates over the nature of God and the proper ways to approach him. In the early 1600s a politically dominant group of religious
scholars set out to extirpate what they saw as "pantheistic" teachings by
burning books and executing those scholars whom they opposed (see Chapter 5). Two centuries later, in nineteenth-century Aceh, self-styled uphold-
ers of orthodoxy were reported to have put to death religious teachers claiming to have special access to God through their practices of chanting and
meditation (Snouck Hurgronje 1906, 2:13–14). In West Sumatra, similar
disputes over religious teachings and authority in the late eighteenth century led to the often violent "Padri movement" of 1807–1832. The Padri
leaders, inspired by Wahhābi reformist teachings in Arabia, called for a return to the Qur'ān and hadīth as the sole sources of religious knowledge
and authority (Dobbin 1983).

For Gayo people in the 1980s, however, the intertwined levels of lan-
guage-related dispute invoked by Alimin and Asyin—speaking religion,
interpreting scripture about such speech, debating such interpretations—recalled a more recent period of religious controversy, developing out of the
international religious current called *modernist* or *Salafiyyah* (Ar. *salaf
as-sālihīn*, the pious ancestors), that began in the late nineteenth century.
Modernists were most directly inspired by the writings of the scholars
Jamāl al-Dīn al-Afghānī (1839–1897) and Muhammad 'Abduh (1849–
1905). The movement became highly influential in Egypt, where Muhammad 'Abduh became Mufti (Hourani 1983), but it soon attracted adherents

in South and Southeast Asia as well. Muslims in the Dutch East Indies first learned of modernist ideas in the 1910s and 1920s, when students from West Sumatra returned home after years of study in Mecca and started new schools and newspapers. These students called on their fellow Muslims to purify religious practices of improper accretions and to adopt modern educational and scientific methods (Abdullah 1971; Noer 1973).

In the Gayo highlands, arguments over the relative merits of older and newer understandings of Islam were most impassioned between about 1928, when a group of West Sumatran (Minangkabau) traders set up a branch of the Muhammadiyah modernist organization, and about 1953, when the outbreak of rebellion against Jakarta turned Gayo attention away from internal religious disputes toward issues of political autonomy, national pluralism, and sheer survival. Public debates, impassioned sermons, and the appearance of new religious organizations marked the period. In the debate between Alimin and Asyin, Alimin invoked closure on this period when he claimed that the pan-Aceh assembly in 1948 had resolved the disputes; Asyin retorted that it also should have ended all talk about these matters.

During this period of about twenty-five years, many religious scholars and teachers in the Takèngën area came to identify themselves with one of two religious orientations. Those who sided with the modernist movement came to be known as the "new group" (*kaum mudë*; Ind. *kaum muda*). They claimed affinities with the Indieswide Muhammadiyah movement or with other networks of schools and associations. Those scholars who affirmed long-standing religious practices were referred to as the "old group" (*kaum tuë*; Ind. *kaum tua*). They associated themselves with a different set of schools and organizations outside the area, most notably in West Sumatra and Medan. The two labels were of general archipelagic currency, and I shall gloss them as "modernists" and "traditionalists."[2] Other Gayo tended to identify themselves with one or the other of the two camps. Villagers tended to see themselves as old group to the extent that traditionalist scholars defended some of their ritual practices (though they were silent on others), whereas most supporters of modernism lived in or around the town of Takèngën.

ON MODERNISTS AND TRADITIONALISTS

Here I offer an ideal-typical characterization of the two positions as they were developed by Indonesian scholars in general, and by Gayo scholars in particular. The positions are redolent of points made by Muslims elsewhere and in earlier times (see Hourani 1983). As Max Weber (1958a:47–48) emphasized (d. 1920) regarding his own use of ideal types in historical expla-

---

[2] I use these terms only as glosses of the Indonesian and Gayo labels; they may have different meanings in other contexts. As we shall see in the next chapter, Gayo developed links to several brands of modernism, each with its own religious, social, and political emphases.

nation, such characterizations are only valid for particular purposes; here my purpose is to provide an initial, general idea of the issues formulated and contested by these two groups of scholars. In this and subsequent chapters I shall examine more closely the differences within each camp, and the complex relations between the public positions taken by religious scholars and popular religious and ritual practices.

At the heart of the modernist position are sharply articulated visions of the self-sufficiency of scripture and the moral responsibility of the individual. Of course, virtually all Muslims consider the Qur'ān and hadīth as authoritative sources. Since the founding of the religion, scholars and other Muslims have based their opinions about proper conduct on the messages that God sent to humankind through the prophet Muhammad, whether collected as the Qur'ān or embodied in statements and actions by Muhammad, "The Messenger" (rasūl) (see Chapter 4). These latter statements and actions are recorded in the reports called hadīth, of which there are several authoritative collections. The reports were written down only after they had been transmitted orally across several generations, and religious scholars have evaluated them in part by scrutinizing the reliability of each link in the chain of transmission. Deciding on the correctness of a particular religious practice often turns on the reliability—itself to be judged from the moral character—of each transmitter.[3]

Ordinary Muslims as well model their religious conduct on the life of the prophet Muhammad. Many Gayo know the general meaning of a number of hadīth, and they can tell stories about Muhammad and other prophets. When fixing the form of worship, instructing people how to behave at funerals, or deciding how best to celebrate a feast day, the Gayo often justify their decisions by referring to Muhammad's example. The historical orientation of much Muslim discourse contributes to what William Graham (1983:63) calls its "fundamentally ritualist orientation," meaning its overriding concern with conformity to norms set by Muhammad.

The distinctive feature of the modernist position is not, then, that it relies on the Qur'ān and hadīth, but that it denies absolute authority to other written religious texts. Commentaries on scripture, no matter how venerated their authors, are valuable to modernists only to the extent that they clarify what is already in scripture. In religious matters we must strictly follow scripture, argue modernists; we should use our powers to reason, but not add or subtract one iota of information. Altering what scripture says is improper innovation (bid'a).[4] No detail is too small to be scrutinized for its rit-

---

[3] On the science of hadīth interpretation see Juynboll (1983), Graham (1977), and Fischer and Abedi (1990:95–149); on Qur'ānic commentary see Rippin (1988), Ayoub (1984), and the translation of Tabarī's commentary (Tabarī 1987).

[4] This strict opposition to bid'a is not limited to modernists; compare the similar positions taken by scholars in Morocco (Eickelman 1985:116–18) and India (Metcalf 1982:148).

ual correctness, say modernists. If, for example, we know that Muhammad raised his arm during worship, then we must follow suit; if this fact is in doubt, then we must not do it. There is no middle way. This rule applies only to matters of service and worship of God (*ibëdët*; <Ar. *'ibādāt*), however. Modernists often quote the prophet Muhammad to the effect of "you know best your own affairs." Science, modern forms of education, and business are all open to the Muslim to pursue as he or she sees fit.

Following God's commands is the responsibility of each individual Muslim. Although solidarity in the worldwide Muslim community (*umët*; <Ar. *umma*) is important, more important from a strictly religious perspective is each person's accountability for his or her own conduct. No one can worship, or fast, or pay alms for another. Furthermore, in each religious action the actor's intent is as important as the outward behavior; I often heard modernist friends declare that "everything depends on intent [*niët*; <Ar. *niyya*]." One must sacrifice, worship, or make the pilgrimage for the sake of God, not in hope of augmenting one's trade or gaining prestige.

Because of the importance of proper intent, one must understand the meaning of the words pronounced in worship and the reasons behind acts of worship. Modernists emphasize the religious importance of translating scripture into vernaculars: not to enable people to judge and interpret freely on their own (for that you need specialists), but so that they will know what they say in worship and thereby formulate the correct intent.

According to the modernist view, scripture is clear once we properly understand it. Scripture has only one set of correct interpretations, and people must be taught this and told to ignore all else. Modernist teachers see their task as shaking people away from the habits and ignorance of former days so that they will listen to the correct message. Teachers may need to be harsh, shrill, and direct, even if such conduct violates cultural norms. Transgressions of culture may be required before people will walk the straight path in religion.

Traditionalists, by contrast, counsel reliance on the collective wisdom of past scholars. They do so because they find scripture to be ambiguous in its pronouncements—not, as claim the modernists, crystal clear. Often one cannot tell from scripture what the prophet Muhammad did, or one finds evidence that he carried out ritual duties in several different ways. Such is the case for his method of reciting the surah al-Fātiha, for example: sometimes he pronounced the opening line out loud, but sometimes he said it softly, to himself (see Chapter 13).[5]

---

[5] Note (1) that the modernist scholar Muhammad 'Abduh also cited the need to interpret an often unclear Qur'ān as an argument for the importance of individual reasoning (*ijtihād*) (Hourani 1983:147), and (2) that the positions set out here do not capture all possible modernist and traditionalist, or Shafi'i, views.

For traditionalists, two conclusions follow from these ambiguities and interpretive difficulties. The first is that one ought to follow one legal tradition (*madhhab*) for the coherence that it offers. Indonesians generally follow the Shafi'i tradition, named for the ninth-century scholar Imam Shāfi'ī. The early scholars had an unsurpassed grasp of scriptural knowledge, say traditionalists, and one should profit from that expertise (compare, for India, Metcalf 1982:144). One therefore should not urge everyone to interpret the Qur'ān or hadīth for themselves, lest they err and lest their sins rebound onto the heads of their teachers. Traditionalists have been skeptical of efforts to translate the Qur'ān into vernaculars, although they have supported the teaching of Arabic.

Second, because two or more distinct ways of carrying out religious duties may be appropriate, one should accept variety in ritual form. Traditionalists' idea that scripture offers alternatives is in direct contrast to modernists' conviction that scripture offers only one correct set of ritual forms. This idea also leads many traditionalists to urge tolerance of what may appear to be non-Islamic ritual behavior. For example, when people hold ritual meals with special foods and incense, they may intend these objects as symbols of devotion or as ways of bringing people together to worship God. In such cases traditionalists would find the foods and incense acceptable. If worshipers considered the foods to be offerings for spirits, however, the matter would be quite different. Intent clearly cannot be construed from the objects themselves, and therefore one should not be quick to criticize the religious practices of others.

Even though modernists and traditionalists agree that the intent involved in the performance of a ritual is important, they conceive of intent differently. For traditionalists, as we have seen, intent is relatively independent of outer form. One may therefore wish to formulate a statement of intent independent of one's act of worship. Modernists disagree, stating that intent is always present in any action (see Chapter 13 on the resulting controversies). For modernists, having the right intent at worship (salāt), for example, means meditating on the words one utters and on the overall sense of submission to God that those words imply. In this view it becomes all the more critical to render the outer form of ritual correctly: by uttering the wrong words or acting in the wrong manner, one creates erroneous intents. Ritual forms that imply the worship of other spirits (such as the offering of foodstuffs at meals) are intrinsically and doubly wrong: they are improper additions to religious ritual, and they signal the individual's polytheistic (and thus execrable) intent to worship spirits.

Although traditionalists follow the teachings of the early scholars, they urge people to accept innovations when such changes help spread the religious message. They consider that there is as much good as bad innovation (cf. Goldziher 1981:230–45). Indeed, the early legal scholars had to create legal traditions precisely because scripture is not preadapted to any and all contexts of use. As examples of clearly legitimate innovations, Indonesian traditionalists cite such technological advances as the use of a public-address system to broadcast the call to prayer (a device used by modernists and traditionalists alike).

Traditionalists also underscore the moral obligations of Muslims toward each other as members of a community. These obligations do not end with death. The dead are not pieces of wood to be tossed around, but bodies with real, if tenuous, connections to souls and to God. One thus has an obligation to work for their benefit by chanting, teaching, and praying. These acts of uttering sacred words create merit because, as God's words or words in praise of him, they carry intrinsic power. He hears them and, moved, lightens the load of the departed soul (see Chapter 11).

Many of the differences between the two groups of scholars derive from their contrasting views of how one ought to read scripture. Modernists find scripture to be ultimately clear and complete, and thus to require no mediation by a legal tradition. Scripture provides a single standard for religious actions to which people ought to be strictly held. Traditionalists, by contrast, find that the ambiguities and lacunae in scripture do require additional interpretation. They highly value the work of the early scholars, are reluctant to encourage the direct popular interpretation of scripture, and hold a relatively latitudinarian position on ritual diversity.

Yet the very possibility of argument between these scholars implies an agreed-upon set of terms and assumptions. In Takèngën as elsewhere in Indonesia, the debates among religious scholars gradually defined a space for religious discourse, one that could encompass divergent readings of scripture but that excluded other possible ideas about religion and ritual. Modernists and traditionalists confined their discussions to those features of religion (Ind. *agama*; Ar. dīn) that were communicated to humans through the Qur'ān and hadīth. Nonscholars today understand "religion" in the same restricted sense. When I asked Gayo in Takèngën or Isak what was meant by religion or Islam, I was invariably told about the five pillars of Islam (the confession of faith, worship, fasting, alms, the pilgrimage), Qur'ān and hadīth, the rituals of birth, death, and marriage, and, sometimes, appropriate beliefs or faith (*īmān*). Not even village healers mentioned such practices as healing or speaking to ancestral spirits when they answered this question, even though they understood these practices to be dependent on the powers of scripture, prophets, and God.

In their impromptu debate, Alimin and Asyin showed how this idea of religion sharply limits and shapes what one may say in defense of a particular practice (and how individuals apply the general modernist and traditionalist positions adumbrated above). Both men continually strove to occupy the high ground of scripture and to avoid any other rhetorical foundations.

Alimin opened the discussion by denouncing those who approved of tahlīl (mortuary recitations) and telkin (the catechism recited at the grave). Asyin understood that his own poetry was being attacked. He responded not by defending these practices but by trying to outflank Alimin by criticizing Alimin's decision to attack the practices of others. "We should rise above conflicts," Asyin said, quoting, in support of this position, the final line from a well-known Qur'ānic verse (109:6), "to you your religion and to me my religion."[6] In support of religious compromise he also mentioned the agreement by leading Gayo religious scholars to alternate between two forms of worship ritual in the main mosque.

Alimin responded by limiting the applicability of the maxim Asyin had offered. He drew on a general distinction between two modes of religious reasoning. The first is taqlīd (imitation), the term used by traditionalists to mean observing one of the four major Muslim legal traditions. Alimin, following other modernists, derided this mode of reasoning as not rational at all, but merely "blind obedience" (taqlīd buta, a phrase widely used in the archipelago) and "whatever father did, I'll just follow." In its place, Alimin advocated ijtihād (independent reasoning), which Alimin glossed as "think the matter out for yourself." While one might follow received opinion in matters that are only sunna (recommended), such as whether to pronounce the bismillāh out loud, one must exercise independent reasoning with regard to required (wājib) actions and then strongly oppose those practices that have no basis in scripture.

Alimin tried to further degrade traditionalist views by characterizing some of them as based not even on scripturally justified blind obedience but on mere custom or habit, the sense in which he employed the term ëdët (Gayo norms, institutions, propriety). Asyin strongly resisted this attempt to cast the debate in terms of religion versus ëdët by emphasizing that those who disagree with Alimin "have their proofs, too, and they say that it is twelve to six for them." He cited as an example of such a proof (dalīl) the prophet's statement that one should teach others "from the cradle to the grave." Asyin specified that the hadīth, the report of this statement, was "sound" (sahīh), thereby demonstrating his own familiarity with the science of hadīth criticism and forestalling the usual modernist tactic of claiming that traditionalists' hadīths are unreliable. He thereby insisted that the debate was within the confines of scripturally based religion.

---

[6] Alimin missed a good opportunity to jab back here. Although Asyin understood this verse to command toleration among Muslims with differing views, no less a commentator than Hamka (1973:262–65)—probably the most influential religious scholar in independent Indonesia—construed it as highlighting the barriers between religions (the usual meaning of dīn) and the need to rid from Islam all that is not part of Islam.

To counter Asyin's claim, Alimin emphasized that independent reasoning is only valid if it is carried out by those with solid knowledge of Arabic and scriptural sciences. He objected to taking the hadīth cited by Asyin at face value and argued instead that it must be interpreted through the science of scriptural interpretation (*tafsīr*); ordinary people must follow the interpretations of knowledgeable scholars. In the same vein was his appeal to the decision made in 1948 by a group of religious leaders from throughout Aceh to forbid the talqīn and other rituals surrounding death. Against Asyin's plea for tolerance, he argued that only those individuals who "have been told what really is in the Qur'ān and hadīth" are capable of making correct choices. The decision of the provincial authorities should thus be accepted and enforced in public and private venues. For Alimin, the authority to decide ritual matters lies with contemporary scholars, not with secular authorities, traditional wisdom, or popular opinion.

Both Alimin and Asyin assumed that "religion" was wholly contained in scripture and was not augmented through other relations between humans and God (such as continuing divine revelation or intercession). Moreover, in the course of their discussion each became less concerned with specific practices than with overarching issues of scriptural interpretation: how tolerant one should be of different views; who has the authority to interpret the Qur'ān; how much supporting commentary one needs when quoting a hadīth. Their exchange was thus rich in metacommentary, or speaking about how to speak properly. Both men's public stances toward religion were highly "scripturalist" (Geertz 1968:56–89) in the sense of drawing exclusively from the Qur'ān and hadīth, as well as "universalistic" in their avoidance of local knowledge and norms as foundations for religious practice.

The scholarly, universalistic Islam that has emerged from these and similar debates among Gayo is represented as a transparent Islam, subject to public scrutiny. Confrontations and debates were the hallmarks of the years 1928 to 1942, the formative period for developing a scripture-based conception of religion in the Gayo highlands. Preachers at Friday sermons took clear positions on a range of ritual issues. In a few cases, people dissatisfied with their mosque's ritual regime built another mosque in which they could worship in a somewhat different way (see Chapter 13). Men carried the arguments away from the mosques into town coffee shops and village prayer houses; women pursued the issues in informal discussions and at women's study sessions. Political leaders organized debates to try and resolve the scholarly disputes (at least in their own minds). One such debate, organized by the most powerful colonial-era Gayo official, the ruler of the Bukit domain, pitted a prominent local traditionalist scholar against his opposite number among the modernists.

By the 1930s, public assemblies on religious matters were common. Sometimes they were occasioned by the visit of a leading religious scholar from Medan or Java; at other times they were called to plan the celebration of a feast day. Here the public character of scholarly Islam converged with (and provided a cover for) efforts to create a political consciousness around the idea of an Indonesian nation. In early 1931, for example, an assembly was held in Takèngën with the explicit purpose of planning the celebration of the upcoming *'īd al-fitr* (Feast of Breaking the Ramadān Fast). But the event was also a celebration of an Indonesian identity. The symbols and language of national identity were displayed in profusion, from the singing of the anthem "Indonesia Raya" to a series of five speeches, in Indonesian, by the founder of the local branch of Sukarno's Indonesian Nationalist Party (Partai Nasional Indonesia, PNI) (Bowen 1991:100–101). Modernist scholars dominated these meetings, in part because modernism was strongest in the town of Takèngën where nationalist sentiment and public gatherings were also concentrated, but also because it was the modernist scholars who called for open debates on religious matters (see Chapter 3).

This scripture-based Islam of the public sphere, as we might characterize it, is not the whole story, of course. But beginning in the 1930s it quickly became the whole *public* story, especially in Takèngën. Islam was constituted in and through a set of social institutions with well-defined publics: schools, publishing houses, bookstores, mosques, and study sessions.

Each such institution, whether modernist or traditionalist in doctrine, based its claims to religious authority not on Gayo knowledge, history, or social norms, but on ties to parent institutions outside the highlands: older schools in such prestigious places as West Sumatra and East Java (and, through them, schools in Mecca and Cairo), publishers and booksellers in the Middle East, and religious scholars and writers throughout the archipelago. The first modernists were associated with Muhammadiyah, the nationwide association inspired by Muhammad 'Abduh's teachings. Takèngën Muhammadiyah modernists' strongest ties were to educational networks in West Sumatra and Java. Traditionalists also borrowed new educational methods and literature from West Sumatran teachers and formed a branch of al-Jammiyat al-Washliyah, the traditionalist organization headquartered in the Sumatran city of Medan. Both groups relied on printed books distributed by these schools and organizations, and both encouraged visits from distinguished teachers.

The cultural communities created through these institutions were supralocal in that each included in its self-definition certain persons and institutions located outside the highlands. Each of the contemporary Gayo scholars whose journeys we trace in Chapter 3 underscores his search for truth outside the homeland, whether this search was carried on by physically traveling to schools elsewhere in the archipelago, by studying with those who had made such journeys, by learning Arabic, or by purchasing and studying books written by scholars in West Sumatra, Java, or, best of all, the Arabic-speaking world.

Books were a critical element in the new, scholarly constructions of religious authority. The Islam of public discussions in Takèngën was and is "an Islam of the book rather than of the trance or the miracle" (as Clifford Geertz [1968:65] characterized "scripturalism" on Java). Books embodied the idea of supralocal authority. Indeed, the first Gayo-language book was a compilation of religious poetry written in Arabic script and published in Cairo in 1938 through the offices of a bookseller in Surabaya, East Java. Books also signaled different styles of education, as we shall see in the next chapter. In the new schools built by modernists and traditionalists in Takèngën, books were carefully chosen from parent schools in West Sumatra or Java, and access to books in Arabic was central to all the new curricula.

Developments since the 1940s have reinforced the tendency to compartmentalize religion as a distinct set of activities and ideas that can be exhaustively grounded in scripture. Local scholars have become more sophisticated in their command of Arabic and of the Islamic scholarly apparatus. Many of the religious offices in Takèngën are staffed by graduates of the State Islamic Institute (Institut Agama Islam Negeri, IAIN) in Banda Aceh, where they receive training in law and Arabic. Indonesian-language law (*fikh*) manuals and collections of hadīth are also widely available, providing the scholar, official, or interested Muslim access to a normative, universalistic discourse on proper Islamic ideas and practices. In state-sponsored Islamic and transconfessional schools, as well as in private religious schools, Gayo children learn about religion as a distinct set of beliefs and practices.

Beyond the explicit teaching of religion as a topic, the very existence of a set of religion-related institutions both defines what is to be taken as religious and furnishes a cadre of local-level officials whose roles are defined in religious terms. In the subdistrict (*kecamatan*) headquartered in Isak, for example, there is a representative (locally called the *Qali* [Ar. *qādī*, judge]) of the Office of Religious Affairs (Kantor Urusan Agama) whose duties include supervising marriages and divorces. There are also various mosque officials; a representative of the Council of Ulama; and a religious official (imëm) in every village who in theory acts as the agent of all the above. In the district (*kabupaten*) there is, in addition to the above-mentioned institutions, a Council of Ulama with several subunits, including the Religious Wealth Unit (Badan Harta Agama) charged with collecting and apportioning the tithe (*zakāt*) and the head tax (*fitrah*). The collection procedures have, in recent years, become increasingly centralized, with a greater share of the total being distributed by the district government. Finally, the district-level Religious Court (Mahkamah Shariah) has exclusive jurisdiction over family-law cases, including the distribution of wealth after divorce or death.[7]

SOCIAL AND MORAL CONTEXTS

These scholarly debates and public institutions have not fed solely on a desire for religious knowledge. They were shaped and motivated by the broader concerns that Dale Eickelman (1979) has termed the "political economy of meaning." Gayo involved in debates over ritual propriety rarely mention the links between scholarly issues and their economic, political, and social contexts. After all, Asyin could no more defend reading a catechism to the dead on the basis of the general importance of ancestor spirits than could Alimin oppose it in the name of a rational modern economy. Yet both men were cognizant of, and in part motivated by, the broad social implications of particular scripturally justified positions.

Let us return to the issues raised by Alimin (all to be examined in subsequent chapters). For most Gayo villagers, the recitations of the telkin and the tahlīl that were condemned by Alimin are moments in a series of interventions by the living on behalf of the dead. By reading the telkin catechism, relatives and neighbors hope to prepare the deceased for an interrogation in the grave by the angels Mungkar and Nakīr. By chanting scriptural passages, they reduce the torment suffered by the deceased between death and the final day of judgment. On the first, third, seventh, and forty-fourth days after death, villagers gather in the home of the bereaved to recite verses and prayers. Food is served throughout the evening. A prayer leader channels the merit of the recitations to the spirit of the deceased (or, say some, to God for the deceased's benefit). The deceased also enjoys the food's spiritual essence. Many villagers continue to set out food for the deceased on certain days of the year, and may dedicate a sacrificial goat or buffalo to an ancestor on the Feast of Sacrifice ('īd al-adhā), held during the month of pilgrimage.

In return, some ancestors help the living. People ask the spirits of former powerful healers for assistance in expelling illness from their families. The founding ancestors of communities have yet broader powers. Besides healing the sick, they are able to protect the rice crop from rats, pigs, birds, and insects. Rice itself is said to have been formed from the body of a daughter of Adam and Eve. It is capable of nourishing humans because it is

---

[7] Compare the description of religious bureaucracy in the early 1950s on Java in Geertz (1960:199–210). Elsewhere (Bowen 1988) I have examined the negotiation of meaning and wealth among ëdët, Islamic, and state codes that is carried out in the religious and civil courts. These negotations form an additional important part of Gayo encounters with religion.

of human substance and because humans can speak to it, urging it to be plentiful and nourishing. Other economic pursuits—tapping sugar-palm trees, planting dry rice or coffee, and hunting deer—also depend on entering into proper communication with spirits, most importantly with spirits of human origin.

For many Gayo, then, practices such as the telkin and the tahlīl are part of the broad nexus of communicative relations with spiritual agents that underlie village society and economy. The dispute over the pronunciation of the bismillāh in worship, on the surface an insignificant matter, similarly implicates the validity of this village nexus. If worship is communication with God, then one should speak clearly to him. Some who take this position cite the prophet Muhammad's statement that the tongue and the heart should work together. Ritual centers on communication with spiritual agents, and such communication is the very stuff of village life. Gayo who see their social lives as embedded in the village also see them as embedded in the continuing web of human-spirit interactions.

For these villagers there is no line of demarcation between healing and farming on the one hand, and worship and sacrifice on the other. True, the former are practical, this-worldly activities that also have a religious and ritual dimension, while the latter are activities directed toward God that, one hopes, will bring practical gain in the afterlife. But most Gayo villagers do not consider the latter to be part of religion and the former to be outside of it. In explaining why they carry out healing rituals, recite farming spells, or sacrifice a goat on the Feast of Sacrifice, villagers refer to their continuing relationships to both spirits and God. They see all ritual activities as informed by the same practical logic of speaking in powerful ways with spirits.

Village ritual practitioners often explicitly situate what they do in an Islamic context, even if they rarely quote scripture in the process. In explaining how spells work, for example, they may refer to the history of conversion to Islam in Aceh, or to the story of God's creation of the world, or to written compendia of prayers and spells. They consider their discourses with spiritual agents to derive from their access to the broader world of Islamic knowledge.

Here lies the irony of traditionalist scholarship. Precisely by engaging modernists on the field of scripturally defined religion, traditionalists have contributed to the gradual suppression of older village ritual practices. In public debates, traditionalists can advocate only those practices that they can support with citations from the Qur'ān, the hadīth, or the learned interpretations of religious scholars. A practice cannot be defended by claiming it as part of Gayo ëdët or as a useful means for gaining some nonreligious end, such as social solidarity or a good harvest.

Traditionalists therefore plead only for those rituals that are widespread

1. Takèngën Shops

in the Muslim world (or at least in Indonesia) and for which scriptural justification can be found. They have accepted, tacitly or explicitly, modernist
criticisms of a number of practices. Thus traditionalists do not defend offerings made to spirits for the sake of the rice crop or the hunt, practices
strongly condemned as polytheistic by modernists. Nor has the wearing of
talismans and amulets, objected to by modernists, been defended by traditionalist scholars.[8] Thus, although village ritual practitioners sometimes see
themselves as allied with the old group scholars, who advocate toleration of
diverse practices, the official old group position in fact leaves out most of
what these practitioners do.

If most villagers see their well-being as dependent on continual communication with spirits, most modernists, especially those living in the town of
Takèngën, reject these ideas. Their emphasis on the authority of religious
education, their insistence on the obligation to exercise independent reasoning over and against received opinion, and their specific refusal to speak to
or for the dead are all linked in various ways to the political-economic
nexus that emerged in Takèngën in the 1920s and 1930s.

By the 1920s Takèngën had become the agricultural and marketing center
for the highlands, benefiting from the booming colonial export economy on
the eastern coast of Sumatra (Bowen 1991:76–79; Ricklefs 1981:143–54).
The town had a multiethnic, and increasingly Indonesian, character. The
men and women who gathered in the town to engage in commerce and civil

---

[8] Healing and exorcism through the use of Muslim spirits (*jin*) are denounced by some modernists but are employed by others. Healing has thus not become an issue for religious debate.

service spoke to each other in Indonesian, read the developing Indonesian-language literature, and enriched their lives through a shared religious commitment. The essence of that commitment was to religion as contained in scripture and as "uncontaminated" by local ideas.

Townspeople thus could agree on an Islam that was understood as knowledge and practices detached from any particular place—an Islam that, to retain its purity, needed to be explicitly distinguished from local forms of religiosity. The immigrant character of the town contributed to this flavor: the people who arrived there brought with them forms of social, religious, and economic life that could exist apart from a village base. Moreover, the two largest groups of Muslim immigrants, the West Sumatran Minangkabau and the Acehnese, both came from cultures where circular migration was part of life. Men in both regions typically spent years away from their homelands (Kato 1982; Siegel 1969). These migratory traditions accentuated the sense of detachment from place that characterized the new socioreligious ideas.

Among the Gayo men and women who moved into Takèngën in the 1920s and 1930s were traders, civil servants, and a small but influential group of men and women who belonged to the traditional elite but who had been bypassed by the hierarchical system of rule recently established by the Dutch. These people were the core of the new modernist group.

Gayo who came to the town as traders generally worked as individual entrepreneurs, often in unofficial partnership with a supplier of capital. For the owner of a retail store, coffee mill, or transport company, economic responsibility was largely an individual or family matter.[9] Although the move from a largely agricultural existence to a commercial one shifted the focus of social life away from the multiple webs of social affiliation and responsibility found in the village, these people generally maintained their ties to the surrounding communities. Many of them continued to live in the villages and work in the town; others visited their natal villages frequently for feasts and celebrations. No migratory culture emerged here.

Ample occasions thus arose for conflict between traders and village farmers. Villagers demanded assistance from their better-off kinsmen qua kinsmen even after they moved to town. Demands came in the form of requests to donate buffalo for feasts, to rent out rice fields, or to support a student or needy child. Townspeople viewed such demands as incursions into capital that would be better used in other, more rational ways. No trader ever met all such demands, and many were (and continue to be) accused privately of "forgetting who their relatives are." In the 1980s, one of the two wealthiest merchants in Isak was rumored to have been unable to complete the pilgrimage because of his usury (*riba*) and to have ignored the material needs of

---

[9] Compare similar social forms of trade in Java (Geertz 1963a) and in lowlands Aceh (Siegel 1969).

2. Isak Shops and Mosque

his son, and the other merchant was the object of covert denunciation in a
Friday sermon because of her failure to pay her rightful due in alms
(zakāt). Poorer villagers invoked the general norms of Islam to formulate
an effective moral critique.

Many traders found a certain degree of moral support for their activities
(and for their social isolation) in modernism's emphasis on the accountability of the individual to God. To defend the sale of land to an outsider to finance their children's schooling, traders could quote the many verses and
hadīths on the overriding importance of knowledge. Trade also offered a
number of positive religious images. After all, the prophet Muhammad was
a trader. And, explained one leading teacher, the traders' wealth enabled
them to support religious activities without hope of personal gain. For modernists, the contrast between proper and improper relations of economy and
religion was epitomized by the trader's selfless endowment of a school on
the one hand, and the greed of a village prayer leader who recites chants for
food and money on the other. A certain "elective affinity" (Weber 1958a)
thus emerged between the social logic of small-scale trade and modernist Islamic ideas.[10]

Trade also provided direct material support for Gayo who wished to pursue religious education. Beginning in the early 1930s, profits from trade enabled Gayo men (and, fewer and later, women) to seek learning outside the

[10] Weber's argument was that ascetic Protestantism and capitalism supported each other in
early modern Europe; the argument was directed against one-way causal theories. On the logic
of this argument see Alexander (1983:33–45) and Giddens (1971:127–32); on its comparative
Indonesian applications see Geertz (1963a:48–51) and Peacock (1975:184–95).

highlands. Gayo view this support as decidedly nonethnic in nature. An Arab trader on the north coast, for example, not only taught several of the future Gayo Arabic teachers, but even paid for their further schooling on Java. Minangkabau, Acehnese, as well as Gayo traders and teachers supported Gayo men during their studies in West Sumatra and Java.

The partial socioeconomic detachment of townspeople from village life created a field of moral tension between two divergent yet proximate moral economies. This tension was also cultural in nature. In particular, Gayo who worked as civil servants in the colonial era were more likely to have attended town schools (labeled "infidel schools" by some villagers), to have become literate in Indonesian, and to have found friends among other Indies natives. Many read newspapers and novels in Indonesian, learned to play Western musical instruments, and taught in colonial or religious schools (Bowen 1991:94–96). For them, the most attractive elements in Islamic modernism were its view outward, toward new modes of education, writing, and discovery, and its supraethnic, universalistic message that ties of common membership in the Muslim community superseded ties of family and village.

Prominent among leaders in the Gayo modernist movement have been the children of the traditional village elite who had not been selected for office by the Dutch and who had therefore sought other pathways to advancement. In many cases these would-be rulers chose to attend religious schools (Bowen 1991:100–102), and their schooling exposed them to nationalist ideas as well as religious ones. Their attachment to modernism was often reinforced by their rivalry with those rulers whom the Dutch had chosen to install, because the local rulers tended to oppose religious modernism on the grounds that it challenged their authority. (In fact, it usually was intended as such a challenge.) Thus nationalist and modernist sentiments coincided with the older rivalries in Gayo villages to create multistranded cleavages in the villages.

A comparative analysis within the Takèngën area supports the hypothesis that involvement in town life strongly favored modernist leanings. In the colonial era, the Takèngën area was divided into two major political domains, Bukit and Ciq (See Map 2.1).[11] As it happened, members of the Bukit domain, centered on the community of Kebayakan, became the most active participants in the new town mode of life. Takèngën was located in this domain, and Bukit people tended most often to become civil servants. Further, the Bukit ruler Rëjë Ilang had acted as the protector of the modernist Muhammadiyah organization in the late 1920s and had encouraged Bukit residents to study at the Muhammadiyah school. But within the Bukit domain there were subregions that remained isolated from the new modes of

---

[11] The third precolonial domain, Syiah Utama, became part of the Bukit sphere of influence under colonial rule (Bowen 1991:80).

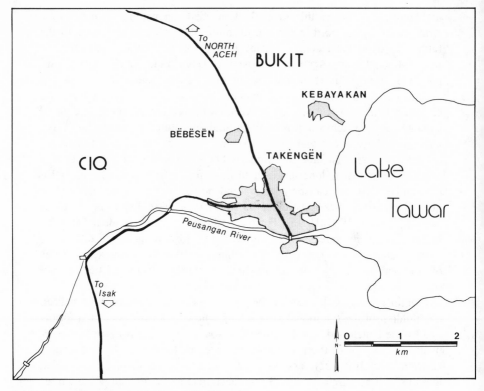

2.1 Takèngën Showing the Bukit and Ciq Domains

livelihood and worship, and, most important, religious leaders in Bukit villages located along the shore of Lake Tawar remained traditionalist.

Town life appears to have been the distinctive feature that supported and
encouraged a modernist religious orientation within the Bukit domain. The
domain experienced a cleavage that cut across all areas of social life: Those
who moved into town tended to enter trade and government, to pursue modern-style schooling in Dutch and later in Indonesian, and to adopt relatively
modernist religious views. Those who remained in Bukit agricultural villages tended to oppose participation in the colonial administration and the
style of schooling that had been introduced in government schools and
adopted by Muhammadiyah. Until recently the home community of Kebayakan was itself strongly divided along religious lines.

The importance of the new multicultural milieu in shaping religious orientations is further demonstrated by the case of the other sociopolitical domain in the Takèngën area, the Ciq domain centered on the community of
Bëbësën. Ciq people were even more involved in commercial ventures than
were Bukit people, but these were agricultural ventures pursued within the

domain itself (Bowen 1991:76–81). The majority of the dammar pine (*Pinus merkusii*) and coffee estates that were the basis for the political economy of the highlands in the colonial era happened to be located in the Ciq domain. At a time when Bukit people were moving into town to become civil servants and traders, Ciq people were moving out to their coffee gardens and to the dammar estates. The last ruler of the domain was called the Dammar King for his overriding interest in his dammar lands.

The Ciq domain consequently remained relatively united and inward-looking in its political economy, cultural orientation, and religious attitudes. Ciq religious leaders by and large have remained traditionalist in their positions on religious matters and strongly tied to their natal villages. They may have introduced modern-style educational methods, but they did not openly condemn village ritual forms. Even in the late 1980s the contrast was marked: the major traditionalist scholars (generally from Ciq or lakeshore Bukit villages) lived in villages or maintained strong links to them, while the major modernist scholars (generally from Bukit or the town area) lived in Takèngën and were active as schoolteachers.

Rather than commerce per se, it thus appears to have been the combination of a multiethnic town community, fluency in Indonesian, and involvement in commerce that supported an enthusiasm for modernist innovations in religion (especially religious education) in 1930s Takèngën. "Internal conversion" (Geertz 1973:170–89) to religious modernism in Takèngën was associated with the broad cultural detachment of Gayo individuals from preexisting loyalties, and occurred most densely when the Gayo found themselves shifting loyalties simultaneously on a number of fronts.

And yet the detachment of Gayo modernists from village life, though broad, has always been partial. Modernists have not conjured images of a new mode of life, free of village constraints, as James Siegel (1969) describes for Acehnese reformists. Instead, they have carved out a distinct religious sphere of activity in which people of diverse backgrounds could participate and which would also allow for the continuation of nonreligious activities and ties (largely in the villages). Gayo modernists thus have underscored the line between matters of religion, where one must follow scriptural norms, and all other matters, where, in the words of Muhammad, "you know best your affairs." They also have kept alive, as a critical part of their own identity, their objections to the ideas and practices of "backward" villagers. Controversies over ritual matters have for this reason retained a greater salience in the Gayo highlands of the 1980s than in the Acehnese lowlands (or, for that matter, than in most of Sumatra).[12]

---

[12] On Aceh see Siegel (1969); on the Sipirok Batak see Rodgers Siregar (1981). My understanding of the Minangkabau case, where there has yet to be a thoroughgoing study of Islamic ritual and religion, is largely drawn from conversations with the historian Taufik Abdullah.

Gayo modernists continue to engage in a double enthusiasm: vigorously casting off old ways of life, and equally energetically seeking to create a new texture of communication based on using scripture rather than communicating with spirits. They object to the latter form of communication not only because such practices are unsupported by scripture, but also because they keep people from carrying out their proper religious obligations. Reciting verses for the dead suggests that others can mitigate the punishment or augment the reward due the deceased. "If that were true," said one modernist, "then we would never have to worship; we could just get others to do it for us."

Although much of the force with which modernists denounce older practices comes from what they see as the threat those practices pose to the true vocation of the Muslim (education, worship, and the study of scripture), part of it comes from the diacritic or oppositional nature of religious modernism itself. Gayo modernists have created new identities by renouncing their own past and by actively detaching themselves from the village setting. If traditionalists and most villagers have the privilege of remaining embedded in the agricultural, ancestral, local mode of communication, modernists must be continually distancing themselves from that context as well as creating their own set of alternative social, moral, and economic relations. In defining their new selves by erecting new boundaries, modernists have frequently relied on the tropes of old and new, ignorant and learned, and, as general symbols of the problem, Gayo ëdët as the rule of the unreflecting villager versus universal Islam as the scriptural guide for the learned individual. Modernist rhetoric thus often casts into the category of ëdët all that they view as improper (as Alimin did in his debate with Asyin).

For Gayo of all religious orientations (and, as the next chapter suggests, the divisions are far more complex than simply into two camps), the motivations behind religious differences extend far beyond religion in the narrow sense. The older political economy of meaning depends upon continuing events of communication and exchange between humans and spirits. The town-based equivalent (shared by rural traders and teachers) depends upon education, worship, and a consequential interpretation of scripture. Modernists have embraced an outward-looking, scripturally informed, individualistic identity that explicitly renounces the older, two-way forms of communication in favor of the uniquely privileged messages delivered by God, through Muhammad, to humans. The "space of dissension" (Foucault 1972:152) in Gayo Muslim discourse is much broader than is the space defined by debates over scriptural norms for religious ritual.

Chapter Three

ISLAMIC KNOWLEDGE
IN THE HIGHLANDS, 1900–1990

GAYO RELIGIOUS SCHOLARS created a public sphere of religious discourse largely through education. By the 1930s, Takèngën-area religious schools, whether modernist or traditionalist, constituted religion as a definable, distinct sphere of knowledge and practice. They did so by teaching Arabic, by defining a religious curriculum through a set progression of textbooks, and by returning to Qur'ān and hadīth as the basis for all religious knowledge. This disciplined knowledge then provided the base for spreading "truth" to the populace through public debates, religious poetry, and Qur'ānic education. The new schools also projected into the public sphere their own distinct ideas about religion's role in social and political movements.

Language itself embodied these new commitments. Students had formerly learned to write and recite (but not translate) Arabic and to read Arabic-script Malay for religious knowledge. Now students began learning to read scripture and other religious writings in the original Arabic. They learned to read novels, newspapers, and didactic religious works written in Roman-script Indonesian, thereby becoming part of a reading public that stretched across the archipelago, and could attend lectures given in Indonesian by traveling religious speakers and party organizers. Indonesian became the language of nationalist commitment and social change; Arabic became the optimal (though not the only) language of religious study.

In this chapter I trace the paths of several leading Gayo scholars (*ulama*; <Ar. *'ulamā'*) across this changing landscape of religious knowledge. I focus on three men, chosen for their public activities in promoting particular ideas of religion. Tengku Asaluddin[1] combines a strong respect for the past generation of Isak villagers with an active life in the Muhammadiyah modernist movement. Tengku Ali Salwany leads the traditionalist association in Takèngën and works to preserve its links to village society. And Aman Murni is the heir of the "radical reformist" wing of modernism, the Takèngën Islamic Education school. Each sees himself as bringing a rational, critical, and modern perspective to religious and social affairs.

---

[1] The title *Tengku* indicates respect for a man's religious learning (it is never used for women); *ulama* (<Ar. *'ulamā'*) refers to such men collectively. Sometimes modernists use the plural form *tengku-tengku* to indicate, roughly, "half-baked, self-styled scholars."

These scholars, and many other men and women who have acquired formal religious education, place their own stories against a broader background narrative of Gayo religious enlightenment. Yet even scholars who agree on doctrinal issues may evaluate the effects of the enlightenment in clearly distinct ways. For some modernist scholars, such as Tengku Asaluddin, Gayo lost a deep (if uninformed) piety even as they gained in knowledge; for others, such as Aman Murni, Gayo escaped a virtual "pagan era" (*zaman jahiliya*) and entered a period of learning and religious progress.[2] Scholars otherwise categorized as modernist or traditionalist fashioned specific identities through their particular understandings of knowledge, language, and history.

LANGUAGES OF PAST PIETY AND LEARNING

My own teacher on religious matters in Isak, Tengku Asaluddin, combines a modernist religious education with a deep reverence for the religious sensibility of the past. He was born in Isak about 1914, and came of age during a transition from older to modern styles of learning, reading, and knowing. Despite his strongly modernist sympathies, acquired during his travels to Takèngën and beyond, his accounts of his own past are characterized more by nostalgia for a now-lost spiritual richness than by a progressivist enthusiasm for expanded scriptural knowledge.

Tengku Asaluddin and those of his generation began their religious studies in Isak by learning to write the letters of the Arabic alphabet.[3]

> We studied first with the Tengku Qali [registrant of marriages and divorces; <Ar. qādī] in my own village, Kutë Rayang. There were very few books then, and a book might cost as much as a water buffalo. We wrote on bamboo skins with ink made from roots, then wiped off the ink and reused the skins. People called this stage of learning 'using bamboo skins' [*berneniyun*].
>
> Finally I was able to buy a book of the Juz 'Amma [the last of the thirty divisions (*juz*) of the Qur'ān]. Tengku Qali taught me how to recite well; he kept me for a long time over how to end a phrase. [He then began to sing softly the

---

[2] Gayo distinguish between a period lodged well in the past ([*jëmën*] *pudah a*), a period of middle distance (*tengah a*), and a period of recent events, referred to in a number of ways (among them *oya wa* and *ini a*). The oldest category of [jëmën] pudah a is often used as a reference point from which change is narrated; it may be shortened to *jëmën: jema jëmën* thus means "people in the olden days," usually referring to people who were born before the Dutch invasion. The use of the Malay/Indonesian equivalent *zaman* indicates an Islamic frame of reference. The phrase *zaman jahiliya* derives from the Arabic term for pre-Islamic history, and its use here likens Gayo practices before modernism to Arab behavior before the coming of Islam. On comparable uses of these period terms in Malaysia see McKinley (1979).

[3] These excerpts are all transcribed from taped interviews with Tengku Asaluddin.

3. Tengku Asaluddin at Home in Isak

three letters] *alip*, *lām*, *mīm*. I moved on to the stage of Qur'ān, and finished reciting it under Tengku Qali. I then began to study with Tengku Ramasan, also called Tengku Ubit, in Kutë Robel [also in Isak], in order to improve how I recited. He taught me how to pronounce the letters; only later on did I study Arabic grammar on my own from books in Arabic.

Years later, after I had learned Arabic, Tengku Ramasan would come to me with an Arabic phrase and ask what it meant. Once I translated a phrase for him: "Everything leaves us except God's love." It is true, because our father and mother and body leave us and only the soul [*nyawa*] is left, and it says in the Qur'ān that the soul is not a matter for created things but only for the Creator [here he recites a Qur'ānic verse]. And the Qur'ān also says: "God is with you wherever you go," because the soul is in his hands. When I explained all this to Tengku Ramasan his body began to shake with excitement. His life was very simple. People of the old days truly believed in the hereafter. There are four worlds: the world before birth, the visible world, the world of the grave, and the world of the hereafter. Everything comes together in the hereafter, because God's determinations [*janji*, promises] are twofold: *wahat* [<Ar. *wa'd*] and *wahid* [<Ar. *wa'īd*]; good and bad. As they say in Acehnese:

wa'at wa'id amar nahī	good and bad, absolute authority
kalām rabbī sikrèt saja	the speech of the Lord, just one word
buteu paham amar nahi	just understand the absolute authority:
tema ngeun janji surga neraka	it all is set out, [who goes to] Heaven and [who goes to] Hell.

Tengku Ramsan often used Acehnese because everyone shared it, and sometimes the lowlanders [Acehnese] did not know fine points of the Acehnese language that we did. Acehnese had a lot of scriptural speech in it, for example the Hikāyat Perang Sabīl [Story of the Holy War].[4] I memorized parts of it and even copied it down from the original book. I recited some of it in 1945, and people became incensed and were ready to leave right away to fight the Dutch at the [Medan and Karo] front. The Kejurun [ruler of the Isak domain] grew angry; his ears were red. He said that the Hikāyat hadn't been effective when they had fought the Dutch before.

People had real belief back then and it showed in all that they did. My grandfather's teachers in Isak were Tengku Balé and Tengku Sufi. They had given up eating rice; they just chanted *zikr* [a spiritual exercise], sometimes eating just a handful of rice or some puffed rice. Both men had studied in Meulaboh. People went back and forth freely between Isak and Meulaboh back then. My grandfather's teacher could put down some iron over there [he points to the other side of his eating platform] and call it to him, tapping on the floor as he did so [he demonstrated]. He had gone to Meulaboh to meditate alone [*berkalut*]. He did not study much and rarely recited the Qur'ān, but certainty of faith [*keyakinan*] was the key.

Tengku Asaluddin's memories of religious life during his youth concern the piety of older people (especially his successive teachers) and the inspiration they derived from religious language. To an extent never realized thereafter, religious speaking and writing embodied the authority and power of piety. Tengku Asaluddin's sense of the religiosity of language involves not only the Arabic of the Qur'ān, although he takes great pride in his command of both the language and the Book, but also the older forms of speech, especially proverbs in Gayo and Acehnese, that to him best convey the fundamental truths of religion.

---

[4] The Acehnese text and Dutch translation of the work, know in Acehnese as *Hikayat Prang Sabi*, are given in Damsté (1928) and excerpted in Siegel (1969:74–77); see also Bowen (1991:67–68).

He also holds close to his heart the old printed and handwritten books that he first saw as a child. Prominent among these are "Jawi books" (*kitëb Jawi/Jawëi*), short manuals of religious instruction written in Arabic-script Malay, which formed the written core of early twentieth-century religious learning. Once a pupil in Isak or in the Takèngën area had studied Arabic letters and had read completely through the Qur'ān, he or she would proceed to the stage of the Jawi books. The Arabic-script writing (also called "Penang Malay" because of the importance of the Penang publishing houses) was the major written medium of religious instruction in the archipelago in the nineteenth and early twentieth centuries, and is still in use today.[5] Many of the Jawi books are translations or adaptations from Arabic works; some were printed in Mecca or Cairo for distribution in Southeast Asia, an indication of the far-reaching networks of translation, publication, and dissemination of Islamic instructional material.

In a sense these Jawi books supplied much of the content of Islam, while its sacred origins and nature were guaranteed by the sounds and shape of the letters concatenated in the Qur'ān. In the 1920s and 1930s, four Jawi books were used for religious instruction in the Gayo highlands.[6] The first book of the series, a short pamphlet called *Masā'il al-Muhtadī* (Questions of the Path-Seeker), is a written version of an ideal dialogue between teacher and student. The *Masā'il*, as it is known in the highlands, covers the basics of faith (*īmān*), and in particular religious law (*fiqh*) and proper understanding of God (knowledge of his unity, *tauhīd*). It is still widely available and used by (mainly urban) students as a guide to basic religious questions.[7] Its lessons are structured as a series of problems or questions (*su'āl*) followed by answers (*jawāb*), such as the following (p. 6):

> "question": If we are asked by someone: how many elements are there to the completeness of the confession of faith? "answer": that there are four elements to the completeness of the confession of faith: first, understand it through its proofs [*dalīl*]; second, pronounce it with the tongue; third, confirm [*tashdīq*] it with your heart; fourth, have certainty in your heart.

---

[5] See van Bruinessen (1990); Nor bin Ngah (1982); Roff (1967:43–45) and Yunus (1979:175–76). The term *Jawi* referred to the scholarly use of the medium; its distinction from vernacular Malay was appreciated by eighteenth-century European scholars who had in mind the model of Latin vis-à-vis vernaculars (Sweeney 1987:55–58).

[6] These books were also used in Aceh (Kreemer 1922–1923, II:504–5; Snouck Hurgronje 1906, II:1–10; Yunus 1979:175–76), but not in West Sumatra (on the West Sumatran curriculum at this time see Yunus [1979:18–77]).

[7] The full title of this anonymous work is *Masā'il al-Muhtadī li ichwān al-mubtadī* (n.d.); it is continually reprinted. In 1989 I purchased a copy of it, printed as a small-format pamphlet of thirty-nine pages, in Takèngën for 500 rupiah (about U.S. $.30). Martin van Bruinessen has told me that it is used throughout Aceh in traditional religious schools; see also Hasjmy (1983:382–84).

In the words of a Gayo scholar, the question-answer format "emphasized the ability to respond quickly to any [religious] issue" (Hanafiah 1974:10).[8] The student who completed the *Masā'il* then worked through the *Bidāyat* (*Bidāyat al-Mubtadī bifadl Allāh al-muhdī*, Initiations of the Beginners with the Grace of God the Guider). It, like the *Masā'il*, was probably in large part a translation from Arabic catechisms.[9] Much of the knowledge contained in these books is organized as lists: the six basic beliefs, the twenty characteristics of God, the ten inner uncleanlinesses. These lists were and are convenient ways of storing knowledge, and older Gayo people often organize their religious discourse around such lists.[10]

The next books in the series were structured in a very different way, and presented serious linguistic problems for most Gayo students. The third book, the *Sīrat al-Mustaqīm* (Straight Path), was written in 1634 by Nūruddīn al-Rānīrī, the leading scholar at the Acehnese court. Written in Malay, it has been printed in Mecca and Malaysia.[11] A Gayo student was considered learned if he (rarely she) had read the *Sīrat*, but because it includes Arabic-language passages that few could understand, it became a quasi-sacred companion to scripture that was read aloud but rarely studied for comprehension. Tengku Asaluddin recalled that "people in Isak used to have copies of al-Rānīrī's *Sīrat al-Mustaqīm*—he was the Mufti to the Sultan [Iskandar Muda]. I used to have a copy, too. People used to recite it but they did not understand it."

The fourth work, the *Sabīl al-Muhtadīn* (Way of the Guided), was written by Muhammad Arshad b. 'Abdullah al-Banjarī in 1780 at the request of the Sultan of Banjar, a Malay kingdom on the island of Borneo, because he thought that the *Sīrat* contained too many Acehnese words (Nor bin Ngah 1983:5). (Printed versions of the *Sabīl* contain al-Rānīrī's work in the margins.) Nonetheless, most Gayo students found it, too, to be very difficult; one scholar who studied it when young remembered the very long sentences that rendered it virtually undecipherable (Hanafiah 1974:10).

Jawi books were virtually the only available written expositions of religious law and doctrine through the 1920s (Hanafiah 1974:9–11).[12] In the

---

[8] The organization of teaching around questions and answers is, of course, found throughout the Muslim world; see Fischer (1980) on the pedagogy of the Iranian *madrasah* (religious schools).

[9] Kreemer 1922–1923, II:504–5. Nor bin Ngah (1982:47) lists an anonymous *Bidāyat* printed in Penang in 1838.

[10] Compare the organization around lists of the *Bihishti Zewar*, a reformist compendium written in the early 1900s in Urdu and intended for the education of Muslim women (Metcalf 1990).

[11] Kreemer (1922–1923, I:7) notes an 1892 printing of the *Sīrat* in Mecca.

[12] Snouck Hurgronje states that, around 1900, only a few Gayo had access even to this level of learning (1903:319–20), in contrast to the wider use of Jawi literature in lowlands Aceh (1906, II:4–5).

1980s many of the same books were still sold in Takèngën markets, but appear to be intended for older men and women, and more for Acehnese than for Gayo.[13]

Romanized Indonesian has largely replaced Jawi as the popular medium for religious instruction in the highlands, so few Gayo growing up today have occasion to study Jawi. At age five or six virtually all Takèngën-area children enter school, where they study in Latin-script Indonesian. Whereas in Malaysia Jawi books and newspapers continue to be seen as a way of strengthening Malay Muslim identity (Nagata 1984:164, 188), many Sumatran Muslim scholars, especially modernists, have preferred to use Latin-script Indonesian and Arabic as languages of instruction. Many of these teachers were active supporters of the nationalist cause and found Indonesian to be a more appropriate vehicle for creating a nationally oriented, Muslim public culture. For gaining direct access to worldwide religious writings they consider Arabic to be most appropriate (van Bruinessen 1990:227–40).

In place of the older Jawi books, Gayo today consult short Indonesian-language pamphlets entitled "Tauhīd" (God's Unity) or "Sifat Duapuluh" (Twenty Attributes [of God]). They can choose from a wide selection of books and pamphlets (for example, Said 1977; Ya'qub 1977), many costing less than 1000 rupiah (U.S. $0.60) in the Takèngën market. The pamphlets are structured around the six basic beliefs—in God, his angels, his scriptures, his messengers, the hereafter, predestination—and the twenty attributes of God. They convey essentially the same information as did the *Masā'il*, but they are organized as a series of lists without the question-and-answer format of the older book. Although such lists also enter into religious discourse (as the example from Tengku Asaluddin below illustrates), they are less explicitly tied to oral discourse than is the question-and-answer format (Goody 1977:74–111).

For men and women of Tengku Asaluddin's generation, the older literature in Jawi retains something of the moral value of the past. Tengku Asaluddin owns a variety of books in Jawi, both printed manuals and hand-copied notebooks, some of them handed down to him from his grandfather, the religious leader of Isak in the 1930s and 1940s. He also owns, and frequently reads from, Arabic-language books on religion and wisdom. For him, these books combine the more properly organized and deeply felt religiosity of an

---

[13] Other Jawi books also have long histories of use in the Malay-Sumatran world; some have been translated into several area languages. For example, Snouck Hurgronje (1906, II:189) mentions an Acehnese verse rendering of the Arabic *'Aqīdat al-'awāmm* by Abu'l Fauz al-Marzūkī (or Ahmad al-Marzūqī al-Mālikī al-Makkī; cf. van Bruinessen [1990:252]). Roff (1967:45) mentions a widely used Malay version of the same work, and in 1989 I purchased a (possibly revised) Malay version (Z. A. Syihab 1986) in Takèngën.

earlier generation with the wisdom found in Arabic religious writings. His books serve as guides for reflective thinking and as a cultural-religious archive. He keeps most of them in a locker on the raised eating platform where, as in most Gayo homes, conversations with friends and neighbors take place. He may pull one out to seek inspiration, to look up a point in response to a question, or to initiate a discussion on a topic close to his heart. He always does so with the enthusiasm of the preacher and the warmth of the pious. Even when he does not consult one of his books, his prodigious memory is likely to make available a hadīth or a proverb (the latter more often in Acehnese than in Gayo or Malay) that bears on the topic of discussion. Some of his neighbors and relatives shy away from him because of his "preacherly" tendencies, but they also acknowledge his learning and seek his advice.

In any single conversation Tengku Asaluddin usually combines information from several of these genres, especially lists of religious elements, quotations from scripture, and Gayo or Acehnese proverbs. The following excerpt was from one of the many conversations we had about the importance of knowledge (a natural topic, given our relation as student to teacher):

> In education it is important to have both general knowledge and religion. We are told to do *amal* [good works] for this world and for the hereafter. If people did not have clothing they could not worship and serve God, and clothing is of this world. God's Messenger himself did not meddle in the affairs of this world. "You know best worldly affairs," he said. So, he did not erect limits around our knowledge of worldly things. But in matters of serving God he said: "Worship in the manner you see me worshiping." [In this and the following case he recited both the Arabic hadīth and an Indonesian gloss.]
>
> For a religious life you need proofs [dalīl], and for those you need Qur'ān and hadīth. There are five sources [of fiqh]: Qur'ān, sunna [Muhammad's example], *ijmā'* [consensus], *qiyās* [analogy], and ijtihād [legal reasoning].[14] But the last three have to lean on the first two, as they say in Acehnese:
>
> | dalil agama wahai tolan | Religious signs, oh you there, |
> | o teu simpan dua saja | only two are treasured: |
> | pertama quran kiteub ullah | First, the Qur'ān, the book of God, |
> | kedua sunna rasul mustafa | second the example of the Messenger, |
> | | the Chosen One. |
>
> Ijmā' comes from the Messenger's immediate followers. Qiyās is comparisons and analogies. For example, how we measure cows and buffalos for figuring the tax (zakāt) is done by analogy to rice and corn. Ijtihād is measuring everything with reference to the Qur'ān and sunna. So [again in Acehnese]

---

[14] On the sources of Islamic law see the brief discussion in Denny (1985b:216–24) and the survey by Schacht (1964).

meng maksud teu paham bujelah	if you want to understand clearly,
usoy fika ta belajar	then study the bases and laws
	[of religion].

Tengku Asaluddin takes both structure and comfort from the diverse discourses he controls. Lists of Islamic categories provide an irrefutable hold on the flux of the world: things can be sorted into degrees of permissibility, kinds of knowledge, attributes of God, duties of the Muslim. This knowledge fundamentally concerns organization, differentiation, and control, and the list format itself contributes to its function.

The Acehnese sayings give him the opportunity to express a warmer tone than that conveyed by the legalistic lists. They elaborate the scripture-based truths and also recall a time when such truths were held closer to heart. The Acehnese language itself evokes a certain period in Gayo history when Gayo and Acehnese people intermingled.

Tengku Asaluddin's life (to which we return shortly) is to a great extent filled with such comforting religious texts. He enriches his worship with carefully chosen Qur'ānic verses and often performs supplementary worship and prayer. He continually constructs a discursive world of worship composed of proverbs, scriptural selections, and enumerations of the elements of religion.

In a deep sense, his language mixing (or "heteroglossia") is part of his purchase on the past. The rich layering of commentaries across languages and genres unites the unlearned past with his own scripturally competent present. Tengku Asaluddin's scripturalism, if that is what it is, involves following truth across multiple forms of expression, rather than drawing it back into a single source. His bookishness allows him to remain at the juncture of contemporary scholarly discourse and older ways of relishing religiosity in the body of language.

THE DEVELOPMENT OF TRADITIONALIST SCHOLARSHIP

Despite their label, traditionalists played a central role in transforming Indonesian religion. In the Gayo highlands, traditionalist scholars were the first to teach Arabic grammar, and they were quick to adopt new methods of instruction developed in Sumatra.[15]

It was a traditionalist scholar who first taught Arabic grammar in the Gayo highlands. Men born in the nineteenth century (the generation before

---

[15] Modernists have written the major studies of the history of Indonesian Islamic schooling, in which they highlight their own teachers' contributions. The standard work on the topic is *Sejarah pendidikan Islam di Indonesia* (*The History of Islamic Education in Indonesia*), by the modernist scholar H. Mahmud Yunus (1979), the first edition of which (1960) is frequently cited by Indonesian scholars (for example, Abdullah 1971; Noer 1973).

Tengku Asaluddin) rarely engaged in serious study of Arabic, and women virtually never did so. In Isak, a few men in each generation would travel to the west coast of Aceh to study scripture. Takèngën-area men who wished further religious studies most often traveled to the north coast to study at the Awé Geutah religious school (Yakub 1980:324). There students read through the Qur'ān and then studied the series of Jawi books. Although some then undertook the study of Arabic and mysticism, most returned home after completing the Jawi series and became teachers in villages around Takèngën, using the Jawi books they had brought back with them. In the 1920s, most men who regularly taught religious subjects in Takèngën had themselves studied at Awé Geutah (which closed in about 1938).

The elder generation of religious scholars in Takèngën today began their educations in the 1930s under the tutelage of these Awé Geutah graduates. By then the virtues of the school had become legendary. The Takèngën modernist leader Tengku Ali Jaidun remembered its reputation for strictness and purity. For example, students were not allowed to smoke. "Anyone who had completed the studies in Sufism there was clean inside and outside," he said in 1978. "The students learned to rid themselves of inner uncleanlinesses, including self-admiration, greed, hypocrisy, pride, hate, envy, and betrayal. The Awé Geutah graduates gained many followers in the fight against the Dutch because they were believed to have truly become pure. Many resistance fighters (*Muslimin*) were graduates of Awé Geutah." One hears in this modernist's reminiscences the echoes of religion as piety and power that Tengku Asaluddin evoked for an earlier generation of Isak men and women.

In the mid-1920s Gayo men began to study Arabic at recently opened schools in Aceh and West Sumatra, and some of them returned to teach Arabic grammar in Takèngën. The most famous of this generation was the traditionalist scholar Ahmad Damanhuri, known as Tengku Silang. In 1989 I asked for information about him from Tengku Ali Salwany, the head of the Takèngën branch of al-Jammiyat al-Washliyah, the association of traditionalist scholars based in Medan. Ali Salwany is the scholarly heir to Tengku Silang, and his cousin (his mother's brother's son) as well. In telling of Tengku Silang's life he placed great emphasis on the educational pedigree that he brought to Takèngën:

Before Tengku Silang, Gayo people did not study Arabic books, only the Jawi books, and if they left the area at all it was only to study those books, perhaps at Awé Geutah. Tengku Silang's generation was the first to study in Arabic. He went first [about 1926] to Bireuën [on the north coast], to study at the Perguruan Islam under Haji Mustafa, then to Langsa [East Aceh] to study with a Minangkabau man, who then sent him on to Candung in West Sumatra [about 1930]. There he studied for three years with Syeh Suleiman al-Rasuli Candung. Syeh Suleiman was one of the eight major scholars ['ulamā'] in West Sumatra at that time; they were known as the Eight Tigers. Syeh Suleiman's school was called the Tarbiyah Islamiyah; Tengku Silang entered at the fifth grade level and left after completing the seventh. The school taught only according to the Shafi'i legal school, from thick Arabic law books. At night [the students] were encouraged to discuss and debate among themselves what they had learned during the day.[16]

Tengku Silang had intended to continue his studies at Pulo Kiton [in Bireuën], but Tengku Pulo Kiton asked him three questions when he arrived and gave him until the following morning to answer. Tengku Silang asked if he might answer right then and did so, after which Tengku Pulo Kiton told him he did not need to study with him and should return home. He arrived back in Kebayakan in 1934, where the next year he opened the Tarbiyah Islamiyah school. It had just one classroom, with benches made by driving stakes into the ground and placing boards on them. In 1939 he moved his school to the new prayer house in Batin, his home neighborhood in Kebayakan. The building burned down in the same year, but the district ruler, Ampun [Kejurun] Zainuddin, gave him the money to build a new prayer house and school. Tengku Silang had served as Zainuddin's religious official since 1939, and had been very successful at bringing in the zakāt. The new school, called Mersah Atu [Stone Prayer House] opened in 1940. Tengku Silang opened branches of his school, all called Tarbiyah Islamiyah, in Bëbësën and Tritit.

His character was what Arabs would call *waraq*, calm and pious [<Ar. *wara'*, piety]; he used few words but effective ones, never raising his voice. He was very pious [*sālih*] and always worshiped. He was a clear contrast in his style with Tengku Jali [the leading modernist spokesman at the time], who laughed raucously. The two scholars met in small debates and discussions from 1938 on, but the big debate took place in 1941, at Ampun Zainuddin's house. Nobody won, although supporters of each side said their man had won. Tengku Silang was able to correct Tengku Jali's Arabic pronunciation and show how his incorrect reading of vocalizations changed the meaning of the words. Tengku Jali knew a lot of words but Tengku Silang knew about every domain covered by scripture.

Tengku Silang died in June 1942. Tengku Jali lived much longer and so could train more students, and that is why they took over the town and control of the town mosque. But everyone in the villages is for us, perhaps one hundred to one. Tengku Rahman had been Tengku Silang's student and assistant, and took over leadership of the school in Kebayakan. He taught there until 1946 when it and many other religious schools in the area were converted to

---

[16] Compare Eickelman (1985:98–104) on the importance of peer learning at an early-twentieth-century Moroccan school.

state primary Islamic schools [Madrasah Ibtidaiyah Negeri, MIN, initially called Sekolah Rakyat Islam, SRI].[17] He then called all the local scholars to him and told each that he had to become a teacher.

Ali Salwany portrays traditionalist scholarship as modern in every way. He describes the importance of rational, critical discussion at the Candung school, as well as the "thick Arabic books" on which students relied. In stressing the significance of open debate and a command of the Arabic sources, his account resembles those given by modernists about their schools. He emphasizes Tengku Silang's superior command of Arabic in his debate with the modernist Tengku Jali. To describe Tengku Silang's character, Ali Salwany selects an Arabic-derived word, *waraq*, that is un-familiar to most Gayo, rather than a near equivalent in Gayo (such as *mukemèl*, has a sense of shame, reserve), as if to suggest that long familiar-ity with the Arabic language had made the teacher more of an Arab than a Gayo.

Tengku Ali Salwany's account also includes a mention of the graded sys-tem of education at Candung and Tengku Silang's erection of benches for his students at Kebayakan. This seemingly unimportant detail became a symbol of modern educational methods for Sumatran teachers. The older style of teaching, often called the "circle" (*halaqah*) method, involved students of different ages and levels of knowledge seated on the floor around the teacher. The best students would help the beginners, and the teacher, in theory, kept each proceeding at his or her level. Beginning in the 1910s, modernist teachers in West Sumatra adopted the Dutch govern-ment system of graded schools as the model for their own religious educa-tion, and the system quickly became the basis for the influential network of Thawalib schools in West Sumatra (Abdullah 1971:55–63; Noer 1973:45–50). Teachers also substituted rows of writing benches for the circle of stu-dents. This move in itself aroused some opposition, as school benches had been a mark of colonial schools; thus, some older teachers attacked the new schools as "infidel schools." The benches became a symbol of the innova-tions in educational method embraced by modernists and many tradition-alists in Sumatra. The innovations are often summed up by the word *kelas*, which can mean both "grade," as opposed to mixed levels, and "class-room," as opposed to prayer house. In the school at Kebayakan, the instruc-tional program gradually developed into a graded system as the number of students rose.[18]

---

[17] This change meant that only civil servants could teach at the schools. Many religious teachers in Takèngën have refused to enter civil service in order to preserve their indepen-dence. The conversion of private schools to state schools has thus been seen by some of these teachers as a means for the state to blunt their effectiveness.

[18] Compare Fischer (1980) on the "semicircle" style of teaching in the Iranian madrasah, and Mitchell (1988:69–92) on the creation of discipline in and through schools in colonial Egypt (in which benches also figure).

The travels of Tengku Silang coincided with a period of rapid pedagogical change in Sumatra. His first stop was at the modern-style school of Haji Mustafa Salim, who had brought the kelas method from West Sumatra to Aceh (Yakub 1980:335). Tengku Silang's final school at Candung was the current center for innovative traditionalist scholarship. The Madrasah Tarbiyah Islamiyah at Candung had been founded in 1907 by Syeh Suleiman al-Rasuli and was the birthplace, in 1928, of PERTI (Persatuan Tarbiyah Islamiyah, Association for Islamic Education), a network of religious schools that held to Shafi'i law (Yunus 1979:97–98).[19] The creation of PERTI took place about two years before Tengku Silang's arrival, and his years there were a time of exciting and edifying expansion, as students were sent out to establish new Tarbiyah Islamiyah schools in their home regions. The final episode in his wanderings confirmed his readiness to teach. He presented himself to Tengku Pulo Kiton after completing his studies at Awé Geutah, the major older-style place of learning for Gayo teachers. Tengku Pulo Kiton's declaration that Tengku Silang had nothing more to learn was not only a certification of his knowledge but an acknowledgment from a master of the older generation of teachers that this product of the new teaching system was every bit as good as those who came from the old.

Indonesian commentators on religious education often focus on the selection of books as the most telling index of a school's orientation. The Kebayakan school used what the modernist writer Mahmud Yunus (1979:53–62) called the pedagogy of the "transitional period."[20] Although modern in its structure and in its focus on learning Arabic, it generally drew on older texts and ideas. The teachings were all in accord with Shafi'i teachings; the school was divided into three classes; and three subjects were taught: law (fikh), Arabic, and Qur'ān. Entering students studied Arabic along with the religious subjects, and teachers used Arabic-language books for the other courses. Courses in law and theology used the same literature as had been used by previous generations.[21] (A few schools, notably the Pesantren Pasir near Kebayakan, continued to use these books into the 1970s [Hanafiah 1974:22–23].)

[19] The association was created in opposition to contemporary modernist developments (see below) and in reaction to modernists' disapproval of al-Rasuli's leadership of a local Sufi lodge, a Naqsyabandiah *tarekat* (Steenbrink 1974:63).

[20] Mahmud Yunus classifies curricula with reference to the period when they were used in the most progressive West Sumatran schools. He identifies the years 1900–1908 as the period of "transition" to modern education in West Sumatra; it was the curriculum developed in this period that continued to be used at the Tarbiyah Islamiyah Candung.

[21] For the study of Arabic syntax and inflections students used the books locally referred to as the Awamil, the Bina, and the Jurumiyah (for identifications see van Bruinessen 1990:241; see also Snouck Hurgronje 1906, II:7; Yunus 1979:43–45). They learned law from the Arabic book *Fath al-Qarīb* and theology from the *Kifāyat al-'Awāmm*, books that had long been in use throughout Sumatra (van Bruinessen 1990:252; Yunus 1973:54–55). The latter may have been in Jawi or Arabic; a Jawi version was still used in Takèngën in the late 1980s.

The school was also transitional in its approach to scripture. For the first two years of a student's career the Qur'ān course consisted only of recitation practice. When Tengku Ali Salwany attended in the 1930s, "only in the third year did we begin to discuss the meaning of verses, and then only short ones. We never read a commentary; our teacher Tengku Rahman would provide us with the meanings. And we only discussed verses that bore directly on legal matters: the fast, zakāt, marriage. Tengku Rahman in turn relied on the *Tafsīr Jalālayn*."

By reading from the Arabic commentary *Tafsīr Jalālayn*, Tengku Rahman both continued a long-standing feature of Malay-world education and joined an innovation in approaches to scripture. This *Tafsīr* had been the basis for what was then the only Qur'ānic commentary written in the Malay language, the *Tarjumān al-Mustafīd* by 'Abdurra'ūf of Singkel (d. 1693). The *Tarjumān* was first circulated in a print edition in 1884 and was subsequently printed in Singapore, Jakarta, and Penang (Riddell 1990). It is still used extensively in Malaysia and Sumatra. Tengku Rahman thus continued to follow what had become standard interpretations of the Qur'ān (previously studied through the Malay *Tarjumān*), but in using the Arabic original rather than the Malay translation, he embodied the new idea of direct access to the Arabic-language sources of religious knowledge.

Graduates of the Kebayakan school were encouraged to deepen their still-elementary understandings of Arabic and of scriptural sciences. Those who chose to do so could pursue their studies by climbing a hierarchy of schools, all within the traditional Shafi'i orbit, before reaching the best, innovative schools in West Sumatra. Modernists and traditionalists alike looked to West Sumatran schools for advanced study in Arabic and in matters of law, theology, and Sufism.

. . .

Tengku Ali Salwany's own life exemplifies the traditionalist's trajectory at mid-century. In 1941, after completing his studies at the local Tarbiyah Islamiyah school, he left Takèngën to study at secondary (*tsanawiyah*) schools in Aceh and then at advanced schools in West Sumatra. He began at the Kuta Tablang school in Samalanga, on the north coast of Aceh, and then shifted to the Madrasah al-Muslim in Peusangan (where his teacher in Kebayakan, Tengku Rahman, had once studied). Al-Muslim was one of the new progressive religious schools that had sprung up throughout Aceh under the patronage of local rulers. The school had been established in 1930 by Teuku Abdul Rahman under the protection of the Peusangan ruler (*ulèëbalang*), and was the birthplace of the Acehnese reformist movement PUSA (Persatuan Ulama Seluruh Aceh, All-Aceh Ulama Association), of which Abdul Rahman became the vice-chairman in 1939 (Reid 1979:23, 25; Yakub 1980:336–38).

In 1949, following his studies at al-Muslim, Ali Salwany arrived in Padang to study under Kiyai Sirajuddin Abbas at his Kuliah Syari'ah school. Sirajuddin Abbas had graduated from the Arabic medium al-Irshād school in Jakarta and had returned to Padang to teach at the Kuliah Syari'ah, where general subjects were offered alongside religious ones (Yunus 1979:103). Abbas wrote at least two instructional books in Arabic that were used by schools in the traditionalist PERTI network (Yunus 1979:100), and then wrote a four-volume set in Indonesian, *40 Masalah Agama* (Forty Religious Issues), in which he provided substantial grounding in hadīth for the traditionalist position on the major issues under dispute. These books are frequently reprinted and serve as handbooks for traditionalists throughout Sumatra.

After five years studying under Sirajuddin Abbas, Ali Salwany moved to Darul Hikmah, the advanced school in nearby Bukittinggi. Darul Hikmah had been founded only the year before, in 1953, and was designed to produce judges for Indonesia's Islamic courts (Yunus 1979:138). Ali Salwany never completed his studies. In 1958 rebellion broke out in West Sumatra, and he had to choose between joining the rebels or leaving the province. He decided to return to Takèngën, where he immediately worked to create new religious schools along the lines of the Kuliah Syari'ah.

Upon his return Ali Salwany joined with two other local scholars to found a Takèngën branch of the traditionalist association al-Jammiyat al-Washliyah (Society for Unification). Al-Washliyah had been established in Medan in 1930 by students at the Maktab Islamiyah school. Its founders intended it to serve as a forum for discussion of doctrinal differences and to dampen the escalating disputes between Medan modernists and traditionalists. The association's charter directs its members to teach religious affairs through publishing instructional books, sponsoring discussions, and founding new schools, all of which would disseminate the Shafi'i legal tradition (Yunus 1975:194–95). By 1955 al-Washliyah had created 266 elementary-level madrasahs, general schools (certified as equivalent to the state schools), and a teacher's training college (Yunus 1979:198).[22]

The Takèngën branch of the association overreached itself in the early years, creating three madrasahs and, in 1970, a university. The university lasted five years and graduated nineteen students; all the madrasahs had closed by 1980, when the association opened a standard-form high school. The 1970s were a period when students throughout Indonesia shifted away from Islamic schools toward those state schools that would best prepare them for employment as civil servants. The organization retreated to other activities: weekly Qur'ān study sessions held at private houses, public lec-

---

[22] In Medan the association took on an ethnic cast, with a largely Mandailing Batak leadership, in contrast to the predominantly Minangkabau composition of the modernist organization Muhammadiyah.

tures (*dakwa*), and informally resolving disputes over ritual and other religious matters.

Today, Tengku Ali Salwany's only office is his desk at the Central Aceh Council of Ulama (Majelis Ulama). The Council of Ulama consists of the heads of local religious organizations and other prominent teachers. It advises the district head (Bupati), the district parliament, and the district religious court (Mahkamah Syari'ah) on matters of religious education, marriage laws, and religious consciousness in the villages. Because modernists and traditionalists on the council must cooperate, they tend to avoid taking up controversial questions of law or ritual. Council members also give Qur'ān recitations and deliver talks in village prayer houses on such topics as the meaning of an upcoming feast day or the importance of regular worship. A subunit of the council, the Badan Harta Agama (Religious Wealth Unit), collects the portion of the zakāt due the subdistrict and district governments. The council once issued binding opinions (*fatwā*) as well, but now that right is restricted to councils at the national and provincial levels.

It is at home that Ali Salwany is free to speak and act as a partisan of the traditionalist viewpoint. He conducts al-Washliyah business there or in local prayer houses. Because of the relative dominance of modernists in town affairs, he and other traditionalists consider themselves marginalized in Takèngën, thus his compensatory remark (heard from other traditionalists as well) that *villagers* preferred traditionalists to modernists "perhaps one hundred to one." He does receive large numbers of visitors from nearby villages who wish to have questions about ritual or legal matters settled by a religious authority, while far fewer villagers ever seek advice from his main modernist rival, Tengku Ali Jaidun, much to Ali Salwany's satisfaction. The difference in popularity between the two stems in part from reasons of personality (Ali Salwany is relaxed and approachable, Ali Jaidun tends toward the schoolteacherly), but more importantly from what villagers perceive as Ali Jaidun's uncompromising opposition to many village ritual practices.

Ali Salwany spends little of his time alone. On one occasion when I was visiting, a delegation of women arrived to request that he deliver a talk in their village the following day; the head of a Takèngën-area subdistrict was waiting to ask his opinion on proper ritual for the Feast of Sacrifice ('īd al-adhā); and Ali Salwany had spent the entire previous day discussing the proper form for the funeral catechism with the other leading traditionalist scholars.

Ali Salwany's approach to history is typical of the traditionalist scholar. He never refers to the local past, quotes no Acehnese proverbs, and evinces little nostalgia for people of the past. But neither does he base his opinions solely on scripture or on the prophet Muhammad's example. His view of Islamic history features the period of the great scholars of Islam: the "four great imāms" who founded the four main Sunnī legal traditions, including the Shafi'i. Consider part of his discussion on one rather detailed issue of worship: whether one should state one's intent just prior to worship. This "*ushalli* controversy" was so named after the standard phrase many recite just before the initial "Allah Akbar" that signals entry into worship:

> Granted, the prophet Muhammad did not say the ushalli. There are many things we do that he did not: wear wristwatches and sunglasses, or use a microphone for the call to prayer. But these things are all good. They are "innovations" [bid'a], but there are two kinds of innovations, good and bad. The four great imams distinguished the good from the bad. They were the last people capable of doing so, the last *mujtahid* [one who exercises ijtihād, independent legal reasoning] capable of memorizing 300,000 hadīth. They set out the Qur'ānic verses and hadīth for us, and none of us today are capable of doing what they did. We all read their books in deciding religious affairs, so if Ali Jaidun says he does not follow a legal school it is a lie [this thought had diverted him from the ushalli and, lost, he asked me where we were in the conversation].

For Tengku Ali Salwany, the history of religious knowledge may include local, partial progress (such as the growth of schooling in Takèngën), but it takes place within a broader historical plot with three major moments: revelation through scripture and the example of the prophet Muhammad; the sifting and collating of scripture by the four great imāms; and, after the "gates were closed" on further independent legal reasoning in the ninth century, our continuing duty, as people of lesser powers, to follow the imāms' teachings.[23]

MUHAMMADIYAH: SOCIAL AND RELIGIOUS INNOVATION IN THE HIGHLANDS

The traditionalist scholars honed their arguments in large part against the modernist challenge to religious life in the highlands (as Ali Salwany's responses indicate), but the modernists active in Takèngën since the 1920s have hardly spoken with one voice. They have included Muhammadiyah teachers educated in West Sumatra who have emphasized social reform, politically active graduates of schools in Aceh who developed strong ties to provincial movements, and religious reformers educated in Arabic-language schools on Java who have stressed the need to rid the highlands of improper religious practices. Beyond their shared commitment to the renewed study of scripture, twentieth-century Gayo modernists have taken diverse positions on issues of social reform, political loyalties, and the appropriate tone of religious campaigning. Within highlands modernism the field of discourse is thus extremely dispersive.

---

[23] On the question of whether in the ninth century the "gate of ijtihād" was indeed closed, see Hallaq (1984).

Muhammadiyah was the first modernist organization to influence highlands thinking. In the 1920s Minangkabau traders from Padang, the West Sumatran port city, were attracted to Takèngën by its thriving cash-crop economy (Bowen 1991:76–81). Some of the traders had studied in the innovative schools of West Sumatra and most followed modernist strictures regarding worship, funeral meals, and other issues. In Takèngën they soon built their own prayer house (still referred to as the "Padang prayer house") where they could gather for congregational worship along modernist lines (see Chapter 13). They presently attracted a small number of Gayo men and women as well, and in 1928 created a Takèngën branch of the Muhammadiyah association. Muhammadiyah had been founded in 1912 in Java, but its rapid spread throughout Indonesia was due in large part to the efforts of West Sumatran teachers and traders. Muhammadiyah gave first priority to building modern-style schools. In Takèngën, Muhammadiyah quickly established religious schools (madrasah) as well as a seven-year school, modeled after the government school, in which both secular and religious subjects were taught. The new schools were staffed chiefly by Minangkabau teachers with Gayo assistants; this pattern continued into the 1950s despite the increasing Gayo composition of the membership in the Muhammadiyah association (Bowen 1991:97–98).

Arabic grammar was a cornerstone of all Muhammadiyah-sponsored education. The same was true, of course, of the contemporary traditionalist schools, especially Tengku Silang's Tarbiyah Islamiyah school in Kebayakan. But Muhammadiyah schools made a complete break with the pre-existing curricula of Aceh by borrowing methods and teaching materials from West Sumatra, especially from the Thawalib schools. They replaced Jawi books with hybrids that used Latin-script Indonesian to explain the meaning of Arabic phrases. Advanced students read books written entirely in Arabic.

The current leaders of Muhammadiyah were among the first students at these new schools. The chief spokesman for Muhammadiyah, Tengku Ali Jaidun, entered the Tarbiyah Islamiyah in Tritit, north of Takèngën, but in 1940 shifted to the recently opened Muhammadiyah school nearby. There he studied largely religious subjects, in particular religious law and Arabic grammar. The books he read were by West Sumatran authors, especially Mahmud Aziz and Mahmud Yunus, whose *Ilmu Musthalah Hadis* (Science of Hadīth Interpretation) became the standard work on the topic for Muhammadiyah schools, and Abdul Hamid Hakim, one of the pioneers of modernist education in West Sumatra.[24] Few copies of these books were available, so students copied from the teacher's books into their own notebooks. Ara-

---

[24] These authors had founded the Normal Islam teacher-training school in Padang in 1931 (Abdullah 1971:13–14, 213–16; Yunus 1979:102–8, 156–58).

bic-language books at first were purchased from West Sumatran booksellers and later ordered directly from Cairo.

Many men and women in the northern part of the highlands received their first instruction in Arabic at one of the Takèngën-area Muhammadiyah schools. The message of this concentration on language skills was that, as one scholar told me, "once you know Arabic you can find out the rest on your own." Tengku Asaluddin's enjoyment of his own command of Arabic is not atypical of the men and women of this generation.

But Muhammadiyah's impact was as much social and political as it was religious. Muhammadiyah set up separate organizations for each gender and age group. The central organization was governed by men, while women ran the parallel Aisyiah organization (named for the prophet Muhammad's wife 'Ā'isha). Since its inception circa 1930, the Takèngën branch of Aisyiah has promoted Qur'ān recitation, the study of commentary, and such *sosial* (social welfare) activities as working for the town orphanage and bringing food to bereaved families. Girls joined the Nasyiatul Aisyiah, and boys entered the scouts organization Hizbul Wathan.

Modernist-leaning women and men in Takèngën invariably mention the adoption of new styles of women's clothing in the 1930s as part of the modernist revolution. Women who joined Muhammadiyah renounced the clothing associated with Gayo ëdët: the shorter blouses and skirt-cloths that were sometimes embroidered with Gayo designs. In their place they adopted the Malay-Indonesian *kebaya* blouses, long *sarung* cloths, and head scarves. The change in clothing signaled a double shift in socioreligious consciousness: toward a heightened concern with covering the body, as well as the adoption of "Indonesian" clothing styles. The kebaya, sarung, and scarf have become mandatory women's wear for all public functions; men have adopted the black *peci* hat popularized by Sukarno, worn with a sarung and, for special occasions, a Western-style suitcoat. Other changes have accompanied these shifts: widespread use of Indonesian, friendships with non-Gayo residents of the town, even knowledge of Minangkabau, the language of the first Takèngën modernists. But the shift in women's clothing, with its double significance of greater modesty and an opening outward to the nation, is the most-remembered marker in Gayo modernists' accounts of their social awakening.

Tengku Asaluddin, my Isak religious teacher, entered Muhammadiyah in the 1930s. In remembering his early days in Muhammadiyah, he celebrated his discovery of a wider, Indonesian world. His autobiographical conversations with me have travel and study, rather than religious reform, as their leitmotif. He wandered in part to avoid registering with the Dutch government and paying a head tax, but also because of a personal and intellectual restlessness that he still displayed in his late seventies.

In 1933, when he was sixteen and one year out of the three-year Isak

elementary school, he left Isak to continue his religious studies in
Takèngën.

In Takèngën I joined the youth group of Muhammadiyah, the Hizbul Wathan.
We joined together to defend our land. We learned "Indonesia Raya" [Greater
Indonesia, the nationalist anthem, banned at that time by the Dutch], but we
sang it with different words as the Hizbul Wathan anthem. It went [he sings to
the tune of "Indonesia Raya"]:

Agama Islam berdasar Quran	Islam is based on the Qur'ān.
agama perintah Tuhën	Religion is the command of God,
dibawa oleh Nabi Muhammad	brought by the prophet Muhammad,
sallā Allāhu 'alayhi wa sallam	May God bless him and grant him peace.
marilah kita sekalian	Come, let us all
ta'luk menjalankan	obediently carry it out.

There are other verses. The Controleur [Dutch district officer] would just sit
and listen, nodding to it, not understanding what it meant to us. In the Hizbul
Wathan we learned what Indonesia was. We recited together:

Wahai bangsaku lekas berdiri	Oh my people: quick! stand up!
karena matahari sudah tinggi	because the sun is already high.
apakah kamu masih tidur	If you are still sleeping,
nasi sudah jadi bubur.	the rice will have turned to porridge.

These lines raised our spirits. Our teachers were all from the Thawalib
schools. Each day I studied Arabic at the Muhammadiyah school with Nasarud-
din, who wanted to take me back to Padang with him; he had no children of
his own. My grandmother would not let me go. I worked at the Muhammadiyah office as well.

At night I studied Arabic grammar with Saleh Sarip from [the Thawalib
school at] Batu Sangkar. Saleh Sarip was a political type; he refused to work
for the government. He had taught in the Tapanuli region first [south of Aceh]
and then came to Aceh. He had cooked rice crisps in Aceh, then made a living
here by making things out of wire, making shoe soles. He had studied Arabic
under Hasbi [ash-Shiddieqy, the Acehnese modernist teacher]. Later he moved
to Meulaboh and worked as a trader, and then moved to Kota Raja [later
Banda Aceh], where he worked for Hasbi on his magazine, al-Hakam [The
Judgment]. Sarip sent for me, and I came [about 1939]. I worked with two
other people laying out the magazine, and three times a week studied Qur'ān
with Hasbi. I also would carry copies to Meulaboh; I would have to sell them
to return, for I had no money at all.

Tengku Asaluddin's life found its channels in what we might call the so-
cial-modernity side of Muhammadiyah. Upon his return to Isak in 1943 he
began to teach Qur'ān recitation in a village prayer house, but delighted
more in teaching children how to play flutes for a performance on 'īd al-fitr

than in correcting adults' erroneous religous ideas. Although he agreed to serve as the first Isak religious official after independence, he retired from the office after two years and moved, with his family and his herd of water buffalo, to a new community north of Takèngën that had been founded by Isak modernists. He served as head of the Takèngën orphanage in the early 1950s, and remained in that position until his retirement in 1979.

Tengku Asaluddin became head of the Takèngën Muhammadiyah organization during the Darul Islam period in the 1950s. He was tolerated by the government precisely because he had kept clear of politics—specifically, he had not joined the Masyumi party, which was suspected of being pro-Darul Islam by the government. He had also refrained from strongly modernist statements, focusing instead on setting up Qur'ān study sessions at Muhammadiyah. "The Communists and Nationalist Party people came as well as those in Masyumi; I could go back and forth among them."

The year after he retired, Tengku Asaluddin and his wife performed the obligatory pilgrimage to Mecca; he repeated the pilgrimage (this time by himself) in 1986. On both occasions he delighted in being the unofficial guide for many of his fellow Gayo pilgrims (in 1980, thirteen people from the Isak subdistrict accompanied him). He loves to tell how he was able to find food and water for his group, locate the graveyard of the prophet Muhammad, and converse with a Palestinian man about war and its dangers.

Whereas Tengku Ali Salwany considers himself and other traditionalists marginalized in the town, in the village it is the modernist Tengku Asaluddin who feels isolated. In the public forum of the mosque, he rails against backward and ignorant understandings of religion. But these public stances cut him off from the majority of Isak people. In everyday life he revels in solitude. Waking early, he takes long walks downstream. He prefers to spend as many of his days as his health permits net-fishing by himself or staying with his wife in a small house downstream from Isak where he keeps his water buffalo. (He knows a fair amount of veterinary science and encouraged one of his daughters to take an advanced degree in the subject.) His sense of community comes less from everyday interactions with fellow villagers than from his access to the wider religious community.

If Tengku Asaluddin exemplifies the social wing of Muhammadiyah, its religious reformism is better illustrated by his erstwhile companion, Tengku Joharsyah. Tengku Joharsyah was born into the descent line of the Clever Chief in Isak, one of the two major precolonial political offices. His elder brother worked as a foreman on a Dutch dammar pine estate. Together, his parents and brother were able to finance his education at a succession of modernist schools in the 1930s. He was one of the very few Gayo men who could afford to attend school in West Sumatra, considered the center of modernist learning. He studied at the Thawalib school in Padang Panjang from 1939 through 1944. "I had heard about Thawalib, that the Dutch suspected it of being anticolonial. It taught you to work for the independence of Indonesia. My eyes had already been opened then and I wanted to go to a school like that."

Tengku Joharsyah's understandings of religious history contrast markedly with those held by Tengku Ali Salwany and other Takèngën traditionalists. For the latter, the great ulama of the past have no equals today and therefore we should follow their teachings. Tengku Joharsyah learned quite differently.

> At Thawalib we studied the Qur'ān, not what "the tengkus" have said. Many hadīth have been invented, so you have to choose carefully among them. But people back in Gayo just followed what "the tengkus" said. For instance, when someone dies you should bring the bereaved some food to ease their suffering, but here people would descend on the house and torment them by eating lots of food. Thawalib included none of that kind of thinking.

Tengku Joharsyah returned to Isak in 1945, where he taught religious school with Tengku Asaluddin. The Japanese quickly named him subdistrict religious official, largely because of his high-status position in the Clever Chief line. From 1946 to the outbreak of rebellion in 1953 he was head of the subdistrict. In 1953 the government removed him under suspicion of siding with the Darul Islam secessionist movement (a charge he denies). During his time in both offices he tried to change how Isak people thought about religion by directly intervening in rituals.

> Together with Tengku Asaluddin I would visit the bereaved after every death. We would bring food and drink with us. One of us would stand up and say that we should all pray together for the deceased, not hold recitations for him. No one ever dared read the telkin [catechism] when they knew we were coming, nor would they dare serve meals for the guests. People really obeyed authority back then. . . . I did not just tell them to stop; I set an example.

Tengku Asaluddin rarely mentioned these confrontations; Tengku Joharsyah loved to recall them.[25]

---

[25] Tengku Joharsyah's mixture of religious reformism and political activism reflects Thawalib teachings, and the differences in emphasis between his own reflections and those of Tengku Asaluddin mirror the general contrast between Thawalib schools and Muhammadiyah. In West Sumatra this difference was sharper, especially after the transformation of the Thawalib association into the more explicitly nationalist Permi (Persatuan Muslim Indonesia, Association of Indonesian Muslims) (Abdullah 1971:130–35). Thawalib teachers accused Muhammadiyah of neglecting political activity, while Muhammadiyah suspected Thawalib of diluting religious activities with political concerns, and even of having lingering pro-Communist sympathies (Noer 1973:77–78).

RADICAL REFORM THROUGH ISLAMIC EDUCATION

The sharpest challenge to traditionalist teachings came not from Muhammadiyah but from the Gayo teachers at the religious school called Islamic Education (Pendidikan Islam, PI). Their strongest connections were with Java rather than Aceh or West Sumatra, and they were inspired by two specific developments: the creation of the Arab-sponsored school network al-Irshād, and outpouring of strongly reformist publications from the organization Persis (Persatuan Islam, Muslim Unity).

Al-Irshād (Jamī'at al-Islām wal-Irshād al-Arabia, Association of Islam and Arabian Guidance) was founded in Jakarta in 1913 by a group of Arab traders. The organization's founders chafed at the deference demanded of them by those Arabs in Indonesia who claimed the status of *Sayid*, or descent from the prophet Muhammad. They formed al-Irshād to promote equality and educational advancement within the Arab community. They found religious backing for their emphasis on social equality in the writings of modernist Muslims and consequently turned increasingly to religious education. Their religious leader was Syeh Ahmad Surkati, born in Sudan in 1872. Surkati had taught in Mecca, where he was impressed by the writings of Muhammad 'Abduh. He was recruited by the Indonesia Arab community and arrived at Jakarta in 1911. From 1913 until his death in 1943 he served as the spiritual leader of al-Irshād (Noer 1973:62–69). The organization quickly established schools throughout Java, and in the 1930s the Surabaya branch created a two-year course to train religious teachers (Noer 1973:65).

Persis also had a strongly international flavor. It was created in Bandung in 1923 by several families of Palembang (South Sumatran) origin who had been attracted to the modernist teachings of Muhammad 'Abduh, the Thawalib group, and Syeh Ahmad Surkati (Federspiel 1970:11–12; Noer 1973:83–85). The group developed its distinctive stance under the direction of Ahmad Hassan. Born in Singapore in 1887 to an Indian father and Indonesian mother, Ahmad Hassan remembered that even when he was small his father would abruptly leave a funeral at which a talqīn catechism was read, and, later, he encountered debates in Singapore and in Surbaya over the ushalli, the expression of intent to worship (Noer 1973:85–88).

Ahmad Hassan and his colleagues in Persis engaged frequently in public debates over religious issues. In a series of periodicals published in the 1930s they provocatively attacked traditionalist teachings. The periodicals included columns wherein a Persis scholar, usually Ahmad Hassan, answered questions from readers on religious topics. These sections were written in plain Indonesian, with Indonesian translations of all quotations from Qur'ān or hadīth, and they were very popular. The columns were reprinted in several volumes as *Sual-Djawab* (Questions and Answers), and a one-volume edition of this work continues to be reprinted and sold throughout Indonesia as a manual for modernists (Federspiel 1970:20–24). Persis also founded schools called Pendidikan Islam (Islamic Education) throughout Java (Noer 1973:89–90).

Al-Irshād and Persis were linked in several ways. The two organizations shared positions on many issues, and both urged Muslims to reject any teachings not based on the Qur'ān and hadīth. Ahmad Hassan also backed al-Irshād's strongly felt criticisms of those Arabs who claimed to be Sayyids and demanded special respect (Federspiel 1970:63–66). Many scholars were involved in both organizations, and al-Irshād graduates often drew on Hassan's writings in their own efforts to reform religious practices in their home towns or villages.

The dual involvement most consequential for Aceh was that of Hasbi ash-Shiddieqy, a graduate of the al-Irshād school who then became a member of Persis and a champion of Ahmad Hassan's views (Shiddiqi 1987). After his return to Aceh he distributed Hassan's magazine *Pembela Islam* (Defender of Islam) as well as his own *al-Hakam* (The Judgment), and founded a school modeled after an al-Irshād school in Lhokseumawe on the northern Aceh coast. He turned over the responsibility for the school to Syekh Mohd. al-Kalali, a trader of Arab descent who had helped found the important Malay Islamic journal *al-Imam* (Roff 1967:64; Yakub 1980:335), and then established his own center for teaching and publishing in Kuta Raja (to which Tengku Asaluddin traveled in the early 1940s). It was through the school run by al-Kalali that Takèngën men and women were exposed to Ahmad Hassan's argument. Several men who had studied at the coastal school then went on to the Surbaya al-Irshād. Their return to Takèngën in the late 1930s and early 1940s signaled the beginning of a heightened debate in the highlands over doctrinal issues, a debate that brought the concerned attention of provincial officials and inspired the creation of new artistic forms and educational institutions.

In 1939 the Takèngën-born Abdul Jalil Rahmany, known as Tengku Jali, returned from several years of study at the al-Irshād school in Surbaya. In 1989 I discussed Tengku Jali's impact on Gayo society with his successor, Tengku Abdul Jalil Bahagia, known by his teknonym Aman Murni (Father of Murni) to distinguish him from the other Abdul Jalil. Aman Murni lives in a spacious, two-story house in the community of Balé, overlooking Lake Tawar. He has devoted the first floor to a classroom, in which are arranged rows of benches facing a blackboard.

Aman Murni has developed the general progressivist attitude of modernists into a Mozartian drama of enlightenment's triumph over corrupt darkness. When I first asked him to talk with me, he said he preferred to write out a history as an outline for our discussions. In the space of a week he produced a seven-page, single-spaced, Indonesian-language document entitled "The Development of Religion in Takèngën, Central Aceh." The paper was in outline form, with three levels of headings organizing highlands history into a dark ages, a period of moderate reform, and then the final "renewal" (*pembaharuan*) under Tengku Jali.

Aman Murni's history begins with the negative characteristics of "the people of Central Aceh" (he avoids the ethnic label "Gayo" in order to emphasize religious rather than cultural differences) before renewal. People worshiped trees, rocks, and graves; they held ritual meals (kenduri) that wasted resources; they relied on village healers who often caused illnesses in order to have the occasion to heal them; and rulers stirred up rivalries between villages and between the Bukit and Ciq domains.[26] Causing the chaos were

> the influence of adat, rulers, phony ulama, ulama drugged on heroin, no local education, blind obedience to the legal traditions; the clever taking from the stupid; the rich taking from the poor; the healers taking from the sick.

True ulama came to Takèngën through the efforts of several parties: Muhammadiyah; the enlightened ruler of Balé who, with the support of local traders, founded the Islamic Education school in 1938; and, finally, the arrival of Tengku Jali in 1939. At this point in his written narrative Aman Murni introduces himself. Born in 1925, he graduated in 1939 from both the government school and the Muhammadiyah school (both six-year courses) in Takèngën, and that same year met Tengku Jali, who had just returned from al-Irshād in Surabaya. "I, Tgk H. Abd. Jalil Bahagia," he continues, "after six years with Muhammadiyah then studied [Arabic] with Ustaz Abd. Jalil [Tengku Jali], and the six years of study were not equal to one year [with him]." Just twenty years old in 1939, Tengku Jali became the Arabic instructor at the newly created Islamic Education School. Aman Murni studied under him until 1942, when he became his teaching assistant. In our discussions he described the school's methods:

> Pupils studied while seated on mats, and wrote on long benches, facing the blackboard; the teacher used no table whatsoever. All the books were ordered from Salim Nabhan's store in Surabaya; he had his own printing press in Egypt and a store in Surbaya for books on Islamic law. . . .[27] Each year each student had to pass an oral examination in front of the public. Most impor-

---

[26] At this point other modernists often mention the purported campaign by C. Snouck Hurgronje circa 1900 to sap Gayo resistance to the Dutch by introducing improper methods of worship (Bowen 1991:32–33).

[27] Van Bruinessen (1990:232) mentions the Surabaya store in his review of religious literature.

tantly, each student had to be able to memorize the answers to questions taken from the *Mufradāt al-Qira'at ar-Rashīda* (Lexicon of Correct Readings). Every morning the students had to wake up early and work at memorizing their *Mufradāt*. Those who lagged received blows or canings, and not even their parents could intervene.[28]

Like Muhammadiyah, Islamic Education sought to create students who were socially modern as well as religiously literate. On 'īd al-fitr, the students sang the school anthem in front of the houses of the two major Gayo rulers near Takèngën. They learned to play musical instruments purchased by the school, including trumpets, harmonicas, flutes, and drums, despite protests from traditionalists that they were, as Aman Murni put it, "trying to be like the infidels." Women who taught at the school started a Garden for Girls where they gave cooking lessons, including European dishes in their repertoires. After independence the school sponsored political courses, taught by the head of the Takèngën middle school, "because people did not understand 'independence,'" explained Aman Murni. "They thought it meant being given food without having to work anymore." The school also built mosques in several villages outside town.

These activities were sponsored by the wealthier traders in the village of Bale Bujang who wished to rid the area of mistaken beliefs, continues Aman Murni in his document. "And thus each day more and more of the old group's followers admitted that their positions were not based on evidence. If before, 75 percent of the people followed the old group, now the tables are turned and only 25 percent follow them, while 75 percent follow us and Muhammadiyah."

Shortly after his arrival in Takèngën, Tengku Jali initiated a series of debates on issues of ritual propriety, the best remembered of which was the debate in 1941 at the house of the Bukit domain ruler Rëjë Zainuddin in which Tengku Jali debated Tengku Silang. The debate lasted "from dusk until nearly dawn," wrote Aman Murni, "using all the books that discussed the talqīn, ritual meals for the dead, and other matters." Each side was asked to bring forth the arguments for or against the practice concerned. "In the end Raja Bukit Zainuddin closed the debate without determining who had won or lost, only saying: 'We now know where lie the better proofs and the weaker ones, even though they [advocates of the latter] will not admit it.'" The argument continued from each side's mosques. Friday sermons were frequently devoted to these disputed issues. The debates led to a

---

[28] The four-volume *Mufradāt al-Qira'at ar-Rashīda* is an Egyptian text in modern written Arabic that was used for Arabic instruction throughout the archipelago (van Bruinessen, personal communication); Yunus (1979) lists it among the books used for elementary instruction at the Medan al-Washliyah school, at the Sumatra Thawalib schools, at the Persis school, and elsewhere on Java.

final resolution at the provincial level, which Aman Murni then described with glee in his written account:

> Because Central Aceh had taken the [modernist] truth so seriously, some thought that the debates would lead to conflict, so the issues were taken up in Banda Aceh, as is set out in the *Maklumat Bersama* [Joint Proclamation] of 20–24 March 1948, which was signed by the head of Islamic affairs, in the name of all ulama, in the name of religious school heads, by the head of the religious courts, by the head of the Office of Religious Affairs, by the Religious Official for Aceh: that the nine practices under dispute do not exist in Islam.
>
> It then was clear that the arguments of the old group had been due to personal desires [*nafsu*] and were invalid. As the Messenger said: "Those who go astray because of us, on Judgment Day their sins will have to be borne by the ulama who misled them through their teachings."

This moment of vindication forms the climax of the narrative. There is, however, a denoument that shows the close but highly undependable ties of religious modernism to trade. Aman Murni describes how, in 1946, the traders who supported the Islamic Education school formed a corporation, PAT (Perusahaan Aceh Tengah, Central Aceh Enterprise). They sold shares in the company but retained majority control. A portion of the profits were to be used to benefit the school, its associated mosque, and the town orphanage. But both the cooperative and the school fell victim to the forces of materialism. "In its heyday, Islamic Education leaders eagerly took in the profits from PAT and paid less attention to religion," said Aman Murni, but devaluations of the Indonesian currency and oversold shares eventually cut those profits to a negligible level. Long before Tengku Jali's death in 1974, "people grew proud of new secular schools and neglected religious education, Qur'ān study, and village religious schools, despite the fact that from Qur'ān study and religious schools comes the true educational capital."

Aman Murni succeeded Tengku Jali as the head of Islamic Education in 1968. Three years later he campaigned for the government party Golkar at the behest of the district head. He was the only leading scholar in Takèngën to support Golkar (the others supported the Islamic parties), and the hostility he generated led the Islamic Education governing board to dismiss him in 1976. He then accepted the government's offer of financial assistance to build an alternative religious school (*pesantren*) on his property in Balé (thereby, in the eyes of many, further compromising himself). He sees his electoral activity as having no intrinsic religious implications and as justified by the support he received for his school.

By the end of the 1970s the Islamic Education school had followed its rivals in al-Washliyah into nonexistence, as students (or, more precisely, their parents) chose state schools for their greater promise of employment.

Aman Murni continued to teach, however, giving afternoon and evening classes in Arabic grammar and Qur'ān recitation at his new school. The course of study takes students between three and five years to complete. Twenty-five of his graduates are now continuing their studies in schools on Java, and in 1989 he reported a recent increase in the number of students; this increase, he concluded, reflected a return to religion. Aman Murni composes his own instructional materials on his typewriter; as of 1989 he had written a grammar of Arabic, a book of the prayers said by the prophet Muhammad, and a two-volume guide to religious ritual. His publications are kept on file at a local photocopy shop, for purchase by his students. All emphasize memorizing Arabic words, Qur'ānic verses, and prayers. (He gave his own son five rupiah for every Arabic word he memorized.)

Interpreting Scripture

In sharp contrast to the traditionalist teachers, modernists emphasized the importance of rendering scripture into the vernacular, or tafsīr. Although *tafsīr* literally means "explanation," and specifically scriptural interpretation, it includes what one might call "translation." Because the inimitability of the Qur'ān belies the idea of a translation, all renderings of its words into other tongues are generally considered to be interpretations.

In the 1930s most traditionalist scholars held that students should not be exposed to tafsīr, on the grounds that only someone with appropriate training can interpret scripture. Abu Bakar Bangkit, the former head of the Islamic party Masyumi, explained his own reticence to interpret partly on technical grounds: nonexperts do not know exactly how to recite the Qur'ān, and thus may misread it. "Even today I do not attempt to interpret the Qur'ān myself," he said. "I read the commentaries of others. . . . As people say: 'I do not translate the Qur'ān, I only interpret it.' We do not really know the *lafaz* [<Ar. *lafz*; the correct pronunciation and thus reading of the written text]; we can only say what we think it means." This hesitation before interpretation is not unique to Gayo or Indonesian Muslims; in the Arabic-speaking world as well, understanding and interpreting the Qur'ān has often been reserved for a late stage in religious education (Eickelman 1985:64; 1989a:304–15).

For Aman Murni, by contrast, tafsīr is a symbol of the modernist struggle. As he explained in a conversation with me:

> The Dutch would not let people interpret the Qur'ān. Sermons were all in Arabic, not Indonesian. Dutch spies listened to the sermons and reported anyone who translated a verse. Slowly, in part because of Muhammadiyah, we began to render some verses in Indonesian, first at religious meetings and then, by the late 1930s, in the Friday sermons, but even then we had to choose the

verses carefully. The Qur'ān warns the people about the infidels; that is why the Dutch were afraid of its message.

Aman Murni considers the rendering of scripture into Indonesian a political act, one that was seen as intrinsically such by the Dutch and thus prohibited. I found little support for this interpretation of Dutch attitudes among other modernists, but it points to Aman Murni's sense of the importance of vernacular renderings of scripture in the overall struggle for religious enlightenment. It is not surprising that Aman Murni and, in the past, other Islamic Education teachers have spent considerable time leading Qur'ān interpretation sessions (*tafsīr Qur'ān*) in nearby towns and villages. In the 1980s Aman Murni led such sessions at the Takèngën mosque every evening after the dusk worship session. He would typically link issues of practical religion and religious history to his explication of the Qur'ānic passage, as in one session I attended in June 1989:

About twenty men and boys gathered around Aman Murni after the evening prayer. Approximately the same number of women and girls sat about ten yards farther back in the mosque, separated from the men by a cloth hung over a cord. Aman Murni sat on a chair with his Qur'ān placed in front of him on a table; the other men and women passed out Qur'āns from the mosque's collection. The older men knew right where they had left off on the previous occasion.

That night Aman Murni read from Sūra An-Nisā', verses 97 to 104. Aman Murni's method was to read a few words, give a quick translation, and then add a sentence or two further glossing the meaning. In a few cases he gave an extended example. The first verses began with a group's complaint to the angels that they were unable to practice religion where they were, and the angels responded that they ought to move [*hijrah*] somewhere else. Aman Murni said that such was the situation confronting Tengku Hasbi ash-Shiddieqy in Lhokseumawe [when he established the al-Irshād school]: people did want to accept his knowledge, and he could not teach them, so he moved to Jakarta.

The following section dealt with the rules for shortening the number of ritual units [*rak'a*] to be performed in worship. Aman Murni spoke at length about these rules. The Department of Religion had fixed at sixty kilometers the distance from home at which you may begin to foreshorten worship, but you may change the way you worship if you need to, he explained, as did the prophet Muhammad when riding on a camel.

Aman Murni concluded the session by reminding everyone that its purpose was to expand the amount of knowledge we all possess [this remark may have been for my benefit]. Tea was then served and everyone waited for the time of the evening worship, which they performed together.

By moving between the time of scripture and the present, tafsīr highlights the immediate relevance of Muhammad's life and statements for solving current problems in religious life. No intermediate interpretations by the great legal scholars are required for acquiring this knowledge.

Other discursive forms send similar messages about scripture and history. Of particular importance in bringing modernism to the villages was religious poetry. In the 1930s and 1940s scholars and poets worked together to create tafsīr-like poetry called *saèr*, from Malay *sha'ir*. The earliest known composer of the poetry is Tengku Yahyë, from the Peugasing area west of Takèngèn. In the mid-1930s Tengku Yahyë wrote short verse works in which he translated passages from the Qur'ān or hadīth. Many of these passages were noncontroversial—they included the opening verse al-Fātiha and several shorter verses—and he intended the poems to be a vehicle for making available, and enjoyable, the sense of the Arabic. The *al-Tafsīr al-Gayo*, the printed collection of Gayo verse published in Cairo in 1938, included many of Tengku Yahyë's works.

Tengku Yahyë also asked other poets in the Peugasing area to compose verse renditions of particular passages. Some of these men then continued to compose and sing saèr, often along with their *didong* poetry; such was the case with the poet Muhammad Yassin (Asyin) who continued to perform as late as 1990 (Bowen 1991:186). One of these poets added a much sharper tone of religious and social criticism to his works: Abdurrahim Daudy, known as Tengku Mudë Kala, studied poetry with Tengku Yahyë and Arabic with Tengku Jali at the Islamic Education school. Tengku Mudë Kala's compositions begin with Arabic passages and Gayo renderings, following the form created by Tengku Yahyë, but then elaborate the translations into often scathing attacks on contemporary Gayo practices—the holding of funeral meals, the use of talismans, or the blind obedience of ulama. It was Tengku Mudë Kala, with the support of a Gayo trader, who collected the poems published in 1938. He collected a set of his own poems in 1950, and wrote a long verse history of the Gayo highlands in 1959.[29]

For some older Takèngèn men and women, the creation of religious poetry was a signal event in the development of local religious consciousness. Inën Muhammad, my "mother" in Takèngèn, often sings bits of poems to herself after a meal, when she thinks no one is around. Her favorites concern sentimental subjects: the fate of orphans, or the story of the prophet Joseph. Her own sense of Takèngèn religious history gives the poetry an

---

[29] I have examined the verse history at length in Bowen (1991:242–46) and plan to devote a future work to the saèr genre.

important role in changing popular practice. "People used to put on huge ritual meals here," she once told me, "but then the poets and Islamic Education came along and they stopped doing it, some of them."

Public Debate, Divergent Memories

Through tafsīr sessions and religious poetry, and above all in Friday sermons, Tengku Jali and his followers have lashed out at those who continue practices that cannot be traced with certainty to the prophet Muhammad. Their religious vision admits only one set of correct practices, and thus contrasts sharply with the views of traditionalist scholars such as Tengku Ali Salwany, for whom much of practical religion is not explicitly dictated in scripture, and thus is of necessity shaped by the views and interpretations of various scholars.

The sharp differences about religious truth between Aman Murni and Ali Salwany include very different memories of public religious debate. As we saw earlier, Aman Murni recalled the 1941 public debate between Tengku Jali and Tengku Silang as a clear victory for Tengku Jali. He remembered the debate as having dealt only with matters regarding death, particularly the telkin catechism and ritual meals. He was thus able to portray it as having led directly to the 1948 assembly of scholars in Aceh where certain mortuary practices were condemned.

But other Gayo scholars (including some modernists) remember the public debate as having been much broader in its coverage and thus only loosely related to the 1948 assembly. At the debate were disputed the statement of intent before worship (the ushalli controversy), the insertion of a special prayer (*qunut*) into the morning worship service, the number of additional worship units (collectively called *tarāwih*) to be performed at night during the month of Ramadan, and how much of the head must be wetted in the ablutions prior to worship.

In contrast to Aman Murni's narrow memory of the debate, Tengku Ali Salwany emphasized its breadth as part of his overall argument that no single, definitive solution to religious disputes is possible:

> These issues can never be resolved because they are questions of ijtihād [independent reasoning] and of the opinions of ulama. For example, the Qur'ān orders you to wet your head before worship; our disputes turned on what was meant by "the head." Tengku Jali said that the Arabic was of such and such a form and thus it was the entire head that should be washed, but others said that if only a bit was wetted then the ablutions were legitimate. No one won, although supporters of each said their men had vanquished the other.

Tengku Ali Salwany himself concluded that "Tengku Jali knew a lot of words, but Tengku Silang commanded every domain."

The two scholars had similarly divergent views of the message sent in 1948 by the assembly of Acehnese scholars. Aman Murni considered the Joint Proclamation to be a watershed event in local religious history. In August 1948, five months after the assembly, the Takèngën Office for Religious Affairs issued a small-format, twelve-page booklet that contained the proclamation and instructions for its dissemination in the area. The office was staffed largely by Islamic Education scholars, and the last page of the booklet contains an advertisement for PAT, the trading enterprise that sponsored the Islamic Education school.

The proclamation itself condemned nine widespread practices, all but one of which had to do with treatment of the dead. The first three practices were forms of kenduri (ritual meals): commemorative kenduris for the dead, kenduri Maulid (for the prophet Muhammad's birthday), and kenduris held at graves. The document also censured offerings made in connection with burial, the practice of guarding the grave, reciting the call to prayer when lowering the corpse into the grave, building any sort of structure around the grave, chanting near the grave, and reciting Qur'ānic verses at the home of the deceased, "because it [recitation] is thought to be part of Religion, whereas it is not." The statement declares that each such practice is not allowed by religion and must be halted.

The next to final page (before the ad for PAT) contains a quote from the prophet Muhammad that is much loved by modernists (italics by the authors of the document):

> The Jews after the prophet Moses split into 72 factions. The Christians after the prophet Jesus split into 72 factions. The Muslims after the prophet Muhammad split into 73 factions. All of them [are/will be] in Hell, except for *only one faction*, that which follows my example and that of my companions.

The booklet, especially the quote from Muhammad added to it by the local compilers, exemplifies the sharpness of Islamic Education attacks on older ritual practices.

Tengku Ali Salwany, however, interpreted the 1948 proclamation not as an authoritative statement of universal validity, but as a specific intervention by Acehnese scholars into a social problem of importance in lowlands Aceh. As on other occasions, Ali Salwany stressed that one must consider an actor's intent when evaluating his or her religious practices:

> The proclamation was directed at people in Aceh who kill one or two buffalo for a funeral meal. It is fine if we call people to come and eat, and our intentions [niët] are proper and we are not proud [riyë]. It is different if the person cannot afford to put on a large meal and yet the village religious leader says he must do so or his parents will be tormented in the grave. What we ourselves

do: we come and pray for the deceased and then people may give us a *sedekah* [<Ar. *sadaqa*; a free gift, referring to the meal served]; that is different.

People did not accept this proclamation here. Daud Beureueh was a great fighter, but in matters of religious practice he was not in accord with most people. He did not want people to say prayers over him when he died, but people did so when he died, including all the ulama in Aceh; some even brought their own food with them!

Yet, in the same conversation, Ali Salwany also set limits on acceptable ritual forms.

We *do* and should oppose setting out special dishes at kenduris with four bananas and an egg, and forty *apam* cakes, and using incense. The plates are left over from the transition period between Hindu times and Islamic times. People had to be given things before they would willingly enter Islam, so they were told that they could eat these special foods in the mosque after worship because the four bananas stood for the four companions of Muhammad and the forty apam cakes stood for the forty people needed for Friday worship. *This* is what the proclamation meant by a kenduri for the dead. Incense, further, is fine if it is intended as a way of making things fragrant, but not as a way of calling a person's soul or the angels.

Takèngën traditionalism as exemplified by Ali Salwany does not embrace *all* local practices, but defends those to which a religiously proper intent can be imputed. The difference between incense, which can be given a religious reading, and apam rice-cakes, which, in his mind, cannot, signals the limits of scholarly traditionalism and thus of public Islamic discourse.

Tengku Asaluddin, Tengku Ali Salwany, and Aman Murni illustrate some of the distinct paths pursued by Gayo religious scholars at mid-century. The topics they and their teachers discussed in the 1930s continued to be the subject of lively debate in the 1980s, and the divisions continue to animate scholarly activities. In 1989 and 1990, for example, Ali Salwany convened two local congresses of traditionalist scholars to discuss the telkin catechism and the issue of serving food after funerals. These congresses were intended to reform local ritual practice and thereby to dull the force of the modernist critique. These disputes never led to the kind of physical conflict that many had feared they would, and neither did they become the primary division in Gayo society because of the crosscutting effects of political struggle and conflict.[30]

---

[30] Compare the analysis in Laitin (1986) of the relative public importance of religious versus ethnic divisions in Nigeria.

Some scholars did not take sides in the religious debates, preferring to become politically active. Of particular importance for the development of this brand of religious scholar was the Islamic Teachers' College (Normal Islam Instituut) founded at Bireuën in 1939 by the Acehnese ulama association (PUSA). The college was directed by the son-in-law of PUSA chairman Daud Beureueh (Yakub 1980:355). In 1946 it moved to Banda Aceh, where several future Gayo leaders attended. Principal among them were Abu Bakar Bangkit, for many years the head of the Takèngën branch of the Islamic political party Masyumi; Tengku Ali Jaidun, today the principal spokesman for Takèngën Muhammadiyah; and Ilyas Leubé, the man who led the Gayo forces in the provincewide Darul Islam rebellion of 1953–1962. (The last two men became relatives when Ali Jaidun married Ilyas Leubé's first cousin.)

The Gayo men who studied at Normal Islam learned a politically sensitive brand of modernism. They were willing to moderate their religious views for the sake of politics, and they were inspired by Daud Beureueh to devote their political lives to advancing the status of religion in the province. The college was particularly important in shaping Gayo participation in the Darul Islam rebellion. During his four years at the college, Ilyas Leubé formed a strong personal tie to Daud Beureueh: he was described by Ali Jaidun as Daud Beureueh's "favorite child-by-way-of-study [anak didik]." Other Gayo students developed strong personal loyalties to Leubé, in part through the years of study and later political activity, and these ties became the basis for the command structure of the Gayo unit of Darul Islam.

After independence the highlands were never free of internal political conflicts. A brief coalition between members of the Nationalist party and proponents of an Islamic state fell apart once the Dutch were definitively driven out of Indonesia in 1950. The Darul Islam rebellion pitted nationalists against the pro-Aceh religious leaders from 1953 until 1962. Three years later, in late 1965, some of the losers in the earlier conflict participated as victors in the massacre of accused Communists, only to find themselves shut out of New Order politics from the 1970s on (Bowen 1991: 106–25).

These political divisions have cut across doctrinal lines. The scholars who urged the rejection of older Gayo institutions in favor of a truly Islamic society included many modernists (particularly those from the Islamic Education school) and some traditionalists from village areas. Those who favored a blending of Indonesian, Gayo, and Islamic institutions also included scholars from both doctrinal camps. Many traditionalists felt under attack for their participation in a wide range of village ritual practices (especially those connected with death) and thus opposed the idea of an Islamic state. But so did some modernists, such as Tengku Asaluddin, who conceived of Gayo social norms as the protector of religious norms, as "the rope you use to tie the buffalo" when sacrificing it for religious purposes (Bowen 1991:113–14).

Scholars of traditionalist and modernist orientations joined in debates that defined religion along scriptural lines, and created institutions in which Gayo could develop a modern approach to religion, society, and politics. But in doing so, this public sphere of Islam excluded a broad range of village practices, founded on quite distinct ideas of language, truth, and power.

PART TWO

Powerful Speech
and Spirit Transactions

Chapter Four

SPELLS, PRAYER, AND THE POWER OF WORDS

ABANG KERNA was puzzled and a bit worried. Once sure and proud of his vast command of spells (one for nearly every purpose), he had recently begun to doubt whether such spells were a proper part of a good Muslim's life. On a June evening in 1989 he had voiced these doubts to a learned friend who had come to Isak for a visit. The matter concerned a verse from the Qur'ān (61:13):

> And He will give you another blessing which you love:
> help from God and present victory.
> Give good tidings, O Muhammad
> to believers.[1]

Shortly before his friend's visit, a religious scholar had told Abang Kerna that God revealed the verse to Muhammad at Medina as a message of peace. God instructed Muhammad to cease fighting the Meccans and to ask permission to visit the city. Muhammad followed these instructions, and a year later he entered the city without bloodshed.

Yet, continued Abang Kerna to his friend, many years earlier he had learned these same lines as part of an invulnerability spell (*doa kebēl*). Veterans of the war against the Dutch taught him how to activate the spell's power by reciting the lines in Arabic (which he only now knew to be from the Qur'ān), followed by a plea in Gayo:

> Let my strength be from God,
> my resistance to blows from Muhammad,
> my invulnerability to iron from Adam.

After these lines he would repeat the Arabic and close the spell with an appeal in Gayo:

> Let my blanket be from God,
> my cloak from God,
> my shawl from God.

---

[1] Abang Kerna recited only the last three lines of the verse; others have quoted the entire verse to me. The verse is frequently cited by Muslims in a variety of contexts; in late 1990 it was used by Saddam Hussein in claiming eventual victory for Iraq against the U.S.

For English translations of Qur'ānic verses, I have drawn rather freely on the translations by Pickthall, Yusuf Ali, and Arberry, and have been assisted by Peter Heath.

To make the spell effective, Abang Kerna would focus his attention inward and imagine that, as he uttered the spell, a garment of invulnerability descended upon him. As he concentrated his thoughts on the image of the garment he would pass his arms over his head and body, as if putting it on. Once activated, the spell had protected him against blows, bullets, and knives. He had shared it with his companions during the period of rebellion in the 1950s. He considered it to be one of the most important spells in his repertoire of personal protection.

He was thus shocked to learn that the Arabic lines were part of a command to *cease* fighting. Someone, he said, must have wrested the verse out of its proper tafsīr (by which he meant its context in the Qur'ān) and inserted it into the invulnerability spell. Who would have done so? Not God, surely; perhaps the Devil? If so, he asked his friend, have I been sinning all these years by using the spell?

Rather than answering him directly, his friend related a story about Ali, the son-in-law of the prophet Muhammad. Ali invariably worshiped by Muhammad's side. One Friday, as he was walking to join Muhammad for worship, he met a man dressed in the white garb of a religious scholar who asked him where he was going. When Ali told him, the man said the hour of worship had passed. In Ali's eyes the sun indeed appeared to have passed the point for the service. Deeply disappointed, Ali returned home. Muhammad delayed the service as long as he could before proceeding without him. When Muhammad next encountered Ali, he asked him why he had been absent. Ali explained. Muhammad replied that the man was the Devil, who often disguised himself to lure pious men from the straight path.

Although his friend drew no explicit conclusions, Abang Kerna understood his point. God allows the Devil to trick people, he explained to me; most likely it was the Devil who had authored the invulnerability spell, with its section taken from the Qur'ān, and who had then made sure that those who used it would think that it had worked, thus sinning both in their misuse of God's word and in their pride. Abang Kerna was now even more worried that, overly enthusiastic in his embracing of powerful spells, he had been beguiled by the Devil.

Most Isak men and women have occasion during their lives to use spells. They recite spells, some of which have Arabic sections, in order to improve the rice harvest, ward off harmful spirits, or heal a sick child. Some, like Abang Kerna, are experts in the use of spells in one or more domains. In 1989 few of them were as deeply worried about the propriety of spells as was Abang Kerna, but most were aware of sharp differences in local opinion on the subject.

Many, probably most, Isak residents feel they may legitimately use the power of words, including scripture, to convince, constrain, or reward spir-

4. Abang Kerna

its, whether place spirits, human souls, or God. Others, a smaller number and most of them modernists, sharply delimit the range of legitimate discourse with spirits. They argue that one may only ask God for help, and that even then his actions are unfathomable. One may not consult or entreat other spirits; to do so is to risk committing the sin of polytheism. Scripture, under this interpretation, is God's message to us, to be understood and reflected upon.

Abang Kerna's perplexity and anxiety in mid-1989 was due in large part to his changing sense of his life's priorities. Long a wielder of curing spells, a practice that depends on trafficking with some highly disreputable spirits, he now was nearing sixty, confronting his own mortality, and becoming more concerned about his standing in God's eyes. Somewhat convinced by the arguments against spirit communication, he had begun to seek alternative ways of curing. To further settle his mind, he requested that I ask Tengku Asaluddin about the verse quoted above: Could it be used for protection even though it came from the Qur'ān?

Tengku Asaluddin knew the verse by heart, quickly located it in his Qur'ān, and explained it to me:

> It tells you that God is near and victory is at hand. So, God will help you if you improve yourself through worship and other meritorious acts. You may ask God for protection and he may help you if you are sincere [ikhlās] in your request. If a pious man recites the verse and then asks God for invulnerability to bullets, God just might grant the request. People often used to recite this verse and the following one [Qur'ān 61:14] for protection against iron and also against water [floods or drowning].
>
> The situation is just the same as it was for the prophet Ibrāhīm when he was thrown into the fire. The angels pleaded him to ask God for help so that, responding to his [God's] orders, they could rescue him. Ibrāhīm replied that he would not ask for help. God knew he was there, after all, and could send down Jibra'il anytime he wanted to. Finally God did send Jibra'il, who protected him from the fire. If God wills it, he helps us.

Without condemning outright Abang Kerna's use of the Qur'ānic verse as a means to acquire invulnerability, Tengku Asaluddin sharply undercut the view of linguistic power implied by such practices. We cannot fathom God's will. He may decide to help us, but our requests must be properly motivated and our lives must be pure. The practical significance of Qur'ān 61:13 is thus not as a magical implement but as a guide for living, a source of inspiration to live in such a way that we will receive God's help. Indeed, because God knows all, requests are unnecessary, as the story of Ibrāhīm and the fire is intended to show.

The main thrust of Tengku Asaluddin's response thus was to deny not the legitimacy of reciting verses and making requests (unnecessary though they may be), but rather the idea that the recitation can bring about direct results. This denial is one of the modernists' most frequently emphasized points, and it strikes at the heart of older Isak ritual practices. Uttering spells, exorcising spirits, and reciting scripture for the benefit of the deceased all depend on the idea of a direct causal link between an utterance and the receipt of a benefit. The denial of such a link by Tengku Asaluddin and others elicits frequent, sometimes angry, retorts, such as the following counterclaim by an Isak village head (and close relative of Tengku Asaluddin) to the modernist teacher's assertions:

> But even the prophet Muhammad said *doa* [spell, prayer], and we follow him in all things. Even the verses of the Qur'ān are doa. For example, when the prophet Muhammad was chased by the Pharoah's war chief, Jibra'il revealed to him the Qul hu [Qur'ān 112]. With his enemy poised to kill him, Muhammad recited the verses. Immediately the sword fell from the war chief's hand, and his horse was swallowed up by sand.

In direct (and explicit) contrast to Tengku Asaluddin, this speaker stresses the immediate, striking, and apparently automatic relation between the recitation of the verse and the beneficial effect. His choice of example—a Qur'ānic verse and a Qur'ānic context—was, of course, a strategic one. By showing that a Qur'ānic verse was effective for Muhammad in a direct, automatic way, the use of verses by others is placed beyond reproach: "even the prophet Muhammad said doa, and we follow him in all things."

The disputes we will examine in the remainder of this book—over spells, appeals to ancestors, or chants for the dead—turn on these contrasting ideas of language and power. Put baldly, the issue is as follows: Do humans have the power to change the actions of spirits by uttering certain phrases? And if they do have such a power, should they exercise it? Village ritual specialists answer in the affirmative to both questions. They say that they are able to convince some harmful spirits to leave patients and to ask God's assistance to expel the remainder. They also offer prayers and food to ancestor spirits so that they will heal the sick or rid the crops of rats. Such powers are given by God, they say, and we use them as he intended us to, in the interest of general well-being.

These rituals of healing and exorcism, used for people or for crops, are the topic of Part 2 of this book. Disputes over the Islamic character of the rituals take place in varied village settings, but not in the public forums defined as religious, such as the mosque or the sessions of the Council of Ulama. Rituals for farming, hunting, or healing are not included in the scholarly definitions of *religion* because they cannot be shown to have been prescribed by scripture. Even traditionalist scholars, who may be sympathetic to such rituals, avoid mentioning them publicly. But, though absent from the public sphere of debate, discussions of the Islamic character of such rituals are important to most Gayo villagers, who depend on these practices for health, good crops, and the continuing welfare of their ancestors.

In Part 3 we turn to a different class of rituals. Celebrations of the Prophet's birthday, sacrifice to God, observance of rituals for the deceased, and the daily worship of God are legitimate and important to all Gayo Muslims. Disputes over these explicitly Islamic events concern their correct form and interpretation, not, as in the case of agricultural or healing rituals, whether they should be performed at all. These disputes turn on the same issues of language and power, however. Is it possible and proper to provide spiritual benefit to the dead by holding special meals or by chanting special phrases, as most villagers believe? Or, as modernists argue, does death definitively cut all such ties, making further communications and exchanges impossible? Do we have the power to transmit merit and material benefit through sacrifice, or should sacrifice only be in celebration of and obedience to God? And (in a more fine-grained set of disputes) is worship of God a matter of communicating with him or of strictly following the way the prophet Muhammad worshiped?

DISTINCTIONS AMONG DOA

These debates focus on *how* particular practices fit into an Islamic worldview, not whether they fit at all. Those who disagree on the legitimacy and effectiveness of doa nonetheless agree that the argument turns on specific ideas about Islamic historical and scriptural knowledge. Practitioners of spells believe that the spells' powers derive from holy scripture, from the intercession of prophets, and from the continuing presence of God in the world. Most Gayo conceive of Islamic history as mediated by powerful speech: in the great world-shattering events of revelation and prophecy, in stories of conversion and holiness, and in the yearly and daily cycles of reciting God's words and speaking with his angels and prophets. Questions concerning the meaning of scripture and the logic of sacred history thus extend far beyond scholarly debates to the everyday situations of Gayo men and women in the world.

Gayo use the term *doa* to refer to a broad range of communicative acts. Most Isak Gayo use the term to indicate any utterances directed to God or to spiritual agents. The category includes personal appeals to God for his assistance, the words spoken during the worship ritual, and spells designed to make iron soft and spirits flee.

Isak Gayo distinguish among types or modes of doa, and I shall gloss these types as *spell*, *request*, *recitation*, and *prayer*. A spell implies a particular desired goal and usually mentions that goal in its text, such as, in an invulnerability spell, the phrase "may my body be as hard as iron." It usually has a fixed form, which must be memorized. It may contain a combination of phrases in Arabic, Gayo, or Malay/Indonesian, and may also include semantically opaque phrases said to be "Batak" or "Kluët" (referring to peoples living to the south and west of the Gayo). Often the spell is given a label that indicates its specific goal: "invulnerability spell" or "beautifying spell." The spell may be addressed to a particular spiritual agent or it may invoke the powers of God and the prophets. It functions relatively automatically once certain conditions are met.

A request is also directed toward a spiritual agent and is intended to lead to a specific outcome, but it works through persuasion and may be close to ordinary speech in form. Its success is less certain than that of a spell. A request may be referred to as a *manat doa* (request doa; <Ar. *amāna*, trust, responsibility); by the verb *bermanat*, "to request"; or by phrases that stress that the speaker converses in an ordinary manner with the spirit: *becerak orum [N]* (to speak with [N]), *iprin ku [N]* (it is said to [N]). A request may be directed toward a spirit, an angel, or one of several sentient objects (such as eggs and the *mungkur* citrus) that can aid the speaker by revealing the future, healing the sick, or expelling a harmful spirit.

A recitation of scripture is directed toward God in order to please him. The fixed Arabic phrases recited during the ritual of worship (G. *semiyang*; Ar. salāt) are usually referred to as *doa semiyang*. At ritual meals people often recite one or more of the shortest verses. At rituals held to honor and assist the recently deceased, a recitation leader chants a long series of verses, collectively called *samadiyah* or tahlīl. The more familiar segments are then repeated by all the men and women present. The recitations generate merit (*pahla*; <Ar. *falāh*, success), and the participants ask God to transmit that merit to the spirit of the deceased.

One prays (*berdoa*) only to God. Although doa is a broad category, its verbal form is reserved for prayer alone. Uttering an invulnerability spell, for example, is referred to as *[mu]baca doa kebël* (to recite an invulnerability spell), never as berdoa. Prayer may be said in public, at a feast or assembly, or in private, to oneself, after worship or on other occasions. Public prayer often includes a set sequence of prayers for the welfare of the deceased and his or her family, for the family of the prophet Muhammad, and for all Muslims throughout the world. Public prayer is entirely in Arabic. Most Gayo prayer leaders raise their hands toward the sky during prayer, and all others present follow suit. Each line of prayer is punctuated by the collective repetition of *amīn*. One might also pray silently to God in Gayo, stating in a straightforward way one's hopes and wishes.

The distinction between spell, request, recitation, and prayer refers to types of speech events, distinguished by the modality of address, the range of possible addressees, and the hoped-for outcomes. Spells involve a stronger expectation that the hearer will be persuaded or coerced by the words than do requests. Both can be addressed to many different kinds of spirits, whereas recitations and prayers are humbly offered to God and God alone. Prayers contain specific requests; recitations repeat God's own words to humankind.

These modes of speech are often combined in a single social event. In a ritual meal for the dead, for example, the liturgy involves sequences of recitation and prayer. The moments of prayer are marked off from the recitations by raising hands and repeating *amīn*. The prayer directs the recitation toward a chosen beneficiary. A healer will usually work the entire range of modalities when he or she tries to cure a sick person: starting from polite requests to spirits, proceeding to spells of exorcism and healing, and accompanying all these efforts with prayers to God for assistance.

Alternatively, the same phrase may be uttered in two or more modes of doa. (Put concisely, the four-way distinction among doa types is in terms of function and does not neatly segment the range of doa forms.) Certain important religious statements occur across all four modes. The first part of the confession of faith (*lā ilāha illā Allāh*, there is no deity but God) appears in spells and requests to spirits, is recited in zikr, and may be inserted in prayers. When a speaker includes this phrase in a personal protection spell he is summoning the power of God to aid him in his appeal to a potentially protective spirit (or in his warning to a potentially harmful one). According to a popular story, a religious scholar converted the ruler of Aceh to Islam by teaching the confession of faith as a gambling spell: the ruler's success at the gambling table strengthened his piety. Repeated as a zikr, the phrase earns generic merit in the eyes of God, which may then be directed toward a particular beneficiary. In a petitionary prayer, the phrase signals the piety and submission of the speaker. The same form, then, may be construed within particular interpretive frames (given by the surrounding social and speech context) as a spell, request, recitation, or prayer.

To be successful, doa in all four categories must be accompanied by mental and physical actions. Spells, prayers, requests, and recitations are effective only if they are uttered with the right intent (niët; <Ar. niyya) and with sufficient concentration or *maripët*. Maripët (<Ar. *ma'rifat*, gnosis) is perhaps best glossed as "powerful depictive imagination." One imagines with maripët the goal or intended result of a spell or prayer (a loved one, or a desired cure) and thereby guides the speech to its results.

Doa also are accompanied by objects or bodily movements, the *isharat* (<Ar. *ishāra*, sign) of the speech. These signs are most elaborate for curing: curers may use eggs, fruits, leaves, and other objects as the material embodiments of intended actions. Requests and prayers also have their required outer signs in prostration or the raising of hands.

In formulating and reciting doa, Gayo make different use of the available repertoire of languages. Gayo, Malay/Indonesian, Arabic, or phrases said to be in Batak carry specific associations with religion and society. Gayo is the language of everyday speech, and a ritual practitioner may use it to convey a set of personal appeals to a spirit. Gayo segments of a spell are less likely to be fixed than segments in other languages.

In the Gayo village context, Malay and Indonesian are virtually the same language: Malay has been a lingua franca in the archipelago for centuries.

Until the colonial period its primary use among Gayo was for religious learning, as in the Jawi books discussed earlier. Malay is frequently used in spells (sometimes with Gayo pronunciation), and this use reflects the older associations with religious learning. In the 1920s Indonesian became the language of nationalism and of interethnic communication; today it is the national language and is used by government officials in public settings (even when speaking to an all-Gayo audience). The use of Indonesian in a public speech reflects these newer associations with officialdom.

Arabic is associated with Islam, of course, but the local effects of its use may vary. In a spell the inclusion of an Arabic word or short phrase conveys the power of the Qur'ān and of Islamic history. In a public address, speakers may rely heavily on long Arabic prayers and phrases. They may also pronounce in Arabic fashion words that have been borrowed into Indonesian and Gayo in order to emphasize the importance of religious norms. Finally, "opaque" words—those which speakers cannot define—invoke the local idea that people to the south of the Gayo, especially the Karo Batak, have especially powerful spells at their disposal.

Code-switching between different sound systems, especially among Gayo, Indonesian, and Arabic, is a special case of the strategic selection of languages. Gayo make use of its possibilities when pronouncing the word *doa*; different pronunciations signal different types of doa or distinct opinions about certain doa.[2] In Isak, people generally say the word as /*dowa*/, with a smooth flow of sound from /o/ to /a/. But in some instances Isak residents bend their pronunciation toward the Arabic source word *du'ā'*. (Those Gayo who may be unaware of the Arabic derivation follow the example of those who do know the Arabic form.) They may say something closer to /*do'a*/, inserting a brief glottal stop between the two vowels, or perhaps /*do'ā*/, with a lengthened and somewhat accented final /ā/. Less frequently, a speaker (a modernist sermon-giver, for example) may replace the glottal with the throaty Arabic *ghain* sound and thrust the first vowel toward the front of his mouth, thereby approximating the Arabic pronunciation /*du'ā'*/.

Each step taken toward the Arabic sound—glottalization, lengthening or fronting the vowels, substitution of the ghain—further highlights the Islamic status of the term and with it the idea of supralocal, scriptural standards by which the associated linguistic practices are to be judged. Most

---

[2] Although the word *doa* (and cognate forms) is found throughout the Muslim areas of the archipelago, in some societies it is reserved for petitionary prayer. In Java (Geertz 1960:42; Woodward 1988:79), the cognate *donga* refers to prayers in Arabic or, apparently less often, in Javanese. In the Malay societies of southern Sumatra (Collins 1979:240) and Malaysia (Laderman 1991:43) prayers (doa) are lexically distinguished from spells (*jampi*). Lois Beck (personal communication) reports that some Muslims in Iran shift pronunciation to indicate different types of doa in ways similar to those described here for the Gayo.

Isak speakers adjust their pronunciation toward *do'ā* as they participate in more broadly acknowledged Islamic events. The same speaker who told me how Muhammad used Qur'ānic verses as spells (pronounced /dowa/), if officiating at a feast will ask everyone to join him in saying prayers (pronounced /do'āl/). His shift in pronunciation signals his recognition of a distinction between spell and prayer, a distinction that has been made more salient by the twentieth-century modernist critique of village practices.

Modernist-leaning members of the community tend to favor the glottal (thus *do'ā*) as a sign of the importance they attach to Arabic sources of Islamic knowledge, just as they prefer the Arabic *salāt* to the Gayo *semiyang* for worship, and Arabic rather than Gayo terms for worship periods (e.g., Arabic *dhuhur* for midday worship over the metathesized Gayo *rohol*). Modernists sometimes couch their denunciations of older spell practices as critiques of current usage of the term *doa*. They condemn the idea that all the speech events commonly referred to as *doa* share certain properties. Specifically, they argue that making requests of spirits is tantamount to polytheism, and that such requests should therefore be sharply distinguished from proper acts of prayer and recitation. Thus Tengku Asaluddin responded to my question about the various ways *doa* was pronounced by expanding the range of forms through a cross-linguistic borrowing:

> *Dowa* is how Gayo say *do'a*, but *dowa* has two more meanings [in addition to "prayer"]. One is "permission." Someone will say: "It is in my dowa" to mean "I permit you to do it."
>
> It is also used to mean *dowa-dowa*, things you say that bring about this or that result. But to say *do'a* really is to praise God or to ask God for something.

Here Tengku Asaluddin distinguishes between the correct pronunciation of the word (/do'al/), with its attendant meaning (prayer), and the several incorrect ways that Isak people use the term, pronouncing it idiosyncratically as /dowa/. He explains that Gayo extend the term's root-meaning when they say, for example, "your journey will be in my prayers" in order to grant permission for someone to leave on a trip. They also use the form to mean "spell." He then further delegitimizes this use by suggesting a more linguistically correct substitute form for the use of *doa* as spell, namely, the reduplicative *dowa-dowa*. This form is not current in Gayo speech but is used in Indonesian to mean "like doa but not really doa." (Other reduplicators are used in Gayo, although not as frequently as in Indonesian.) Through this cross-linguistic borrowing, Tengku Asaluddin represents spells as outside the proper referential field of do'a.

Tengku Asaluddin manages here to concisely ridicule the use of spells by claiming that they are based on a popular misunderstanding of what words mean. Spells are mistaken uses of language, he and other modernists argue;

people utter them under the illusion that words can produce automatic effects. Their mistake is proven by the fact that they mispronounce the word *doa*. Such evaluative acts of metalinguistic commentary are typical of modernists, who argue for the superiority of their own position by pointing out deviations in local speech practice from what they claim to be the correct (because closer to Arabic) speech norm.

THE EFFICACY OF SPELLS

Despite these criticisms, spells are an important element of everyday living in Isak (and will be central to the discussions of farming, feasting, and healing in later chapters). Most Isak Gayo understand spells to be fixed utterances intended to bring about a specific end. Often they are accompanied by manipulating objects or concentrating the imagination on a desired object.

Most Isak residents have used spells to attain specific, individual goals. Boys learn invulnerability spells (doa kebël) to protect themselves from bullets or blows. A "body fence" spell (*pëgër-n-bëdën*) builds a protective wall around the body and wards off physical attacks and malicious spells; it is often said just before setting off on a journey. A "hitting" spell (*doa derë*) makes one's own blows more forceful.

Men and women of all ages make use of spells designed to enhance the qualities of the speaker in the eyes of others. A "roarer" spell (*penggentur*) makes one's voice highly persuasive, while a "sweetener" (*pemanis*) makes one appear attractive to the opposite sex. My friends offered me this type of spell more often than any other. A spell to call the vital force (*[pen]talu semangat*) of someone may be used either to attract someone's attention (usually a desired partner) or to recall a wandering vital force whose departure has disturbed or sickened someone.

To earlier anthropologists, such spells fell into the category of *magic*, defined by its false theories of instrumental power over insentient objects, as distinct from *religion*, defined by its practices of communicating with deities. Even two such otherwise contrasting figures as the eloquent armchair-anthropologist Sir James G. Frazer (1935) and the irascible fieldworker Bronislaw Malinowski (1935) agree on this sharp categorical distinction. Although they offer quite different accounts of why people resort to magic, they both argue that a magical spell involves the automatic relation of cause to effect, while religion involves propitiation and reflective thought. This distinction relegated practitioners of magic to a "primitive" position in the world vis-à-vis practitioners of religion.

Although anthropologists have more recently recognized that people may engage in highly reflective thinking about spells, and that religion, too, has its automatic character (Brown 1985; Geertz 1975:174–75), some anthropol-

ogists have continued to postulate a general category of "magic." Stanley
Tambiah (1990:73–74, 80–83), for example, who has underscored the importance of a spell's "social pragmatics" (what it communicates to other
people), assumes that local theories of a spell's efficacy rely solely on technical notions of causality, rather than on the interactions with spirits associated with religion.[3] For him, as for Frazer and Malinowski, magical spells
and religious ritual are two distinct kinds of practices. Note, of course, that
this distinction is the same one made by Gayo Muslim modernists in their
critique of village ritual, as in Tengku Asaluddin's distinction of (religious)
do'ā' and (magical) dowa-dowa. Here the received anthropological categories weigh in firmly on the side of modernists, despite anthropologists' general preference for things deemed "local."

By starting from Gayo categories for speech events and from specific
spells, we can explore the ways Gayo combine different modes of speech
without our making an a priori distinction between magic and religion.
Gayo spells do include the kind of utterances that anthropologists often take
as epitomizing "magical speech." Yet, in the same spells, Gayo also invoke
God's power and Islamic history. They do so in order to remind the object
of the spell, who is assumed to be listening, of the authority of the speaker:
his or her God-granted right to demand protection and power.

The Islamic Framework

The Gayo men and women who employ spells understand them as part of a
larger body of Islamic history and knowledge. The links between the spells
and the Islamic context may appear explicitly in the spells themselves or in
the way spell users explain and classify them.

Gayo explain all spells in terms of their relation to scripture. Spells that
come directly from God are *wahyu* (<Ar. *wahy*, God's revelations). They include all spells that contain Qur'ānic verses, as well as other spells that are
believed to have been sanctioned by God. The latter group is in the category of *ilmu ladani*: powerful knowledge that is not in the Qur'ān but that
"has its own book [*kitëb*]."[4] My neighbor Abang Das, an inveterate spell-
user, explained that ladani spells were revealed at the time of Muhammad
and were immediately written down. They draw their power from God's

---

[3] Because Tambiah's writings on magic often involve references to Malinowski's ethnography of the Trobriand Islands, it is worth noting that Malinowski himself was uncertain as to
whether Trobrianders considered gardening spells to have automatic effects on their crops or
to involve communication with spirits (1935, II:229–30).

[4] The term is from Ar. *'ilm ladunnī* (divinely inspired knowledge, lit., "knowledge from
me") and is mentioned in Qur'ān 18:65 (see Schimmel 1975:18, 73). Note how the Gayo term
kitëb combines the senses of writing and authority in the same way as does the Arabic *kitāb*
from which it derives; see Graham (1987:79–91).

willingness to grant gifts to his people. "We invoke the name of God and ask for something in the name of God."

Spells that come from God often directly invoke the example of the prophet Muhammad and may call on him or other prophets for assistance. Spells intended to improve the speaker's appearance or voice, or to make him or her attractive to members of the other sex, may mention the prophet Yusuf (Joseph), especially in the form: "Just as Sitti Zulaika [Potiphar's wife] was attracted to the prophet Yusuf, so let [Name] be attracted to me." Similarly, the prophet Daud (David) is called on to make the speaker's voice sweet; Muhammad's daughter Fatimah is asked to ensure a healthy birth; and Fatimah's husband, 'Ali, is evoked for success at war.

Gayo consider certain other kinds of knowledge and power to be legitimate but to derive from extrascriptural sources. People obtain "Sufi knowledge" (*ilmu sufi*) or "image knowledge" (*ilmu bayan*) by drawing near to God. By meditating, eating "light" foods, and abstaining from sinful behavior, they can receive special insight into the future. They may be able to tell someone's fortune, for example. One common method is to pronounce a spell that transfers (*seduëi*) the person's fortune onto an egg, place the egg in the person's shadow, and then gaze upward to see an afterimage that is either white (a good sign) or black (a bad sign).

Other spells come from harmful spirits (perhaps from the Devil) and are designed for evil purposes. These spells of *ilmu sihir* (black magic, <Ar. *sihr*, magic) may turn ordinary paper into money, make one invulnerable, or cause harm to people in various ways. They often require one to do the reverse of normal or divinely sanctioned behavior, such as fornicating, not bathing, or eating uncooked food. Most Isak people agree that the prophets before Muhammad (especially Moses) had (properly) used *sihir*, but that Muhammad himself had not; some conclude from this fact that the followers of Muhammad should not practice it either.[5] These types of knowledge are dangerous because they lead the practitioner to sins of pride or avarice, they say, or because they depend on an alliance with a harmful spirit and thus are likely to cause harm to innocent parties.

Invulnerability and the Knowledge of History

In some spells, the speaker's power over a spiritual agent comes from the history that the speaker and the spirit share. These empowering histories may be referred to in the spell or may be the subject of separate narratives that speakers tell friends or those to whom they are teaching the spell. Such narratives usually place the spell in an explicitly Muslim context in which

---

[5] Compare Antoun (1989:134–36) on a Jordanian preacher's presentation of magic as obsolete, pertaining to the period before Muhammad, rather than as simply false or evil.

God, archangels, or prophets invest certain phrases with transformative force.

When a Qur'ānic verse is used as a spell, it is usually supplemented by a Gayo-language text that clarifies the intent and use of the verse. The verse may be inserted into a Gayo-language spell text, as with the invulnerability spell that contained Qur'ān 61:13. Or the verse may be explained by a parallel narrative, as when the village headman cited Qur'ān, Sūra 112, as an example of a powerful spell, and then told how it had come to be revealed to Muhammad and how Muhammad had used it to defeat his enemy. Through telling this sacred history the headman situated the verse in a doubly Qur'ānic context, in which its power derived from its provenance (from God by way of Jibra'il) and from the context of its revelation (Muhammad's need for military assistance). The force of such narratives is quite profound. Because God intended the verse to be used as a spell (an intent discernible from the way it was revealed and how Muhammad employed it), use of it for instrumental purposes can hardly be criticized. The argument legitimizes the use of verses as spells (and, as the headman's conclusions make clear, spells in general) by placing the idea of a spell's direct instrumentality into the context of sacred history.

Most spells are explicitly directed at a specific goal, such as making the speaker invulnerable, increasing the nourishing power of cooked rice, or exorcising a harmful spirit. Such spells give the speaker control over a specific feature of a particular object: the hardness of iron, the fertility of rice, or the power of a particular fruit to hold a spirit for exorcism. Not only do these spells empower the speaker, they also explain the speaker's right to claim such powers. They do so by referring to the historical relation of the object to humans, a relation that empowers the speaker in a particular way.

These historical references often include statements about the object's origins and names. Spells addressed to the rice plant tell of its origin as a daughter of Adam and Eve; those addressed to harmful spirits name the spirits and describe how they were once defeated and commanded to obey humans; those addressed to the mungkur fruit (used in divination, purification, and exorcism) remind it how God ordered it to serve humans. In other cases, the origins of the addressee are part of the speaker's understanding of how the spell works, but are only hinted at in the spell. Thus a spell to make the speaker appear beautiful to others (doa pemanis) is directed to the *jejerun* plant, the first plant to exist on the earth. Speakers know that the plant's powers to beautify the speaker come from its special status as the first plant, but the spell makes no mention of this status.

Isak Gayo men have placed particular importance on acquiring invulnerability spells that protect the body against bullets, knives, and other weapons made of iron. Iron is used to make productive tools as well as destructive weapons, and Gayo see iron not as evil but as impetuous and thus requiring human control. Invulnerability spells are designed to soften iron or to proclaim one's own hardness against it, as in the following spell:[6]

Hé besi	Hey, iron.
Ya buduhu ya rasuluhu	Oh, His servant; oh, His messenger,
sawa tubuhku dengan besi[7]	make my body together with iron.
Kun kata Allah	"Be," said God,
payakun kata Muhammad	"and then it was," said Muhammad;
hukumtumhu sujud ko ku Tuhën	his judgment for you: bow down before God.
Hé ta'asan hé ta'usèn	By Hasan, by Husayn,
Zat laksin namamu besi	Laksin [?] essence is your name, iron;
hip nama ibumu	hip is your mother's name.
Kun kata Allah	"Be," said God,
payakun kata Muhammad	"and then it was," said Muhammad;
hukumtumhu	his judgment for you.

The speaker begins by hailing iron. Once he has iron's attention, he then asks Muhammad (the servant and messenger of God) to make his body as hard as iron. He includes a phrase similar to one that occurs several times in the Qur'ān, *kun fa-yakūn* (" 'Be,' and it was"). This phrase evokes God's power to create from a single command, as when God creates Adam (Qur'ān 3:59). In the spell, however, Muhammad is quoted as the author of the report on the effects of God's utterance. Muhammad, therefore, is by God's side as he creates the world. The spell empowers Muhammad by way of this altered scriptural quotation. It then quotes God's command to iron: that iron must prostrate itself before him. The speaker attests to his own knowledge of iron's name and the name of its mother, and does so in the name of Hasan and Husayn, the prophet Muhammad's grandsons whose martyrdoms serve as a perduring symbol for Shi'ite Muslims.[8] The spell closes by once again recalling God's (and Muhammad's) words of power.

Considered rhetorically, the spell contains pleas, reminders, and evocations intended to forcefully persuade iron not to harm the speaker. Unlike what one would expect under the dominant anthropological notion of a magical spell, every line of this spell is addressed *to* iron, or intended to be heard by iron, as a way of convincing it of the powerful resources available

---

[6] Some spells soften all nearby iron; friends warned me never to recite them while riding a motorcycle or truck lest the spell melt the hard automotive parts.

[7] *buduhu* from Ar. *'abd*, servant; *sawa* from Ar. *sawā*, together.

[8] The Gayo and virtually all other Indonesian Muslims are Sunnī, but Shi'ite influences abound in the archipelago: for example, in the celebration of Ashura, the frequent evoking of Hasan and Husayn, and the stories of Muhammad Hanafiyyah, their half-brother.

to the speaker. The spell is thus a vehicle of forceful persuasion for a potentially harmful listener.[9]

Considered narratively, the spell alludes to a number of histories. It is
a kind of index to a larger narrative set. When Isak Gayo told me an invulnerability spell they would invariably go on, without further prompting, to
fill out the spell with its historical context. This history, identical in its
main features from one teller to the next, is part of a larger narrative of
human origins. It begins with the attempts by God to create Adam. (God's
difficulties with this task provide the starting point for several other stories
as well.) When God first created Adam, his body was soft and Adam could
not stand up. God ordered the archangel Jibra'il (<Ar. Jibrā'īl, Gabriel)
to fashion pieces of iron into bones for Adam. As one Isak man then continued:

> Jibra'il went to take a piece of iron from the column of iron sticking up out of
> the earth, but the iron said that it was God and was not about to give up any of
> itself to Jibra'il. So Jibra'il returned to God and told him what had happened.
> God told him what to say to iron, and Jibra'il did so and iron came crashing
> down.
>
> Iron then became part of the earth. Jibra'il took thirteen pieces of iron out of
> the earth, but only used twelve of them to place inside Adam. A long piece of
> iron stuck out of Adam's body; Jibra'il cut it off and threw it away, and it be-
> came the iron in the earth. Jibra'il asked it if it would become the source of
> life for humans [for tools] and it said it would, but that it would destroy those
> humans who did not know what its name was and where it had come from.
> But the thirteenth piece of iron, the one not placed in Adam, was angry at God
> and said that God did not keep his promises, and that it would not listen to re-
> quests from humans. So invulnerability spells will not stop it because it will
> not bow down to men. Because it disobeyed God it is called "treacherous
> iron." But men rarely are killed by it.

The same elements that are sufficiently powerful to keep iron from harming humans when uttered in the spell are arranged here in narrative form.
Iron is by nature proud and angry. It sets itself up as God, and the portion
not used for Adam's body turns against humans. Iron is only domesticated
by God's powerful command, spoken by Jibra'il, and by its insertion into
Adam's body. After God's words are spoken the column of iron comes
crashing down, in effect prostrating itself before God (the word used is
sujud [<Ar. *sujūd*], the term used for prostration in worship). The iron that
was cut from Adam's body becomes the iron used to make tools and weap-

---

[9] Compare the San Blas Kuna healer's chant, in which he lists the parts of a snake's body in
order to convince it that he knows it intimately and therefore has power over it (Sherzer
1990:242–65).

ons. This iron agrees to serve those humans who know its name and the story of its origins, but says it will destroy all others. It shares a common origin with humans because it was used to make Adam's bones and is thus particularly responsive to human commands. Because the human body contains iron it can be made as hard as iron (as in the spell quoted above). Yet the possibility that an invulnerability spell might not work is also foreseen: a bullet or knife made from "treachorous iron," that which Jibra'il left aside, will not respond to the spell.

Spells against iron work because of God's demonstrated power over iron; the common origin of iron and humans; and the historical pact among iron, Jibra'il, and humans, in which knowledge of names and origins is made the condition for future human safety. The speaker refers to each of these sources of power in iron's earshot. The historical reminders in the spell thus function as a license that recalls the powers of God and Muhammad and guarantees the safety of humans.

Other invulnerability spells contain different combinations of the same elements: pleas for hardening of the body ("if iron comes let the skin be iron; if wood, then wood"), repetitions of the names of iron or the words with which God prostrated iron, or evocations of the power of creation represented by God and Muhammad. One such spell consists of repetitions of the phrase "'Be,' said God, 'and then it was,' said Muhammad"; another, of the line "*Alip* [the first letter; God] does not die; *bë* [the second letter; Muhammad] does not die; I will not die." Each spell comes with conditions that must be fulfilled for it to work: speakers must have faith in God, or they must add certain prayers to the spell, or the spell can only be used in battle and thus cannot be tried out beforehand.

The key role played by knowledge of iron's origins is shown by the nature of the countermeasures one can take against someone with an invulnerability spell. One such measure is to wipe one's own semen on the cutting edge of a blade intended for use in a fight. Because humans are of greater importance than iron, semen (the embodiment of human origins) outweighs the invulnerability spell (reminders of iron's origins). Semen itself is a sign of humans' priority over steel and their power to use steel for whatever purpose they choose, including the killing of other humans.

Gayo classify the above spell as part of ilmu ladani, divinely inspired, though extra-Qur'ānic, knowledge and power. Gayo sometimes use spells that come from the domain of black magic. One healer admitted to having tried the powerful knowledge called *rëjë sujud* (ruler [through] prostration), so called because the speaker orders iron to bow down before him as it once did before God. In activating this knowledge, the speaker puts himself in God's place and claims power for himself. When the healer tried it, he abstained from bathing for a year. He would only scrub himself with a cloth to stay clean. "You don't get dirty," he claimed, "it's more clean than bathing." But once during the year, on the fourteenth day of the pilgrimage month, he held a ritual feast and bathed.[10] When bathing he wiped the liquids from his eyes, ears, and nose over his body. At the ritual feast he said (in Malay/Indonesian):

> I bathe in the estuary of the Berhud well.
>
> Zuru is your name, iron;
>
> When you became iron, Abillah was your name.
>
> When you were first created
>
> it was forbidden [haram] for you to harm me, iron;
>
> If you do harm me
>
> Allah taala will be ashamed [malu] of you.

The bodily liquids are the "Berhud well," said to originate in Hell and to flow out of the ground at Babylon. In another version of this spell one would bathe in one's own excrement. Bathing in one's bodily fluids brings out the protective power, derived from spirits, that lies within us. It places that power around us for use as a protective cover. The healer who had tried these spells contrasted this process with the divinely derived use of Qur'ānic verses as a garment of invulnerability: the one comes from spirits; the other, from God. Because of the source of these powers they have side effects: the user's toenails die, for example. (He mentioned several men whose nails had died, and showed me that several of his had, too.)

Both ilmu ladani and ilmu sihir, in fact, come ultimately from God. God leaves it up to humans to decide which they will use, and to accept the ultimate consequences for their decisions. As is apparent from the above spell, ilmu sihir draws on the same sources of linguistic power as does ilmu ladani: spells in both modes claim knowledge of the origins and names of iron and of the restrictions placed on iron by God, and both cover the individual in a protective garment. They differ in the sources of protection: scripture, other divinely inspired speech, or spirits.

QUR'ĀNIC KNOWLEDGE AND POWER

Scripture itself is understood as powerful speech. Isak Gayo study and recite the Qur'ān for the merit, knowledge, and power to be derived from it. Not only are certain verses of the Qur'ān considered to be imbued with special efficacy, but recitation of any portion of the Qur'ān, because it pleases God, may lead him to grant the reciter special favors. Qur'ānic recitation thus is always powerful (even when that power is not immediately tapped, it builds up as merit [pahla] to the credit of the reciter).

---

[10] For those on the pilgrimage this day marks the end of the pilgrimage proper and the easing of the remaining ritual prohibitions.

Reciting Scripture

The Qur'ān was and is an oral "recitation" (the meaning of the Arabic word *qur'ān*). Its verses were revealed to Muhammad in the voice of Jibra'il, who recited from the heavenly book. The earliest revelation in the Qur'ān, chapter 96, begins with the command to Muhammad: "Recite!" Thereafter, Muslims have placed special emphasis on the recitation and transmission of the sacred verses through oral/aural means (Graham 1987; Nelson 1985). Muhammad himself was illiterate, and both his illiteracy and lack of previous poetic skills are cited as proofs of the Qur'ān's divine source. At a time when written Arabic lacked markings for vowels, punctuation, and intonation, the reciter, not the transcriber, was the authoritative transmitter (Fischer and Abedi 1990:97–149; Graham 1987:96–102). Muhammad also commanded that his followers recite the heavenly speech in a melodious way: "Embellish the Qur'ān with your voice." Qur'ānic recitation thus became the pious imitation of revelation itself (cf. Berque 1980:194–215).

Qur'ān recitation is an important link among local, national, and worldwide Islamic contexts. In Isak, virtually all children begin to recite the Qur'ān about the time they enter primary school. Usually they study with a village religious official or another learned man. Community recitation classes often are held in the Isak mosque. For most of 1989, for example, the religious official of Kutë Baru village held nightly sessions in the mosque. About twenty children, boys and girls from all five villages, attended the sessions regularly. The students were divided into two groups. The beginners worked their way through the Juz 'Amma, a separately bound collection of the final thirty-seven chapters of the Qur'ān. These chapters are the shortest in the Qur'ān and are often recited in worship and on other occasions. The second group had completed their recitation of the Juz 'Amma and were reciting the entire Qur'ān. A child completes the study of the Juz 'Amma or the Qur'ān by correctly (in the judgment of the teacher) reciting every chapter. This criterion does not imply memorization, although the students are encouraged to memorize the shorter chapters. At each of the two stages of completion a small feast is held for the student and the teacher.[11]

Most Isak residents have recited the Juz 'Amma but not the entire Qur'ān, although many have learned and retained the principles of recitation sufficiently well to be able to recite any part of it. Many of the younger men and women have studied the art of melodious recitation or cantillation (*tajwīd*) of Qur'ānic verse (cf. Denny 1988). This art is shared by Muslims

[11] Compare the similar processes of earlier Qur'ān study described for lowlands Aceh by Snouck Hurgronje (1906, II:3–4), for Morocco by Eickelman (1985:57–65), and for Iran by Fischer and Abedi (1990:27–30); and compare Messick (1989) on the related tension between oral and written forms of legal documents.

throughout the world and draws authority from the prophet Muhammad's declaration: "He who does not recite the Qur'ān melodiously is not one of us." Every two years there is a national Competition in the Recitation of the Qur'ān (Musabaqah Tilawatil Qur'an, MTQ). Competitions are held at each level of national administration, in Isak as elsewhere in the nation. In each of the five Isak villages as many as twenty persons compete in three age groups. The half-dozen best in each group then compete in the Isak mosque for the subdistrict title. Further contests are held at the district, provincial, national, and international levels. The rotation of the national contest site around the provinces is part of the government's national development strategy. Years before the event, everything from road building to the writing of local histories picks up pace in the designated province. The winning reciters thereafter perform frequently on national television.

Performing or hearing these cantillations of Qur'ānic verse is emotionally gripping (to me as well as to Gayo and other Muslims) in a way that a bare description of the art cannot be. One realizes why it is that recitation is held above silent reading. As William Graham says of his own listening experience: "It is in the moving oral rendition of the text that the Qur'ān is realized and received as divine" (1987:101).

The Qur'ān also provides a repertoire of scriptural resources for personal use. Along with Muslims elsewhere, Gayo often say verses to themselves for special comfort. One finds the same selection of verses singled out as especially powerful in Sumatra, Pakistan, or Egypt as a pan-Muslim tradition about how to use scripture. At moments of danger, some people recite the "Seven Verses," a selection of seven verses from different chapters of the Qur'an, each of which celebrates the power of God.[12] Others derive a reassuring sense of God's power and majesty from Qur'ān 2:255, the Throne, or from Qur'ān 36, the chapter (sūra) titled Yā Sīn after its first two letters (cf. Graham 1987:109; Padwick 1961:117–19). Both selections affirm God's powers. Sūra Yā Sīn also describes the Resurrection and Judgment, and is sometimes recited during a long illness or when death is feared.

Most Isak Gayo use and appreciate the Qur'ān for the combination of personal reassurance, physical protection, and generation of merit that recitation provides, as in the following illustration:

In July 1989, Aman Déwi's mother had left on the pilgrimage to Mecca. He was troubled during her absence, often awakening in the middle of the night and worrying about her safety. At such moments he would arise and recite from the Qur'ān [ngaji]. He usually began with the chapter Yā Sīn. I asked him why that one, and he said that it

[12] The verses are as follows: Taubat (9:51), Yunus (10:107), Hud (11:6, 56), Angkabut (29:6), Fatir (35:2), Zumar (39:38).

5. Aman Déwi

was because many people read it, and because it was easy for him to find; he just had to look for the first two letters and then start reading. Then he continued on to other chapters; it did not matter which ones. But before he recited he would ask God to give to his mother the merit produced by the recitations: "the merit [pahla] from reading your voice [*lingmu*], your verses [*ayatmu*]." He asked God to lessen her troubles, to calm her feelings, and to guard her.

At other times as well Aman Déwi would recite verses before going to sleep, especially if he was worried about the family finances or the state of his farm. At his farmhouse he keeps an old Qur'ān, with two of its sections [juz] missing, perched high up on a shelf. Harmful spirits [jin] fear it, he told me, and will not enter the house.

Along with many other Muslims, Aman Déwi derives both reassurance and a sense of accomplishment from reciting verses. Arising at night, troubled, he calms himself by his recitation. He knows something of the content of these verses, especially Yā Sīn (which, since childhood, he would have heard people recite at troubled moments). He is also able to direct the merit he creates toward the person whose circumstances worry him.

Aman Déwi also profits from the physical power of the written Qur'ān to keep spirits away from his home. If the oral Qur'ān was and is primary, the written Qur'ān and its individual letters also participate in the book's heavenly character. Written letters were the first objects to emerge when the universe was created, and they can convey the power of God's creation. Written on scraps of papers, Qur'ān verses have served the same purpose as invulnerability spells. A slip of paper inscribed with one of the names of God, the confession of faith, or the names of prophets or other figures from Islamic history may be carried in a small bamboo tube, placed inside a shirt, or kept in a home as protection against harmful spirits.

Qur'ān and Power

On first glance, the talismanic use of the written Qur'ān, widespread in the Muslim world, might seem in conflict with the primacy of Qur'ānic orality. Indeed, a tension between the Qur'ān as oral revelation and recitation on the one hand, and the received, written form of the Qur'ān on the other, not only dates from the beginnings of Islam but is presaged in the Qur'ān itself.[13] In the chapter titled Cattle, which highlights the contrasts between Islamic and pagan practices, the reasons for choosing oral revelations over written ones are set out. Among them:

> Had we sent down to you a writing [kitāb] on parchment
> so that they might touch it with their hands,
> those who do not have faith would say:
> "This is nothing but obvious magic."
>
> (Qur'ān 6:7)

The Qur'ān distinguishes itself from a mere written object, which might be taken to be a magical device. Yet the Qur'ān also proclaims itself as kitāb, a word used to refer to any kind of writing.

---

[13] Until the collection and codification of the Qur'ān in written form under the third caliph, 'Uthmān (r. 644–656 C.E.), qur'ān would have meant "recitations" and not a fixed collection in written form (Graham 1987:88–95).

> Truly it is a noble Recitation
> in a hidden Book,
> which none shall touch but the purified—
> a revelation from the Lord of all beings.
>
> (Qur'ān 56:77–80)

The specific revelations of this book, and of those books (the Psalms, Torah, Gospels) given to earlier messengers of God, are based on an original, heavenly scripture. This divine writ is referred to in the Qur'ān as the *umm al-kitāb*, literally "mother of scripture," in the sense of prototypical writing. The Qur'ān also refers to the *lauh al-mahfūz*, "well-preserved tablet," on which God first recorded all earthly scriptures and, in some interpretations, all existents (Graham 1987:84).

The distinction conveyed in the Qur'ān between its own mission and a possible, and erroneous, magical interpretation is not, therefore, that of oral and written media per se. It is, rather, the distinction between the Qur'ān as the revelation of previously (divinely) fixed messages (a fixing that was both spoken and written), and the Qur'ān as merely an object, a thin writing, with nothing behind or prior to it (cf. Werbner 1990:160). One may interpret the apparently magical use of the Qur'ān to fall either within or without the range of its self-proclaimed legitimate use. Following the dominant Isak view, one may consider a talisman fashioned from Qur'ānic verses to be the written form of God's speech. Under this interpretation it is not magical in the sense intended in Qur'ān 6:7, but a secondary concretization of the original revelation—a revelation that was itself secondary to an original divine inscription. (As we shall see in Chapter 5, the original fixing of form and meaning is the cosmogonic key to understanding the sources of religious power.) Of course, others condemn talismans as merely playing with verses (and also as trying to second-guess God about the future).

Some Qur'ānic verses are considered especially meritorious (cf. Padwick 1961:108–20). Qur'ān 112, al-Ikhlās (Sincerity), has been mentioned as a source of aid in times of trouble. The chapter reads in its entirety:

> Say: He is God, Unity
> God, the Eternal
> He neither begets nor was begotten
> And there is none comparable to Him

One of the shortest chapters, al-Ikhlās is also one of the first that children learn. Because virtually everyone has memorized it, the chapter is frequently recited in worship. It is also specially favored because of its content.[14] It reaffirms the oneness of God, his tauhīd, by declaring God's eternal quality (that he is not created but Creator), his transcendence of bio-

---

[14] If the two chapters that follow 112 are considered to be prayers rather than proper chapters, then al-Ikhlās is the concluding chapter of the Qur'ān (Pickthall n.d.:454).

logical kinship (in explicit distinction from Christian notions), and his incomparability (in opposition to polytheisms of any kind). God's unity, when explicated in this way as a series of affirmations and denials, can be thought of as the primary message of Islam. Chapter 122 is therefore often said to sum up the Qur'ān and to contain its essence (as is also said about the first chapter, al-Fātiha).

For all these reasons—its brevity, familiarity, and embracing message—al-Ikhlās is, along with al-Fātiha, the centerpiece of scriptural recitation. When men and women gather to transmit the merit of their recitations to deceased loved ones, when they hold a feast to celebrate an Islamic holiday, or when they gather for a ritual to mark the start of the agricultural season, they invariably recite al-Ikhlās. The chapter, usually referred to in Isak as the "Qul hu" after its first two words ("Say: He"), is often recited in sets of three. Some Isak people hold that three such sets are equivalent in merit to having recited the entire Qur'ān: "Three Qul hus and you complete [tamat] the Qur'ān." The equivalence is due to the chapter's affirmation of God's unity, a message that so pleases him that he grants great merit to those who recite the verse. For these Isak Gayo, the rich semantic meaning of these verses grants temporal power to the reciter by way of God's predictable pleasure.

Isak modernists disparage what they see as the cavalier, instrumental way in which others treat this and other chapters: "It is the Surat al-Ikhlās," said Tengku Asaluddin to me, disapproving of my reference to the chapter as "the Qul hu." "Its contents indeed are wide ranging," he admitted, "but reading it three times is certainly not the same as reading the entire Qur'ān. That would be far too easy!" Al-Ikhlās and other commonly read verses (he mentioned Qur'ān 2:255, the Throne verse, and Qur'ān 36, Yā Sīn) can give a reader power, he explained, but only because they contain powerful meanings. Reading such verses reinforces one's sense of inner strength and builds confidence.

Because each verse has its own message, Tengku Asaluddin selects verses for his own daily worship based on the kind of message he needs on that day. The significance of verses for him lies primarily in the instruction and comfort their recitation in worship can bring (cf. Graham 1987:94–95, 102–3; Padwick 1961). Whereas healers recite the Seven Verses as spells to drive off harmful spirits (who fear the power of God), Tengku Asaluddin recites them in worship to reassure and calm himself.

While al-Ikhlās and certain other verses are said to bring general merit and power, some verses are assigned more specific functions.[15] Verses that

---

[15] Verses such as al-Ikhlās also appear as part of goal-specific spells, but in such cases the goal is specified by the Gayo or Malay/ Indonesian portion of the spell. For a detailed analysis of similar ideas among the Sudanese Berti see Osman el-Tom (1985).

tell of a particular gift from God or of the power of a particular prophet are often thought to lend the same sort of power to the person who recites them, once he or she has met certain conditions. Thus, in order to gain invulnerability, Abang Das recites verses 10–11 of Qur'ān 34 (Sabā):

> And We gave David grace from Us:
> O hills and birds, echo his psalms of praise.
> And We made the iron soft for him,
> Saying: Make thou long coats of mail
> and measure the links
> And do right.
> For surely I see what you do.

For Abang Das, this passage describes God's grant of invulnerability to the prophet David. The gift took the form of an iron garment. During the dangerous days of the Darul Islam uprising, Abang Das sought out invulnerability spells and was directed toward these verses. To activate the spell he prayed to God for protection and declared that he would use the spell for good, not evil. He then recited the Qur'ānic passage and passed his hands over his arms and legs, covering all the areas to be rendered invulnerable, as if washing them or putting on a shirt and pants: "You are putting on your iron clothes when you do this." Like others who use this passage, Abang Das obtained his protective garments in a dream in which Jibra'il appeared and placed the iron shirt on him.

ACQUIRING POWER AND EXPECTING RESULTS

One can acquire a spell, and the power or knowledge to activate it, by a variety of means. Certain kin groups retain the power to effectively use spells—especially the more public, ritually embedded spells. Thus one descent line in Kutë Robel village has provided the most powerful curers in Isak since precolonial days, and a descent line in Kutë Rayang village has furnished the rice ritual specialists for the community. Others who have tried to exercise these functions have failed.

Most spells, however, are potentially available to any individual, man or woman, who is able to prepare himself or herself to receive them. Some spells are the property of individuals, and one must give something to the spell's owner in exchange for the spell. In the case of Qur'ānic verses used as spells, one already knows the text; what is needed is the divine authorization (ijazah; <Ar. ijāzah, license or diploma) to use it for a particular purpose. Solitary meditation may be required to obtain that authorization, or perhaps just purity of heart and the right intentions.

The notion that divine authorization is needed to activate a Qur'ānic verse as a spell addresses a potential problem with the local theory of powerful scripture. If scripture had intrinsic power, then anyone, regardless of personal qualities or divine favor, could acquire divine power merely by memorizing the appropriate verses. Scripture would then resemble classic anthropological notions of a magical spell. Such a result would be intolerable to Isak people. It would cheapen the power of spells, as "bad spells" uttered by totally undistinguished people would, like bad money, drive out good.

Indeed, one can formulate an underlying principle for all spells in Isak: spiritual power involves something more than mere recitation, whether that "something more" is the purity of the reciters, their powers of imagination and concentration, or a special capacity, either acquired or inherited, to deal with spiritual agents. A corollary of this principle is the comparative idea that the more individuating or extraordinary the particular "something more," the greater the powers the person exercises. Thus the ritual practitioners of greatest renown are those who have inherited a healer's power or have acquired it through meditation. These individuals are considered to have gained special access to God's grants of power.

Solitary meditation (*kalut*), in which the practitioner eats little food and recites scripture, is a particularly effective way to acquire the power to use a Qur'ānic verse as a spell. Abang Kerna described his own, only partially successful attempt to gain such powers through meditation:

> To make a doa effective you have to obtain the ijazah to use it by meditating; this enables you to internalize it [*amalën*] for future use. You cannot just read off a doa and expect it to work!
>
> I only lasted a week at meditating. When I was herding buffalo I built a hut up on Bur Lintang and meditated. I ate puffed rice [*bertéh*] and said zikr, "lā ilāha ilāllāh." Then what I was told would happen came about: I was tested by several visions. First a tiger appeared, growled loudly, and sprang at me. This I could resist, and I kept on chanting. Then a long, thick snake slithered out of the woods and wrapped itself around me, leaving only my neck and head. This I resisted, and I kept on chanting. Then a huge wave of water came rolling over the earth at me, and I was swimming, and then drowning, taking in water, and finally I died. But I resisted and kept on chanting. But then a corpse came walking toward me, and at that I fled. I have always been very scared of corpses and avoid places where people have just been buried.
>
> If I had resisted all the trials an angel would have given me an invulnerability doa, just for me, with a special way I was to recite it. The doa might have been just an ordinary Qur'ānic verse, but there would have been a tag, a *hu* or *ya*, just for me. This did not happen, but an angel did enter my dreams shortly after I returned from meditating and gave me a garment to wear. It was woven from tiny mīm letters, for Muhammad. After that I could utter a doa and it would make me invulnerable. I also found that I could light a cigarette with

my breath. But I put these doas aside long ago, when I had children. I worried that in a moment of anger I might hit one of my children lightly, and that the doa's power that was in me would hurt the child.

Activating a spell is described as putting it on (*pasang*) as one would a suit of clothes, or concentrating reflectively on it (amalën) as one would a section of scripture, a proverb, or a lesson learned from life.[16] It may also involve drawing on resources in the body. For example, Abang Kerna and Abang Das, in activating their invulnerability spells, pressed down on their eyelids to create points of light in their vision; this light, the Light of Muhammad, is the inner counterpart to the external power provided by the spell.

The process of acquiring an invulnerability spell involves learning the spell itself, gaining the authority or license to use it, and activating the spell. When people describe how they acquired a spell they give different weights to these three elements. For the more generally available spells such as Qur'ānic verses, spell users emphasize the need to acquire special authority. For the more restrictively transmitted spells, which may be re- vealed by fellow humans, an angel, a spirit, or an ancestor, such special au- thority is already implied in the mode of transmission and thus does not ap- pear as a separate element.[17] When a Qur'ānic verse is transmitted as a spell, it may be given an individuating tag that transforms this once gener- ally available text into a restrictively transmitted spell. In these cases the function of meditation or the special dream appearance—to assign the text to the individual as a spell—is embodied in the new form of the text itself.

Most modernists do not deny that one may obtain special powers through meditation, reinterpreting this accepted fact as God's gift of a miracle to the purified meditator. Thus Tengku Asaluddin discussed how men used to meditate and chant and be subjected to images of danger and death (these images were much like those described by Abang Kerna). "Some of the men asked for invulnerability and others for strength," he said. But then he situated this practice in a Qur'ānic context: "As when the prophet Muham- mad meditated in a cave and was given the Qur'ān by Jibra'il." Spiritual gifts from God are thus gifts granted the pure, not spells licensed for those who pass certain tests. The tests and the gifts are, in Tengku Asaluddin's words, God's miracles (ma'zizët).

Purity can also explain the powers an individual exercises over inanimate objects. Tengku Asaluddin often recounted the extraordinary powers of his

---

[16] The verbal forms of *amal* convey something like the expression "to take to heart," com- bining the activities of concentrating, reflecting, and putting to use.

[17] Compare Evans-Pritchard's (1929) analysis of Azande and Trobriand spells in terms of their modes of transmission, secrecy, and relation to social groupings.

grandfather, Tengku Twenty-Two. Tengku Twenty-Two could control iron. He could call to an iron object from the other end of a longhouse, and the object would come slithering across the floor to him. He once healed a foot that had a piece of iron stuck into it by uttering a spell that turned the iron into bone. Tengku Asaluddin accounted for such powers in terms of the shared origins of iron and humans: like the exegeses of invulnerability spells, but with a twist:

> How can humans have this power over iron? It is because both humans and iron were created from light. Light became the air, the air became mist, mist became clouds, clouds became rain, and then rain became water, rivers, and foam, and then moss, earth, gravel, stone, coral, and finally iron. Humans also were created from light, and have iron in them. That is why humans and iron are one of a kind and humans can control iron. But the only humans to obtain this power are those who have purified themselves so as to become light-like and holy.

Both this account and the exegeses of invulnerability spells assert that iron and humans share history and substance, yet the two views disagree on what exactly is shared. For the utterer of a spell, humans share a history of commands and events with iron: God's powerful speech to iron and iron's promise to God. Spells coerce iron by reminding it of its history and thereby subordinating it to human will. By contrast, Tengku Asaluddin and other modernists contend that power is lodged not in speech, nor in iron's role in creating Adam, but in the precorporeal sharing of substance. Human power over iron is realized by remounting the ladder of creation, from flesh to the light from which humans were formed.

The critical distinctions between these two narrative formulations are not in their implied histories, for they draw on a shared cosmogonic tradition, but rather in the emphases made in and the practical conclusions drawn from these histories. In the general Isak view, the origins of humans and the generic power they possess over iron explains their capacity to transform iron. This history also legitimates the use of spells. In Tengku Asaluddin's account the power over iron is not inherent in humans; rather, it is conditional on the purity and piety of the individual.

These different interpretations of sacred history lead to different notions of the relation between speech and outcome. For Abang Kerna, once God has given him a verse for his own use, that use yields virtually certain results. Verses recited for the sake of a deceased person or to bring merit to the reciter also generate merit in a predictable way, albeit by way of God's pleasure. Powerful speech always involves communication, but much of the time the responses to that communication are highly predictable.

Tengku Asaluddin takes the opposite view, stressing our inability to fathom, much less predict, God's will. For him, the effectiveness of verse recitation lies not in a causal relation with the external world but in the verse's ability to soothe the spirit of the reciter and, ultimately, to render him or her spiritually improved and, just perhaps, more likely to receive gifts from God.

Both approaches contain inevitable tensions. For Abang Kerna, as one of the more reflective and inquiring of healers, it is difficult to reconcile the use of verses as spells with his knowledge of their contexts of revelation. If verses were intended as messages to Muhammad, then how can they be reinterpreted by us as spells for invulnerability or curing? For Tengku Asaluddin the tension lies between his theory of divine unpredictability and his experience that meditation leads to regular outcomes. Thus for Abang Kerna the tension between alternative ways of understanding the power of speech emerges from the instrumental use of verses in the face of their authorship by God, and this tension surfaces in self-doubt. For Tengku Asaluddin it derives from the predictable power of spells in the face of God's unpredictable control, and surfaces in admissions of ignorance.

By starting from specific units of discourse—the spells Gayo utter—we have been able to explore their capacity to combine diverse kinds of speech—evocations of God's power, of historical events, of the Qur'ān—all of which remind spiritual healers of the God-granted authority of the speaker. Gayo spells are imbricated in a communicative matrix that is itself oriented toward particular practical ends. But they also are grounded in historical and ontological conceptions of God, spirits, and humans that draw from Qur'ānic sources and other Muslim traditions. To speak religiously is to speak powerfully, and, when spirits are in question, vice versa.

Chapter Five

THE SOURCE OF HUMAN POWERS IN HISTORY

FOR ALL THEIR disagreements, Tengku Asaluddin (and other modernists) and Abang Kerna (and other users of spells) agree that speech alone does not change the world. To exert power through spells or prayer one needs to communicate with spirits, and to do that one needs to combine the right words with mental concentration and the use of certain objects and gestures.

But how is such communication possible? When I first began to learn about spells, recitations, and prayers, I suspected that people saw them as automatically effective, something like what anthropologists have called "magic." My teachers made allusions to the reasons spells worked—the primordial compact between iron and humans, for example, or the divine nature of the Qur'ān—but I did not understand from their remarks how humans could reach the spirit world with questions, pleas, or threats.

It was only as I asked for fuller accounts of spells that several teachers began to explain the mechanism behind these human powers. Each of these Isak ritual practitioners—for I had approached them as expert wielders of spells, not as theoreticians—couched his explanation in historical terms: the history of the cosmos, or of the creation of humans, or of the coming of Islam to Aceh. Although some of these accounts were quite brief and partial, while others were more encompassing, they all relied on the assumption that God's initial creative acts have left their traces in our spiritual and material being. These ideas come from a broad tradition of Sufi Muslim speculative thought, which Gayo have employed to understand and change their immediate, practical world.

THE CREATION OF THE WORLD

Isak men and women describe a chain of creation that links all beings (whether humans, animals, or spirits) to the prophet Muhammad and, through him, to God. The chain is based on the distinction between "inner" and "outer" reality, a distinction that underlies all Gayo thinking about ritual. This distinction has both an absolute and a relative sense. In the absolute sense it describes the difference between the outer world (*lahir*; <Ar. *zāhir*) and its complementary inner world (*batin*; <Ar. *bātin*). In the outer world are tangible, visible, and audible things and events. The inner world contains invisible, hidden entities, such as spirits and souls, and also the mental states that correspond to physical events.

In this model of the world, the image I form in my mind of an object is the inner version of a physical, outer object. The medicinal compound I apply to a patient, when accompanied by the proper words and images, may serve as the outer vehicle for a message I send to a harmful spirit in the inner world. The coexistence of two parallel worlds explains why objects and mental states must accompany spells: the objects anchor the spells in the outer world, while the mental imagery constructs their counterparts in the inner world.

But the terms *lahir* and *batin* may also describe the relative distinction between two states of being. In this sense we can think of the pair of terms as describing a continuum extending from the most outer, physical states to the most inner, spiritual states. At one end of the continuum are the solid objects of the visible world; at the other end is God, the most spiritual of all beings. Along the continuum are a range of other beings: the Light of Muhammad is next to God in spirituality; our souls are further along the continuum, and our shadows further still. A shadow is spiritual or inner relative to a body, but it is material or outer relative to its invisible counterpart, a spirit called the "black boy" (*bujang itëm*). Along with many other Muslims, Gayo evoke images of light, shadow, and letters to convey the movement from inner to outer states along the continuum of being.

This chain of being is not merely a matter of theoretical speculation, however. Humans who possess the proper knowledge can remount this chain and draw on the power of the relatively inner, spiritual beings to heal or, if they wish, to destroy.

The distinction between outer (lahir) states and inner (batin) ones is the consequence of God's initial act of creation. Isak people draw on diverse images to describe the relation of God to Muhammad in the beginning. Some mention the primordial appearance of two lights in the universe: the light of God (*nur Allah*) and the light of Muhammad (*nur Muhammad*). One political leader and poet, Rëjë Hasyim, described the origins of these lights as follows:

> In the beginning there was only the word of God [*kalam Allah*] and a single object that was round like an egg. God gave a command and the egglike object split in two. One of the halves became the light of Muhammad and the other became the light of God. . . . All things on the earth then were created from the light of Muhammad.

This narrator counterposes the original word of God against the lights of God and Muhammad that were created by the word. The active power to reveal and command is God's alone, but the first object to exist in the world combined the lights of God and Muhammad. The rest of the world then is made from the light of Muhammad. Muhammad thus appears as coeval with God in terms of objecthood, though he lacks God's power of creation.

Abang Das, an enthusiastic narrator and spell user, emphasized the interdependence of God and Muhammad through a series of images:

> Nur Muhammad was the first created thing. God made him so that there would be someone to say God's name so that God could hear it.[1] So, there would be no God if there were no Muhammad and no Muhammad if there were no God. Muhammad exists, but God is the one in control. God's light is that of the sun; Muhammad's is that of the moon. That is why Muhammad took the moon and split it and put one half up one sleeve and one half up the other, because it is his light.

In this narrative God and Muhammad have distinct kinds of temporal priority. Thought of as letters, they are "the shadow of the *alif* and the mīm." The letter alif [ا], the first in the alphabet, stands for God (Allāh); the letter mīm [م], for Muhammad. In the beginning of time these letters were but shadows or reflections of the yet-to-be-written forms. Abang Kerna described what then happened: "The letter mīm was written. Then from this dot, which is the starting point for writing each letter, was written the letter alif." Although the word of God was the first element in the universe, the mīm of Muhammad was the first letter to be written. "After all," said Abang Kerna, "you must first make a dot before you can make a straight line." The mīm thus signifies Muhammad's status as the first outer manifestation of reality, the first object. (Recall that Abang Kerna's dream-bestowed garment of invulnerability was woven from many little mīms.) This disharmony of precedence between God and Muhammad led them to argue, as Abang Kerna explained:

> God told Muhammad to recite the confession of faith. The confession mentions God first [there is no deity but God], and only then Muhammad [and Muhammad is his messenger]. Muhammad refused, saying that it should be the other way around. So God said: "All right then, let us each hide and try to find the other." God hid and Muhammad could not find him. God can truly disappear. Even though God has an object in the letter alif, God is not the same as the letter alif and can exist independently of the letter.
>
> Muhammad, however, could not disappear. When he tried to hide, God found him. He remains mīm and is always an object. So God won, and the confession of faith was fixed as God had commanded it, and in that form it was taught to the prophet Adam.

---

[1] This statement is a virtual paraphrase of the extra-Qur'ānic divine declaration, "I was a hidden treasure and I wanted to be known; therefore I created the world." This statement is quoted in Schimmel (1985:131) and discussed below.

The scriptural reference point for this particular letter symbolism is an extra-Qur'ānic divine revelation (*hadīth qudsī*) known throughout the Muslim world: "I am Ahmad [another name of Muhammad] without the *m*" (Schimmel 1985:116). The letter mīm is thus what separates God from Muhammad. Muhammad stands for the first outer aspect of reality to have come into existence, but he is also restricted by his outer status or objecthood. As Abang Das put it, "Objects were uncreated before God drew the initial dot and then the initial line. That is why God was the first inner state, but Muhammad the first outer state."

As God proceeds to plan and then create the objects of the universe, he adds his own divine essence to the objecthood that is signified by the mīm. Abang Kerna continued:

> God then planned in his mind what was to be in the world. He planned all the souls [*ruh*] that eventually would descend to the earth and wrote the letter lām [ل] on his tablet. All the souls were contained in this letter lām. First he planned things, and these plans were in the lām, and then as he created [these things], as they became manifest [lahir], the alif was added to the lām so that the things became *lām-alif* [لا].
>
> The essence [*zat*] of each thing was from the mīm, but its light, that which gave it life, was from the lām-alif. The mīm is Muhammad and the lām-alif is the light of God and the light of Muhammad.

God first plans the existence of each thing that will have empirical being. He then inscribes the souls of these potential existents on his heavenly tablet, the *luh mahful* (<Ar. lauh al-mahfūz, preserved tablet). The state of having been inscribed is signified by the letter lām. Finally, God adds his own alif to the lām to produce a material object. While the letter mīm is the sign of objecthood relative to God, the double letter lām-alif is the sign of an object brought into being by God after having been infused with his light and that of Muhammad.

This entire sequence of creation can be stated in terms of pairs of relatively inner (batin) and outer (lahir) qualities or states, which are represented by the relative pairs God/Muhammad, alif/mīm, and lām/lām-alif. They form a chain of signs leading from God, the most inner form of reality, to empirical things in the world.

In using images of light and letters to represent the relations between lahir and batin, Gayo thinkers echo writings from elsewhere in the Muslim world. The image of Muhammad as an everlasting light is nearly as old as Islam itself. Since at least the eighth century, theologians, poets, and peasants have figured this eternal spirit as the Light of Muhammad (nūr Muhammad), citing a Qur'ānic passage called the "light verse" (*āyat an-nūr*) (24:35):

God is the Light of the heavens and the earth
the likeness of His Light is as a niche
wherein is a lamp
(the lamp in a glass,
the glass as it were in a glittering star)
kindled from a Blessed Tree,
an olive that is neither of the East nor of the West
whose oil wellnigh would shine, even if no fire touched it;
Light upon Light;
(God guides to His Light whom He will).

Sufi thinkers compared Muhammad to the lamp through which the Divine Light shines on the world. In the ninth century an Iraqi Sufi, Sahl at-Tustari, further interpreted the phrase "likeness of His Light" as the Light of Muhammad. This light, he wrote, was the first created thing, and existed as a primordial column of divine light, bent in worship of God. From the Light of Muhammad was created Adam, and Muhammad in his terrestrial form was later fashioned from the same clay used to make Adam. Muhammad himself is reported as having said "I was a prophet when Adam was between water and clay" and "The first thing that God created was my light" (Schimmel 1985:124–30).

Sufi writers found a reference to the Light of Muhammad in the divine revelation: "I was a hidden treasure and I wanted to be known; therefore I created the world" (Schimmel 1985:131). For the writer Ibn al-'Arabī (1165–1240), the "hidden treasure" saying became all-important because it explained creation itself. God's desire to be known led to his creation of the Light of Muhammad as the first knower of his greatness (as in the story by Abang Das quoted above). The rest of creation was, in turn, fashioned to know Muhammad.

Sufis have also accorded special significance to certain letters. The lām-alif, for example, may be taken to form the word *lā*, "no," and thus to begin the confession of faith, "there is no deity but God." It also may be taken as a negation of the material world followed by a drawing near to God's alif, or as a symbol of the simultaneous separateness and union of God and humans.[2]

The images and ideas of Middle Eastern Sufi writers were taken up by the earliest known Sumatran scholars. By the late sixteenth century, theologians living in Aceh were engaged in a lively debate about the presence of God in the world. Those involved in the debate drew on the writings of

---

[2] On the lām-alif, and on the equally widespread idea of the letter mīm as the "shawl of createdness" standing between God and Muhammad, see Schimmel (1975:418–20).

Muslim intellectuals in South Asia and the Middle East, and indeed were in frequent communication with them.

The earliest known contributor to this debate was Hamzah Fansuri, who was born on the northwest coast of Sumatra and died about 1590 (al-Attas 1970:3–30; Drewes and Brakel 1986:1–25). Hamzah knew Persian and Arabic, and traveled extensively in the Middle East. During his travels, probably in Baghdad, he was initiated into the Qādirīyah order (al-Attas 1970:10–11). On his return to Aceh he wrote a number of prose and verse works in Malay in which he developed a monistic theory of being. Hamzah relied in particular on the theories of Ibn al-'Arabī and al-Jīlī (b. 1365) (Johns 1957:31–32).

Hamzah and his follower Shamsuddin of Pasai (d. 1630) were denounced as pantheistic heretics by Shamsuddin's successor at the Aceh court, the Malay-speaking Gujerati scholar Nūruddīn al-Rānīrī (d. 1658). Al-Rānīrī accused them of failing to recognize the basic distinction between Creator and created, and ordered books written by them burnt. He himself fell out of favor in 1644 and left Aceh.

The Sufi line of thought was continued by 'Abdurra'ūf of Singkel (d. 1693), a Sumatra-born theologian best known for his translation of and commentary on the Qur'ān. For twenty years 'Abdurra'ūf studied in the Yemen and in Medina, where his teacher Ibrāhīm al-Kūrānī (d. 1689) composed a work on creation for the edification of the people of Aceh (Johns 1978). In 1661 'Abdurra'ūf returned to Aceh and began to write religious works in Malay under court protection, which he enjoyed for the remainder of his life. Although 'Abdurra'ūf disagreed with the theories of Hamzah and Shamsuddin, he also promoted certain ideas and spiritual exercises associated with Sufism. Under the name Syiah Kuala (Syech of the Estuary, because of the location of his grave), he is revered as the bringer of Islam to Aceh.

These writers left a legacy in the scholarly and practical Islam of the region. They argued that God was the single reality rather than a distant creator. This view, often called the "doctrine of the unity of being" (*wahdat al-wujūd*) or *Wujūdiyah*, held that creation was a process of five successive determinations or manifestations of that underlying reality. The first of the five determinations created the qualities of knowledge, being, sight, and light, which were the first outer (zāhir) aspects of the pure, indeterminate, unknowable, and inner (bātin) essence. Muhammad appears as an archetypal spiritual being, a Logos who mediates between God and his creation, giving it form and spirit. The spirit of Muhammad is one form in which the Holy Spirit (*rūh al-kudus*) is manifested; other forms include the most-exalted pen, the first intellect, and the preserved tablet.

Hamzah followed earlier Sufi writers in celebrating the eternal Light of Muhammad, as in his interpretation of the divine saying quoted earlier:

I created Creation for thy sake, thee I created for My sake (that is, Creation came into being from the Light of Muhammad; that Light came into being from the Divine Essence).[3]

This theory of creation and of Muhammad's role in it is echoed in accounts given by Gayo practitioners, and may have been the historical source of those accounts.[4] Although Hamzah's works were effectively obliterated by al-Rānīrī, many of his ideas and images left their mark in popular thought. Water and the ocean, for example, provided Hamzah with just the right vehicle for steering between naive pantheism and orthodox blindness: just as clouds and raindrops remain identical with the ocean in their substance even after they have emerged from it, so, too, is God immanent in his reality and yet transcendent in his form. Hamzah translates a Persian text to make his point:

> The sea is timeless; when it heaves it becomes just waves,
> People say "waves" but in reality [haqīqat] it is just the sea.[5]

Read in isolation, this passage might suggest the naive pantheism from which Hamzah took pains to distance himself. (Indeed, such passages were later taken as proof of Hamzah's heresy.) He avoids this effect, however, by superimposing on the waves a second imagery, one of shadows and bodies, in another verse. The world is only the image or shadow of what God knows as the initial possibilities:

> As to the world, although it is existing it is yet
> nothing but the shadow of the Known.[6]

God not only knows those things that appear in the world, he also manipulates them. Hamzah depicts God as a distinct actor in the world rather than as equivalent to, or substratum of, it:

> It is He that causes Hamzah to move so that he can move. If He does not cause him to move, Hamzah cannot move, for Hamzah is but a shadow. If the

---

[3] *Asrāru'l-'Arifīn* (The Secrets of the Gnostics), 42. All citations of Hamzah's prose works are from al-Attas (1970) and are given with manuscript page numbers.

[4] An early, incomplete form of this argument is found elsewhere (Bowen 1987). A more complete argument would consider the similarities between Hamzah's five-stage scheme of creation and the Gayo creation story, and would contrast both to the seven-stage scheme that dominated all Sufi writings in Aceh after Hamzah. The seven stages were developed by Shamsuddin in 1601, based on a 1590 treatise written in India by Fadlullāh, a scholar in the Shattārīyah Sufi order. Fadlullāh's *al-Tuhfa al-mursala ilā rūh al-nabī* (The Gift Addressed to the Spirit of the Prophet) was to become the touchstone for later theological disputes in Aceh (Johns 1965:126–48). Hamzah's legacy may thus have been best preserved in highlands oral traditions.

[5] *Asrāru'l-'Arifīn*, 55.

[6] *Asrāru'l-'Arifīn*, 77.

Possessor of the shadow does not cause him to move, how can Hamzah move?[7]

Understandably, 'Abdurra'ūf (Syiah Kuala) took even greater pains to distinguish between a naive pantheism and the idea developed by Ibn al-'Arabī and Hamzah of creation as determinations of a divine reality. Just as the reflection of something in a mirror is neither the thing itself nor completely separate from it,

> . . . all these things are manifestations of Him, they are not He, nor are they other than He. (Johns 1955:151)

'Abdurra'ūf also elaborated letter symbolism in ways similar to Gayo speculations. In his scheme of creation he uses the written dot, the mīm, as the object that contains or prefigures the line, the plane, and all other shapes (Johns 1955:68).

Despite the bitter controversies, the idea of creation as governed by a series of determinations perdured in Aceh and elsewhere in Indonesia (Johns 1965; Lombard 1967:163–64; Woodward 1989:125–34).[8] The Shattārīyah order brought to Sumatra by 'Abdurra'ūf spread throughout the archipelago and remained strong in Aceh through the nineteenth century (Snouck Hurgronje 1903, II:18).[9] Ibn al-'Arabī's teachings concerning the primordial Light of Muhammad, developed by Hamzah, Shamsuddin, and 'Abdurra'ūf, became the standard beginning for narratives of the prophets' lives (Snouck Hurgronje 1903, II:172, 184). 'Abdurra'ūf had also introduced the teachings of the Qādirīyah order regarding Sufi spiritual exercises (Riddell 1990:232–38), particularly the zikr, and by the late nineteenth century these exercises had become widespread under the name *ratib* (Snouck Hurgronje 1903, II:216–57).

An explicit sense of continuity between the writings of Hamzah Fansuri and nineteenth-century Sufi ideas was preserved through the spiritual genealogies, *silsilah*, that gave each local Sufi order its historical identity. Snouck Hurgronje (1903, II:19) reports that 'Abdurra'ūf was included in the genealogies of many Acehnese orders and that he was almost always described as

---

[7] *Asrāru'l-'Arifīn*, 76–77.

[8] Strong dualistic reactions to the general monistic line surfaced throughout the archipelago, however. Of particular importance was the introduction of the writings of the "sober" Sufi al-Junayd (d. 910) (Drewes 1977).

[9] By the end of the nineteenth century, however, the Shattārīyah order had declined in importance, despite the general popular veneration of 'Abdurra'ūf (Snouck Hurgronje 1903, II:18–20). Only in the twentieth century did other Sufi orders develop in Aceh. In particular, the Naqshbandiyah, which had already become strong elsewhere in Indonesia, became important on the west coast of Aceh. On the development of Sufi orders in Indonesia see Lombard (1985) and Kraus (n.d.).

"of the tribe [*bangsa*] of Hamzah Fansuri." On the west coast of Aceh the influential religious figure Habib Seunagan also claimed to disseminate the ideas of Hamzah Fansuri (Snouck Hurgronje 1903, II:14).

In the Isak of the 1980s, the Sufi views of the earlier Aceh writers underlie the theology even of some modernist thinkers. Tengku Asaluddin, for example, expounds a set of ideas about creation and being that echo those of Hamzah. For him, creation was a process of successive emanations (*pancaran*) from the Light of Muhammad, just as the Light itself was an emanation from God. He also used many of the images employed by Hamzah and 'Abdurra'ūf:

> Nur Muhammad was created from the essence of God, and Nur Adam was in turn created from Nur Muhammad. Nur is the nature of the soul and of reason. Like the fire in a lamp: where does it go when it burns out? The same with the soul at death. . . .
>
> Water always exists [here he said he was paraphrasing 'Abdurra'ūf], but waves only exist when the wind comes up. The waves are the shape and color of the water, just as a bottle gives color to clear water. All things but God are temporary and were created by him so that he might be in the knowledge of another being, so that there would someone to know him.
>
> We move, like the wind, from not-being, *'adam* [Ar.], to Adam, and back to not-being [here he wrote the Arabic for each word on a sheet of paper for me to see], just as the water moves from being still to having waves to becoming still again.

Tengku Asaluddin owned a very old manuscript copy of a work by 'Abdurra'ūf, which he had inherited from his grandfather. The manuscript consists of poems written in Jawi (Arabic-script Malay), some of which are commentaries on Arabic proverbs. Tengku Asaluddin enjoyed reading and commenting on favorite sections to his visitors. He thought 'Abdurra'ūf had understood very well the relation of God to humans:

> On the one hand, there is an absolute difference between the Creator and the created. On the other hand, we feel God in ourselves; we have a "feeling of godliness" [*rasa ketuhanan*]. This is because he has a hold on our souls at all times. Some people can become complete and closer to him, such as prophets but also the older teachers in Isak who needed little food. They are the Insan Kamil [Perfect Man].

Tengku Asaluddin did not know the name Hamzah Fansuri. He thought that Shamsuddin was a wandering Sufi whose teachings were received especially well in western Aceh, and who taught that man and God were the same. In each village, he said, Shamsuddin would try to extract money by offering to cure people. He also tried to seduce village girls. Tengku Asa-luddin mentioned al-Rānīrī's attacks on Shamsuddin, and the warnings by ulama since that time about Sufis who wear Arabic head-garments and spread lies. Yet he remained an intellectual descendant of Hamzah and Shamsuddin.

THE HUMAN EMBODIMENT OF CREATION

In order to use their speculative knowledge of creation, Gayo must extend it to the human realm. As they do so they continue to draw on the Islamic framework, but they refract it through a set of Indonesian ideas about the body, the spirit, and the organization of the world into sets of four.

In relating the story of human creation, Abang Kerna highlighted the di-vine trace left in each human, a trace that he and other healers can manipu-late. He depicted this trace in the form of the combined letter lām-alif:

God told Jibra'il [Gabriel] to make Adam from the thirty letters of the alphabet and to pattern him after nur Muhammad. Nur Muhammad already existed as a transparent film. From this film Jibra'il could make out the shape of Muham-mad's body, and from this image he traced the shape of Adam. Then God put a soul [nyawa] into Jibra'il's hand and told him to take it and to place it in Adam's body.

But as he flew down to the earth Jibra'il opened up his hand to see what it was that was so heavy and yet seemed to be without substance. As he did so the soul flew away and became all the *jin*. Then God gave Jibra'il another soul to put into Adam, but this one could not find a way into Adam's body. It tried to enter through every opening in the body, and the body trembled at these ef-forts and fell apart. So Jibra'il had to construct the body all over again. This time God said that Jibra'il's days as an angel would be over if he messed up again, and gave him a third soul.

The third soul said that it did not want to descend to earth unless the lām came down to earth with it, because all things on the earth first were in the lām, in God's plan for the world, and then when they became real in the world they became the alif. The alif is the thing in the world and lām is the plan. Like when you build a house: you have to finish it before you start it: finish it in your mind, in the lām, before you start building it in the world, in the alif. The soul did not want to be far from God, from the lām of his plans, so God sent down the lām as well to be the place for the soul.[10]

Jibra'il then brought down the soul and placed it on Adam's head, on the fontanelle where the bones had not grown together, and said: "Open, sit down,

---

[10] In some versions of this story, the soul is carried in a mungkur citrus fruit.

close." The lām-alif inside Adam opened to receive the soul; the soul lowered itself inside, and the lām-alif closed over it, just as a baby's bones close over the space in its head. When the lām-alif opens up again that is when our soul leaves us and we die [Abang Kerna then drew a diagram of the successive states of closed, open, and then closed again with the soul inside].

Because the human soul contains the lām-alif, it embodies the logic of creation itself. Souls are connected to creation through the trace left of its sequence. Accounts of this trace are practically motivated. Ritual practitioners describe two distinct, task-specific pathways from human spiritual components to objects in the world. Each of these two pathways proceeds from relatively spiritual (batin) states to those that are relatively material (lahir). The first pathway is that of the *embodiment* of the spiritual in the material world. Ritual practitioners use it to seek signs of a person's well-being or to send messages with spirits of the external world. The second pathway concerns the *empowerment* of humans through their links to spiritual agents.

I consider here the totalizing schema explained to me by Abang Kerna. Through many conversations that extended long into the night, he gradually moved from piecemeal descriptions of healing to a systematic exposition of the logic of creation and power. I also talked with the other major Isak healers about these topics, and their schemas were consistent in overall structure with his. (I consider variation in healing ideas and practice in Chapter 6.)

In his account, the presence of the divine light in the human body is the critical link between the general theory of creation outlined above and the specific features of human composition that are important to ritual practitioners. As was the case for creation, it is through Muhammad's mediation that the divine lights become concrete images or reflections (*bayan*). Muhammad's light is first manifested in each human body (and in other sentient beings) as a "white image" (*bayan putih*). The individualized presence of the Light of Muhammad enables humans to communicate with other spiritual agents. Thus, as Tengku Asaluddin pointed out, iron hears our spells because humans and iron were both formed from light and thus retain similar white images.

Each white image has a corresponding "black image" (*bayan itëm*), which also derives from Muhammad but at a slightly greater remove. It therefore is more material or lahir than the white image. It is the basis for destructive conduct. Both the white and black images are necessary for well-being, and in the healthy individual they are in balance. Healers use the white image to heal the body and the black image to attack harmful spirits. The two images are sometimes described as the individual's internal reservoirs of healing substance (*tawar*) and poison (*tubë*).

These "four images" (*bayan opat*) of God, Muhammad, black, and white stand in the order of creation shown in Diagram 5.1.

Light of God → Light of Muhammad → white image → black image

Diagram 5.1: The Four Images.

Taken together, the four images furnish a spiritual substratum; in Abang Kerna's words, they "approximate the soul [*nyawa*]." But in fact, Gayo speak of four kinds of souls and spirits that reside in the human being. The soul proper (nyawa) secures life. It remains in the body during life, but may rotate slightly and give off a changing reflection; this reflection, if askew, is the sign of an ailment. Jibra'il brought the soul to Adam and thereby brought him to life. Death occurs when the archangel Izra'il (Ar. 'Izrā'īl) wrests the soul from the body.

The reflection of the soul affects the state of the vital force (*semangat*). All living things have souls and some also have vital forces. The vital force lends strength and well-being to the individual. Its departure leaves a person lethargic and open to invasion by spirits, but does not itself lead to death. The vital force may be attacked by those who wish the individual harm, but it may also be strengthened. At the time of the rice harvest, for example, people utter spells to strengthen the vital force of the rice plant just before it is cut.

The spirit (ruh; <Ar. *rūh*) can roam in and out of the body. It is itself a sentient being, and its wanderings at night produce dreams. When we are awake it is divided among the five senses and enables us to think. Some Gayo say that it becomes the spirit of the deceased (*arwah*; <Ar. *arwāh*) at death; others say that the two are separate entities and that the arwah only leaves the body at (or shortly before) death.[11] After death it is this spirit that can hear the speech of humans.

Although these four terms may be used to distinguish among four spiritual entities, more often Gayo use them to differentiate states of well-being, emotions, wakefulness, and life. The distinction between spirit (ruh) and vital force (semangat) is in part a distinction between the cognitive faculties and general well-being. Abang Das formulated the difference in terms of the location of the two entities. The spirit resides in the liver and head, from where it spreads throughout the senses, he explained. It leaves during dreams and during the last stages of life when we begin to lose the use of our senses. By contrast, the vital force flows out from the heart through the veins. It moves upward within the body when we become angry or excited.

---

[11] In Arabic, *arwāh* is but the plural of *rūh*. Gayo have mapped the distinction between pre- and postmortem states of the spirit onto the Arabic distinction of number.

These two entities may best be thought of as idioms for human faculties and states. The English expression "in good spirits" is somewhat akin to the Gayo assertion that someone has "good vital force." Some commentators stress the closeness of the spirit and the vital force. "They are the same thing, like two brothers," said hunting-magic expert Aman Renim. Spells sometimes mention the combined "spirit-vital force" (*ruh-semangat*) of an individual. Gayo may also use *nyawa* to refer to a person's entire soul-spirit complex.

The Embodiment Pathway

These four spirit entities (nyawa, semangat, ruh, and arwah) are embodied in the four elements of the afterbirth: the amniotic fluid, blood, umbilical cord, and placenta. Born after the human infant, they are considered to be his or her "younger sibling" (*ngié*). They are also the infant's "four companions" (*së[hë]bët opat*) and link him or her to the four elements (earth, water, wind, and fire) of the natural world. In Gayo culture, as elsewhere in Indonesia, sets of four stand for internal completeness or wholeness.[12]

Among the four companions the placenta plays the most important role. It carries the infant's vital force (semangat) until the moment of birth. Shortly after birth the placenta is cleaned and buried, but it remains an important link to the natural world.[13] It also continues to be the material substratum for the vital force. A child's vital force is only weakly attached and may leave the body and wander away. In the spells uttered to call it back, a healer invites it to return to its comforting abode in the placenta (speaking as if the placenta and the child's body were still united).

Inën Segah, in 1978 an elderly woman who often attended women giving birth, used the following vital-force calling spell (*doa talu semangat*) to lend healing power to the infant, to the bath water, and to the mother's milk (an infusing of power called *nëbës* or *rajah*):

Kesah uri	First, the amniotic fluid
keduë ketubën	second, the darker fluid
ketigë tali pusët	third, the umbilical cord
keempat tembuni	fourth, the placenta.
Ko sedaging ko sedarah	You are one flesh, you are one blood

---

[12] Similar ideas about the four components of the afterbirth, their correspondence to other elements in the world, and their continuing importance to one's welfare are found throughout Southeast Asia; the Balinese system in particular is strikingly resonant with that of the Gayo (Hooykas 1974:93–128). For an account of Javanese classifications see van Ossenbruggen (1977).

[13] The afterbirth of a girl is buried under or near her house, "to keep her from wandering"; that of a boy, near the edge of the village "to give him strength" in his travels, or near the prayer house so that he will perform his religious duties.

ko setikar ko sebantal	you are one mat, you are one pillow
ko semakan ko seminum	you eat as one, you drink as one.
Sidang tetap sidang mu'min	Lord of the earth, lord of the water
sidang salih sidang salihin	lord of the wind, lord of the fire.
Jangan ko begempar-gempar	Do not shake,
sëbët opat wan ni rembëgë	the four companions in the body
sëbët tungël si mujëgë	the single companion who guards [against]
si ilët dengki	those who connive and hate.
Berkat do'a ni rasulullah	Blessings [from] the prayers of God's Messenger.

Inën Segah addresses the spell to the afterbirth as the material counterpart of the vital force (semangat). Other healers might speak directly to the vital force, or add to the four elements a fifth, the person's body.[14]

The four companions have a double semiotic importance. First, their former physical connection to the individual survives as an inner link. The placenta in particular provides a continuing basis for communication with the natural world: as it merges with the earth, the placenta creates a pathway between the individual and the natural elements.

Second, the four companions represent the individual in terms of an interdependent set of four elements. Ritual practitioners map this human set onto the four elements of the natural world, the *nasir opat* (<Ar. *'anāsir*) of earth, water, wind, and fire. The four-way array thus adds a symbolic dimension to the material link between humans and nature. Gayo also postulate another four-way set that serves as a mediator between humans and nature, the "four lords of the elements" (*sidang opat*).

Abang Kerna distinguished between an outer and an inner aspect of the afterbirth to explain how this mediation worked; his account illustrates how different entities can be linked in terms of relative states of inner and outer reality:

> If we follow the tie from the four companions to the outside, they become the four lords of the elements. After a child is born the afterbirth is buried in the woods. This burial generates the four lords of the elements for you, to which you can appeal when you are in the woods. Everyone has their own four lords of the elements, just as they have their own four images and four companions. The four companions are the afterbirth's inner aspect, the four lords of the elements its outer aspect. They [the lords] are outside of us even though they are from us. They are the images of what was buried.

[14] The spell may also include a mention of the four stages that the organism undergoes as it develops into a human fetus: *di* (separate male and female elements in the man and woman); *wa'di* (the coming together of the man and woman); *mani* (the ejaculation of the male element, sperm); *manikum* (the mixing of male and female elements to form the human fetus). Compare the Karo Batak techniques discussed in Steedly (1988).

The embodiment pathway stretches from the individual's spiritual elements to the elements in the external world. It is open-ended, in that it can be extended to reach other powerful spirit foursomes. Healers may call, for example, on the "four Syechs" (*siah opat*), spirits associated with the four cardinal directions, to augment their power to communicate with the outside world.

the four images (*bayan opat*) → human spirit (*ruh-arwah, semangat, nyawa*) →

the afterbirth (*sëbët opat*) → lords of the four elements (*sidang opat*) →

the four elements (*nasir opat*) → the four Syechs (*siah opat*)

Diagram 5.2: The Embodiment Pathway.

The embodiment pathway is useful in two distinct ways. It provides an external, material foundation for spiritual entities, as when Inën Segah reminded the vital force that it had a secure home, and it also provides a channel for communication with the lords of the elements. As we will see in subsequent chapters, healers rely on their own and their patients' links to the environment to expel harmful spirits, as do rice ritual specialists when repairing damage to crops.

The Empowerment Pathway

The embodiment pathway provides a grounding for human well-being and communication. It explains how it is that humans are spiritual (and connected to God and Muhammad) and yet also corporeal (and able to affect the physical world). The empowerment pathway then provides the means for converting inner (batin) reality into an instrument for the manipulation of the outer (lahir) world.

The four images of God, Muhammad, black, and white not only form a spiritual substratum in each individual, they also can be constructed into a spirit agent, the "single companion" (*sëbët tungël*) mentioned by Inën Segah in her spell. The single companion guards the boundary of the body against harmful spirits, against "those who connive and hate." Travelers often invoke it to stand guard while they are sleeping.

The single companion is visible as the shadow, which in this context is called the black boy. The shadow extends the chain of creation outside the body and thus can be called on to mediate between the body and the external world. One can read one's fortune from the state of the shadow, or send the shadow to do one's bidding. Just as the four images contain the possibility of both good and bad, the single companion and the shadow can be called on to perform good or evil, as personal guardians or as carriers of black magic.

The shadow in turn has a lahir counterpart in a humanlike spirit, the Old Hunter (Pawang Tuë), who lives in the hills. In some accounts the Old Hunter is a spirit that descends from Cain; in others it is an ordinary person who wandered up from the agricultural area to the hills and remained there; in still others it grew out of Adam's afterbirth. In each case it is a spiritual agent connected by ties of siblingship to each human and able to reward success or failure in the hunt. Hunters can call on it for assistance because of the connection between the shadow and the Old Hunter. Some healers also rely on this connection, appealing to the Old Hunter to assist them in expelling spirits.

The Old Hunter is in turn embodied in the afterbirth—thus the burial of the afterbirth in the woods, the Hunter's domain. Both the Old Hunter and the afterbirth are considered to be the sibling of the individual (a relationship we will explore at length in Chapter 9).

the four images (*bayan opat*) → single companion (*sëbët tungël*) →

black boy/visible shadow (*bujang itëm*) → Old Hunter (*Pawang Tuë*) →

the afterbirth (*sëbët opat*)

Diagram 5.3: The Empowerment Pathway.

The afterbirth thus appears as a terminal point in both pathways. It provides an embodiment for each individual's spiritual entities (and in particular for the vital force) and allows others to heal the soul by urging it to return to the afterbirth. The afterbirth also provides a material base for empowerment by way of the Old Hunter and the single companion. Both pathways connect the individual to the natural elements, but they do so with respect to two distinct functions: embodying spirit in the material world, and empowering people to manipulate spirit.

Few Gayo are able to completely articulate this complex system (those who did so were substantially in agreement with Abang Kerna). But most Isak adults are familiar with all the entities in question; many make active use of them for various ritual practices. These practices draw on specific linkages in the two pathways I have discussed. Some of them are listed in Figure 5.4 below and are examined more fully in later chapters.

Each of these ritual practices connects a delimited portion of the empirical individual's experienced self (internal feeling states, shadows, the afterbirth) to specific postulated spiritual agents (the solitary companion, the Old Hunter, the four lords), and regulates how appeals may be made to those agents. The pathways cut across the corporeal boundaries of the empirical human individual: he or she is pulled, punched, and guarded by diverse agents and aspects of existence. These agents are not united as

a firmly bound individual, but have different links to the outside and demand quite different interventions in the case of illness, danger, or ritual
exigencies.

Inner-Outer Relation	*Ritual Practice or Domain*
Light of Muhammad / white image	all speech to spirits, spells
four images / human souls and spirits	healing by direct repair
souls and spirits / afterbirth	recalling the vital force
black image / single companion / visible shadow	exorcisms and protection
visible shadow / Old Hunter	hunting magic and healing
Old Hunter / afterbirth	birth ritual
afterbirth / lords of the four elements	agricultural ritual

Diagram 5.4: Practical Uses of Relations between Inner and Outer Reality.

How does the ritual practitioner manage to travel along the pathways described by these theories? The key to powerful ritual action is maripët, powerful depictive imagination. Gayo describe maripët in everyday life as a
kind of pictorial memory. As it was explained to me, newly arrived from
the United States:

> You use maripët to imagine what your village looks like when you are not
> there, when you are here with us.

Gayo use maripët to reach from outer to inner reality in order to communicate with the spirits who, inhabiting this inner domain, are responsible
for many of the events or states in the outer world. One may use maripët to
induce someone else to do one's bidding, to see events in the future, or to
cause a spirit to leave the body of a patient. In all cases, using maripët requires one to imagine an object or person, to concentrate on that object,
and to mentally suggest the desired outcome. One must practice and train to
concentrate well, which some healers have achieved by spending weeks or
months meditating in seclusion and chanting the name of God or the confession of faith. Once they develop the ability to concentrate they can see into
the inner aspects of anything. According to Abang Das,

> it is like a coconut: there is the husk, and then the meat inside that, and then
> the water inside that, and then the oil on the water. You have to get yourself to
> think only about the oil inside the coconut. That is maripët.

Our access to maripët is due to the presence of the Light of Muhammad
inside each of us. Abang Kerna showed me how to see that light by press-
ing down on the eyelids: the spark that appears in our vision is the Light of
Muhammad. He explained our access to that light by referring back to the

story of creation and to the embodiment of creativity in each human individual. Because we each have God's plans and the Light of Muhammad inside ourselves we can see inside each other:

> This light is also the source of maripët, the path [for the light] between you and other people. You can see if someone else is alive and well and whether they will continue to be so by placing him or her in your own lām-alif. If you can call up this image [of the person in your lām-alif] and put it together with your own image in your maripët, then the person will be healthy; otherwise he or she will fall ill or die. This is because the lām is the place of God's plans, and we have access to those plans through our maripët, through our own light, since this light is our connection with God.

One aspect of maripët's power is thus the insight it gives us into God's plans for the future. We gain this insight by manipulating others' spirits and indirectly knowing what God has in store. We use this insight in a variety of contexts, including, as the above passage suggests, expelling harmful spirits.

Gayo ideas about maripët as power may be explored in the broader context of Sufi traditions about gnosis (ma'rifat).[15] Gnosis involves knowing things in the mode that God knows them, "participation in God's knowledge of things" (al-Attas 1970:98). In Isak, Tengku Asaluddin drew a connection between ma'rifat and the Gayo use of maripët. The religiously devoted person travels along a succession of states, he explained, as he or she endeavors to approach God: sharī'a, the exterior behaviors appropriate under Islam; tarīqa, the path to knowledge; haqīqa, appreciation of the truth and reality of God; and ma'rifat, gnosis. When I asked about the relation of gnosis to maripët, he replied as follows:

> The two words are really the same. The Arabic word ma'rifat means true knowledge accompanied by certainty about that knowledge. This knowledge can be of anything: of a person, a spell, or of God. It must be total [bulët, lit., "round"] before it can be called maripët. So a healer who maripëtën [-ën: transitive suffix] a spell or an image is by the strength of his certainty causing that image to be realized, or that spell to reach its goal. It's the same with knowledge of God.

We thus may view Gayo exegetical practice as a transformative elaboration of Sufi writings in Sumatra and elsewhere. Gayo have reimagined the Sufi stage of ma'rifat as an imaginative vision that draws its power from the presence, in each human individual, of the Light of God and the Light of Muhammad.

---

[15] I have developed this argument elsewhere (Bowen 1987).

THE COMING OF ISLAM TO ACEH

Gayo have also transformed the history of early Sumatran Sufi writers into a story about conversion, spirits, and powerful speech. The clash in the seventeenth-century Acehnese court over the presence of the divine in humans left a narrative legacy. In Gayo stories the figures of Shamsuddin and 'Abdurra'ūf enact the clash among competing Sufi ideas. The founder of the Qādirīyah Sufi order to which 'Abdurra'ūf belonged, 'Abdul Qādir al-Jīlī (Jīlānī) (1077–1166), also appears in these stories. However, all three appear not only as historical figures, but also as spirits who continue to harm or to heal humans. The narratives thus insert history into the immediacies of healing. They also highlight the issue of moral responsibility for the powerful speech that we considered in Chapter 4.[16]

ABANG KERNA ON THE ISLAMIZATION OF ACEH

Syech Shamsuddin worked as a *syech* in Mecca, someone who took care of pilgrims arriving for the Hajj. But then his intentions [niët] changed, and he drifted away from Islam. One day when he was escorting pilgrims to the mosque to pray, they all entered but he was unable to do so; the door was suddenly too small for him![17] He knew that this meant he would be unable to enter Heaven. He decided to enjoy the things of this world, since he had no more hopes for the hereafter.

He had already begun to visit Aceh, to spread Islam, returning to Mecca each year at the time of the Hajj. But after he could not fit through the mosque doorway in Mecca he returned to Aceh to stay. He began to make Aceh into a *jāhilīya* [pre-Islamic, thus pagan] country, one with no rules or customs. You could sleep with your sister. Infant girls were killed if they were not needed as wives, since they were unfit for waging war, the only thing deemed important. Things were even worse than in a Christian country! People could call jin to emerge from rivers and obey them. These conditions were the result of Shamsuddin's influence, as before him Aceh had enjoyed rules, even if it had not yet become Muslim.

Syech Shamsuddin had two younger brothers in Mecca: Abdul Qadir Jilani was the middle brother, and the youngest was Abdurra'uf. When there had been no word from Shamsuddin, Abdul Qadir Jilani was sent to follow his tracks. He was not able to enter Aceh because of the strength of Syech Shamsuddin's efforts to keep away Islam, so he traveled further south to

---

[16] I have heard the following story many times from different narrators with only incidental variations. The following is a composite of three accounts from the same narrator, Abang Kerna. The accounts, told in 1978, 1980, and 1989, differ only in their details. A similar story from lowlands Aceh is found in Snouck Hurgronje (1906, II:311–12).

[17] Similar stories are told in Isak about local men and women who are unable to enter buildings in Mecca because their riches were ill-gained.

Langkat [an East Sumatran coastal kingdom] where, under the sultan's protection, he spread Islam. So Langkat became Muslim before Aceh.

The sultan of Langkat had designs on the kingdom of Aceh. At that time they were separate kingdoms, but Langkat bowed before Aceh [acknowledged its suzerainty]. So the Langkat ruler invited the ruler of Aceh to come and gamble with him; gambling was common at the time. The two rulers rolled dice under coconut shells. Abdul Qadir Jilani stood behind the sultan of Langkat and used his powerful vision [maripët] to see the dice underneath the shell. The Langkat ruler won all the goods and territory of Aceh. The ruler of Aceh was reduced to poverty. He sent his son out to fish each day, and then they would sell the fish to buy rice.

Now word got back to Mecca that Abdul Qadir Jilani had been unable to enter Aceh. So Syech Abdurra'uf was told to follow him. At first he did not want to leave Mecca, because it is land forbidden to Hell [tanoh haram] and so after death one's soul must go straight to heaven. Aceh, however, was open [halal] to Hell, and Abdurra'uf feared that if he died there his soul would go straight to Hell. To prove him wrong his father took him to see the Zamzam well, to which angels had transported the corpse of a man who had died in Rum after defiling a mosque. His corpse was hung above the well and the angels were tormenting him. Abdurra'uf's father said that there was another well at Babylon, called Berhud, the water of which flowed from Hell.[18] So wherever you died your soul could be transported to Heaven or Hell.

Abdurra'uf then agreed to leave. He arrived in Aceh at the estuary of the river and built a small hut in the rushes. He was afraid to say who he was; Syech Shamsuddin was still in power and the sultan had been reduced to poverty. He saw the sultan's son out fishing in the estuary, and he too went to fish. He caught a lot of fish and shared his catch with the boy. After several days like this he told the boy that he caught so many fish because he knew fishing doa. He then taught the boy the doa:

> Aūzbillah min al-syaitān il-rajīm. Bismillāh irrahmān irrahīm
> [I take refuge in God from cursed Satan.
> In the name of God, the Merciful, the Compassionate.]

Abdurra'uf called on God for his assistance—if he had not been helped by God he never would have made it into Aceh. The boy started to use the doa and caught many fish. God will help people in anything, good or bad, as long as they pray to him. The person who requests bad things ends up in Hell, but he, too, receives God's help on earth. God gives anything he is asked to give; that is the only just [adil] way.

Abdurra'uf then gave the boy more doa. For gambling he taught him the confession of faith ["I testify that there is no deity but God and that Muham-

---

[18] Recall the black magic spell in Chapter 3 that refers to the practitioner's bodily fluids as "the Berhud well."

mad is His messenger"]. The boy studied these, and he had certainty and belief [*yakin dan percaya*] in their effectiveness, so they worked.

The boy's father, the ruler of Aceh, then asked to meet Abdurra'uf. Abdurra'uf asked him if he would like to win back his kingdom. Of course, he
replied. But he had to promise that he would put into effect Islamic law
throughout Aceh. Abdurra'uf said: "You are sure to win back your posses-
sions, because I am close to the angels, and whatever you want will be communicated [*itèlèk*, lit., "telexed"] straight to God." Abdurra'uf then taught him
and his son the basic elements of Islam [*rukun Islām*], including the recitations
[doa] for worship. The son went on to master all doa and, as Syiah Kuala
[Syech of the Estuary], spread Islam throughout Aceh; the father never got
past the basic elements. But the father began to gamble in the villages to raise
capital. He had to win what today would be about 14 million rupiah before the
ruler of Langkat would be interested in gambling with him.

Finally he had raised enough money and they invited the sultan of Langkat
to come and gamble. When the invitation arived at Langkat, Abdul Qadir
Jilani consulted his book,[19] saw that things were not propitious, and advised
the sultan not to accept. But the sultan insisted on going and said that they
would take lots of capital, and so they did: gold, silver, and other valuable
things. Abdul Qadir Jilani stood behind the sultan of Langkat and Abdurra'uf
stood behind the sultan of Aceh. Abdurra'uf put up a partition [*ijab*; <Ar.
hijāb] that made him invisible. He also blocked the power of Abdul Qadir
Jilani's doa so that he could not see the dice in his inner self [batin]. Abdurra'uf let him see the dice on some rolls, when he told the Aceh sultan to
place small bets, but blocked his view on the others, when he had the sultan
place large bets.

The Aceh ruler quickly won back all that he had lost before. But he had
promised he would not covet Langkat territory, so they fixed the boundary between the two kingdoms. Everyone was circumcised and studied the confession of faith. Abdurra'uf became the chief judge, and Syiah Kuala the chief
ulama.

The story traces the passage of Aceh from the darkness of its pagan days
to the light of Islam. Some tellers of the story wax eloquent on the many terrible things Aceh people did prior to conversion. The process of conversion
depends on the power of sacred words. The ruler of Aceh and his son are
convinced to follow Abdurra'uf by the effectiveness of the sacred phrases
he teaches them: the confession of faith and the basmala (bismillāh irrahmān irrahīm). The son becomes learned because he believes in the power of
the words he studies. Conversion is less a matter of faith or belief than the
willingness to employ sacred words for practical ends and the certainty that

---

[19] His kitëb, book; this reference could be to a divination book or to the Qur'ān itself, often
used to determine whether a venture would be propitious or not.

the words will be effective. The narrative thus affirms the practical power of all doa, whether spells, prayers, or recitations.

The narrator steps back from his story to affirm that God accepts and assists in the use of doa as spells. God's assistance does not reflect his approval, only his fairness in granting requests to anyone who makes them (an evenhandedness we will revisit in discussing exorcism practices). The use of the basmala as a gambling spell does not need to be justified, although the eventual conversion of the two kingdoms is available as a justification; its use is merely noted.

The events of conversion play out the controversies of the seventeenth century, with the ulama of the earlier period as practitioners. Here, Shamsuddin is no longer the court judge in an Islamic kingdom, but the impious ruler of a pagan land. Abdul Qadir Jilani, the founder of the historical 'Abdurra'ūf's Sufi order, is here portrayed as Abdurra'uf's rival. Abdurra'uf himself is given credit for the conversion of the province. But the tale is not a simple one of good versus evil. The three men are brothers, after all, and Syech Shamsuddin worked as a guide in Mecca before straying from the religious path.

Gayo usually tell this story in one of two practical contexts. In the first, a healer may do battle with the spirit of Syech Shamsuddin, in which case the fate of this wayward teacher is described: In one version he is tricked by Abdul Qadir Jilani into entering a padlocked, wooden box. Abdul Qadir Jilani then removes him from the box, rips him in half, and throws one half toward the sunrise and the other toward the sunset. Both halves become malevolent spirits that bring sickness from both directions. In another version, Abdul Qadir Jilani makes Syech Shamsuddin very small and places him into a gold box. He then tosses the box into the middle of the ocean, where Shamsuddin becomes the jin of madness. These stories make scholars of the seventeenth century into figures who bring immediate benefit or harm to everyday folk.

Ritual specialists concerned with farming or hunting also tell these stories, but they identify two of the figures, Abdul Qadir Jilani and Abdurra'uf, as powerful local ancestors. In these accounts Abdul Qadir Jilani was buried at Gerpa, a village near the origin site of Lingë, but arose alive from the grave. Only after he had died and arisen twelve times did he remain buried and become known as the Gerpa Ancestor (Muyang Gerpa). Abdurra'uf is identified with several distinct ancestors in the Gayo highlands, each of whom also demonstrated his power by rising from the grave after burial. Other local ancestors may be associated with these two figures: a founding ancestor in the Serbëjadi domain, Muyang Bunin, is said to have accompanied Abdurra'uf to Aceh. In this way the tale provides Islamic identities for the ancestors, rendering the local geography both powerful and sacred.

Gayo ideas of local power and knowledge thus echo both the long tradition of Sufi speculative thought and the political struggles engendered by it. Gayo articulate into an explanatory whole the creation of the universe, human capacities for interchanges with spirits that result from creation, and the relation of inner to outer reality that differentiates and connects humans and spirits. These ideas are the outcome of Gayo transformative elaborations of broader Muslim traditions. In elaborating these general Islamic formulations, Gayo have added a set of specifically Indonesian ideas, including the role of the placenta, the figures of the shadow and the Old Hunter, and the correspondence across sets of four.[20] In the next several chapters I explore how Gayo have applied these Islamic and Indonesian ideas as a system of thought to the practical problems of healing, exorcising spirits, and ensuring successful crops and hunts.

[20] For comparisons elsewhere in the archipelago see Hooykas (1974) on Bali, Laderman (1991) and Skeat (1967) on Malaysia, and Sibeth (1991:85–98) and Steedly (1988) on the Karo Batak.

Chapter Six

THE HEALER'S STRUGGLE

THE ELDERLY WOMAN, one side of her body paralyzed, had been lying in Aman and Inën Tauhid's house for two days. An Isak native (from Kutë Ryëm village), she had lived north of Takèngën for the past few years. When no healer in her new community succeeded in improving her condition, she returned to Isak to seek Aman Tauhid's help.

Before beginning his cure, Aman Tauhid tried to determine who was responsible for the illness. Paralysis is generally assumed to be caused by the actions of harmful spirits (jin) sent by a malicious human, often another healer. By concentrating his powers of imagination (maripët) and saying the names of potential spirit-senders, Aman Tauhid was able to depict, in his inner vision, the person responsible. "If I say a name and it is that person," he explained, "then his or her image will immediately enter my maripët; if it is not that person the image will definitely not appear." The first name he tried, that of Aman Risa (another Isak healer who was frequently Aman Tauhid's rival) immediately brought up the man's image. "But I knew it was him in any case," he added, "because yesterday we were drinking coffee together in the coffee shop and he said: 'She [the patient] won't be cured until her flesh separates from her bones.' Of course you die if your flesh separates from your bones, so talking like that meant that he was the one who sent the disease."

Although Aman Risa could have sent one of several possible spirits to cause the illness, Aman Tauhid knew that he most often used the jin called "one thousand dangers" (bëlë seribu). To carry the jin to its intended destination, Aman Risa usually called on the Old Hunter (Pawang Tuë), the spirit of human origins that roams the hills. Armed with this knowledge, Aman Tauhid chose the most appropriate approach. He began with the least invasive level of treatment, which involved relieving the woman's symptoms by applying medicinal substances and politely asking the jin to leave her body. Because her legs felt cold "as if there were water inside," he treated them with a compound made up of hot medicinal substances: two types of seed that burn the mouth and make it feel tingly, a leaf with a pungent odor, and the oil from a rotted coconut to make the substance stick to the skin. The hot substances would warm the patient's legs and the odorous ones would drive off the jin and allow her blood to flow again. Aman Tauhid chopped and pounded the substances into a fine powder that he then mixed with the coconut oil.

As he applied the compound to the woman's legs, Aman Tauhid appealed to Rëjë Kaharollah, the ruler of all jin (<Ar. *qahr Allāh*, God's power), to call off the one thousand dangers. The spell, called a *doa rajah* (or *perajah*), was recited over the medicine just before it was applied, so that the compound would carry the spell's message into the patient:

He pintu langit	Oh, [at the] door to the sky,
ko Rëjë Kaharollah	you are Rëjë Kaharollah;
Seribu seratus sembilën puluh	One thousand one hundred ninety
angkan rayatmu	are your subordinates.
Ikë i matahari	At the sun
Rëjë Semah anak jin pari	King Obeisance, child of *jin pari*,
nama panglimamu	is the name of your warlord.
Ikë i dunië ni	On this earth
Rëjë Jihim name panglimamu	King Jihim is the name of your warlord.
Kerna ini mayo terkidingé	Because this entered through her legs,
tangkohën ko terkidingé miyën	draw it out again through her legs.

Aman Tauhid explained that he could request favors of the ruler of the jin because he had made the ruler's acquaintance when he first became a healer.[1] The ruler comes when called and orders the jin to leave the patient. But often the jin refuse to obey him. "This is not so different from people here in Isak," explained Aman Tauhid. "When their ruler tells them to go and clear land for coffee gardens they find something else to do instead." The healer then needs to take stronger measures to drive the recalcitrant jin from the patient.

Indeed, on this occasion the polite request to Rëjë Kaharollah did not work and the patient's condition did not improve. Aman Tauhid tried another measure: asking the Old Hunter, whom he suspected of having brought the jin into the patient, to leave the body. Because the Old Hunter often helps people he must not be attacked or driven away. Instead, he must be given a sign that a human healer is aware of his presence, that the healer gives him all the honor he is due, and that he would like to remove the discomfort from the patient.

To pay proper respect to the Old Hunter, Aman Tauhid assembled substances that would signify the spirit's special relation to humans. They included leaves of the wild sirih plant, which grow in the forest (the Old Hunter's abode); the leaves of the *karé* orchid, which are long and pointed, resembling the spear from which they originated (the weapon of the Old

---

[1] He had done so by rolling a sirih leaf (see below), lighting incense, and asking the ruler to come when called. Other healers also made appeals to this ruler. Some knew that the ruler's title meant "God's power." The choice of this name for the ruler of all jin might once have been taken to equate him with God, an equation that would be consistent with the general idea that all power is ultimately God's. Aman Tauhid did not intend this connection, however.

Hunter); and the black tendrils of the sugar-palm, which suggest the Old Hunter's broom. The last two items "form a tie between him and us" because they remind him that he is of human origin and that he left the community to hunt in the forest (a story discussed in Chapter 9). Aman Tauhid boiled the three kinds of leaves in water, sprinkled some of the water on the patient, and then stroked her gently with leaves of the *reringën* (lit., "lightweight-like") plant (*Flemingia congesta*, Roxb.), "so that the heavy elements causing the illness will leave her."[2]

In order to better assess the damage caused by the spirit intrusion, Aman Tauhid employed a second diagnostic technique. He duplicated the signs of the patient's illness in a chicken, a process called *seduëi* (from the Acehnese "*sa, dua*" [one, two]). He moved a live chicken counterclockwise over the patient while counting from one to ten and imagining (with maripët) that the illness had entered the chicken. When he cut open the chicken he found that its arteries were hard and that black blood had collected at the base of the heart—both signs that the blood of the chicken (and thus that of the patient) had been prevented from flowing freely. In other respects the internal organs of the chicken appeared normal, suggesting that the patient would recover quickly. Aman Tauhid then took a *sop* leaf, chosen because its name began with the same Arabic letter (*sin*) as the woman's name (Senah), and dripped water from it onto the chicken's heart and artery. This action appeared to "loosen up" and redden the organs, and was thus prognostic of a quick recovery. He told the patient to drink water in which the leaf had been soaked, because it appeared to be beneficial for her.

Aman Tauhid, Aman Risa, and other healers in Isak possess a broad repertoire of curing techniques. In shaping and understanding what they do, healers select appropriate elements from the broader Muslim tradition, including the notion of maripët; theories about the balance of elements in the body; the powers of jin, prophets, and angels; and the willingness of God to help humans. A practical discourse, healing by powerful speaking is also a locally constructed Muslim discourse.

HEALERS AND KNOWLEDGE

Most residents of Isak consult a guru (healer; practitioner of spiritual sciences; teacher) to rid themselves of a persistent somatic complaint or a psychic disturbance. Because of the particular vulnerability of a child, a healer is usually called in to treat any childhood illness. Most villagers consider

[2] For this and other plant identifications I have relied on Kreemer (1922–1923, II:548–56) and Burkill (1966). In the field I obtained plant descriptions and cross-linguistic glosses (usually Gayo to Javanese) but did not systematically collect specimens. An independent botanical study of plant uses in the highlands is thus highly desirable.

the skills of the healer and those of the government paramedical-worker or doctor to be complementary: whereas "village illnesses" (*penyakit kampung*) are better addressed by healers, many others can be best cured by doctors. Because one is never sure of the nature and cause of an illness, some villagers will employ both kinds of medicine at the same time (and, following the same logic, will visit several doctors and combine the pills they prescribe). By "medicine" (*waq*) Gayo mean both the leaves and roots that form part of the corpus of local knowledge and the medicines available at the local clinic (puskesmas) or from a pharmacist in the nearby town of Takèngën.

Following a healer's cure can take months or even years. A child who is born with an illness, seems ill at ease, or will not eat may be brought to the healer monthly for the first few years of his or her life. At each such visit the parents of the child host at least a minimal ritual meal (kenduri) of a plate of puffed or glutinous rice. At times more elaborate meals must be provided, with small gifts of cigarettes or cash for the healer. A major gift must be made to complete the healing process. One healer would ask his patients to buy a sheep from him and then give it back to him. (He used the same sheep in this way for several years.)

Isak men and women acquire and practice the knowledge that allows them to negotiate with spiritual agents. Women carry out children's initiation rituals and attend to difficulties in conception and delivery, and they are often engaged as healers or to utter the spells required to ensure the fertility of a rice crop. The healers most often consulted to resolve serious or chronic illnesses, however, are men. I have heard only of men performing exorcisms in Isak, although both men and women were suspected of having sent harmful jin.

In the 1980s, six men enjoyed particular renown as healers and were appealed to frequently by a wide range of afflicted persons, while many other men and women were recognized as competent healers, sometimes for one or two specific illnesses. Each of the six best-known Isak healers had obtained his knowledge (*ilmu*; <Ar. *'ilm*) by requesting it from one or more older healers, usually a close relative of the preceding generation (father, wife's father, or mother's father). Five of the six were Isak natives; the sixth had married into the community from the nearby Peugasing district.

Much of the knowledge possessed by all five Isak natives derived either directly or indirectly from one descent line in Kutë Robel village, the line of the Healer to the Four (Guru Si Opat) (the title refers to the four principal domain lords of precolonial Gayoland). Bearers of this title descend from the founder of Kutë Robel. The founder had two sons. The elder son succeeded his father as village ruler while the younger son inherited the power to heal. The younger son was buried in a spot known as Gergung, located about one mile upstream from Kutë Robel. The son's spirit and the grave site are known today as Datu Gergung. This son's healing powers have been transmitted to eldest sons in each succeeding generation (Bowen 1991:48). In precolonial times the Healer to the Four might be called on to cure a patient anywhere in the highlands, and, in particular, to attend to relatives of the ruler of the Lingë domain, the Kejurun Lingë. In Isak the Healer also performed the public rituals designed to ward off smallpox.

In the 1980s the direct descendant in the Healer to the Four line, Aman Arjua, performed no public rituals. He did, however, have privileged access to the healing powers held by Datu Gergung. His assistance was often sought, especially by residents of Kutë Robel or the offshoot village Kutë Baru. He had studied the art of healing with his father, Aman Mok, but had received the powers required to activate his knowledge after his father's death—his father had appeared to him in a dream and bestowed the powers on him.

Aman Mok had also taught the art of healing to his son-in-law, Abang Das (who had married Aman Mok's eldest daughter). Because Abang Das was not the son of Aman Mok, he had to formally initiate the teaching process. He "requested spells" (*nuntut doa*) from his father-in-law by presenting him with a set of objects. These objects represented the tie that would henceforth bind them as teacher and pupil. They included a measure of milled rice, a needle (standing for the strength of their connection), and three betel nuts (which "open the path" for many kinds of formal encounters; see Bowen 1991:157–58). In some cases (but not in this one) a set of clothes is also given to the teacher. At the end of the teaching process the pupil "closes off" (*bermungën*) the exchange with a second presentation, or sometimes with a small ritual meal.

Other Isak healers also had acquired their knowledge from the Healer to the Four line. Abang Kerna studied with Aman Mok and with his own wife's father, Mpun Kali, a close kinsman of Aman Mok who had studied healing in West Aceh. Aman Tauhid, in Kutë Robel, was instructed in part by Abang Kerna and in part by Aman Mok. Aman Risa in Kutë Rayang (Aman Tauhid's frequent adversary) was given his knowledge of healing by his father, who had received it from his father, who had obtained his skills from the Healer to the Four at the time. Only Aman Méja, born outside Isak, had no direct connection to the Healer to the Four tradition.

These individuals became healers for a variety of reasons, and some were later highly ambivalent about their choices. Abang Kerna first dabbled in spells as a matter of personal protection. He was an avid performer of didong competitive poetry, an avocation that put him at great risk of sorcery attacks from his opponents. Like many other men who came of age during the period of revolution and rebellion in the late 1940s and 1950s, he sought out invulnerability spells from as many sources as possible. Gregarious by nature and an intelligent devourer of spells and their lore, he offered to heal friends and family, and his services began to be called on by many in the community. By the late 1980s, however, the strain these demands placed on his family, and his growing doubts about the religious validity of what he did (described in Chapter 4), had caused him to limit his accessibility as a healer.

Aman Tauhid also studied healing as a form of self-protection. Because he was closely related to the famous healers in Kutë Robel, others in Isak assumed he had been given an assortment of spells and cures, and "tested" him to see how much he knew. This testing took the form of spells sent against him, which, he said, caused him and members of his family to become ill and forced him to become proficient at the healing sciences. In the late 1980s he began to be the object of such attacks again, and some attributed his wife's death to his involvement in the dangerous practices of healing and exorcism.

The core of healing knowledge in Isak is transmitted orally or in the form of handwritten notebooks, although people may also consult printed books of protective spells and prayers that are sold in Takèngën. Although some printed materials may have been used in the past for divination,[3] healers learn how to identify the jin responsible for illness, to apply techniques of divination, medicinal application, and exorcism, and to understand the power of spells and maripët from direct contact with teachers. The partial centering of authoritative knowledge in the Healer to the Four line may lend a greater consistency to healing knowledge in Isak than in some other highlands communities. Healers who enter Isak from elsewhere (such as Aman Méja), or who study elsewhere in the highlands or on the coast (such as Abang Kerna's teacher Mpun Kali), have, however, introduced new elements into the local system.

The steps in healing include the diagnosis of the illness and its cause, efforts to restore balance among the elements that make up the patient, requests or other measures taken to induce harmful spirits to leave the patient, and, finally, the exorcism of a recalcitrant spirit and its return to the sender (healers in Isak generally try to persuade spirits to leave the patient before attempting to expel them). Healers take a trial-and-error approach to their use of medicinal compounds and spells, drawing on Islamic sources of knowledge and power to make their diagnoses, attempt cures, and exorcise harmful spirits.

Each healer has his or her own particular strategies and schemata, which derive from a common set of ideas about the nature of the spirit world and

---

[3] I encountered one man in the village of Owaq, downstream from Isak, who used healing spells found in the *Taj al-Mulk*, a frequently reprinted Jawi manual written in Aceh in the late nineteenth century (see Snouck Hurgronje 1906, II:33). In Isak the only current use of the book is to determine auspicious days or dates, including the setting of dates for the agricultural year. Aman Tauhid said he tried using its medicinal prescriptions but they never worked.

the possibilities of communicating with it. All healers combine powerful depictive concentration (maripët), spells (doa), and objects that act as tokens (isharat) of intended effects. These objects may have their own independent efficacy (the heat or smell of a leaf, for example), but they also serve to transfer, carry, or embody the healer's message.

FINDING THE JIN

Many complaints of bodily pain or discomfort do not involve spiritual agents. Colds and fevers, for example, come from changes in the weather. Major stomach and liver ailments are physical problems to be treated by doctors. But many other sicknesses do result from the action of a spirit, whether harmful or otherwise, and thus can be remedied by a healer. The symptoms of jin-caused illnesses range from persistent diarrhea to poor appetite (especially for infants) to possession by spirits.

The causes of some illnesses may be apparent from their unique symptoms. The symptoms of smallpox or measles are relatively unambiguous and require no further diagnostic procedures. All smallpox is (or was) caused by a single spirit, called simply "Ruler" (rëjë), who must be asked to leave the patient. In other cases the circumstances of the illness strongly suggest its type and cause. An infant who is born with an illness is said to have brought the illness as his or her "baggage"; it is given by God as part of the child's fortune and can only be treated in a specific way.

In other cases an illness could be the result of an internal imbalance of elements within the patient or the intervention of a jin. The healer may then employ two kinds of diagnostic procedures: he may inspect, either directly or by means of a proxy, the internal state of the patient, or he may attempt to identify the jin responsible for the patient's condition.[4]

One common way of checking for internal damage is to reproduce (seduëi) the illness in another object, often a chicken or a chicken egg. The healer must concentrate with maripët on the intended transfer, hold the object over the patient so that its shadow falls on him or her, and then move it in a counterclockwise direction over the patient.[5] The shadow acts as a path from the patient to the object. In performing the seduëi, Aman Tauhid and Aman Méja merely count from one to ten; Abang Das recites the confession of faith, the basmala ("In the Name of God, the Merciful, the Compassionate"), and the names of the four archangels, with the intention that one of them will carry the illness over the path and into the chicken or egg. The process does not remove the illness from the patient, but merely copies it onto the new object.

---

[4] Similar diagnostic techniques are used by Karo Batak healers (Sibeth 1991:89–92).

[5] Counterclockwise movements attract an element (illness, jin, or fortune) into an object; clockwise movements expel it.

Once the illness is in the object, the healer can dissect it and discern the location and nature of the patient's affliction. In the case discussed earlier, Aman Tauhid used this technique to perceive the seriousness of the elderly woman's illness. As in that case, the color, fluidity, and volume of the patient's blood is generally a crucial sign of the type and severity of the ailment. This process is used frequently, not only to examine an illness but also to tell a fortune or expell a jin. An egg, or a mungkur citrus, or even four piles of colored rice (*oros opat*) may serve as the raw material for the transfer. (Abang Das frequently uses an egg). Each object has distinct semiotic properties: the egg substitutes for the chicken, which in turn substitutes for the patient; the mungkur was ordered by God to act as a purifying agent for humankind; and the four-colored rice serves as a sign of the four elements of the human body.

If the healer suspects that a jin has lodged itself inside the patient's body, he may begin by calling out the names of the most likely spirits. If a spirit fails to respond to his name, the healer may threaten him, declaring that God will be angry if he does not leave the patient. If the spirit is indeed present it generally will respond. The response may be verbal—protests and threats uttered through the mouth of the patient—or nonverbal—an uneasy sensation in the healer's stomach, a movement of the patient's arm, or a tremor that can be felt by the healer. Healers are then able to identify the spirits by certain signature movements.

The healer may or may not seek to determine who has sent the spirit. He may try several names and wait for an affirmative sign (such as the image that came to Aman Tauhid's mind). As with other divinatory practices that involve responses to suggestions from the healer, this method tends to confirm preexisting suspicions.[6] Abang Kerna usually did not try to discover the sender's identity, on the grounds that the process of ridding the patient of the jin did not require such knowledge. A spirit sender often appears in Abang Das's dreams as a tiger; in Aman Tauhid's dreams his father sometimes tells him who has caused an illness.

Most often the healer finds that the illness was caused wholly or in part by a malevolent spirit sent by someone who wished to do the patient harm.[7] (The unintentional harming of a patient also occurs, usually by an ancestor who hails a relative as he or she passes by the grave and thereby, unwittingly, causes the passerby to suffer a stomach ache.) The human agent may be an individual with a grudge against the patient (as in cases where spirits were supposedly sent by young men to possess the women who had

[6] The classic case of self-confirmation is the Zande oracle described in Evans-Pritchard (1937).

[7] In theory, all harm from jin comes from the ill intent of another human (see below), but in healing practice not all spirit-caused illnesses are diagnosed as being so caused.

jilted them), or another healer who wishes to test his rival or create a clientele for his own healing services.

Healers vary in the ways they label spirits, but they share the general idea of a spirit hierarchy. At the top of this hierarchy are certain harmful spirits such as the one thousand dangers, certain favored intermediaries such as the Old Hunter, and certain helpful spirits such as Rëjë Karahollah, who can persuade the harmful ones to leave the patient alone.

Gayo generally use the term *jin* to refer to one or more harmful spirits, or the entire category of such spirits, as in the all-inclusive expression *jin iblis sétan* (jin, devils, Satan; <Ar. *jinn Iblīs, shaitān*).[8] But there are good jin as well as harmful ones. These "Muslim jin" (*jin Islam*) are the souls of people who had been extremely pious during their lives and were therefore spared death and were instead transmuted into spiritual beings. Also referred to as *aulië*, "saints," or *salihin*, "pious ones," they live in certain clearings in the forest, where, rarely, a favored human may come across them. The most influential Isak teacher of the 1920s, Tengku Ubit of Robel village, is said to have been escorted by such Muslim jin to their village and to have worshiped together with them. (He himself died a normal death, however.) And a man of Kramil village who was "killed" by the local militia during the 1965 massacres reportedly became a Muslim jin.

Jin also inhabit the human body, from where they order external jin to do harm. These internal jin are the rulers of the external ones, as the healer and hunter Aman Renim explained in 1979:

Everyone has jin in their hearts.[9] The heart has two main layers, one jin and the other Muslim. When we are confronted with a choice, each will come forward with its own intention [niët]. The jin part will say, for example: "Go ahead and eat that durian fruit that is lying there," whereas the Muslim part will say: "No, you must ask permission first." Whichever is the stronger will win and determine what we do. Usually the jin wins, and that is why the world is in such bad shape. Both are us [roané kitë]; there are two distinct desires, wills [kenaké], that speak, and one wins out over the other.

The jin in our heart is the ruler of jin [rëjë jin] because it can command the jin who are on the outside to do its bidding. They originated from the soul that Jibra'il released when he was flying down to place it in the prophet Adam. After death the jin in our heart becomes external jin: *sidang bèla* or *apah konot*, or some other kind. The Muslim part goes straight to God. God allows

---

[8] For an extensive description of Moroccan Muslim ideas about jin see Westermarck (1926), and for the Sudan see Boddy (1989:187, 272–75). Geertz (1960:16–29) and Laderman (1991) provide comparative accounts from within the archipelago.

[9] The term *até* anatomically refers to the liver, but on emotional and moral planes it has the resonances of English *heart*.

the jin to tempt us so that the Devil will have companions in Hell. Such is God's evenhandedness: he accepts good and bad, but punishes humans for the bad on the day of judgment.

In this view, jin are but the externalizations of the harmful intentions within us.[10] (Others modified this account by saying that jin only enter humans from time to time to tempt them.) The converse, that the harm a person does comes from a jin inside him, is also true. This view, kept alive in everyday conversations by such phrases as "it was the jin in him that did it," somewhat lightens an individual's moral responsibility for a harmful action (and the intensity of blame leveled by others).

Certain jin are associated with particular illnesses. The [*segunyë*] *sidang bèla*, for example, frequently causes illness in infants and small children. It lives in the forest and sometimes inhabits birds and humans. It has no will of its own, but humans can order it to bring sickness to someone else. The *jin gilë* (jin of madness) was brought by Syech Shamsuddin from Mecca to Aceh. It is often sent to possess people and is frequently directed at girls by jilted boyfriends. The bëlë seribu (one thousand dangers) could be responsible for diverse prolonged physical ailments in adults. The *burung* (Mal. bird) lives in birds and can cause a similar array of diseases. If a spell aimed at removing the one thousand dangers fails, a healer will try spells suitable against the bird. There are short and long ghosts (apah konot and *apah naru*); these jin are the spirits of the dead that appear in the community to signal a coming illness and sometimes cause severe stomach cramps in the living. Other jin inhabit particular places: *jin awang-awang*, named after the place halfway between Heaven and earth, scatter dust that causes discomfort; *jin sani* (of which there are subtypes) inhabit the rivers, swamps, and fields and can bring about burning and itching sensations.

Healers are less concerned with the precise taxonomic relations of these and other jin, however, than with the general relations between symptoms and successful cures. Some spells mention a number of jin against whom the spell should be effective. Thus Aman Tauhid often used a spell that contained the names of what he thought to be all the major jin that ever harmed people. As with the broad-spectrum antibiotics frequently prescribed in Indonesia, this sort of spell is given in the hope that one of its components will do the trick. If it works, the healer neither knows nor cares which one it was. Or an appeal may be made to the ruler of all jin (Rëjë Kaharollah) to expel his subordinates from a patient. If this appeal is heard and the patient recovers, then the healer need not know precisely which jin was responsible.

---

[10] The interaction of internal and external jin is similarly a significant cause of illness in the Malay view (Laderman 1991:62).

RESTORING THE BALANCE

The first measures a healer takes after diagnosis are intended to directly re-arrange, rebalance, or return components of the patient's body and spirit. Sometimes these measures alone restore health and obviate the need for the more taxing attacks on jin and their human senders. One source of illness lies in the condition of the souls and spirits. An individual who seems out of sorts, ill at ease, weak, or subject to frequent illness may have lost his or her vital force (semangat). The vital force is then called back, using spells such as the one given earlier.

Other illnesses are due to an imbalance of elements in the patient. The idea of balance as crucial to well-being extends across specific configura-tions of elements, organs, and states of being. Each of the healers in Isak drew on idioms of balance in explaining how the body worked, incorporat-ing the symbolically rich configuration of elements into fours that runs across all domains of Gayo (and, more generally, Indonesian) ritual and reli-gious life. The Galenic attribution of illness to imbalances in one of the four natural elements, prominent throughout the archipelago (Laderman 1991), was given more importance by some healers than by others. In each case, it was the general idea of balance between health-causing and illness-promoting elements, rather than a specific four-way medical totalization, that informed healing practice.

The most encompassing schema was that drawn by Abang Das. In re-sponse to my questions about healing, he took out a sheet of paper and began to write. At the top he wrote "Allāh," and underneath, "Muham-mad," both in Arabic. Below he wrote the names of five organs and an as-pect of their functioning, and below them he constructed a table of corre-spondences, structured around the four elements. To each element was matched an archangel, a sacred book, a daily worship period (leaving out the night period), and a bodily position in worship (cf. Hooykas 1974).

Allāh Muhammad

Lungs are the wind	Heart is the Baitul makmur	Liver is the ruh's judge	Gall bladder is poison	Spleen is the place of the wind of blood
tanah [earth]	*air* [water]	*angin* [wind]	*api* [fire]	
Jibrail	Mikail	Israpil	Izrail	
Turid [Torah]	Zabur [Psalms]	Injil [Gospels]	Kur'an	
subuh	*duhur*	*asar*	*magrib*	
salam	*rukuk*	*sujud*	*kiam*	

Diagram 6.1: Correspondence among Elements, Organs, and Religious Figures, from Abang Das.

The list of five organs appears to structure how Abang Das understands and explains the process of healing.[11] He interpreted the chart to me as conveying not only the associations of elements across domains, but also the general truth that the divisions in the human body were all roads to God by way of Muhammad. The bodily organs transmit the four natural elements inside the body, and they need to be in balance to function properly. Thus the lungs are the seat of wind or air, which is mixed with blood in the spleen and then pumped into the heart. If the heart is too hot or cold, he explained, then the blood will be deficient and will cause the individual to fall ill. The blood then goes to the liver, where we first feel the good or bad effects of the state of the blood. The gall bladder is the base for all attempts to harm others either with poison, which is stored in the gall bladder, or with spells propelled by maripët. The gall bladder also controls one's potentially offensive actions, such that it is said of someone who cannot control their actions that he or she has no proper sense of shame (*gërë mukemèl*) and also has no gall bladder (*gërë mpau*).

The four elements provide the material bases for the body: earth, the physical body itself; water and fire together, the blood; air, the wind that circulates through the lungs. The elements are interdependent within the body as well as in the outside world:

> The body is like a pressure lamp. The glass is from earth and serves as the container. The fire makes wind possible but depends on water, the kerosene. So with the body: only with water does the fire become blood, and only when it is pumped around the body is there wind. So if someone is breathing too hard we know that there is too much wind and that this is because there is too much fire pushing the wind around. So he or she must drink water to cool himself down and we must ask Izrail to keep down the level of fire in the body.
>
> The wind can be used to carry jin to harm people or to send back jin; it is addressed as "Rahim tungël" in those instances.

Despite Abang Das's claim that he would call on specific archangels to redress specific deficiencies in the body, in his curing practice he tended to call on all four archangels together. Indeed, the primary significance of the schema for healing was the symbolic richness it gives to the ideas of completeness and balance, which themselves are central guides to healing practice.

Abang Kerna represented the balance of competing elements as a white

[11] Several others in Isak had charts that contained the same or similar elements in varying arrays: Tengku Asaluddin, for example, possessed a notebook written by a religious and military leader in the 1910s, Kepala Rahim, with correlations of worship positions, the four elements, and bodily organs. Abang Kerna relied on correlations among angels, organs, and elements for his curing. Aman Renim correlated colors, positions, and lords of the elements. Each of these three schemata differed from the others, however.

and a black image in the body, each of which, as we saw in the last chapter, reflects the Light of Muhammad. The black image is further manifested as a reservoir of poison (tubë); the white, as the antidotes (tawar) to the poison. These are contained in the two sides of the "structure" (*gedung*, *gedung ilmu*, or *gedung Saidina Ali*) that lies right next to (and is concealed by) the heart. The structure is the home of the lām-alif, God's presence in each individual human. As Abang Kerna explained:

> God put equal quantities of poison and antidote on opposite sides of the structure that houses the individual's lām-alif. If there is too much antidote in the structure, the individual will have no desires [*hawa nafsu*]; he or she will just sit around and await death. If there is too much poison, he or she will fall ill; Adam will be uneasy because there is too much fire.

Abang Kerna and Abang Das have rendered the internal relations among elements of well-being in divergent ways—Abang Das, as a matter of flow and substance; Abang Kerna (and Aman Renim), as a matter of spiritual elements. But these somewhat varying pictures of the body converge on the general principle that healing requires restoring the balance of poison and antidote. The healer restores this balance by using his own internal reserves of each. Abang Kerna, more than the other healers, imagines himself entering the patient and, with the aid of the four archangels, repairing the patient's heart, liver, lungs, or other organs. His practice relies the most strongly on this kind of imaginative play. But in their spells all healers invoke the ever-present reserves of tawar and tubë to return the patient to health.

When Abang Kerna recites a counteractive spell he sends it through his maripët to the four archangels, who are asked to assist in the cure. The spell addresses the four images that connect patients to divine sources of power, asserts the healer's own humanity and claim on that power, and singles out the white image as the source and sign of counteractive medicines. While Abang Kerna recites the spell, he blows onto the patient's afflicted organ from within himself, from the side of his own spiritual structure that contains the antidote:

Kesa bayan allah	First, the image of God,
keduë bayan Muhammad	second, the image of Muhammad,
ketigë bayan itëm	third, the black image,
keempat bayan putih	fourth, the white image.
Tatkala ko berdiri	When you stand
ari bumi sawah ku langit	from the earth up to the sky;
Engko menyatakan ujud dirimu	You present your own body,
aku menyatakan ujud diriku	I present my own body.
Hé bayan putih	Hey, white image:

Kusuruh sekejëp seketikë   I order you to immediately
   menawari [Name]   heal [Name].
Sah tawar sah tawar   Work, antidote; work, antidote;
Ini tawar ni Tuën Derham Dangi This is the medicine of Lord Derham
                                Dangi.

After the spell Abang Kerna addresses the four archangels in everyday Gayo speech, asking them to repair whatever is damaged in the body. He piles up phrases such as the following:

Gelah si rusak itetahën   Please fix that which is broken,
   si kurang itamah   add to that which is insufficient,
   si mèrèng itetapën   righten that which is crooked,
   . . . .

The healer also applies an external medicine to the patient. If the patient coughs excessively, his or her lungs are too dry. The dryness is due to an overabundance of fire in the body, and the healer will apply water from medicinal leaves. If the patient suffers from a swelling of the stomach (*busung*), he or she has too much water and thus a drying agent such as garlic will be used (cf. Laderman 1991).

Manipulating Medicines

Diverse objects can be used as medicines along with the spells. Certain leaves provide medicinal effects by way of their cooling or strengthening properties. They are known collectively as the "forty-four remedies" (*petawarën empat puluh empat*) and include leaves used throughout the Malay archipelago for healing and promoting well-being. The most commonly used, with their probable identifications, are

   dedingin, cold-like (*Bryophyllum pinnatum*, Kurz)
   batang teguh, tough plant (*Eleusine indica*, Gaertn.)
   bebesi, iron-like (*Justicia ptychostoma*, Nees?)
   celala (*Celosia cristata*, Linn.?)
   jejerun (*Sida rhombifolia*, Linn.?)
   reringën, lightweight-like (*Flemingia congesta*, Roxb.)

The first four plants (*dedingin, batang teguh, bebesi, celala*) are invariably included in a bundle of leaves used to sprinkle water and thereby impart fortune and health to a newly married couple, to men or women who have been reconciled after a fight, or to an infant. The plant may be chosen to convey specific healing qualities: Aman Tauhid used the reringën plant to "make light" the heavy qualities causing paralysis. Healers often use the dedingin, the leaf that is thought to cool the patient most effectively (and

6. Abang Kerna Reciting a Spell

which does indeed feel cool to the touch) to reduce the fire in a patient. The
jejerun was the first plant in the world; it and the closely related *pelulut*
have a cooling and strengthening effect.

Abang Das, Aman Méja, Abang Kerna, and Aman Risa also frequently
used a *selensung* in their healing. The selensung or sirih roll is constructed
by making a streak of lime on a sirih leaf, rolling it into a tight cone, pushing a small betel nut inside the top (a slice of gambir is optional), and then
folding over the top flap. A very effective vehicle for sending a request to a
prophet or spirit, the selensung derives its communicative capacity from the
use everyday of its components. Chewing a mixture of sirih, betel, lime,
and gambir is an obligatory opening step in any formal encounter, whether
a negotiation session over bridewealth, a ritual speaking session at a wedding, or, in precolonial days, a dispute-resolution session between two villages. Casual social intercourse, especially among women, is livened by

the sharing of the same substances. These exchanges signify the respect that each individual has for the other.[12]

Just as the exchange of sirih and betel conveys respect among humans, the presentation of a sirih roll signifies the human sender's respect for the spiritual agents that reside outside the human community. Hunters frequently place a sirih roll on the ground to send a request for game to the Old Hunter and to the other spirits of the forest and hills. Some healers, usually men who have used the sirih roll for the hunt, regularly call on the Old Hunter for assistance in curing patients.

Calling on Prophets

Healers may also address requests for assistance (accompanied by a sirih roll) to various prophets. Isak healers and ritual specialists ascribe control over the elements to particular prophets (*nabi*, prophet, or *nabiollah*, prophet of God). When about to cut down a tree, a man will ask permission of Nabi Nuh (Noah), the prophet of the trees. Nabi Kedemat guards the earth, and his permission is sought for its cultivation. In activities involving the rivers and streams, protection is sought from Nabiollah Yakub (Jacob), the prophet of rocks and stones, and Nabiollah Yati, the prophet of the water itself (for Malay equivalents, see Skeat [1900:99]).

Nabiollah Yati is of particular importance in healing. He is asked to remove the impurities that come into the world along with childbirth. He carries requests for help to the Ruler at the Center of the Sea, who can order jin to desist from harming a patient. Yati also transmits offerings made to place spirits at propitiary agricultural rituals. Healers equate Yati with the prophet Hilir (<Ar. al-Khidr), a figure associated with the sea in Muslim traditions (Wensinck 1953b). Nabi Hilir was the teacher of all the other prophets until Muhammad, said these healers; Muhammad, because he was the greatest of all prophets, could not be asked to study from any other being, so angels gave him Hilir's wisdom directly. As Abang Das explained in 1980, with his usual passion for punning:

> Nabi Hilir was on the earth as soon as there was water. He was made from water whereas Adam was made from earth. He instructed the other prophets but he was never made a messenger. His miraculous power was to see into the future. He is called "Nabi Hilir" [Mal. *hilir*, downstream] because he flows downstream, but that is not his real name. Anything to do with water must be preceded by a request to him. He flows into the sea, to the Center of the Sea.

[12] See Bowen (1991:157–58) on betel-chewing and communication. The sirih leaf is also attributed religious significance. I was told that the first sirih plant was planted when the prophet Muhammad was born, and that he chewed betel and sirih (*bermangas*) throughout his life. Chewing in the four months associated with his birth (the Maulid months), and only in those months, brings the chewer religious merit.

Hilir wanders the earth, sometimes in human form. He visits mosques and sometimes worships together with everyone else. You can detect him by shaking his hand, because he has no thumb bone. Several individuals told me versions of the story found throughout the Muslim world of Hilir's encounters with Moses (Nabi Musë).[13] As Abang Kerna told it in 1979:

> Nabi Hilir approached Moses and asked him if he was ready to become a prophet. Moses said he was, and Hilir replied: "We shall see." He told Moses to follow him but to refrain from questioning anything he might do. They set out walking. After they had gone a short way Hilir came upon a very beautiful woman. He took out his sword and slew her! Moses was astonished and asked why on earth he had done such a thing. "That's why you're not ready yet [to become a prophet]; you're not supposed to question things I do." Then they came to a beautiful house and Hilir burned it to the ground. After that they came upon a filthy urchin, whom Hilir washed and took care of. And finally they arrived at a broken-down hut that he repaired.
>
> He told Moses that he could see into the future, could tell all that would happen. The woman would have spread Judaism, the beautiful house would have become a gambling den, the child was going to encourage people to worship, and the old house would become a place of worship.

The prophet Yati/Hilir thus combines the important practical function of carrying requests to commanding spirits with the mysterious, esoteric side of Islamic prophethood.

ASKING A SPIRIT TO DEPART

In the steps described above, the curer attempts to heal the patient with the help of angels, prophets, or other spirits, and by applying objects, such as leaves, that have curative powers. These attempts to restore balance are often insufficient, however, and the healer must then try to induce the harmful spirit to leave the body.

Just how a healer addresses a malevolent spirit depends on the relative powers it possesses. Should the spirit be of great power, the healer must proceed extremely cautiously and must ask, rather than order, the spirit to leave. Misjudging the proper mode of communication with a spirit could be fatal to both the patient and the healer.

Some illnesses come from God and thus cannot be driven away. The various kinds of illness that a child brings into the world, generically referred to as *penyakit dena*, are "God's gifts" and cannot be expelled. They may, however, be transferred to another object and thus neutralized. The illness

---

[13] The story is in the Qur'ān (18:60–82); for a discussion see Wensinck (1953b). See Soeratno (1978) on al-Khidr in Malay literature.

is itself helpful in this regard, for it lets the healer know (through maripët) the object that will best contain its harmful effects. It may ask for a chicken, a dove, or a length of wire, usually gold at either end, which is then worn around the wrist.

An older midwife, Inën Segah, distinguished between two material elements that may be born with the baby. One, the *gënggemën*, is a projection of the child's vital force (semangat). The gënggemën serves to protect the child but must be given whatever it asks for. The other element, the *dimerën*, causes illnesses at regular intervals in the child. On such occasions it must be given feasts of puffed rice (bertéh). The two elements appear as green, hard places in the umbilical cord. An attentive midwife is sometimes able to spot them at birth and squeeze them back toward the afterbirth.

God is also directly responsible for certain other illnesses. Isak Gayo often mention the respect that one must have for the Ruler (rëjë) whom God sent to bring smallpox (*rëjë kul*, Greater Ruler) and measles (*sempirèn* or *rëjë kucak*, Lesser Ruler) to humanity. Along with these diseases the Ruler brings antidotes. As does God, the Ruler dispenses beneficial and harmful things alike and thus is never to be opposed, only besought for assistance. Abang Kerna explained the peculiar mission given to the smallpox-causing spirit:

> God ordered the spirit to bow down before Adam, but he refused, saying that he, not Adam, was the ruler. So God gave him a mission, to travel around the world and collect souls for himself. He takes those who have a certain kind of blood. We all have different kinds; that is why doctors can inject some people with frog blood but not others. The Ruler cannot be destroyed. Other spirits follow him and cause other illnesses; still others are sent by people.

The Ruler is sometimes given a more concrete identification, as one of two rather distant, powerful spirits, both of whom can be appealed to for aid. The Rëjë Pusët Lot (Ruler at the Center of the Sea) exercises control over all harmful spirits. His services are also important in ridding the rice fields of pests. He is said to have originated from the umbilical cord of the prophet Muhammad, which was tossed out to sea at his birth. His counterpart on land is the Rëjë Pusët Dunië (Ruler at the Center of the Earth), who is the source of other medicines and antidotes. He is often identified as Abdul Qadir Jilani ('Abdul Qādir Jīlānī), the ambiguous figure in the stories of Aceh's Islamization who, although he opposed Aceh, was the one to rid Aceh of the evil Syech Shamsuddin.

The Ruler may visit someone in their house, where he must be treated well. ("Abang Kerna once chased after the greater ruler with a machete," said one man, "and so he cannot cure it effectively.") He is described as a ruler with a large army behind him. Some people mentioned hearing the sound of their army boots passing through the community late at night. Or he and his army are seen carrying green and yellow lanterns across a ridge to the north of Isak. One woman who had suffered from smallpox said that the Ruler's army had come to her and said they intended to kill her. She resisted and asked to see their commander. He came and gave her an antidote, and ever after she has been very successful in curing people of the disease.

In November 1978 I talked with several women in Kutë Kramil village whose children had just contracted measles. As we talked one afflicted boy lay feverish in bed, where he cried and refused the tea he had just asked for. The women were careful not to get angry with him. If they gave the child a shot it would be worse; the disease would get angry at them. But before the disease appears you may give shots. One of the women, Inën Dar, said that perhaps when the child was born the midwife tossed his afterbirth into the water rather than burying it as she should have done, and the semangat is now weak or angry, and should be given something to appease it.

To deal with illnesses brought by the Ruler the healer cannot use his normal techniques. He cannot order the Ruler to leave or even empower a medicine to drive it out with a rajah spell. Rather, he must show respect by making him a formal offering of food. (The women interviewed above had held an offering meal before I arrived.)

When Abang Das's son came down with the measles in 1978 he made a food offering (kenduri) to the Ruler. The offering, set out in the house at night, consisted of puffed rice, one hard-boiled egg, four rolled-up sirih leaves, and four bananas. To be complete, the offering had to contain four elements (*opat perkara*); cooked rice and flat apam cakes could have been substituted for the egg and bananas. The one essential ingredient in the offering was the sirih roll, which Abang Das used to convey the right amount of respect to the Ruler.

When the offering was ready, Abang Das arranged it on a plate and lit a small piece of benzoin incense. The sweet odor of the incense attracts the angels and the Ruler to come and hear what he has to say, explained Abang Das. He later explained that the prophet Muhammad was the first to burn incense. He did so when a follower complained that he disliked eating at the house of another man because of the unpleasant odors there. Burning incense is recommended (*sunët*; <Ar. sunna), he said: it brings us merit (pahla), but we do not sin if we refrain from it. However, it is important to burn it so that the spirits and angels hear us.

Abang Das then picked up the plate with the offering and began to speak very softly and in the style of his everyday speech:

Bismillāh irrahmān irrahīm	In the Name of God, the Compassionate, the Merciful.
Si ringën-ringën osa	Give us the light things,
enti si berët-berët	not the heavy ones.

Ini kendurimu	Here is your food offering;
selensung opat	four sirih rolls,
awal opat	four bananas,
tenaro sara	one egg,
bertèh sara pingën	one plate of puffed rice.
Berharap aku sunguh	I strongly hope and expect:
numë kurang ni matangku	it is not lacking, in my vision,
numë jis ni atèngku	there is no resentment, in my heart.
Si mulo merai	Call back the early ones;
si lemëm bernampi	await the later ones.
Tawar ari Tuhën	Tawar from God,
tawar ari Nabi Muhammad	tawar from the Prophet Muhammad,
tawar ari Rëjë si Limë	tawar from the Five Rulers.
Rëjë Kedah	The Ruler of Kedah,
Rëjë Cina	the Ruler of China,
Rëjë Pagaruyung	the Ruler of Pagaruyung,
Put Almarhum	the Sultan of Aceh,
Pera'un	the Pharoah.
Ini mana tubuhé	Here is the body [of the offering].

The five rulers named at the end of the spell are the five possible guises of the Ruler, the five diseases he might bring. "It is like the governor, the district officer, the subdistrict officer: they are different people but you have to behave in the same way toward all of them." And by saying all their names you are certain to address the one who is in fact responsible for the illness.

At the end of the spell, Abang Das set down the plate, turned slightly, and held his hands over the burning incense. He spoke in the direction of his son, and mentioned the name of his own teacher, Aman Mok. He did so in the hope that the teacher's spirit might hear and help in the cure. The next night his son's face was hot, so Abang Das applied healing leaves to him, holding them in a bundle, dipping them periodically in a basin of water, and moving from the head down toward the legs, asking the Ruler to follow this downward movement and leave his son's head. Because the Ruler likes antidotes, he may follow the counteractive leaves downward and out of the body. Abang Das's son eventually recovered, verifying the course of action Abang Das had taken to cure him.

For illnesses other than those brought by God, the healer may (and does) induce a jin to leave by means of a rajah spell, transmitted through a substance applied to or drunk by the patient, or through an exorcism (*penulang*). The healer takes care to strengthen the patient's body beforehand so that the jin will not harm it when it leaves. Abang Das frequently uses such "completing the body" spells (*pelengkap ni bëdën*), which call on all the elements of the body to remain together, but Abang Kerna uses them less often.

The same spells that call on angels to bring medicines can also be used, in slightly modified form, to request poison for use against the jin. Thus, when Abang Kerna drives out a jin he often uses the counteractive spell given above, but for the last three lines he substitutes the following:

Kusuruh sekejëp seketikë	I order you to immediately
menubëi perbuëtën iblis syétan	poison the work of devils and Satan
di ujud ni [Name]	in the body of [Name].
Sah tubë sah tubë	Work, poison; work, poison;
Ini tubë ni Tuën Derham Dangi	This is the poison of Lord Derham Dangi.

As we saw earlier, Qur'ānic verses are often used as spells against jin. They can also be used to invest a substance with spiritual power for purposes of healing. In 1989 Abang Das used the chapter called The Calamity (al-Qāri'a, Qur'ān 101) to treat a woman suffering from a sprained ankle. The short chapter ends by revealing the "blazing fire" that will afflict people. Abang Das prepared an infusion of several roots and recited the short chapter seven times, blowing into his hands at the end of each recitation. After he finished he inserted his right index finger into the mixture, which his patient then drank. (He also had her consult a specialist in foot massage.)[14] Healers may also worship and then make a request to God at the conclusion.

One can transmit the force of a rajah spell along diverse channels. Reciting the spell with the proper maripët sends it to the archangels whose help is requested. One can then "enspell" (rajah) the person directly, investing him or her with the spell by speaking it into the fontanelle, where it is closest to the spiritual structure inside. One can also enspell a glass of water, which the patient then drinks or the healer sprays from his mouth (*puruh*) over the patient. Aman Tauhid enspelled a packet of cigarettes in 1979 on behalf of a neighbor's son. The son worked in the sugar factory north of Takèngën and was the victim of malicious gossip from his coworkers. The spell was intended to make his boss look favorably upon him once they had smoked from the pack together.

Two specific ideas shape the healer's efforts to directly cure the patient through spells and maripët. One is balance, a concern that is linked to the prominence of the four-way schemes of classification in the overall struc-

---

[14] I was unable to get a response from Abang Das concerning the particular appropriateness of this Qur'ānic chapter; I think that, in this case, he had heard that the verse was effective and did not have a theory about the relation of its contents to the desired effect.

ture of thought. The second is care not to offend. In dealing with the Ruler this care is terribly important, but in other cases as well the healer is safer if he or she can persuade rather than threaten a spirit.

None of these spells directly implicate the possible human senders of sickness. Should these measures fail, however, then the healer turns to his last weapon: an exorcism that, by returning the harmful spirit to its source, both exacts retribution and heals the patient.

Chapter Seven

EXORCISM AND ACCOUNTABILITY

AMAN TAUHID'S CURE of the half-paralyzed woman (see Chapter 6) did yield positive results, but he planned to complete his cure by returning the jin to the person who had sent it. He had identified the sender, his frequent rival Aman Risa, with the help of a recent dream. "I am doing this so that in the future he doesn't harm other people," he said. Using a mungkur citrus as his vehicle for capturing and expelling the jin, he ordered it to return to whoever had sent it (sending it with his maripët as he spoke the words).

In several weeks the woman's condition improved and she was able to return home. Aman Tauhid claimed that his success in sending back the jin had frightened Aman Risa. The two practitioners met in the coffee shop shortly after the exorcism had taken place, and Aman Tauhid declared he would begin to fight back against whoever had sent the jin. As Aman Tauhid recalled their conversation, Aman Risa urged him not to do so: "It would only hurt everyone," he pleaded. Aman Tauhid said he was tired and would let the matter drop, as long as the jin was not sent anymore.

The case was closed, but Aman Tauhid considered it part of a continuing struggle between well-intentioned healers such as himself and incorrigibly malicious ones such as Aman Risa. Aman Risa naturally saw things differently. He described his healing practices to me much as did Aman Tauhid his own, and he accused others of sending harmful spirits. He, too, created a world of combat and victories over those who would do harm. Neither requiring nor seeking public confrontation, the healers of Isak fashion social dramas—complete with uncertainties, setbacks, and catharses—out of their patients' symptoms, their own diagnostic procedures, and their casual encounters in coffee shops or on the street. Out of this experienced struggle comes the repeatedly enjoyed exuberance of victory.

In these encounters between healers we can discern the specific social shape of Gayo healing. Rather than confront a suspected sorcerer or make an accusation, the Gayo healer draws on his medical resources to covertly counter the sorcerer's actions and at the same time exact retribution for the harm he or she has caused. Because the healer, drawing on Sufi tradition, can conduct his operations entirely in the hidden, batin realm, he can avoid confronting the sorcerer and yet finish his exorcism with a feeling of personal satisfaction and instrumental success. In a society constructed around relatively egalitarian day-to-day politics, this particular selection and recasting of Muslim elements prevents the harsh feelings and accusations against purported sorcerers from escalating into large-scale conflicts.

CASTING OUT THE SPIRITS

Expelling a jin from a patient is a two-step process. The healer first removes the spirit from the patient's body and lodges it in another object. He then ejects the spirit from that object, projecting it back to whoever had sent it. The spirit works its harm on the original sender, causing discomfort and possibly serious illness. The healer carries out these steps through his powerful imagination.

In the 1970s and early 1980s, Abang Kerna probably performed these exorcism-and-returns more frequently than anyone else in Isak. I followed him through one case in February 1980. A small girl, about 18 months old, had become ill and listless, with a poor appetite and a fever. After trying other remedies, her parents asked Abang Kerna to intervene. He determined that the illness was caused by a jin that someone had sent to afflict the girl. He did not try to determine who the sender was. It was not necessary, he explained, because the exorcism would return the jin to whoever had sent it.

Abang Kerna used two methods to expel the jin from the girls's body. The first was "hitting the mungkur" (*pepok mungkur*), in which the jin was induced to enter a small citrus fruit and then was forced out by a strong blow. Here Abang Kerna followed the empowerment pathway (Diagram 5.3) from the human body to other agents and ultimately to God. The second method involved appealing to the four lords of the elements to send the jin downstream. This process used the embodiment pathway (Diagram 5.2) described by the four-way correspondences between humans and the physical world. The two methods shared a common idea of how communication with and coercion of spirits was possible.

The first vehicle for capturing and sending back the jin was the small, wrinkled citrus fruit called the mungkur.[1] The privileged role of this inedible, soapy-feeling fruit in spiritual communication is explained by recounting how God used it at the time he created Adam and Eve. In some Gayo versions of the story, the archangel Jibra'il held Adam's soul inside a mungkur (after having lost the soul on his first try). Diarrhea flowed out of Adam and Eve after they had eaten the forbidden fruit, and God called on the mungkur to clean up the mess. At that point the mungkur asked that in return for its services it be allowed to serve humans in three ways: as a bod-

---

[1] The mungkur (*Citrus hystrix*, DC.; M. *limau purut*) is used throughout Southeast Asia to wash the hair, to exorcise spirits, and as an internal medicine (Burkill 1966, I:574–75).

ily and spiritually cleansing agent (*penyuci*); as a healing agent (*pemulih*); and as a vehicle for the expulsion and return of jin (penulang). (It is also used to foretell the health of a patient or a rice crop, or the happiness of a couple.)[2] God agreed to these requests and planted the mungkur tree on the border of Heaven, with one branch reaching into Heaven to cleanse and heal, and the other branch reaching into Hell to perform destructive acts when ordered to do so in the name of God.

To lodge the jin in the mungkur, Abang Kerna used the *seduëi* transfer technique. First he ordered the mungkur to follow the directions he was about to give it. His spell summarized the history of the mungkur's relations with humans as a reminder of its compact with God and its consequent duties. The spell also restated the peculiar nature of the mungkur: though a fruit, it has a spirit (ruh) that can work in the inner (batin) realm of being. As with other spells, this one is persuasive because it demonstrates the speaker's knowledge of the object's origins, names, and obligations:

Hé limo si rëjë limo	Hey citrus, king of the citruses;
Aku tahu asalmu jadi	I know your origins.
Nurollah nama nyawamu	"The Light of God" is your soul's name;
Nur Muhammad nama tubuhmu	"The Light of Muhammad" is your body's name;
Ruh batin sebenar-benar nyawamu	The inner *ruh* your true soul.
Hé limo jëlënmu tulu perkara	Hey citrus, you have three paths:
kesa penyuci	the first, to cleanse;
keduë jahat	the second, wicked;
ketigë kin pemulih	the third, as a healer;
Rëjë Rengkan menurun ko ari langit	King Rengkan brought you down from the sky;
Peteri Rengkan menuripën ko ari bumi	Princess Rengkan made you grow from the earth.
Rëjë Rengkan	King Rengkan,
Peteri Rengkan	Princess Rengkan,
Tengku Jumal al-Hakim	Tengku Jumal al-Hakim,[3]
malekat itëm	the black angel.

[2] On the day of a wedding several mungkurs are sliced into a bowl of water, the behavior of the slices is interpreted, and the water is used to wash the bride. Slices that come together signal the future cooperation of the bride and groom; diverging slices warn the specialist of their coming arguments. See Chapter 8 on divination in agriculture.

[3] Identified by Abang Kerna as Lukman al-Hakim, who brought antidotes to the world and now is at the Center of the Sea. Healers request aid from Lukman for childless mothers because he was so beloved by his parents (see Heller 1953).

Hartamu ni maléh kugunëi	Your legacy I will put to use
kin pemulang	as a returner;
kin memulangkan jin iblis sétan	to send back jin, devils, Satan.
Karena ko segër turun orum wé	For you descended [to earth] at the
	same time as he [the patient]
dan tenironmu ngë sawah serlo ni	and your requests come due today
dan turah kugunëi	and I must put them to use.

As is generally the case with Isak spells, the speaker uses Malay for the formulaic sections of the spell, sections that have the strongest persuasive effect on the object. Here that section is the recitation of the origins, names, and true nature of the mungkur at the beginning of the spell. The mungkur is called by its Malay name *limo*. The remainder of the spell tells the mungkur which of its three functions is to be used (the "wicked" one of exorcism and return).[4] These sections are in Gayo, and are more open to variation in form.

Abang Kerna carried out the transfer one evening. After reciting the above spell he moved the mungkur from the patient's head toward her foot, adding a counterclockwise motion. He counted backwards from seven to one, at the same time imagining the jin passing into the mungkur.[5] "It's even more effective if the patient can perform the transfer himself," he commented, "because then the maripët is already inside, and it can be used to push the jin out."

The next morning he continued the cure on the banks of the Isak river, with the girl, her parents, and I present. The jin now was inside the mungkur, and Abang Kerna needed to discharge it toward its original sender. He began this next stage by reminding the mungkur of its task. He repeated the spell to the mungkur that he had recited the previous day, adding at the end:

Enti né musiyër	Do not deviate,
enti né musimpang	do not stray
ku kuën atau kukiri	to the right or the left.

---

[4] The same spell can be used to ready the mungkur for a task of cleansing or healing. One simply substitutes "white angel" for "black angel," and, for the descriptions of sending back the jin, the lines:

Hartamu ni maléh kugunëi	Your legacy I will put to use
kin tawar serta pemulih	as an antidote and curative,
kati [Name of patient] pulih dari	so [Name of patient] recovers
penyakit [Name of illness]	from [Name of illness].
Si bisë tawar	That which hurts, be relieved;
Si mugah magéh	That which is infected, be well;
Si berët ringën	That which is heavy, be light.

[5] I was puzzled that the counting was in reverse, because in similar transfers for purposes of divination the counting is forward. The reason for the reversal, he explained, was that the ultimate purpose of the transfer was not to keep the jin in the mungkur but to expel it.

Ikë ko musiyër atau musimpang	If you deviate or stray,
ko darohaka ku Tuhën	you will be treasonous toward God.

He then told the mungkur what it had to do, specifying only that it return the illness to whoever had sent it:

Ulakën ko penyakit ni [Name]	Return the illness of [Name of patient]
ku si berilët dengki khianat	to whoever connives, hates, betrays.

Abang Kerna emphasized that he did not need to speak the name or imagine the face of the sender, or even know the person's identity. All that was necessary was that he have firmly fixed in his will (*kehendak*) an image of what needed to be done. He chose this way of proceeding, he explained, because it ensured him against error. Were he to imagine a particular individual, send the jin against him or her, but turn out to have been mistaken, then the exorcism would fail. (It was unclear whether harm would befall the erroneously supposed sorcerer.)

Once the mungkur was reinstructed, Abang Kerna placed it on a smooth rock, where it would be steady. As he later explained, he imagined the rock to be the moon, the site of Heaven, so that once the mungkur was placed on it the jin would willingly remain there. The channel of communication with the jin continued to be open throughout this process. Speaking softly, he called on the four archangels to keep the jin firmly in place on the rock, and declared that, although he did not know the identity of the sender, the angels did:

Hé malekat Jibra'il Mika'il	Hey angels: Jibra'il, Mika'il
Israfil Izra'il	Israfil Izra'il:
Ikunul[ën] ko kuini	Place here the
jin si berilët dengki khianat	jin that connives, hates, betrays.
Kerna ko jema benar	Because you are true beings,
ko jema bersuci	You are holy beings;
Kati kuéngon jema iso	So that I can see that being
si berilët dengki khianat	who connives, hates, betrays;
Kerna ko betèh	Because you know [its identity];
aku gërë betèh	I don't know [it].
Enti osah ko pé bluh ku kuën	Don't let it go to the right;
enti osah ko pé bluh ku kiri	don't let it go to the left.
Enti osah ko pé bluh ku atas	Don't let it go upward;
enti osah ko pé bluh ku tuyuh	don't let it go downward.

Abang Kerna then picked up a second rock, which he depicted in his imagination to be the sun. He imagined his outstretched arm to be "God's alif" (the initial letter alif in Allah), raised in the air and ready to strike the mungkur and the jin inside it. Holding the rock above his head he addressed the Angel of Death (Ar. *malak al-maut*), Izra'il, calling on it to strike the jin just as his shadow, the black boy, in a black movement, falls on the citrus:

Hé rëjë Malekal Maut	Hey Ruler Angel of Death!
Datangmu tiada berwaktu	Your arrival has no certain hour;
datangmu tiada berketikë	your arrival has no certain time.
Datangmu gerak itëm bujang [itëm]	Your arrival [is in the] black
	movement, the black boy,
sëbët sudërëngku menyebut	my friend and companion, saying
namaku	my name.
Ko-lë kusuruh seraya	You I order in an instant, a
sekejëp seketikë	moment, a flash
memukul jin iblis sétan	to strike the jin, devil, Satan
si didalam limo ini	that is in this citrus.

As the Angel of Death, following the shadow, strikes the jin, so does his single companion, the inner counterpart of his shadow on the empowerment pathway (see Diagram 5.3). "They strike the jin together," Abang Kerna explained, referring to the single companion and the angel. His command is directed to spiritual agents across several levels of manifestation: to the shadow, the single companion, and the Angel of Death.

He then turned to the citrus and the jin inside it, making clear that it was in the inner realm that the true action was about to take place:

Hé limo	Hey, citrus!
Bukan engko yang kupukul	It is not you whom I strike
melèngkan iblis sétan	but devils and Satan
si berilët dengki	who connive and hate.
Bukan aku memukul ko	It is not I who strike you
pi'ilmu memukul dirimu	but your own conduct that strikes you.
Babu itëm tungël	Solitary black slave,
bujang itëm tungël	solitary black boy.
Tumpah derejët	Let his/her lot spill forth.

As he spoke this last pronouncement he held his arm straight out from his body, and when he finished he swiftly brought it down onto the mungkur. As his arm descended he let out his breath, directing the inner aspect of his breath (the spiritual agent called *rahim tungël*) to aid in expelling the jin. He repeated the action several times until he had thoroughly squashed the fruit, then tossed the remains into the river.

This part of the ritual established two immediately connected parallel universes, one outer, the other inner. In the outer world, the healer's arm brings down a rock to crush a mungkur seated on another rock. In the inner world, the single companion and the Angel of Death strike the jin (till this moment lured by the cool moon) with the unbearably hot sun, throwing it back to the original sender. The visible shadow serves to guide the path of the angel, as the outer form of the single companion. Each outer object is a sign of the inner object upon which the intended action, conveyed by maripët, falls.

Yet the outer objects signify not only their immediate inner counterparts, but also the hidden reality of God at the opposite end of the chain of being. The shadow of Abang Kerna's arm, raised to strike, stands not only for the single companion that he can set against the jin, but also for the ultimate source of power and judgment. As God's alif, his arm's shadow acts as a material sign of God in both his empirical immanence and his transcendent knowledge of things. As a sign of objecthood, the alif recalls God's material effectiveness in the world. As opposed to mīm, the alif stands for God's transcendent nature and knowledge not contained in objecthood.

Knowledge comes from proximity to God, and in Gayo practice so does power. The single companion may be able to expel the jin, but the entire chain of being extending from Abang Kerna's arm to God's alif provides the overall power and direction. God's power and justice is the inner and effective cause of the exorcism, ensuring that the jin will be returned to whoever sent it. The healer's arm, raised to strike, invokes the inner power of God by virtue of its literal representation of God's name and the ability of the healer to imagine it as such. God knows, even if Abang Kerna does not, who sent the jin, and God, acting as the divine dispenser of justice, will direct it homeward. Recall the line of his spell:

> It is not I who strike you
> but your own conduct that strikes you.

The ultimate agent in the expulsion and return is thus God's justice itself. His immanence and his transcendent knowledge provide an ontological and ethical foundation for the exorcism. Abang Kerna may cause harm by sending back the jin (and the possibility does cause him real anguish), but it is God who directs the jin and thus he who is ultimately responsible.

Hamzah Fansuri's commentary provides further enlightenment on the relation of God's acts to our own. Hamzah illustrated God's immanence in the world when he translated a Qur'ānic verse (8:17) concerning the battles of Muhammad against the Meccan forces:

> It was not you who slew them [enemies of Muhammad]
> but God who slew them.[6]

God's immanence in the world links Hamzah's understanding of ma'rifat with Abang Kerna's understanding and use of maripët. Images of the shadow have persisted across this historical process of transformation and application.

---

[6] *Asrāru'l-'Arifīn*, 37.

Hamzah understood gnosis, ma'rifat, as a form of participation in God's knowledge of things. He saw his own movements as the shadow of what God knows ("the world is but the shadow of the Known"). Abang Kerna views his own shadow as the visible endpoint of a chain of being that reaches back to God. The critical difference between the two systems is that Abang Kerna—and generations of Gayo healers before him—extends the Sufi cycle. God is manifested in humans, who then strive to achieve gnosis of God—but now they take the additional step of bringing that achieved gnosis back into the everyday world.

For Hamzah, the lesson to be drawn from Qur'ānic verses such as the above is that God is everpresent in the actions of individuals. The historical proof lies in God's interventions at crucial points in the battles between Muhammad's troops and the forces of the still-unrepentant Meccans. Hamzah likens this proximity of the divine in concrete actions to the transparency of a clear wine in a fine glass, or to the waves in the ocean. In neither case is one element distinguishable from the other. The aim of ma'rifat is to become aware of this indistinguishability.

The point of maripët, however, is quite different. Knowing that God is immanent in the world allows one to direct God's actions through the manipulation of worldly things: speech, objects, bodily movements. This shift in intent brings with it a reversal of the relation between image and body, and, in particular, of the figurative role of the shadow. The Gayo healer desires to change the world, not merely know it. His belief is thus not in the dependence of the visible on the invisible, but the reverse: the human capacity to change the inner world by manipulating its outer counterparts. Shadows are thus cast not by God on the world, but by the world on God. The shadow of the healer's arm brings God's power down on the jin. Humans have seized shadows, less to attain the divine than to use him to better their immediate condition.

The squashing of the mungkur, though the high point of the curing, did not bring it to a conclusion. Before tossing away the fruit, Abang Kerna asked it to help heal the patient. He also recited the Seven Verses of the Qur'ān, each of which celebrates the power of God and thus can be used as protection against jin or other dangers.[7] He then sought to determine whether or not all of the jin had left the girl. He did so by using a second mungkur, this time as an instrument of divination. As he sliced the ends of the mungkur into a pan of water, he asked that they drop face down into the water if the cure worked. As it happened, one end fell face up, the other face down, which meant that the exorcism was incomplete and had to be repeated at a later date.

[7] Abang Kerna linked the Seven Verses to the seven parts of the body, a correspondence that, to him, affirmed the verses' protective value. He also associated each verse with a different protector: God, Muhammad, the four archangels, and Adam.

Abang Kerna then expelled the jin a second time, this time driving them into the river. (Although he may have been further motivated to do so by his finding that the first exorcism had been incomplete, he had already prepared the objects required for it and I believe would have carried it out in any case.) Here he depended on the good offices of the "prophet of the waters," the prophet Yati (or Hilir). He "opened a path" to the prophet by presenting a sirih roll to him. Holding it above the river, he said:

Assalam'ualaikum	Peace be with you [pl].
Hé Nabiollah Yati	Hey Yati, Prophet of God!
Ikë ku toa Pang Kuala	Downstream [you are] Pang Estuary;
Ikë ku ukën Pang ke'ulu	Upstream [you are] Pang "To the source."
Kë kuën mudik	On the right, traveling upstream,
Rëjë Menggala	Rëjë Menggala;
Ke kiri mudik	On the left, traveling upstream,
Rëjë Benang	Rëjë Benang;
Si lah-lah Si Lantak Lulu	In the middle, Si Lantak Lulu,
si ku ukën ku toa	who goes upstream and downstream.
Hélam nama bapamu	Hélam is your father's name;
Hamin nama dirimu	Hamin is your own name.
Karena ko rëjë benar	Because you are a ruler who is true,
karena ko rëjë pulih	because you are a ruler who is healthy,
Ini mana pemeliyënku kin ningko	Here is my token of respect for you.
Karena lo si serlo ni	Because on this day here,
terbilangan si jeroh	when the dates are auspicious,
terketikë si bisé	when the times are fortunate,
Aku sawah ku ko	I come to you
memulihkan maléh ujud ni [Name] ni	to heal the body of [Name] here.
Pulih zat pulih sipët	Heal essence, heal features;
pulih nyawa pulih tubuh	heal soul, heal body.
Dengan berkat	With the blessings from
la ilaha ilallāhū	there is no deity but God.

He let the rolled sirih leaf drop into the water and float downstream, bearing his request to the prophet Yati. He told the parents to bring the child to the stream and have her squat in the water. (She was impressively compliant through all these procedures.) Earlier that day he had arranged four sirih rolls and four colored piles of rice on a large banana leaf. Now he held the leaf over the child's head while calling, in a soft voice, on the four elements and their lords to aid him in expelling the jin:

Hé nasir opat	Hey, four elements!
wëih tanoh rara kuyu	water, earth, fire, wind.

Sidang tetap sidang mu'min	Lord of the earth, lord of the water,
salih salihin	lord of the wind, lord of the fire.
Karena ko si opat	Because you are the four,
karena ko pintu opat	because you are the four doorways.
Ini mana keta oros opat	Here are the four rice [piles].
Sawahën kam renyël ku Siah Opat	Send these along to the Four Syechs:
Siah bediri siah gembèra	Syech of the East, Syech of the South,
siah gemitë [beditë] siah kutup	Syech of the North, Syech of the West.
Si munamat pintu bumi	Who hold the gateways to the earth:
Nur Katun namamu bumi	Nur Katun is your name, earth;
Abdussalam namamu air	Abdussalam is your name, water;
Nur Salin namamu api	Nur Salin is your name, fire;
Rahim Tungël namamu angin	Rahim Tungël is your name, wind.
Terkam denéwé mayo	Its [jin's] entry was via you,
keta terkam dené itangkuhën kam	so via you is the way you expell
penyakit si berilët dengki khianat	this illness that connives, hates,
ni ku dërët	betrays, to outside [the patient].
Keta si ari dërët	And that which is on the outside,
enti né osah kam ku was	let it not enter inside.
Ini mana isharat buktié	Here is the token of proof.
Hé Si Lantak Lulu	Hey, Si Lantak Lulu,
si ku ukën ku toa	who goes upstream and downstream.
Mai ko penyakit ni [Name] ni	Take the illness of [Name]
ku Rëjë Pusët Lot	to the Ruler at the Center of the Sea.
Sawah kahé ko ku pusët lot	When you reach the center of the sea,
kirimën ko tawar putih	send a white antidote
kin pemulih	as medicine
kin tawar ni anggota tujuh ni	as antidote for the seven limbs of
[Name]	[Name].

This spell highlights the four-way correspondences across a series of signs.[8] The four rice piles (oros opat) are offered by the healer on behalf of

[8] In providing translations for the names given to the four Syechs and the four lords of the elements I follow the associations given to me by Abang Kerna. The Gayo names either have different ordinary meanings in everyday speech from those given here (mu'min and salih are from Arabic words and mean, roughly, "pious"; bediri means "stand up" and may derive from the rising of the sun in the east), or, as in the case of gembèra and gemitë (Hazeu [1907, s.v. "Siah"] gives beditë), have no meaning in everyday contexts. Some healers made the same associations as Abang Kerna; others made different ones. The English text thus represents a localized interpretation of the Gayo, valid for Abang Kerna and some, but not all, other healers in Isak.

the patient. They represent the presence of the four elements in the patient; they are the "token of proof" of the child's presence, and communicate that presence to the four elements and to the Ruler at the Center of the Sea whose aid is requested. The four lords of the elements (sidang opat) are the four doorways through which the healer can communicate on behalf of the patient regarding her physical state. The illness entered through the four elements (especially the wind) and is now asked to leave through them. Abang Kerna can call on the four elements to aid him by virtue of his own bodily relation to their four lords. When he does so he emphasizes the unity of the elements outside with those inside the body:

> Nur Katun is the name of the earth when we make it one with the earth that is inside us, and the same is true for the other elements. Rahim Tungël is the wind that leaves us as breath, and that can carry our four elements to the hills, to the world. By saying the names of the elements we bring them together with us and thus can command them to keep jin outside the body of the patient.[9]

But to expel the jin and keep other jin from entering the patient, Abang Kerna called on a further set of four agents. The Four Syechs are better placed to control what happens in the external world through their association with the four cardinal directions. "The Four Syechs know where things have come from, they know who has sent a sickness to us and to whom the jin ought to be returned," explained Abang Kerna. "The four elements protect us, our bodily boundaries, but the four Syechs know the outside world."

After addressing the agents who would carry the jin away, Abang Kerna transferred the jin to the offering (the leaf with its four sirih rolls and four rice piles). Continuing to hold the leaf over the patient's head, he said:

Sara mutesara	One unifies;
Roa tulu	Two, three,
gelah tentu renyël ko	be exact right off, you;
Opat gelah tepat	Four, be on target,
iturut ko perintahku kahé	follow my orders later on;
Limë enti né ko berdëwë	Five, quarrel no longer;
Onom pitu	Six, seven,
gelah tentu kahé sawah boh	be exact when you arrive, right?

This spell, the appropriate maripët, and the counterclockwise movements over the girl's head together transferred the jin to the offering and directed the offering to take the request to its destination. Just before releasing the

---

[9] Aman Das used the same names in his healing spells, but associated Nur Katun with water along with Nabiollah Yati.

leaf in the water Abang Kerna declared that the jin was now separating from the girl. He uttered the three pronouncements that make final a divorce in Islamic law:

Kesa talak	The first, divorce;
keduë talak	the second, divorce;
ketigë talak	the third, divorce.
Sah talak ceré ko penyakit	Work, divorce; leave you, illness,
jin si berilët dengki khianat	jin who connives, hates, betrays,
orum [Name] ni	from [Name] here.
Karena ko nar	Because you are fire,
ini nur	here is light.
Dengan berkat	With the blessings from
la ilaha ilallāhū	there is no deity but God.

As he let the offering go he recited additional spells for healing the child, including the Seven Verses and a request for the four images to bring her health. He watched the leaf float away until it sank—a good sign. (If the leaf is caught in an eddy and appears to be returning toward the patient, that is a sign that the jin is refusing to leave and that the second exorcism has not worked.)

THE SOCIAL FRAMEWORK OF EXORCISM

Other Isak healers also conduct exorcisms, each with his own variations. Abang Das, for example, captures the jin in a mungkur and then calls on the wind (as Rahim Tungël, thus one of the Four Syechs) to return it to its sender. Sometimes he uses an egg for the same effect, or to diagnose a disease. His accounts of how the exorcism works rely on an imagery of shadow and the inner world that closely follows that described by Abang Kerna. Aman Méja uses a mungkur for divination, but to rid his patients of jin he releases into the river an offering identical to that used by Abang Kerna, with four sirih rolls and four colored-rice piles. He calls on the Old Hunter to help him drive away the jin.

In general, Abang Kerna, Aman Tauhid, and Abang Das characterize their art as "working on inner reality" (*main batin*), using maripët to intervene directly to repair a patient or to expel a jin. Each of these three healers traces his knowledge to the Healer to the Four line in Kutë Robel village. The two Kutë Rayang healers Aman Risa and Aman Mëja, by contrast, generally use an intermediary to heal a patient. They often call on the Old Hunter, with whom they also work when they hunt, to find and expel jin from their patients.

In my talks with Isak healers, I found that each was able to describe accurately the techniques used by the others, despite the fact that the details of the techniques were closely guarded. Many individuals who had only been patients also had varying degrees of knowledge about how the techniques worked and about the identity of the harmful spirits. Although the healing process neither requires nor facilitates comprehension by the patient of the healer's speech, the healer frequently discusses with the patient the nature and source of the illness.

The healers' different techniques lead to different areas of sensitivity as well: Aman Méja and Aman Aris, who use the Old Hunter and the single companion in their healing, were very reluctant to discuss these spirits. Because these spirits are widely thought to cause illness, those who call on them for help in healing are suspected of using them for malevolent ends as well. Aman Méja started sweating when I brought it up; Aman Aris reached for a magazine and said, "I stay away from it because it conflicts with belief in God." The other healers were quite free in discussing these spirits because they were not themselves accused of misusing them.

Healing is not primarily a field of theoretical speculation, although much of that goes on, but a field of combat with real exhilirations and equally real dangers. Healers' tales of their careers emphasize their conquests of inferior rivals, not their success in saving lives or easing anguish. In 1989, Abang Kerna recounted how in 1955 he had finally attracted the attention of the foremost Isak healer, the Healer to the Four, Aman Mok. Aman Mok had been engaged in a running duel with a Kutë Baru man of "returning [jin] to each other" (bëlës-membëlës), and Aman Mok was getting the worse of it. He was often sick, and several Takèngën people who came to Isak had attacks of diarrhea ("That is when townspeople began to fear Isak people"). Abang Kerna was able to cure one of the Kutë Baru man's victims and send back the jin so well that he caused widespread illness in the sender's family. The man's wife brought him a large cash payment—"the price of a water buffalo"—to get him to stop.

Aman Tauhid saw his own running battle with Aman Risa as having led, by 1980, to major illnesses in his family and, by 1989, to his own illness and to his wife's death. Aman Risa himself, although denying that he (or Aman Tauhid) ever sent jin to harm people (he accused Aman Méja of doing that), boasted that the Old Hunter spirit that he and Aman Méja used could defeat any other spirit available to Isak healers. "Aman Tauhid doesn't fool around with Aman Méja; he would lose in a contest of inner resources [batin]."

As one might expect, accusations of sorcery follow lines of sociopolitical tension within Isak. In Kutë Rayang village, Aman Risa comes from the kin group of the religious official, while Aman Méja married into the ruler's kin group. These two groups have been at odds with each other since precolonial times, largely because of the rival claims by the ruler and the religious official to political preeminence (Bowen 1991:44–46). Aman Risa and Aman Méja frequently blame each other for spirit afflictions. Furthermore, Aman Méja was an outsider to Isak and in the 1980s was the Isak person most frequently accused of having caused illness and death. Both Aman Risa and Aman Méja tend to be blamed for misfortune by people from other villages, and in particular by healers connected to Kutë Robel.

The discovery that sorcery accusations travel along the social lines of least resistance (and most tension) is hardly new.[10] What is of sociological interest about the Gayo case is how, in the absence of central authority, the specific logic of healing prevents sorcery from generating potentially explosive tensions. The activities of diagnosis, healing, and retribution can be carried out privately and without the cooperation of the person who sent the jin. A healer usually works at home and in private, although others may witness the proceedings. Suspicions never lead to public accusations, and confrontations need never ensue.[11] I know of no person ever to publicly admit sorcery, although one former healer did make such an admission to me in private; this concerned his past conduct, now abandoned. (He said he did it to create business for himself as a healer, but stopped when he found himself made irritable—"my heart was always hot"—by the constant trafficking in spells.)

Keeping such matters out of the public domain indeed runs in line with the general tenor of Gayo social life. Gayo precolonial and, as much as is possible, contemporary village politics emphasize the public reaffirmation of concord and agreement (Bowen 1991:151–54). Informal public behavior, too, is guided by values of consensus and the avoidance of open confrontations. Gayo evaluate and shape their public behavior with reference to the norms of shame or embarassment (kemèl) and having a proper social sense of self (mukemèl). Gayo frequently use these norms to gloss norms in other domains. Thus some Gayo equate religious piety (īmān) with this sense of shame and selfhood, as a person who was mukemèl would necessarily be pious as well.

Someone with this proper social sense refrains from loud speech and quick gestures, avoids those who stand in "heavy" kin relations to him or her (father, or mother's brothers), and employs circumspection in speech. Gayo often use Indonesian terms for such delicate categories as wife and

[10] Among the many fine demonstrations of this sociological point are, to mention only two on quite diverse societies, Fortune (1932) on Dobu sorcery, and Boyer and Nissenbaum (1974) on Salem village.

[11] The available evidence from the period just prior to Dutch rule suggests that public accusations of sorcery were not made at that time either (see the lengthy ethnography of the Gayo compiled by Snouck Hurgronje [1903], who was particularly concerned with issues of authority and politics, and who surely would have reported such accusations had they come to his attention).

husband to avoid the associations of sexual intercourse that are more strongly felt when one's own language is used. Gayo also virtually never accuse each other of anything in public, nor have I ever observed a public fight or argument among Gayo in Isak, except for the arguments carried out into the street by one woman who was said to have no sense of shame. Of course, this general restraint means that much interest is generated by the few activities that do air hostile feelings, such as public didong song contests and women's ritual wailing prior to a marriage.

Gayo ways of healing and explaining misfortune obviate the need for public encounters and yet allow Isak healers to come away from their travails satisfied with the results. Out of their overall interpretations of the patient's symptoms, their own images and dreams, and the responses of others in the community, Isak healers construct a drama of vigorous spiritual combat that rarely, if ever, leads to open accusations and disputes. They fashion an Islamic discourse of healing in just such a way that they can heal and exact retribution in a single event that has no need of a public hearing.

In two respects Gayo differ in healing practice from neighboring peoples in the archipelago (with whom they share, however, general ideas about balance and health). Gayo practitioners do not become spirit mediums, and they have avoided designing objects that are specific to sorcery.

In neighboring societies in which trance and spirit possession are frequently used, such events become public social dramas. People in Malay and Karo Batak societies, for example, make frequent use of trance and spirit possession to investigate the nature of an illness. Karo mediums will allow a spirit to possess them (Sibeth 1991); Malay healers will put themselves and their patients into trances, from which they can speak and act out the sources of their ills (Laderman 1991). The Malay seances are indeed a form of dramatic art. Gayo reliance on a private form of exorcism is consistent with the general social and cultural tendency to avoid public confrontations.

Second, Gayo make only sparing use of charms or other objects. In some parts of the archipelago, objects play a major role in directing the flow of harm to a victim (Lieban 1967; Skeat 1967). The Gayo practitioner has less need of such objects because, through his own imaginative power, he is able to let God's justice direct the spirit back to its sender. The relative absence of sorcery-specific objects has a further consequence: it keeps sorcery and healing out of the domain of Gayo jurisprudence. Gayo ëdët-based rules for determining fault depend on material proof. To convict a person of stealing or fornication, an incriminating object must be found in his or her possession or in the victim's abode. In the absence of specifically harmful objects, no Gayo could or can be convicted of sorcery. When, in the mid-1980s, the (non-Gayo) district public prosecutor attempted to convict a Takèngën-area man for sorcery, the case had to be abandoned not because of problems with the legal status of sorcery (it is actionable), but for lack of material proof: all the objects found in the suspect's home that could have been used for sorcery also had other, legitimate uses.[12]

The Morality of Sorcery

Despite the anger that some healers, and surely all victims, feel toward the perpetrators of sorcery, healers rarely evince a sense of moral outrage or condemnation. The ethos of antisorcery is more agonistic than moral. To some extent the moral tone of Isak sorcery discourse can be explained by the politics of speech and emotion: an outward expression of rage would betoken an insufficiently developed sense of shame and would threaten the fragile, interactive form of political-legal discourse. Yet this reasoning fails to explain how, in an explicitly Islamic context where people talk frequently about sin and punishment, sorcery can be perceived more as a challenge than as a wrong. How do we explain this attitude?

Let us first return to the approach the healers take toward illness and health. The healer is successful to the extent that he or she can call on God and angels, or at least invoke their power. "When we pronounce a spell in the name of God," said Abang Kerna, "we are Adam speaking, calling on all thirty divisions [juz] of the Qur'ān to descend and heal the person. The Qur'ān is the basis of all knowledge and can be used to kill or to heal, to clarify or to obscure." A person can use the power of the Qur'ān to heal or to harm, and in this sense its power is prior to judgment about the ethics of its use. In this respect (though not in others) the Gayo attitude toward religious power resembles the Javanese concept of power. "Since all power derives from a single homogeneous source," writes Benedict Anderson (1972:8) about the Javanese notion, "power itself antecedes questions of good and evil."

In the Gayo view, God is willing to transmit harmful spells as well as beneficial ones. He accepts all requests for assistance, and thus can be called on to destroy someone or to protect him, to send a spirit to do ill and then to send him back to the original source. God and humans are dependent on each other, and, just as humans must worship God, he must receive their requests. But he will hold humans accountable for their actions at a later time.

Furthermore, the activities of healers and spirits are part of a natural, premoral order—recall how smallpox is not only tolerated but commanded by God. Healers, careful to affirm their role as mere technicians in a world where God dispenses ultimate justice, do so by echoing the words of Hamzah Fansuri: God acts through humans, who are but his instru-

---

[12] On the evolving legal status of sorcery in Indonesia see Slaats and Portier (1993).

ments. Aman Tauhid put it in ways that recall the words of Abang Kerna's spells:

> You must remember to call all the objects you use in exorcism by different names, inner [batin] ones. It is not you who are hitting the mungkur, and not a piece of wood you hit it with; these are just the outer forms. Also, you are not sending the illness back to whoever sent it; it is sending itself back. This is important so that you do not sin.

Not that healers are without doubts and worries on this score. Indeed, Abang Kerna, who in 1980 was rather unabashedly boastful of his victories against sorcerers, in 1989 had begun to be concerned that he might have inflicted too much harm on men and women who were not serious sorcerers. "Someone might have been playing around and happened to hurt someone, and then I sent the jin back in all seriousness and really clobbered him." By about 1986, he said, he had ceased performing the direct exorcisms with mungkurs, and relied only on Qur'ānic verses for healing (combinations of the shorter chapters al-Ikhlās, an-Nās, and al-Falaq). The greater concern with God's judgment that comes with aging, and perhaps the effect of a continual modernist critique of spirit manipulation, had led him to shift his moral perspective and to choose more carefully the cases he agreed to solve.

Modernist Ambivalence

Gayo modernists in Isak and Takèngën take an ambivalent stance toward the whole business of spirits and healing. On the one hand, they wish to deny that spirits have the power ascribed to them by healers and their patients, and they whole-heartedly oppose appeals to any spiritual agent other than God. On the other hand, modernists rarely deny outright that harmful jin exist or that some healers do succeed in ridding people of these jin.

For an Isak man such as Tengku Asaluddin, who has enjoyed the richness of his village heritage and yet, by education and by conviction, opposes trafficking in jin, the conflict often emerges as a rupture in the middle of a conversation:

> In 1989 Tengku Asaluddin and I were talking about the miraculous things people have seen and done; he was ascribing to "God's miracles" [ma'zizët Tuhën] anything out of the ordinary. He mentioned the special powers some tigers carry with them. "Tigers know how to find special leaves that make heavy things light or that reflect your own thoughts. Once, three men saw a tiger choosing leaves until he found the right one. He gazed at it and then buried it.. One of the men then dug it up and looked into it, and saw in it the face of his own daugh-

ter. He went home right away. It's just like when you [JRB] close
your eyes and see your son at home." I asked if that was maripët and
he said yes, and when I remarked that healers said they saw jin
through maripët he answered that yes, perhaps that was how they did
it. People often can talk with jin. One man in Java can call back the
souls of people who have died.

But then he straightened himself up and changed his tone of voice
from one of a pleasurable involvement in stories from the past to his
stern teacherly mode. "But God is one," he admonished, "people who
put on feasts and say doa-doa make themselves into God."

One extended case of illness and curing involved my own Gayo family,
that of Abang Evi in Takèngën. A long series of disputes between them and
another family in the town erupted in early December 1980, when Abang
Evi was attacked by a member of the rival family near the town courthouse.
In an action of violence unusual for the highlands, the man leaped from behind a bush and hacked at Abang Evi's face with a razor-sharp machete.
One side of his face was cut clear to the bone, and only after he received
stitches in Takèngën and was rushed to Medan for more intensive care
could he be pronounced out of danger. During his recovery in Medan he
frequently felt pain, often in his stomach as well as in his face, and his
elder brother, who lived in Medan, set out to diagnose these pains and attempt a cure.

Abang Muhammad, the elder brother, soon became possessed by spirits.[13] His face began to twitch, and he beckoned me furiously to come
closer. He dictated a list of ingredients: "seven kinds of flowers, seven needles, three mungkurs, rhinocerous horn, . . . to be bathed tonight." I wrote
out the list and gave it to his mother, who quickly dispatched one of her
granddaughters to buy the ingredients.

That evening Abang Muhammad, already in a light state of possession,
transformed the assembled ingredients into an instrument for expelling the
jin inside Abang Evi. He sliced in half one of the mungkur fruits, cut a slot
in its side to hold one of the flower petals, and stuck the seven needles
around its edge. He floated the mungkur in a large basin of water, and then
added the remaining mungkurs, flowers, and a bit of the rhinocerous horn
powder (if that was indeed what the girl had brought back). Abang Evi then
drank of the water. When Abang Muhammad raised the prepared mungkur
out of the water and over Abang Evi's head, his hands began to tremble
violently. He nearly dropped the mungkur. Regaining control, he began
to move the mungkur slowly along over Abang Evi's body. When he

---

[13] I know of no cases of healing through trance in Isak or other rural Gayo areas; Abang
Muhammad probably picked up this technique in Medan, where he had lived for nearly twenty
years and where mediums are commonly used.

reached the feet he flicked the mungkur outward (a movement that he later told me was to expel the jin). He repeated the process several times, and then used the remaining fruits to rub Abang Evi's limbs and make further flicking motions. (Abang Evi later said that he felt "cool and odd" during the session.)

It was "they" (*paké a*) who possessed him and dictated the steps in the cure, explained Abang Muhammad later. He had no idea who "they" were, but in the past they had come to tell him how to cure people. He had no memory of what they said, nor did he know anything about medicines and healing. His sister, Kak Mus, also used to be possessed in this way. Their grandfather (his mother's father) knew a lot about curing, he added. When I speculated that perhaps it was the grandfather who sent the directions, Abang Muhammad gave me a smile and a half nod. His mother, who was deathly afraid of committing the sin of *shirk* or "duplicating God" (*menduëi Tuhën*) by communicating with spirits, intervened at this point to say sharply that the instructions "came straight from God," that they were *ilham* (divine inspiration). Abang Muhammad remained silent.

Abang Muhammad explained that his possession was "medicine" (*uwak*) and thus not in conflict with religion. He recited a saying of the prophet Muhammad favored by modernists in such contexts: "For every illness there is a medicine." Once, he added, God even ordered Muhammad to gather leaves for use as antidotes. To heal is to follow the prophet's example. What one must avoid is the use of talismans (*tangkal*), such as leaves placed above a door or the six-pointed star of Solomon, that suggest a lack of confidence in God. A talisman used to ward off danger and illness "duplicates God" and "goes ahead of him" because it tries to anticipate what he has planned for us.

In his explanations, Abang Muhammad trod the delicate line between calling on God through one's own inner powers and treating scripture as effective independent of God's will. His mother sought to frame the whole affair as a matter of following God's medicinal instructions rather than as communicating with other spirits, in keeping with the modernist effort to avoid any trafficking with spirits. Abang Muhammad was more willing to indulge in such trafficking, as long as he could avoid direct responsibility for doing so. Possession gives him a way to sidestep such direct involvement.

On another occasion Abang Muhammad made use of an intermediary to avoid the sin of giving offerings to jin. Modernists often condemn food offerings as wasteful (*mubazir*). When Abang Muhammad found out that land he had purchased for a coffee-storage shed was full of spirits, he tried to clear them out in a way that would not conflict with religion. On instruction from "them," he sprinkled water from the well of Zamzam (brought back from Mecca by a relative) around the perimeter of the plot to keep jin from entering. He then took a handful of earth from each of the four corners and used it to mark a path that jin already inside the plot could follow to a nearby swamp. After they had presumably left, he used the water to close the path. He then worshiped on the plot and prayed to God for assistance.

Despite his efforts, Abang Muhammad felt ill at ease over the next two days. He felt sick in his head and stomach, as if a great struggle were taking place inside him. "They" told him that the jin had not left peaceably for the swamp but were congregating around the gate trying to get back into the plot. The jin would only go away if given an offering of four rice piles, seven apam cakes, and a dead, uncooked black rooster. This was their desired food, to be placed in the swamp area at sunset (the time of day when jin move around freely).

Abang Muhammad refused to make the offering because he knew he would be committing the sin of waste, he said. But he told his partner in the coffee business about the request and left it up to him. The partner said he would meet the jin's demands. Abang Muhammad did not ask further about it, but after several days the partner reported that the jin had bothered him for two days and then had left.

Over the ensuing weeks Abang Muhammad entered trance frequently to treat his brother. He recaptured Abang Evi's vital force (semangat) by gulping air from the four cardinal directions and blowing it (perhaps containing the force) into Abang Evi's fontanelle. He would then hold a Qur'ān over a jug containing Zamzam water, and push it slowly down onto Abang Evi's head, moving as if encountering great resistance. He expelled jin by using a magnetic ring to pull a razor blade from Abang Evi's chest and then, at the window, blowing between the ring and the blade. He consecrated a jar of honey for Abang Evi to eat, saying: "Here is the antidote for one thousand and one illnesses, keep it carefully, we are getting tired and cannot come always. . . ."

Abang Muhammad followed many of the same steps as would an Isak healer. He returned Abang Evi's vital force, which had been crowded out by the jin; he exorcised jin using a mungkur; he offered (or arranged to have offered) the same food that an Isak healer would have used to induce jin to leave his land. But he did so while in a state of possession, or on the basis of instructions received while in that state, or through an intermediary. He thus displaced agency to an undefined source. He might believe that it was the spirit of his grandfather who instructed him; his mother, resistant to such ideas, was free to assert that it was inspiration directly from God that directed him. No one engaged in lengthy exegesis; everyone was free to place his or her own interpretation on what happened. Isak healers displace onto God responsibility for directing an exorcised jin back to its original sender. Abang Muhammad, along with other modernists, takes the further step of distancing the responsibility for his actions as healer.[14]

Absent from Abang Muhammad's repertoire are spells and the use of maripët. When Abang Muhammad moved the mungkur over Abang Evi's body, he was not engaged in a simultaneously inner and outer act of intention (or at least he did not remember having been so engaged). He merely carried out what he had been told to do, on the assumption that the outer actions would have an effect on the jin. Here, among modernists who retain their older heritage, we reach the limits of healing through spirit communication, when the healer becomes an automaton in the process.

The logic of Gayo exorcism elaborates Islamic ideas in a way that corresponds to the dominant social and cultural concerns of Gayo villagers. Exorcism is possible (in the Isak view) because humans have the capacity to retrace the chain of creation. Healers can call on inner aspects of their own being, from their shadows to their powerful spirit agents to God himself. His judgments and actions work through human intermediaries.

This religious logic makes it possible for healing and antisorcery practices to develop a vigorously combative texture in what was historically a relatively egalitarian society and a nonconfrontational culture. It also highlights the role of powerful speaking in ritual practice. Spells, divinations, and exorcisms all involve a practitioner speaking (and sometimes sending objects) to a spiritual interlocutor. This speech is evaluated on much the same grounds as is speech among humans. Jin, like villagers, sometimes fail to pay attention when spoken to. Serious speech to spirits requires objects as signs of that seriousness, just as does ritually important speech. Speaking to God must be clear and audible, like speech to other people. The power of speech is realized when it reaches its intended hearer and persuades him or her or it of its message.

[14] Mary Steedly (personal communication) reports that among Karo healers in Medan, and for reasons similar to those suggested here, (female) mediums have suffered less criticism from Christians for their activities than have (male) wielders of spells.

7. Isak Seen from the Rice Terraces

Chapter Eight

FARMING, ANCESTORS, AND
THE SACRED LANDSCAPE

GAYO MEN AND WOMEN speak with spirits not just for individual benefit but at times on behalf of the community as a whole. When they do so they draw on ideas of powerful speech to reaffirm their moral and practical interdependence. In the Isak valley, people feel materially dependent on one another most acutely during the rice-growing season. Farmers (thus nearly all Isak residents) must work together for certain technical reasons: the irrigation system must be repaired by group effort; planting must be coordinated to stagger water use and reduce pest damage; transplanting, harvesting, and threshing are more easily (and enjoyably) accomplished through group action.

But agriculture also has a ritual, spirit-oriented side, and its demands are no less collective. A single powerful ancestor (*Datu*) holds sway over each cultivation district and affects the welfare of all those who farm it. Disharmony among some villagers may displease spirits and endanger the success of everyone's crop. The rituals to expel pests and malevolent spirits, though performed by a specialist, must be attended by people from each village. Individual farmers address the rice plant to ensure its smooth passage from seedling to plant to nourishing food, but the rice ritual specialist (Kejurun Blang, Lord of the Fields) must negotiate the collective relation of the farmers and their crops to the spirits, ancestors, and pests that inhabit the cultivated world and the forests beyond.

Rice rituals not only improve the harvest, they also make visible ideal images of the community. Divination reveals the degree of social and moral disarray in each village, reminding people of the links between their conduct and the material well-being of the entire community. The rituals also enact the ideal images of social structure, in which rulers of right lineage and proper spiritual status exchange formal speeches. In the context of village life, the rituals thus bring together material, social, and religious concerns in a set of public events.

But the rice rituals stand in an uneasy relationship to the public sphere of Islam as interpreted by the ulama. Although some ritual events, such as prayer recitations, are widely acceptable, others, such as talks with long-dead ancestors, are not. Ulama disapprove of the transactions with spirits practiced by the Lord of the Fields as much as they disapprove of most spells. Yet, by varying the degree of publicity attached to each segment of the ritual series, the specialist has been able to keep disapproval from becoming open argument.

Speaking with the Ancestor

In 1979 Aman Jukri was the Lord of the Fields for the cultivation district of Kemulo, on the eastern border of Isak (see Map 8.1). One morning in April he rose early and bathed in the stream near his small house in the rice fields. He then walked a short distance uphill to the place where he could communicate with the spirit of Datu Béwang, the first person to have settled in the area. His first task of the day was to ask the Datu, the Ancestor, for help during the upcoming agricultural season.[1]

Although the Ancestor's site resembled a grave, with stones marking his head and feet, as well as those of his wife, it was not a grave. The ancestral couple had been buried here, but on the evening of the burial they arose together and walked northward. Nearby farmers saw the light of a pine torch leave the grave area and slowly move into the high hills, disappearing when it reached the top. The next day the farmers climbed the hill and found a freshly dug grave on the very top. The original grave was now empty, but the Ancestor's spirit remained where he had first been buried. This spot became a "place for worship" (*persemiyangan*) rather than a grave (*kuburën*). For as long as Aman Jukri knew, the farmers in the area had always asked the Ancestor's permission before cultivating their fields.

At the Ancestor's site, Aman Jukri performed two ritual units (*rak'a*) of worship. At the end he remained seated, stretched his hands upward, and prayed to God. Speaking in everyday Gayo, he asked God to protect the Ancestor, to guard the crops from "whoever connives and hates" (*si berilët dengki*, a phrase common to healing spells), and to transmit to the Ancestor any requests that failed to reach him on their own. "Worship creates a path to God for these prayers," explained Aman Jukri, "and the prayers ensure that God will transmit my words to the Ancestor."

After addressing God, Aman Jukri turned his attention to the Ancestor. He took a pot of water he had brought with him and poured it over the two sites. He began with the site of the Ancestor's wife, pouring from the foot toward the head three times. He then poured some water on the Ancestor's footstone, and knelt by the headstone to talk with his spirit. The stone was the material sign (syarat) of the Ancestor, he said. The stones also helped to transmit the requests to the Ancestor: the prophet Yakub (Jacob), present near stones, sent the words and the cool quality of the water to the Ancestor.

---

[1] I will distinguish between a powerful named Ancestor, a Datu, and ordinary ancestors, collectively called *muyang datu*.

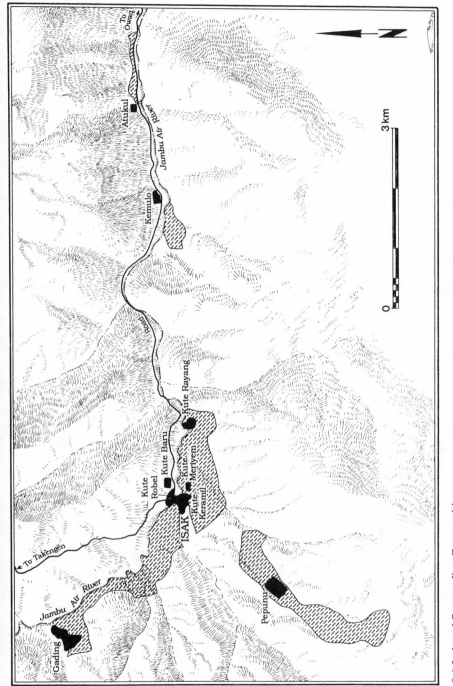

8.1 Isak and Surrounding Communities

Aman Jukri spoke informally, in everyday Gayo. He asked the Ancestor to protect the crop against pests and against the actions of people who are spiteful toward and envious of the farmers. Several days later he told me what he had said:

Aku maléh berlangkah	I am going to enter
ku daérah n Datu ni	into Ancestor's region here;
kerna Datu mulo	because Ancestor came before;
purën aku	later on, me.
Si ilët dengki Datu metéhé	Those who connive and hate, Ancestor knows them;
Datu nulo wé	Ancestor watches out for them;
Datu nelité	Ancestor investigates them.
Si gërë sawah	That which does not reach,
Datu nyawahné	Ancestor makes it reach.
Si gërë sampé	That which does not arrive,
Datu nyampèné	Ancestor makes it arrive.
Aku cukup ërëp Datu	For me, enough just as far as Ancestor.

After delivering these words of request, he lit a piece of incense and asked it to convey his next words to the Ancestor. The incense ensured that the requests reached the Ancestor and that he would take them seriously. "It is like when you come to ask for knowledge from me," he added. "Because you bring cigarettes, sugar, and coffee it is clear that you want something specific. I must give it to you because there is now a tie between us. What was optional [warus] has become obligatory [wājib]." He again asked for aid in farming, added a specific request for permission to farm the land, and ended with an Arabic prayer.

In a short period of time Aman Jukri had created a dense network of communication channels between himself, the Ancestor, and God. He had opened the series of speeches with worship of God, and then Gayo-language prayers. His requests to the Ancestor were carried by God (via the preceding prayers) and by the prophet Jacob (via the lustrated stone), and reinforced by the burning of incense. Taken as a whole, the speeches create a network of spiritual support for the agricultural year.

But in his speeches to God and to the Ancestor, Aman Jukri implied markedly divergent ideas about his relation to each. Worship and prayers to God emphasize submission to him as all-powerful, and Aman Jukri asked him to carry messages to the Ancestor, to protect the Ancestor, and to protect the crops. But when speaking to the Ancestor he failed to mention God at all. Repeatedly he stressed that the Ancestor was the one who would make sure his words reach their destination. And by saying "enough just as far as Ancestor," he explicitly left God out of the picture.

In framing his two sets of speeches differently, Aman Jukri implied two

8. Aman Jukri at the Site of the Kemulo Ancestor, 1979

divergent interpretations about the overall ritual event: one that is focused on God, and a second in which the Ancestor is the main actor. The overall ritual is itself divided into two parts, each acting out one of these interpretations. By compartmentalizing the two views, the ritual specialist prevents an explicit clash between the advocates of each.

The set of events that marks the start of cultivation consists of two parts: the specialist's session with the Ancestor, and the ritual meal (kenduri) that follows. In 1979 the meal took place in a rice field near Aman Jukri's house. While he had been conversing with the Ancestor, other farmers in the area had gathered at this spot and food had been prepared. Aman Jukri joined the group and asked an older man, skilled at scriptural recitation, to say prayers. The man rinsed his mouth with water, lit some incense in a coconut shell, and announced: "Now, together, we shall ask God to keep danger away from the crops." He held his hands over the incense and recited, to himself, an Arabic prayer. He continued his recitation out loud with a long series of short formulaic prayers, including most prominently a series of requests for forgiveness that begin: "I ask forgiveness from God" (*astaghfirullāhal 'azīm*). (These prayer units were used on a number of different occasions, most importantly in recitations for the deceased.) He then led the group in seven repetitions of al-Fātiha, the opening verse of the Qur'an, followed by another long prayer punctuated by unison utterances of *amīn* from all attending.

While the prayer was said, the requirements for a major four-element ritual meal had been set out before the group (explained in Chapter 10). The four ritual dishes that give the meal its name—flat rice-cakes, a mound of glutinous rice, puffed rice, and cooked rice—were then removed, and the food to be eaten brought forth. Near Aman Jukri were reed baskets of rice seeds and a bowl of healing leaves (*petawarën*). The objects contained in a dish set before him—a measure of rice, a needle, and three betel nuts—signified that the community surrendered authority over rice cultivation to him.

After the meal Aman Jukri instructed everyone to begin preparing their irrigation ditches and to soak their seeds on the 17th of the lunar month and sow them on the 20th. He then prepared the seeds and the cooling leaves for distribution to the farmers. Normally he would chew betel and spray the red juice over the seeds and the leaves, but because his teeth were loose he asked Aman Ras, seated next to him, to chew and spray for him. Aman Jukri then said a few quiet words over the seeds and the plants. He reassured the rice seeds that they were to be used for the good of humans and therefore should not fear planting, and instructed the healing plants to cool the fields and the crops during the year. After the meal, he divided the seed and the water from the leaves among the farmers, who later shared the seeds and water with farmers who had not come to the meal. Each farmer was to place a bit of leaf and water in each location where irrigation water entered the rice plot.

As Aman Jukri later explained to me, the ritual meal imbued the water and leaves (and through them, the rice plants themselves) with the power to grow and nourish. Gayo refer to this power as *berkat*, a word from the Arabic *baraka*, "blessing." Unlike the Arabic concept of baraka (Eickelman 1976:158–63; Gilsenan 1982:75–115), however, berkat is a function of the well-being of the rice plant or grain itself, which humans can augment or diminish, rather than a direct blessing from God. At the ritual meal, spraying the seeds and plants with betel juice was an external (lahir) sign of the inner (batin) powers transferred to the seeds. Spraying the juice, said Aman Jukri, brings up the cooling (penawar) element that lodges within every human being (and that healers employ). As the juice passes through the teeth it collects the inner quality of strength that teeth signify. "Our teeth are like iron," said Aman Jukri, as he elaborated the inner-realm equivalences activated by the spraying. "They can break rocks." Finally, he said,

. Aman Jukri and Farmers at the Kenduri, 1979

the betel mixture is itself inherently healing and cooling: the sirih leaf grows in the hills and thus belongs to the "holy beings" (aulië) whom we must placate; the lime is from rocks and thus, like the teeth, has a "hard soul" that can crush all manner of pests; the betel nut is our own because we plant it, and so it takes care of us.

The sequence of events that forms the initial cultivation ritual can be interpreted in several distinct ways. For Aman Jukri, the first part of the ritual requested help from the Ancestor while the second part conveyed the power of growth to the seeds and water. In our many conversations on agricultural ritual, Aman Jukri never mentioned God as an important actor in the agricultural process.

Other Isak men and women consider such entreating of ancestral spirits as tantamount to polytheism or "making God plural" (menduëi Tuhën). But these villagers, generally sympathetic to the modernist position, were not forced to publicly recognize that the rice ritual specialist, in his discourse at the ancestral site, had established the Ancestor as his principal counterpart in the spirit world. They may or may not have known that such were the specialist's words in 1979, but they avoided talking about them as current practices. Indeed, nobody, regardless of religious persuasion, ever publicly mentioned Aman Jukri's speech to the Ancestor. Those who disapproved of such appeals condemned them as part of an unenlightened time. "People used to do such things in the distant past," they would say.

By contrast, the ritual meal was often publicly discussed. Modernist-leaning villagers were able to interpret the meal as an occasion to recite scripture and pray to God. The presence of a person skilled in prayers guaranteed that all villagers would accept the proceedings. No one mentioned the Ancestor, and the words Aman Jukri muttered at the end of the meal to the seeds and leaves could be ignored, interpreted as legitimately Islamic, or played down as "custom" that did no particular harm. I heard people express all three attitudes. Modernists who discussed the ritual viewed the opening words of the prayer recitation, which framed the meal as an opportunity to thank God, as defining the entire event.

Others have accommodated the ritual meal to their religious positions in other ways. In Owaq, fifteen miles downstream from Isak, the meal is held in a house or in the mosque, and never in the fields. As long as the meal was held in the fields it gave nourishment to jin, explained the Owaq headman, and such practice clearly is idolatrous (*mushrik*). But jin will not enter a house or mosque, he added, so a meal held indoors could only be intended to ask for help from the spirits of one's ancestors and thus is acceptable. (Some Isak and Takèngën modernists would have roundly condemned even that practice as idolatrous.) In Owaq the healing leaves distributed to the farmers may only be placed in the middle of the fields as signs that the farmer is asking God for help. The headman tells farmers not to place them in the irrigation canals: to do so would imply that the Lord of the Fields had made the leaves into medicines by his words and gestures, and only God can do that.

For some Gayo, particularly those who live in Takèngën, placing agriculture in the religious domain at all is dangerous because it recalls (and, they fear, maintains) some of the practices from "the distant past" that should not be carried out by good Muslims. For these Gayo the cultivation ritual is best construed as entirely social and technical, with the goal of coordinating farm labor. Indeed, most townspeople with whom I discussed rice ritual described the role of the Lord of the Fields as a technical coordinator; many thought him to be part of the government agricultural service (he is not). In villages near Takèngën, rituals such as that performed by Aman Jukri are held in the Lord of the Fields' home, allowing the continued public pretense that what he does is "only agricultural."[2]

---

[2] This third, sociotechnical interpretation of the specialist and the rituals over which he presides is likely to be the basis on which any eventual centralized coordination of agricultural practice in and around Takèngën takes place. Centralizations using local ritual specialists have occurred elsewhere in Indonesia, for example in Bali (Lansing 1991).

Gayo thus interpret agricultural ritual in three quite distinct ways: as a series of instrumental mediations between the Ancestor, the farmers, and the crops; as an occasion for beseeching and thanking God; or as a meeting of farmers to coordinate their activities. In the first view, the specialist's speech is part of a series of ritually mediated transactions between the living and the dead; in the others, no such ideas of exchange are acknowledged. This interpretive divide stems from the same differences in views of language and power that we explored in earlier chapters.

Gayo even use three different names to refer to the ritual, two of which refer to agricultural aspects alone: "ritual meal for entering the fields" (*kenduri turun ku blang*) and "ritual meal at the headwaters" (*kenduri k'ulu n'wëih*). The first of these is most often used in public announcements or ritual speaking. But in ordinary conversation, Isak Gayo most often use a name that emphasizes the appeal made to the Ancestor: "ritual meal at the Ancestor ['s site]" (*kenduri ku Datu*). The way in which these distinct discourses are socially channeled allows certain people (particularly modernists) to ignore some activities and highlight others. People may hold divergent opinions without ever having to confront their differences publicly.

Aman Jukri's agricultural domain, Kemulo, is just to the east of Isak proper. It is in the community of Isak itself where differences over the propriety of agricultural ritual are most sharply felt. Here, representatives of five villages gather to request help from the Lord of the Fields, and on this occasion invoke an older, still-idealized social order. Here, too, is found the best-known Ancestor in the entire valley, Merah Mëgë, whose powers attract people from Takèngën and beyond. Isak's population also includes modernist-leaning teachers and officials, who are quite critical of the attention paid to Merah Mëgë.

In Isak, the office of Lord of the Fields has been held continuously by members of the Elder Imëm's descent line in Kutë Rayang village, one of the five villages that make up the community. Members of this descent line claim to be direct descendants of Merah Mëgë and to have inherited his spiritual powers (Bowen 1991:45–46). In precolonial and early colonial times the Elder Imëm was responsible for leading community-wide prayers and for pronouncing on Islamic legal matters. The first Lord in Kemulo was Aman Jukri's father, who was adopted into the Elder Imëm's line so as to share in Merah Mëgë's powers. Members of the line claimed that only they were capable of serving as Lord of the Fields. Indeed, Elder Imëm people cite numerous examples of others in Isak who attempted to fill the office and failed. Lords in this line are shown in Diagram 8.1.

The worship site of Merah Mëgë is located on a forested hill above the village of Kutë Kramil near the village graveyard. As with that of Datu

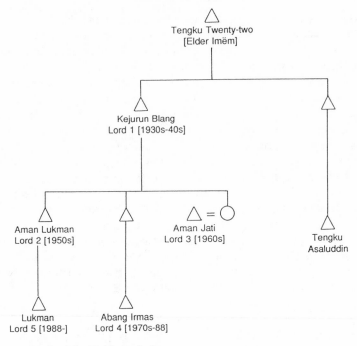

8.1 Lords of the Fields for Isak

Béwang, the Kemulo Ancestor, this site consists of two gravelike areas, each marked by a stone at the head and foot. In this case the space between each pair of stones is filled with gravel, and the entire site is covered by a wooden structure. People visit the site for large-scale rice rituals, personal vows, and, until the late 1950s, an obeisance just before marriage (Bowen 1991:42–43). Whereas the other Ancestors in the Isak valley are only of concern to those in their immediate vicinity, Gayo of Isak origin who have moved elsewhere return to Merah Mëgë in cases of great need. A ritual meal presented to Merah Mëgë usually includes the sacrifice of a goat or a sheep, and has from ten to thirty people in attendance. In part because of the frequency of visits to the site, and in part because of its relative proximity to Isak, the major community in the valley, it is here that differences in interpretation have produced disagreements over proper ritual procedure.

The explicit issue in question has been the location of the ritual meal that follows the Lord's discourse with the Ancestor. The ritual meal used to be held in the open area next to the worship site. At least by the mid-1970s, however, Isak religious leaders, seeking to reduce the visibility if not the importance of what they considered to be improper communications with spirits, successfully urged the Lord of the Fields to hold the meal in the

Kramil village prayer house. (They also tried to discourage people from holding ritual meals at the Ancestor's site on other occasions, but to no avail.) Their action made it easier for those who so wished to interpret the meal—and through it the ritual as a whole—as merely an occasion for the recitation of sacred verse.

When a new Lord, Lukman, succeeded to office in 1988, he declared his intention to return to the original site. However, for at least his first two years he gave in to what he identified as pressure from the religious leaders (including the influential modernist—and his own close relative—Tengku Asaluddin) and held the meal in the Kramil prayer house after conversing with the Ancestor at the grave site.

Unlike the ritual meal at Kemulo and most other sites in the Isak valley, the Isak ritual for the start of the agricultural year begins with the exchange of speeches between the Lord of the Fields and a spokesman for the office of Clever Chief (Kepala Akal). In the late precolonial and early colonial periods, the Clever Chief was the leader of one of two major political blocs in Isak; the Elder Imëm and the Lord of the Fields were members of this bloc (Bowen 1991:38–50). Although the office had been vacant since early in the century, in the 1980s it still represented an ideal image of the entire community in its precolonial state. At the agriculture ritual a headman or religious official from one of Isak's villages speaks in the name of the Clever Chief. In his speech he invokes the names of the precolonial headmen in Isak, names that are only heard on such occasions.

At the 1989 ritual it was the religious official (imëm) for Rerawak village who spoke in the name of the Clever Chief. Seated directly in front of the Lord, he slowly raised his hands in front of his face and began:

Ini oros senari	Here a bamboo of rice,
kapur orum blo	lime and sirih.
Kerna ngë ara doa	Because we already have permission
ari Kepala Akal	from the Clever Chief,
Setië Mudë	the Young Faithful,
Pengulu Gading	and the Ivory Headman.
Kerna ngë ara sara bulën roa bulën	Because it has been a month or two
kami tangkuh ari wan blang	that we left the fields.
Nta ini, kami pé	So here, we also;
Ikë si lapé mengenakan korong	The hungry seek to be full;
ikë si gërë ara mengenakan ara	those without seek to have.
Dan kami mucontoh ku Kepala Akal	And we look to the Clever Chief.
Dan Kepala Akal pé gërë muduëi	And the Clever Chief does not divide [his attention],
serahan ku nama guru	[he] turns over to the *guru*,
muniro doa ku nama guru	asks for prayers from the guru.

Guléwé wëihé	The meat and the water,
ini kuserahan ku nama guru	this I give to the guru,
kati nama guru menyerahan ku	so that the guru will give them to the
malimtë	learned one,
untuk berdowa	so that [he] will say prayers
muniro tolong ku tuhën	asking help from God;
selamat denië	Well-being in this world
selamat ahèrat	and in the next.
Kadang ara berdedingin sejuk	Perhaps there is cool dedingin leaf
bercelala bengi	and cold celala.
Dan kadang ara beras padi tungkët	And perhaps there is rice, the staff
imëm	of piety
si malé kami sokën ku lah ni blang	that we will plant in our fields.

The imëm's speech was in traditional, if unpolished, Gayo ritual-speaking style.[3] He quickly dispatched his task: to ask the Lord of the Fields to accept the food and betel brought by the community, to ask a religiously learned man to recite prayers, and then to prepare the leaves and rice for insertion into the fields. The Lord, unaccustomed to ritual speaking, responded perfunctorily and turned the proceedings over to Aman Bani, the imëm of the host village, Kutë Kramil. The Arabic prayers he recited were much like those at the Kemulo meal in 1979, but they included an appeal to God to show mercy on the soul of Merah Mëgë.

After the prayers, and after the Lord had sprayed betel juice over the cooling plants (as in the Kemulo ritual), the Rerawak imëm again spoke. This time, however, he employed a formal Indonesian speech style, beginning with the Islamic greeting:

Assalamu 'alaikum	Peace be upon you [pl.],
wa rahmatullah	and God's compassion,
wa barakhatu	and God's blessing.

He followed with a formal statement of thanks to God. On behalf of the Lord of the Fields, he instructed the farmers to take the cooling leaves to their fields, to gather materials for repairing the fences, and then to await further instructions. His attempts to Indonesianize what once was a Gayo speech were clumsy, sometimes rendering Gayo words as he thought they would be in Indonesian: thus the name of the host village, Kutë Kramil, became Kota Krambil. After several minutes some yelled out that he should speak in Gayo because some of the women would not understand Indonesian, and he did so.

---

[3] Gayo ritual speaking is examined in Bowen (1991:151–68). Particularly clumsy here is the use of the Indonesian *dan*, "and," as a linking word.

The code switching that took place during the ritual is part of a hesitant refiguring of Gayo public speaking that has taken place in Isak more than elsewhere in the valley. It also, I believe, bespeaks a growing sense of the ritual's compartmentalization into distinct references and functions. Speaking in the name of the Clever Chief harkens back to a long-gone political structure that, despite the abolition of the office after independence (and its lack of power during the colonial period), continues to symbolize for many the legitimate precolonial Isak polity. However inept the speech itself, the recourse to this genre, signaled by its linguistic parallelisms and by the dialogue posture assumed by the two men, revived, momentarily, an older sense of community order.

The prayers to God asked for forgiveness toward the souls of the deceased, and especially for the soul of the Ancestor Merah Mëgë. But they were introduced as simply requests for help from God, in this world and the next, and thus kept the Ancestor's role well in the background.

Finally, the instructions to the farmers were presented as a technical matter, best done in Indonesian, the language of offices and government, despite the fact that all present spoke Gayo (and some only haltingly spoke, or understood, Indonesian). The attempt to accentuate this shift in modes by a shift in language was shouted down. Yet, given the frequency with which Indonesian-language speeches are made in Isak (Bowen 1991:165–68), the shift might be successfully made in the near future, supporting the opinion of those who see the ritual as mainly one of technical coordination of farm labor.

PROTECTING THE CROPS AND THE COMMUNITY

The rituals that inaugurate the agricultural year are but one moment in a long series of activities carried out by the Lord of the Fields. He must choose propitious dates and days of the week for beginning the season and for each ritual activity. The Lord is the first to soak his seeds prior to sowing, and the first to transplant the seedlings forty days thereafter.

About three months after the transplanting, the Lord officiates at two community events designed to protect the crops from harm. The two rituals form a pair and can be performed together. This is a time for the Lord to unite the community in the face of crop damage from rats, pigs, and insects. At the ritual of healing, the *kenduri nayang*, the Lord assesses the extent of the damage, divines its causes, and repairs the damage by distributing healing leaves. At the exorcism of pests, the *tulak bëlë* (lit., "pushing back danger"), he asks God to expel the pests and tells their ruler to leave the crops alone. At both events the Lord draws on the same powers used by healers, employing similar combinations of spells, imagination, and objects.

Finding the Social Causes of Crop Damage

The ritual of healing repeats many of the steps of the first ritual. In Isak the Lord of the Fields visits the Ancestor Merah Mëgë and then officiates at a large meal held at the Kramil village prayer house. Downstream at Kemulo (where the season is usually about four months behind Isak) the Lord calls the farmers to his house; he may or may not visit the Ancestor Datu Béwang beforehand. But in both places the Lord must assess the condition of the crops and distribute healing leaves to the farmers.

In Isak divinations have been held at both the healing ritual and the crop exorcism. In 1979 each of the five villages in Isak brought a bucket to the Kramil village prayer house. Each bucket held some healing leaves, an egg, and a mungkur. (Kramil village had added an extra mungkur for the uplands farming community of Pepunu, peopled largely from Kramil.) The imëm of each village was to have given the mungkur to his headman to hold for a few minutes. By holding the fruit, the headman made visible his own *tabiët* (character; <Ar. *tabi'a*, responsibleness) and *pi'il* (deeds; <Ar. *fi'l*) by transferring them to the fruit. The pure character of the mungkur made it absolutely reliable as a vehicle for making these inner qualities open to outer inspection.

After a meal had been served and eaten, Yusuf, a man generally acknowledged as a descendant of Merah Mëgë, spoke in the name of the Clever Chief. He asked the Lord, Abang Irmas, to give them healing leaves for the crops, and presented him with a measure of rice and a needle as signs of the community's willingness to abide by his orders. The Lord then cut a thin slice from the top and bottom of each of the six mungkurs. He let the slices fall into a large bowl of water, noticing how they fell and moved on the water's surface. Sometimes he prodded them with the tip of his knife to see how they would react. He then broke each egg into the bowl, inspecting each yolk for tears or blood that would indicate community disorder. He poured some of the mixture into each village's bucket, added some rice and sauce from the meal we had eaten (to say to the pests: "You have had your food; now leave"), sprayed everything with betel juice, and instructed the farmers on how and when to distribute the leaves.

I was unsure what the Lord had learned from the mungkurs. He had taken the fruits from the buckets and placed them in a pile near him, never asking from where each had come. Nor did he comment on the movements of the slices to anyone at the time of the ritual. I knew that one could follow several different methods in interpreting the behavior of mungkur slices, and that the specialist chooses an interpretive method prior to beginning. (The slices will sense the officiant's intent and behave accordingly.) One may make the outcome depend on whether the slices land face up or

10. Abang Irmas Divining the Causes of Pest Damage, with Abang Das to His Right, Isak, 1979

face down, on whether the slices move or remain where they fall, or on how they move with respect to each other. The addition of the eggs gave the Lord another possible code for interpreting the general condition of life in the villages.

On the following day I spoke to the Clever Chief spokesman, who had assisted the Lord with the divination. He explained that the Lord had stipulated that the interplay of the first two slices would be a sign of the unity or disunity of each village. If the first slice remained in the center of the bowl, the village ruler was acting as a leader should. If it moved to the side of the bowl or stuck to the knife, the headman was the cause of disorder in the village. (Others mentioned that the second slice moving away from the first indicated that the ruler and his wife were at odds.) "The ruler's actions determine the welfare of the entire village," explained Rëjë Hasyim, former ruler of Kutë Rayang.

As it happened, the first and third pairs of slices had slid in opposite directions on the water, even after the Lord had prodded them with his knife. The others had moved together, although when the fifth fruit was sliced one of the slices stuck to the knife. Yusuf said that the mungkurs from Rerawak and Kramil villages had separated, signaling village disunity, and that the slice that had stuck to the knife had been from Kutë Rayang, betraying problems with its headman. My immediate reaction was: How right these signs are! I knew little about Rerawak affairs, but Kramil was in the midst of an argument over the use of government funds, and the office of Kutë Rayang village headman had become nearly impossible to fill.

A second divination was held two days later at the crop exorcism (tulak bëlë). On this occasion Abang Das assisted the Lord. This time, explained Abang Das on our way back from the ritual, the mungkur slices from Rera-wak, Kramil, and Robel villages drifted away from each other, indicating problems. But, he explained, it was not that simple. The Lord may have been looking for other signs, especially whether the slices landed face up or face down or the first one way and the second the other. He thus had to wait for the Lord's verdict concerning his own village, Kutë Rayang. It was clear, he added, that for the community as a whole the results of the divina-tion were not good; he knew this partly from the fact that three of the slice pairs had separated in the water, and partly from the Lord's demeanor after performing the divination. He had looked concerned and had asked Abang Das to announce that he would have to repeat the ritual at a later time to compensate for the mistakes they all had made.

Over the next few days word circulated in Isak about the results of the two divinations: that disorder in several villages, especially Rerawak and Kramil, had exacerbated the damage to the rice crop. But gossip on this matter was directed less at specific causes of damage than it was at the gen-eral inability of the community to unite and improve its welfare. If the Lord spoke to individual village rulers or their imëms, he did so privately. Aman Jukri, the Lord at Kemulo, said that he thought Abang Irmas was too re-served to speak to the rulers, but no one could remember a time when a Lord did publicly assign blame. At most, said Rëjë Hasyim, the imëm would ask his ruler if he had not forgotten to carry out an obligation to a spirit, for such neglect could result in harm to the crops. Usually an over-sight such as forgetting to fulfill a vow was at the bottom of the problem, he said. Furthermore, then as now, disorder might be the result of a head-man's attempt to enforce a regulation rather than the result of personal defects.

Divination is thus not a mechanism for identifying guilty officials and punishing them for their misconduct. Rather, it serves to illustrate a general proposition about the practical consequences of human behavior. The moral quality of social conduct has a direct effect on the growth of plants and on the extent of pest damage, through a general relation of reciprocity between humans and the other inhabitants of the world. Pests know when a headman behaves badly, and they attack the rice more vigorously in response. Rice refuses to be fruitful when a farmer has not paid his religious tax (zakāt), in part because God intervenes and reduces yields. The rice plants are also receptive to direct human communication and respond positively to proper speech and negatively to an absence of such speech or to improper con-duct carried out near the field. Farming involves a set of morally grounded transactions as well as practically grounded ones. Its success depends on upright conduct in all aspects of one's life. As the visible representative of his people, the village ruler is the most likely to be responsible for crop damage.

It is on this point, concerning the observable results of morally reprehensible conduct, that the views of most Isak farmers converge with those of their religious leaders. Modernists such as Tengku Asaluddin and Tengku Kali emphasize the importance of the moral and spiritual qualities of the Lord and of the farmers for the success of the crops. In the past, a candidate for Lord of the Fields had to show that he had the proper spiritual fitness (*tuah*) to bring prosperity to the community. One means of discerning tuah was to ask God for guidance and then open a Qur'ān. If the page held the opening lines of a verse, that was a good sign; otherwise one would read the lines at the top of the page and interpret them. An exhortation to obey God meant that the farmers would obey the Lord; condemnations of a people might mean that the Lord was not suitable. The idea of harmony or balance is as important here as it is for healing a person. Tengku Asaluddin explained how tuah translates into good crops:

> Humans share basic qualities of life (*benih*, seeds) with plants and animals. There is something of the rat and the deer and the rice grain in each human being, and that is the basis for those creatures' willingness to obey humans. If a person has tuah then she or he will be in harmony [*sesuai*] with these creatures and they will prosper. For example, a coconut tree built next to a house always seems to be healthier than one built off by itself: it benefits from the person's closeness. Whether that is because it is cared for or because it is fertilized, I don't know. Conversely, all disasters—floods or droughts—are the result of the bad qualities of the inhabitants of an area. Even in one descent line some people will have tuah and others will not; that is why the Lord of the Fields had to be selected by inspecting his tuah.

Maintaining harmony (*sesuai*) requires that members of the entire farming community act in morally proper ways. Despite a Lord's best efforts (and personal qualities), disputes in a community or immoral actions by some of its members will endanger a crop. Such was the case, continued Tengku Asaluddin, in the early 1940s, when farmers began to clear the forest area of Jëgët, southwest of Isak, for rice farming. For the first few years they prospered under the Lordship of a pious man, Aman Caya, who agreed to serve as Lord only as long as no one stole. But then "they were tested." They found gold on the ground and removed it. But some became ill and they quickly returned the gold. They then found a huge pair of elephant tusks—Tengku Asaluddin saw them himself. The district ruler, Kejurun Talib, seized them and sold them, and thereafter, because they had taken things from the land, the crops began to fail. Eventually all the farmers returned to Isak and the land fell into disuse.

The Lord looks to several channels along which he may repair the crop.

He may urge people to resolve quarrels and to remember neglected spirits. He also uses healing leaves to "cool" the crops. Eggs may be used for experiments that guide the Lord in selecting the most effective healing leaves. (The eggs that Abang Irmas broke into the bowl along with the mungkurs told him of the condition of the crops.)

At Kemulo, Aman Jukri views social and agricultural welfare as directly linked. He relies primarily on egg divination to divine the state of both. He first slices a mungkur to see if the crops will be receptive to healing leaves. In 1979 Aman Jukri split open an egg and saw that the yolk had separated into three pieces and was dotted with small holes. The fissures indicated that the hearts of his fellow farmers were not united; the dots showed that pests were damaging the crops. Aman Jukri then repaired the egg with the healing leaves. He used the two primary leaves in the Lord's arsenal: the dedingin (cool-like) and the batang teguh (tough plant). At his instruction, his elder brother (who has substituted for him as Lord on occasion) dripped water from these two leaves over the egg. Slowly the three sections merged and the holes in the yolk disappeared. "When the people see this they believe in the Lord again," explained Aman Jukri, "and they come back together." The previous year the yolk had fallen apart, but he was able to repair it with the leaves, so the farmers continued to put their trust in him. "All I can deal with are the rice plants, not the people" he said, "but by curing the rice the people unite."

Ten years later, in 1989, Aman Jukri reflected on changes in the sociomoral conditions for farming throughout the 1980s. He remembered clearly the divination performed in 1979 and the reasons the egg had exhibited the signs of social disunity. Harvests in that and previous years had been good, but people had only grudgingly followed his leadership. The problem had been in the social realm. While the area once had been farmed by people from Kutë Rayang village, in the 1970s people from other villages had obtained land in the area and their presence had led to discord. In 1985 and 1986, many households busied themselves clearing land for coffee in the hills, and no one farmed in Kemulo. When a small group of villagers began to farm again in 1987, they were united and things went well. They built a single fence around the cultivated area and had no problems with pigs or birds. Things are still good, he said, but the pests are returning and he will have to watch for signs of disunity among the farmers.

From the Lord's point of view, then, the problems facing farmers and the effectiveness of rice rituals derive from the general sociomoral condition of the community. The "technical" problems of pest damage and poor growth are just as rooted in the behavior of farmers as are the "social" problems of dissension.

Expelling the Pests

While the first ritual heals the crops, the second, the tulak bëlë, rids them of pests. Aman Jukri's way of carrying out this ritual involves appealing to God and to the spirits who control the pests. At midnight he performs a special form of the worship ritual called the *tahjud* (night worship; see Wensinck 1953c), consisting of two ritual units (rak'a) followed by petitionary prayers. He prays in everyday Gayo, asking God to keep away the pests. The request must be made in the middle of the night, when God's presence (wahyu) comes close to the earth. Aman Jukri then sets out seven measures of glutinous rice (kunyit) as an offering to the spirits who command the pests, and recites Arabic-language prayers to God over the rice. Finally, he takes a fistful of the rice out to the border between the rice fields and the forest, and addresses the pests directly:

Buh, kerna kam, pertama babi	So, because it's you, first the pigs:
enti kunëhi kam hak ëdëm	don't disturb man's domain;
so hak allah peroromëntë	over there is God's domain where you should gather.
Keduë tikus	Secondly, rats:
enti kunëhi kam hak ëdëm	don't harm that which is man's domain;
ini bagiënmu	here is your portion.
kunyit segemul nguk kuaran	I can come up with a fistful of glutinous rice;
hak ëdëmku enti kunëhi ko	as for my "man's domain," don't mess it up.

He then proceeds in the same way for the birds and leafhoppers that also have been eating the plants. He leaves the fistful of rice on the hillside and returns to his house, careful not to turn around and look behind him (an act that would invite the pests to return with him).

The tulak bëlë in Isak is a much more elaborate and public ritual. The Lord of the Fields sends an offering of food, live chickens, and damaged rice plants downstream to the spirit who controls the pests, along with a plea to "take this and no more." Each of the four older villages in Isak contributes a live chicken of a particular color (although in practice any color seems to be allowed); Kutë Robel village, an offshoot of Kutë Dah (today Rerawak), merely sends an egg.

In 1979, as in previous years, the Lord, Abang Irmas, instructed the five village heads to send representatives to a place just downstream from the last Isak rice field. By two in the afternoon, about thirty women had appeared, bringing with them food, mungkurs, and chickens. Only nine men showed up, and all but two of them (aside from Abang Irmas and myself) were from Kutë Rayang. The Lord and several other men began to construct a raft from two sturdy banana stalks and assorted branches. Packages of rice and vegetables were piled on top, along with several assemblages of four rice piles and four flat apam cakes. The Lord arranged the foodstuffs so that the raft would remain in balance, and then added sheaves of rice plants that had been eaten by pests, one sheaf collected from each village imëm. No one from Robel had yet appeared, and the chickens, held by boys, nearly escaped several times. Finally a Robel man arrived with the village egg and the men moved the raft onto the river.

Kneeling next to the river, the Lord picked up the chickens and spoke softly for several minutes. With one sure motion, he then placed the chickens on the raft and pushed it away from the shore. The chickens began to peck contentedly at the rice while the raft drifted into the center of the stream and, buffeted by the swift current, immediately began to fall apart. After the raft had drifted for about thirty feet the chickens flew off and regained the shore. The boys, who had been warned against catching the chickens before we had all left the stream, nonetheless caught them and carried them off.

Piqued by this infraction, Abang Irmas quickly turned and started up the hill toward the house where the ritual meal was to be held. The rest of us followed at a slower pace. The divination described previously followed, after which the Lord, speaking through Abang Das, expressed his displeasure at the poor turnout, the boys' capture of the chickens (which threatened to bring the crop pests back to the community), and the failure of some farmers to observe a prohibition on entering the fields on the day before the ritual. These infractions, along with the disappointing outcome of his divination, meant that he would have to hold a ritual meal of glutinous rice to which each village would need to contribute.

Just before releasing the raft, Abang Irmas had uttered a request to the ruler who commands the pests and who inhabits the water:

Ini lo si selo ni	On this particular day,
bilangan si jeroh	a good date,
ketikë si bisé	a propitious time,
Aku menulak	I push back.
Beras padi tungkët imën	Rice grains and plants, the staff of faith.
Enti né delé si rusak	Let there not be much more damaged,
enti né delé si binasa	let there not be much more destroyed.
Ini ningko	This is for you:
si bernyawa kuosah opat	of things with souls, I offer four.
Rëjë si ku ukën ku toa	Ruler who goes upstream and downstream,
sawahën kirimën	pass on that which is sent
ku rëjë i pusët lot	to the ruler at the center of the seas.

After the initial, formulaic beginning, Abang Irmas declares his intention to repel the pests that have been damaging the crops. The phrase *beras padi tungkët imën* links rice (and, more generally, all foodstuffs) to faith (and, more generally, to all immaterial things).[4] As Abang Irmas later explained to me, the material offerings sent to the spirit ruler are given in expectation that the ruler will command the pests to desist from their damaging activity. He offers the four chickens and asks that there be no more damage done to the crops. The spirit who travels in the streams (ruler of the streams) is asked to carry the offering to the ruler of the pests, to be found at the "center of the seas." The four piles of rice on the raft are the ideal vehicle for the message, because they correspond to the four natural elements (earth, water, wind, and fire) that constitute humans and the spirit ruler alike. They bridge the differences between senders and receiver. "He will then order the pests to stay away from the fields," Abang Irmas assured me, "and they usually do stay away after this." Of course, he added, the chickens fly off the raft, but we may not catch them. Only if they return to the villages of their own accord may we capture and eat them.

Although the ritual has been performed continuously within living memory, the form of the tulak bëlë has varied over the years. In the 1930s, according to Rëjë Hasyim, before the Lord sent offerings downstream, each village took its own protective steps. At the Lord's direction, a village imëm might set up four trays, each made from a bamboo thrust into the ground, with its top split and the ends flared out, on which an offering (*sejeni*) would be placed. Or the imëm would bury apam cakes for the pests to eat instead of the crops. These practices were gradually abandoned at the urging of modernist religious leaders, for whom the offering of food to spirits is probably the most reprehensible of the many village practices that they denounce.

By the late 1980s the assurance with which Abang Irmas and others carried out rice ritual had been dampened by economic, social, and religious changes. In 1987 and 1988, most Isak farmers were lured away from their fields by two new economic opportunities: coffee planting in the hills and wage labor on the road that ran through Isak. Many quickly tired of the strenuous labor on the road and the difficulties of keeping coffee gardens going in the hills while children attended school in Isak, however, and in late 1988 many Isak residents returned to full-time residence in the community and resumed planting rice. Some of the returnees chose the short-term varieties of rice that had just been introduced. Cash poor, they needed a harvest as quickly as possible, and these varieties reached maturity in four

---

[4] One pronounces the same phrase when offering rice to a teacher as a token for the knowledge that one expects to receive, or when speaking directly to the rice plants or harvested rice grains.

rather than seven months. But, for whatever reasons (probably insufficient water and fertilizer), the yields were poor and the taste of the rice unsatisfactory. Most of these farmers thus returned to a traditional variety in 1989.

But the lack of coordination of planting over the previous two years left Abang Irmas virtually devoid of authority. People planted whenever they wanted to. In 1989 he held the tulak bëlë in his house rather than by the water's edge. The village imëms gathered at his house with mungkurs, eggs, and chickens, and he prepared their healing leaves for them, but then he and two other men carried the raft downstream and quietly let it go. Abang Irmas himself said that he did this because he would have felt odd holding the ritual in public when some people were still planting and weeding. But a contributing factor surely was the mounting criticism of the ritual from local religious figures. Critics included Tengku Asaluddin, a close relative of the Lord and a man he respected highly for his learning. Abang Irmas indeed had become more active in religious affairs during the 1980s, abandoning his former didong singing to teach Qur'ānic recitation to children and recite prayers at funeral rituals. Most likely, finding himself with few followers and more vocal critics, he attempted to reduce the visibility of his role as Lord of the Fields by shifting the scene of the tulak bëlë to his own house.

It was in this same year, 1988–1989, that Abang Irmas turned over the office of Lord to his father's brother's son, Lukman. Lukman took up the practice with the assurance that planting could once again be coordinated. But he wanted more than that: a sign that the farmers of Isak were maintaining—or reasserting after a two-year hiatus—their time-honored practices. As noted earlier, he had vowed to return to the site of the Ancestor Merah Mëgë, although he had not yet mustered sufficient support to make good on his promise. He had also declared that he would hold the tulak bëlë ritual as in previous years, in the open and downstream from the fields. The pests needed to be told to leave the crops at a point downstream from all the fields, he explained to me. Otherwise "the pests just stick to the fields as you walk through them to the river."

Lukman's stance shows that religious change does not follow a single, irreversible course. In this instance, Isak farmers have counterasserted, however tentatively, their own "ritual technology" (Lansing 1991) in the face of both modernist objections and new rice varieties ill suited to local conditions.

ANCESTORS AND OTHER SACRED BEINGS

Farming communities in the Isak valley are usually defined around a common source of water. The larger communities also define themselves through their common appeals to the spirit of an early resident in the community who is considered to have special powers: an Ancestor. The network of such Ancestors gives a sacred character to the topography of the Isak valley. In this way ritual technology intersects local religious history.

I have identified thirteen Ancestor worship sites at which appeals are made for the success of the crops, either through a ritual specialist or by individual farmers. This list is not fixed: there are additional Ancestor sites that could become centers for rice ritual if the surrounding areas were made suitable for farming. Moving from west to east, the sites are as shown in the accompanying table:

Place	Name of Ancestor	Source of Appeals
Gading	Teungku Saléh Ibrahim	individuals
Perëgën	Datu Paya Jami	individuals
Pepunu	Datu Gegarang	specialist
Isak	Datu Merah Mëgë	specialist
Kemulo	Datu Béwang	specialist
Atu Kul	Datu Pemung	individuals
Tiro	Datu/Tengku Tiro	individuals
Uning/Panton Nangka	Datu Tinyu Langit	specialist
Géwat/Tenamak	Datu/Tengku Perau	individuals
Penarun	Muyang Bunin	specialist
Gerpa/Serulë	Muyang Gerpa	specialist
Lumut/Lané	Datu Gergung	individuals?
Lingë	Datu Suling	individuals?

Table 8.1 *Worship Sites Used in Agriculture, Isak Valley, 1980s.*

Some of these sites are connected to each other by means of narratives about powerful Ancestors. The narratives often concern several such Ancestors: Penarun residents, for example, tell of the days when the valley was ruled by Datu Gergung, Muyang Bunin, Muyang Gerpa, and Datu Merah Mëgë. Muyangs Bunin and Gerpa are often said to have come together from Mecca or Baghdad, or simply "from overseas." The founding of the Serbëjadi region to the east is sometimes ascribed to Muyang Bunin. The use of *Muyang* (in everyday use, great-great-grandparent) for these two Ancestors implies that they arrived in the valley before Ancestors known as *Datu* (in everyday use, great-grandparent) or merely *Tengku*, a title used for someone learned in religious matters.

Of the two Muyangs, Muyang Gerpa is generally admitted to be the oldest. Aman Jukri claimed that all the Ancestors represented by these sites descended from Muyang Gerpa. Gayo from throughout the valley identify Muyang Gerpa as Syech Abdul Qadir Jilani ('Abdul Qādir al-Jīlī or Jīlānī [1077–1166]) and (as we saw in Chapter 5) assign him a role in the coming of Islam to Aceh. He is credited with bringing Islam to the Gayo highlands after having subdued the heretical Syech Shamsuddin. He used a special rope in his efforts to circumcise the men of the valley. This rope would fly through the air on its own and tie up the candidate, readying him for circumcision.

Muyang Gerpa is said to have died at Gerpa, downstream from Isak, but, as in the case of Datu Béwang, to have risen again from the grave just after burial. He arose and died twelve times in all. His descendants in the eldest male line are known as Tengku Guru, an honorific that combines religious status with healing power. They once were renowned throughout the valley for their curing abilities. These stories link the spiritual power available at Isak valley sites to a more widely recognized set of religious figures, adding Islamic legitimacy to the rituals of healing and agriculture.

Each of these Ancestors is credited with particular spiritual powers. Datu Béwang, the Ancestor to which Aman Jukri appealed, aids hunters as well as farmers, and hunters will often make offerings to him in their search for deer. On occasion this Ancestor appears to Aman Jukri in his dreams to offer solutions to problems, usually in the form of "a large man, very white-skinned, with a reddish beard" (he was intrigued by my own fit to this description). The Ancestor also keeps a tiger, whom he sends to protect people or to deliver warnings to people who fail to keep their promises to him.

While all of the above Ancestors exercise control over the farmland surrounding their sites, some are also the ancestors of current local ritual specialists. In such cases ordinary people must take their requests to the descendant as an intermediary. Such is the case with Muyang Gerpa (descendant: Tengku Guru), Muyang Bunin (descendant: Pengulu Benu), Datu Gegarang (descendant: Healer to the Four), and Datu Merah Mëgë (descendant: the Isak Lord of the Fields). The recent death at an early age of one Isak man is generally attributed to his failure to conform to this requirement. This man had served as the Lord for a group of farmers who cleared land for coffee gardens near Pepunu, in Datu Gegarang's domain. Although the Lord made his offerings and requests directly to the Ancestor in the correct fashion, he did not consult the Ancestor's descendant, the Healer to the Four. His death was attributed not to the Healer, but to retribution from the Ancestor.

Isak residents interpret spiritual power within the double framework of local social organization and the topography of farming and hunting. On the one hand, sites for appeals to spirits serve as points of connection between the spirits of the dead and particular social categories of the living. On the other hand, the range of power possessed by spirits depends on their location in an environment defined by their productive activities.

The powerful Ancestors are part of a dense network of sacred beings who inhabit the Isak valley. Isak people sometimes include these Ancestors in the general category of powerful spirits that they refer to as aulië, *kramat*, or Muslim jin (jin Islam). The different terms reflect different, practically motivated ways of situating spiritual power in a particular place. *Aulië* derives from Arabic *aulia*, the plural of *wali*, a term that refers to a close relationship of care or responsibility, either between persons (a guardian or benefactor) or between God and those beings close to him. The latter relationship is usually rendered as "friends of God," and has its locus classicus in the Qur'an (10:63–65):

> Surely God's friends [*aulia Allah*]—no fear shall
> be on them, neither shall they sorrow.
> Those who believe, and are Godfearing—
> for them are good tidings in the present life
> and in the world to come.
> There is no changing the words of God;
> that is the mighty triumph.

Gayo have assigned distinct meanings to the Arabic singular and plural forms of the term *wali*.[5] Gayo use *wali* primarily to refer to the status of legal guardian, although it can also convey a sense of spiritual legitimacy in the phrase *kramat wali*: "power due to a good spirit rather than a malicious one." Isak residents sometimes use *aulië* to speak of the spirits of deceased humans, and *kramat* to refer to the power associated with a grave or worship site (cf. Skeat 1967:673–74; Snouck Hurgronje 1906, I:165, II:300–301).

The quality of spirituality attributed to these beings is associated with physical lightness, as a maximum of inner qualities and a minimum of outer ones. Inanimate objects can also be high in inner qualities and thus can help someone attain the condition of aulië. Thus if a person wishes to become nearer to God he will eat only puffed rice, a very lightweight food. If he is persistent he will be able to fly through the air with great speed. Isak residents reported how Tengku Ubit, a renowned religious teacher, now deceased, worshiped on Fridays first at Mecca and then immediately afterward in Isak. He and others like him were described as aulië.

As late as 1980 Isak people referred to one living man as aulië: Ilyas Leubé, who had led the Gayo division in the Darul Islam movement and had returned to armed struggle in the 1970s as part of the much smaller Free Aceh movement. Leubé was killed along with others in his band in the early 1980s. After his final disappearance into the hills, Gayo began to recount his ability to disappear just when he was about to be captured and to reappear in a far-removed place. Leubé carried out his struggle in the name of Islam, and his powers were said to result from the intensity of his religious commitment (*leubé* means "religious teacher" in Acehnese).

---

[5] This practice allows Gayo to make more precise distinctions among the several possible meanings of the lexical item. The practice was encountered earlier with the pair *ruh* and *arwah*.

Isak people of differing religious orientations give various descriptions of these aulië beings. Most villagers consider all aulië to be available to help with everyday practical problems, as are powerful Ancestors. The modernist-leaning minority, however, consider the aulië a distinct and exemplary community of worshiping beings who serve as models to whom ordinary humans should aspire. The following description of an aulië community by Tengku Daud (the Isak Qali [<Ar. qādī], supervisor of marriage and divorce) came in the course of a broader discussion of Muslim jin and contained both a religious and a political message:

> There are good and bad jin. The Muslim jin are people who have been taken away [from ordinary life] because they were very pious. They did not die, but became aulië, which is to say Muslim jin. They have a village at Bur Gegarang [several kilometers into the forest], and their mosque is at Kala Mpan. They have bodies just as we do, but we cannot see them unless they take us there [to Kala Mpan] themselves. Tengku Ubit was taken to their mosque once by one of them and saw it, even prayed there. But he died a natural death and did not become one of them. They speak Acehnese there, even if they did not know it beforehand and even if they were Gayo. It isn't hard to learn it.
>
> People say that Sapi'i [a man who lived in Kramil village] who the local police tried to kill during the Gestapu massacres [in late 1965] became a Muslim jin. They could not kill him. He was a good man. They are good; they worship and cultivate rice just like us, but don't talk much. They could not be bad [another villager had said to me that they were]; they are even mentioned in the final part of the recitations for worship [salāt], where you say *salihin* [Ar. sālih, pious].

In characterizing the aulië as a parallel community of humans, distinguished only by their spiritual nature and their exemplary Islamic behavior, the speaker moved freely among the terms *aulië*, *jin Islam*, and *salihin*. (I often heard these three terms used in a nearly interchangeable way in Isak to refer to a spiritual quality rather than a typology of beings.) Tengku Daud depicted the aulië as human in form and habit but superior in quality. They grow rice, live in a village, pray in a mosque, and, by contrast to chatty Isak villagers, "don't talk much." When they do speak, they use Acehnese, the language in which Gayo pursued higher religious education in the precolonial period. From this perspective, aulië exemplify how Gayo ought to be. But they do so anonymously, in contrast to the individualized exemplars who make up the Javanese pantheon of wali (Geertz 1968).

The aulië do, however, include among their number some recognized individuals. Tengku Daud (and others) mentioned Sapi'i, one of four Isak residents killed in the massacres of late 1965. In local accounts he was shot by the police but survived and fled. After some time, tiring of the pursuit, he gave himself up to be killed. Although some thought that he was an aulië, he was not an outstanding individual before his death: he was not distinguished by his learning, personal qualities, or powerful deeds. Talk about his holiness focused on his ability to resist the police; such talk itself is a relatively safe way to express the feelings of loss and rage at the killings, events that cannot be contested publicly without fear of state reprisals (Bowen 1991:119–22).

Others in Isak emphasized the power held by the aulië to intervene in people's lives. Abang Das told of the origin of the aulië in a way that played up the assistance they gave to hunters (he himself is an avid hunter):

> When God created the world he sent down seven aulië. They brought three dogs with them, called Kitmir, Sijeni, and Kumang. That made four with Doloh [a dog that God had sent to earth with Adam's soul and that guarded Adam's body from Satan]. The seven aulië became the beings who inhabit the mountains; each mountain has its own aulië and every expert hunter works with one. To have dogs you must have aulië, since they came down together, and dogs are necessary to protect men. "You work the fields and I'll guard them" said the dog [to Adam]. These aulië are like angels with the shape of humans, but they usually have a veil [ijëb; <Ar. hijāb] so that we cannot see them. If we call them to us, we are their elder brother; if we go to the hills, we are the younger brother.[6]

Abang Das here portrays aulië as mediators between humans and the environment. They control the hills and the fields around the areas of human habitation. In the hills they are in their own territory, and a hunter who ventures there (sometimes with hunting dogs) must supplicate the aulië of that hill for help. When he hunts, Abang Das makes appeals to two specific spirits. Tengku Malim Putih (the "white learned one") controls the hills to the north of the Isak river, and Tengku Malim Itëm (the "black learned one") the hills to the south. The night before our conversation Abang Das had gone hunting in the hills and, although he had left a sirih roll (selensung) for Tengku Malim Itëm, had returned empty-handed. "He is very stingy with his deer," Abang Das complained; "people usually don't even bother to seek deer in his domain."

The distinction between lowlands Ancestors and uplands Muslim jin spiritually demarcates the boundary between the realm of humans (hak Edëm)—the cultivated or settled lowlands—and the realm of God (hak Allah)—the forested hills. People invoke this boundary when expelling pests from their lowland rice-fields. Pests, they say, should retreat beyond

---

[6] The story probably was influenced by the tale of the *ashab al-kahf* (people of the cave) in the Qur'ān (Wensinck 1953a) (the Seven Sleepers of Ephesus in Christian traditions); on the Acehnese version, see Damsté (1939). Abang Das's references to elder and younger brothers links his story to that of the Old Hunter to be considered in Chapter 9.

the limits of human lands to the hills and forests where they may do as they wish. Hunters, venturing into the realm of God, must humbly seek help from its rulers.

Because of this distinction, the ritual side of uplands farming is quite different from that appropriate to the lowlands. In the lowlands, the crucial point for ritual intervention is when pests have begun to damage the crops. It is here that the Lord of the Fields' abilities are tested. The Lord (and the individual farmers) do communicate with diverse spirits at other stages in the farming process, of course: the Lord appeals to the Ancestor at the season's beginning, and farmers speak calmingly to the rice plant at planting and again at harvest. But these other events are relatively unproblematic.

In uplands farming, by contrast, it is clearing and planting that are most critical. Clearing a field constitutes an invasion of territory that is not part of the "realm of humans." When Isak farmers make a clearing in the forest to plant rice, they must direct their pleas for assistance to the spirits who control the realm of God. These are the spirits who "control/own this place" (mpun tempat), a category that includes the spirits to which Abang Kerna appealed in his exorcism: the four lords of the elements (sidang opat) and the Four Syechs who are each associated with one of the cardinal directions. The category also includes Tengku Malim Putih and Tengku Malim Itëm, the Muslim jin who rule over the hills and to whom hunters must deliver their requests. Part of the ritual that is held before planting the uplands garden involves making the claim that the cleared area is now converted to the status of human control, "Adam's right." The activities of the uplands Lord of the Fields (as he is called there, too) thus emphasize the maintaining of boundaries that accompanies all agricultural activities.

The ritual activity accompanying rice production thus makes salient two sets of social relations: those between the human and spirit worlds, and those among humans. Ritual highlights the linkages and the demarcations between human actors in their own domain and the spirits that control the natural world. As is the case in healing the sick, protecting and repairing the rice crop involves recognizing one's connections to external entities. Spirits will listen to, and sometimes act on, human requests because of their shared substance (signified by the four piles of rice) and because of the offerings and pleas that reach them. Humans can reassert their superior claim to their rice fields by demanding that harmful spirits and pests remain on the other side of the boundary between the lowlands and the uplands.

Collective rice rituals also represent the ideal shape of the community: distinct villages, led by rulers who possess proper tuah and the right lineage, sharing material interests and ritual activity. By momentarily highlighting the ancient relations among village headmen (the Clever Chief, the Pengulu Gading, and so forth) the rituals project an image of social order that corresponds to the desired order of the natural world. This image does not "mystify" those who participate, as Bloch (1986) has claimed for royal rituals on Madagascar. People regret the loss of the older order, and contrast the disorderly and harmful behavior of the current generation of leaders. Rice rituals also illustrate the generalized and direct effects of proper and improper conduct on the rice crop—a discourse in which the aulië figure as both exemplars and actors. The Lord of the Fields and those who interpret his divinations and recall past disasters thereby remind residents of the importance of a moral code for human welfare. Rituals also provide a mechanism for repairing damage.

But ritual technology is far from static. Changes in social, economic, and religious ideas are felt, and to some extent shaped, through the form of rice ritual. Lords have been able to compartmentalize the different stages of rice rituals, removing controversial aspects (such as calling on the Ancestor) to the social background and highlighting those that are less controversial (such as saying prayers at ritual meals). The private appeals, prayers, and spells to spirits retain their instrumental character, which is highly objectionable for modernists but which, kept behind closed doors, they can ignore. The public discourse of ritual meals, by contrast, has taken on an increasingly generic quality, with its Muslim prayers, orders to begin planting, and intermittent use of Indonesian. Rice ritual enters into the public sphere of the 1990s as either religious expression or technical coordination, but it continues in an offstage fashion as a means of speaking to important spiritual agents.

The two relational axes represented in the rituals—human-nonhuman relations, and divisions within the community—are very much connected in the minds of Isak farmers. In 1989, the Kemulo Lord, Aman Jukri, recalled how coffee farms had lured away many farmers in the mid-1980s. Those who remained in Kemulo were people with ties to Kutë Rayang village who had farmed in the area for generations. For about two years they felt united as never before. They built one large fence, not between their plots, but around the perimeter of their collective area: a fence that no longer divided families, but united them against the territory that had reverted to "God's right" and the pests that resided there. In those years, and only those years, no pests came. The direct relation of human social unity to a strong defense against damaging forces was here, momentarily, given a clear spatial image.

Chapter Nine

ADAM AND EVE'S CHILDREN

WHEN I FIRST approached Aman Jukri, the Lord of the Fields at Kemulo, and asked to learn about his art, he responded by telling me a long story. The story explained how Adam, Eve, and their son-in-law, the prophet Muhammad, discovered rice. At the command of an angel, Muhammad sacrificed his own daughter, received the first rice grains from her body, and learned, step by step, how to raise and care for the crop. God designed the rituals accompanying rice cultivation, the spells pronounced by the Lord of the Fields, and the characteristics of rice itself.

Just as Gayo healers see themselves as continuing the centuries-old battle of Syech Abdurra'uf with Syech Shamsuddin, the Lords of the Fields consider themselves to be following a ritual pattern established early in Islamic history. Ordinary farmers also tell stories about Adam, Eve, and their children to explain how rice grows and nourishes and how humans hunt game and came to possess chickens, buffalo, and other items of productive wealth. In addition, these stories address the problem of incest, and they describe the origins of the Old Hunter. The characters in these narratives generate wealth and power by creating new distinctions in the world, just as God first generated the world by creating the distinction between inner and outer reality. In telling these stories Gayo combine elements from Islamic and Indonesian traditions to produce an interlinked set of narratives of considerable explanatory power.

THE ORIGINS OF RICE

Aman Jukri's narrative is hardly typical of those told in Isak—it is long, and it is the only one I have heard that makes the prophet Muhammad the main actor. In the story Muhammad plays the very role of a ritual specialist: carrying out ritual, asking God for guidance, leading others in each step of cultivation:

AMAN JUKRI ON THE ORIGINS OF RICE

The prophet Adam and Eve had a child, Tuan Fatima. They lived on leaves from trees and rarely had enough to eat. Tuan Fatima wanted to marry the prophet Muhammad. She talked with him but without touching him, without intercourse—there was a barrier between them; he had seen her but not yet married her. But merely from that contact there was a spark between them, and she became pregnant by him without intercourse. She had a daughter, Maimunah.

God sent word to Muhammad by way of an angel that he should cut the child's throat, cut her up into little pieces (as you would a jackfruit—but you needn't write that down), and scatter the pieces into the field. The pieces became rice seeds, and grew to become rice plants.

Adam asked Fatima where her daughter was. She answered that she did not know. Adam replied that Muhammad was the father of the child and that he had scattered the child into the field. Eve said that Fatima must have slept with Muhammad and must marry him. Fatima swore that she had not, that they had only spoken, with a barrier between them. Then Jibra'il, Mika'il, Abu Bakr, Uthman, 'Ali, and Shi'a all came down from the sky and married the two (Shi'ah sits to the immediate left of God). Muhammad did not refuse.

Muhammad then took Fatima into the field and showed her the rice and Fatima called out her child's name. Maimunah then answered, saying: "Don't look for me anymore, mother; I have become your means of life."

As the story continues, God teaches Muhammad how to harvest, thresh, and cook the rice, and how to perform rituals for healing the crops and exorcising the pests. These are the first such rituals ever held, and Jibra'il scrutinizes Muhammad's preparations to ensure they are correct. When at a loss as to how to proceed, Muhammad performs two rak'a of worship and then asks for divine guidance, just as does the Lord of the Fields. The narrative thereby gives God's sanction to the specific form taken by Isak rice rituals.

The story also highlights the importance of ritual as communication between humans and spirits, and thus the general role of the Lord of the Fields as ritual intermediary between the rice crop and God. When rats begin to devour the rice in the granary, for example, God explains to Muhammad that the rats are orphans, that he loves them, and that, therefore, they may not simply be killed. At this point Aman Jukri stopped to draw out the practical implications of the story, as he did at several times in the narration. All pests come from a set of orphaned siblings, he explained, and thus you may not poison them. "If you poison a rat, one hundred will come out of the forest for each one killed." In the story, God sends Muhammad a "Qur'ānic verse" with which to ask the rats to leave. Aman Jukri recited it for me; it turned out to be an Acehnese-language spell—Qur'ānic, explained Aman Jukri, because it begins with the basmala, as does each chapter of the Qur'ān. You recite it, he added, while circling the granary or the fields and telling the rats that "here is the realm of humans; the hills are your realm, the realm of God."

Aman Jukri's narrative strongly emphasizes the provenance of ritual knowledge from God and Muhammad, and he frequently referred to that provenance in commenting on the religious propriety of his duties. It and similar stories told in Isak place rice growing in an Islamic exegetical tradition and in a local, practical context. The stories lend the authority of recognizably Islamic figures, ideas, and traditions to local rice ritual forms.

Yet the story would hardly please Isak modernists. In the narrative Muhammad kills the fruit of an illicit union, and only later is married to his daughter's mother. The nature of the union between Muhammad and Fatima implies that Fatima gave birth to her child as a virgin. Here the narrative incorporates a Shi'ite Muslim idea regarding the historical Muhammad's daughter, Fatima.[1] This Fatima had two sons by 'Ali, one of whom, Husayn, was killed on the battlefield of Karbala and became the central martyr figure for Shi'ism. According to some Shi'ites, Fatima bore Husayn as a virgin (Momen 1985:235–36), accentuating his patrilineal kin-relatedness to Muhammad and also the general value of patriliny in Islam (Combs-Schilling 1989:90–91).

But the Gayo narrative replaces a male with a female sacrificial victim. It is Fatima's *daughter*, Maimunah, who is sacrificed and who becomes a source of life for her parents. This series of events fits well with the general Indonesian idea that fertility came from a divine female figure through sacrifice (de Josselin de Jong 1965). Aman Jukri's story links this sacrifice to an improper marriage, and this connection, too, is found elsewhere in the archipelago. A story from Sunda (West Java) presents rice as first appearing from the eyes of the corpse of Sangyang Sri, a female deity who was born from an egg but nourished by the wife of the god Batara Guru. She was killed by other gods in order to prevent Batara Guru from committing incest with her (Sukanda-Tessier 1977:74). In a story from eastern Java (Geertz 1960:81) Batara Guru kills his daughter to prevent her from marrying a human. In western Sumba a father kills his daughter rather than give her in marriage (Hoskins 1989:434), or she is the odd one out in a group of intermarrying brothers and sisters, marries improperly (to a rat), and is killed by him (ibid.).[2] (I develop the link between sacrifice and marriage below.)

In Aman Jukri's narrative all events have a divine template; they come from the interaction between God and Muhammad at the beginning of human history. But this template is also culturally a Gayo (and a more

---

[1] This instance is one of many where Shi'ite ideas have been adopted into the otherwise Sunni context of Gayo Islam (note the figure of "Shi'ah" in the narrative, whose identity is unclear).

[2] In a South Sulawesi version (Anwarmufied 1981:31–33), Batara Guru's daughter simply dies. The rice-origins story told in lowlands Aceh is similar to that of the Gayo highlands (van Waardenburg 1979:89–131).

broadly Indonesian) one. It traces the power to nourish to a sacrificed daughter, with whom humans continue to speak generation after generation.

The late Inën Saidmerah was a farmer and healer in Kutë Kramil village. She was careful to speak properly to the rice plants all through the cultivation season. Her account of the origin of rice emphasizes the importance of such communication:

> Adam and Eve had seven daughters; the youngest was called Insën Tinggi [Superior Human]. Her parents had prepared land for cultivation but had nothing to sow, so they asked their daughters which of them was willing to give herself as a means of life. Insën Tinggi answered right away that she would do so. Then three others answered with one voice and said they also would give themselves for their parents; these girls were Mahmani, Reseki, and Surbani. These four names are the ones that we always use in talking to the rice. Two other daughters, Selamah and Maimunah, said nothing, and we can mention their names but do not have to. The seventh and eldest, Kadija, said she would rather become the shadow that eats the rice [kemang] and she did so. You may not say her name, or the kemang will eat the rice so that it becomes white and empty of fruit. The rice was called "Insën Tinggi" because she was from the first human, Adam. Her blood became glutinous rice, with the name Pulut, and her body became normal rice, with the name Kepal.

In this story the sacrificed girls are daughters of Adam and Eve rather than granddaughters, as in Aman Jukri's account. In many Isak versions of the story it is three, four, or seven daughters who are sacrificed, or sometimes a single daughter with seven names. The several daughters, or (as in the above story) the distinct parts of one daughter's body, give rise to the different kinds of rice. Three entities are of special importance in these narratives: ordinary rice, glutinous rice (considered less nourishing), and a rice pest (usually a rat or a grain-eating spirit).

To highlight these distinctions among rice elements, narrators draw on the names of the prominent women in the life of the prophet Muhammad. Ordinary rice is usually called Maimunah or A'isa, whereas Kadija designates either the pest or glutinous rice. Khadija and 'A'isha are the two wives of the prophet Muhammad most often remembered by Muslims. Khadija was his first wife and the mother of Fatima; both Khadija and Fatima are revered in mainstream Muslim thinking as "obedient and reserved wife and mother" (Combs-Schilling 1989:88). 'A'isha, much younger than Muhammad, was his favorite wife and was politically active after his death. She appears in most Muslim narratives as "dynamic, forceful, and childless" (ibid.). The distinctions encoded by use of their names do not correspond to the content of their usual representations in the Muslim (including Gayo) world: revered Khadija becomes the rice-eating pest, for example. Rather, their names provide a code for differentiating among substances, a code that underscores the Islamic quality of the narrative and draws on the salience of a particular contrast in Islamic history.

The powers of rice to hear human speech and to nourish are important in Isak. Everyone in Isak eats rice, and nearly everyone grows it.[3] Men and women work together to plant the rice crop, to ensure that the rice grains multiply on the stalk, and to see that they nourish their human consumers once they are harvested.

Both the productivity and the nourishment of rice comes from its inner productive power, its berkat, which derives from the sacrifice performed by Adam and Eve (or by their children). This sacrifice transformed a human vital force (semangat) into the nourishing power (also semangat) of the rice. When humans ingest rice they are nourished because rice is originally of human substance, yet it is distinct from humans by virtue of the act of sacrifice.

Crop yields and rice's nourishing power are of constant concern to Isak residents. Yields vary widely from year to year, and even a decent yield may be exhausted before the year is up. When rice stores are used up, men and women are forced to take on such low-paying tasks as working on a road crew, cutting lumber, or tapping the sugar-palm. Unusually high demands on the household granary can also bring disaster. Thus some men and especially women wield spells intended to increase the power of rice to fill the stomach and thus reduce consumption.

Isak farmers can speak to the rice plants when sowing, planting, harvesting, threshing, or storing. The period from planting to harvesting the rice is one of uninterrupted growth for the rice plants, and little direct intervention by the farmer is needed. Farmers are careful to obtain some healing leaves and water from the Lord of the Fields after the opening ritual of the rice season, and to place the leaves at the point where water runs into their fields so that it will carry the protective essence to the crop.

Some farmers speak to the rice when they sow their seedbeds. Aman Asil feels that by sowing he is repeating the action of Adam when he scattered his daughters' remains into his fields. "You have to remember the origins of rice." He would say the following words to himself as he scattered the first handful of seed:

---

[3] In one of the five villages of Isak, Kutë Kramil, fifty of fifty-five households in 1979 cultivated irrigated riceland; the remaining households either rented out riceland they owned, or were dependents of other, rice-growing households. During the late 1980s about one-third of these households moved to a newly cleared coffee-garden site. Some of these households rented out their Isak riceland, some continued to farm it, and others abandoned the gardens and, by 1989, returned to Isak to take up rice farming once more.

A'isa, Kadija, Maimunah, Selamah. Water, earth, fire, wind. Water returns to water, earth returns to earth, fire returns to fire, wind returns to wind. This is the legacy of the prophet Adam.

As the rice grows, its vital force grows in strength. "You can feel their vital force if you walk through a field of mature rice plants," said Abang Kerna; "that is why no one is afraid to travel to the end of Isak at night right now, when the fields are full."

When the nourishing power of the rice has matured, it is ready for harvest. Here the farmer must ensure that the rice's power survives the physical cutting of the rice stalk. Inën Saidmerah and some older Isak women and men planted the first seven stalks of rice around a stake made from the *beringin* fig tree (*Ficus benjamina*, Linn.). The beringin comes from 'Ali (the prophet Muhammad's son-in-law), she explained, and protects these stalks with his power. Ideally, leaves from the beringin tree should be placed in the granary (*kebën*) as well.

The rice planted around the stake was the last to be harvested in Inën Saidmerah's fields. These stalks provide continuity of nourishing power over the generations that have passed from Adam and Eve's daughter to Noah and the flood, and down to the current crop, she explained. She said to the seven stalks: "This is what has come down from the prophet Noah; this is my inheritance that has no breaks." Then she harvested the stalks and took them right to the threshing shed. There she summoned their vital force, using the same spell used to call back the semangat of a child, but substituting the names of the rice.[4] "The rice can understand what we say because it is of one origin with us," commented Aman Asil. These seven stalks then called the semangat of the rest of the rice. The rice was allowed to rest for several days before threshing. "It has to sleep first, lest it be afraid when it is threshed," said Aman Asil. "It is the semangat of the rice that gives us berkat, and the semangat will be weak if the rice is afraid."

A second risky moment arrives when the farmer moves the threshed rice into the granary. The semangat of all the rice must once again be called, to ensure that it moves with the rest of the rice, and the newly harvested rice must be "married" to rice from the previous year to ensure the continuity of its power. Inën Saidmerah took the new rice in her left hand and let some of it fall into her right, where she held some of the previous year's rice. Aman Asil commented on the marrying:

> Because the old rice has semangat, the old and new have to be married so that eating the new rice will have nourishing power [berkat]. People who do not

---

[4] One can also call the vital force of one's neighbor's rice so that it leaves his or her crop and augments the yield of one's own. Some people were said to have done that but to have suffered poor levels of berkat themselves as a retribution from God.

have a granary have to get a lot of rice because their rice has no semangat and thus no nourishing power, no sacred power [kramat]. Nourishing power exists because the origins of rice are the same as our own, from the prophet Adam, because he sacrificed his daughters to be our means of life.

Farmers who otherwise use few spells for their crops often do take care to marry the old and new rice in this way. The notion of a continuity of power takes account of a simple fact of self-sustaining agriculture: that, as Abang Kerna put it, "it is from last year's seeds that this year's crop grows." The practice of marrying the rice gives to that fact a historical and spiritual side: that the inner power of the rice, born with the death of Adam and Eve's daughters, is handed down from generation to generation of rice without interruption.

At the same time that she worked to maintain the continuity of rice's power, Inën Saidmerah was careful to keep the spirit Kadija from devouring the rice. "She is our shadow and follows us where we go," she explained. When threshing or moving the rice she hung a piece of cloth far away from the rice, so that Kadija would stay with the cloth to be its shadow and thus not reach the rice.

Whereas the rice plants and the harvested rice grains (both called *rom*) are spoken to as sentient beings, milled rice (*oros*) is a foodstuff, ready to be made into cooked rice (*kro*). Aman Asil explained that he could not call the milled rice by the personal names used for unmilled rice: "If I did it would lose its berkat; it would give no nourishment when cooked." Instead, one addresses it with a phrase we have already encountered: *beras padi tungkët imën* (milled rice, rice plants; the staff of faith).[5]

The phrase is both the name of milled rice and a description of its nature. Cooked rice is given or eaten in return for knowledge and faith, and its growth depends on the possession of knowledge and faith, including the expert knowledge of the Lord of the Fields. The moment of milling is the moment of conversion from one state of berkat, that of the growing power of the rice, to another, that of its capacity to nourish those who will eat it. One can increase this nourishing power through spells; one can also "tie up" the hunger of guests so that little rice is eaten. Cooked rice can be offered at ritual meals to ancestors, angels, and prophets. Its nourishing power, its berkat, can be enjoyed in a worldly way and can also, as an inner quality of the food, be transmitted to spirits.

Uncooked (milled) rice, however, is offered only to spirits that reside outside the community. Specifically, four piles of uncooked rice, each dyed a separate color (white, black, red, and yellow) and corresponding to the four

---

[5] Malay *beras* – Gayo *oros*, milled rice; Malay *padi* – Gayo *rom*, rice plants, unmilled rice. The phrase *tungkët imën* in Gayo means "the staff of faith." Gayo often use Malay in maxims of special importance, thereby setting them off from everyday speech (Bowen 1991:159).

elements of the world (respectively: water, wind, fire, earth), are used to communicate with spirits that control the nonhuman world, the realm of God. Offered by humans, the colors signify not just the natural elements, but the natural elements that connect humans and spirits, facilitating communication between them. At the ritual that initiates the cultivation season in Isak, the Lord of the Fields places the four rice piles on the ground when speaking to the "spirits that own this place" (*si mpun tempat*). When expelling pests at the exorcism ritual, he places four rice piles on the raft along with the chickens to take his message to the ruler at the center of the sea. When initiating an infant into the world on the seventh day after birth, the officiant sends four rice piles downstream on a banana leaf (as did Abang Kerna in the second stage of his exorcism).

In all these ritual uses, the four piles of rice signal the presence of a human sender (in the infant's case, they let the natural world know of the arrival of a new human) and open up a path to communication with the spirits. They add one more set of signs to the four-way symbolic correspondences that link the human to the natural world, from the four spiritual images in the human body to the four natural elements, by way of the four elements of the afterbirth. Rice functions as the ideal substance for these signs because of its human origins. As the human element that has been transformed, through sacrifice, into the nonhuman, rice bridges the gap between the two worlds.

CAIN, ABEL, AND THE MARRIAGE OF TWINS

The rice story is part of a larger narrative repertoire that explains not only the nourishing power of rice but also the divisions between lowlands agriculture and uplands hunting, access to game, and the origins of marriage. Gayo have elaborated on the resemblance between two stories—the Islamic tale in which Cain kills his brother, and the Indonesian story in which rice originates from a sacrificed daughter—in such a way that elements from one narrative explain those in the other.

In the following narrative, Aman Asil explains God's command that Adam sacrifice four of his daughters as a solution to a problem of marriage. Unlike their sisters, the girls who became rice had no brothers whom they could marry:

> Adam had children in boy-girl pairs of twins. Each married the twin of the next sibling in line. But he also had two pairs of girl twins. The angel Jibra'il ordered Adam to kill them so that they would become rice plants, the life giver of humankind. They had no brothers, so they could not marry. Adam cut them up into little pieces and scattered the pieces over the fields and they became rice plants. The four girls were mixed together. Their blood became glu-

tinous rice; their skin, black glutinous rice; and their flesh, ordinary rice. Only ordinary rice can nourish us because it is of the flesh; only it can make us feel full; only it has berkat.

Here it is the leftover status of the girls, their unmarriageability, that destines them to become rice. Some narrators introduce the added complication of a quarrel between two of the sons. The sons, called Kabil and Habil (Ar. Kābīl and Hābīl – Cain and Abel), fought over whom each could marry. Abang Kerna gave particular prominence to this conflict between Cain and Abel in his account of rice origins and rice ritual (note that, as often occurs in Gayo narratives, he reverses the usual roles of Cain and Abel).

> The origin of rice is from the prophet Adam. Adam and Eve had many children; each was to marry a sibling, but not his or her closest sibling in age. Abel, who was the second or third son, wanted to marry the girl born right after him, who was the rightful bride of Cain, his younger brother. Thereupon Abel killed Cain so that he could marry this sister, named A'isa. They had two daughters, Kadijah and Maimunah. Abel then killed one of his daughters to produce rice. Her liver became glutinous rice—both are fatty—while the rest of her body generated the seeds of ordinary rice and those of all other seed-bearing plants.

In this narrative the problem of the first marriages assumes a prominent place. The brothers' conflict over their sisters displaces the sacrifice of the daughter onto the next generation. Abel kills his brother and then his daughter, suggesting that the fratricide may have led to the sacrifice. From a structuralist perspective, Abang Kerna's account suggests that a surfeit of brothers in one generation gives way to a surfeit of sisters in the next.

The marriage dispute was further amplified and set into a scriptural context by Tengku Daud, an Isak religious official. In the period immediately after independence, Tengku Daud had been an active proponent of Islamic law, and in his narratives he emphasizes the authority of God's word and the prophet Muhammad's example over local customs. He broached the subject of Cain and Abel in a casual discussion in his home on how Islamic law and the example of the prophet Muhammad could be incorporated into Gayo society:

TENGKU DAUD ON CAIN AND ABEL

Not all prophets [nabi] are messengers [rasūl] and not all that the twenty-five messengers did should be followed. It was the task of Muhammad, as the final prophet, to distinguish between what is still to be practiced and what is no longer valid. For example, the children of the prophet Adam married each other, but we can no longer do that.

Cain was Adam's eldest son and Abel his younger brother. Adam ordered each brother to marry his next sister, not his twin. But Cain said that because he was born together with his twin he wanted to marry her. He would not let Abel marry her though he had the right to do so. They fought. Cain wanted to kill Abel but did not know how until a devil appeared and showed him how to pick up a rock and let it fall on his brother's head. He did not know what to do with the body and God sent two birds flying overhead, fighting in the air. One bird killed the other, and when the dead bird had fallen to the ground the other bird covered him with earth. And Cain did the same for his brother. Adam made Cain leave his domain, and he ended up in Holland, where there is a place where even today men marry their sisters, but they do it in secret.

Sexual jealousy motivates Cain's fratricide, and his incestuous longings were inherited by people in Holland, who do not realize that marrying one's sister is no longer allowed. In the histories of the prophets told in Isak and Takèngën, certain transgressive practices are associated with each prophet and are valid only for his epoch: black magic with Moses, raising the dead with Jesus, brother-sister unions with Adam.

Gayo frequently tell some version of the Cain and Abel story, in part because it resonates with two themes in Gayo culture: the social and historical prominence of conflicts between brothers, and the calamities that result from improperly close marriages. In Gayo society, siblingship is the primary idiom for talking about kinship, affinal ties, and intervillage relations. Gayo reckon how closely they are as kin in terms of their distance from a shared relative—for example, one great-grandparent—regardless of the gender or kin-group affiliation of the linking relatives. They thus see their kin as more or less distant siblings. Affinal ties are also referred to in sibling terms, as the relation between a "source" (*raliq*) brother and his married-out sister, rather than as categories of wife-givers and wife-takers. Gayo also conceive of relations among the kin groups in a village, and sometimes also the relations among villages, in sibling terms (Bowen 1991:37–50).

The prominence of siblingship as a code for relatedness also makes it the preeminent code for ambivalences. The departure of a sister in marriage is the sole occasion for legitimate ritual wailing, often replete with the bride's recriminations against her brother(s) for allowing her to go. Competition for resources may arouse reactions of mutual support or jealous struggle between siblings. Ambivalence among siblings emerges in the content of tales: stories about brothers' attempts to deprive their sisters of wealth are about as frequent as those about the tearful reunion of siblings.

In Gayo origin-stories, conflicts among siblings are a major force behind the breakup of communities and the dispersal of Gayo over the highlands. A pair of half-siblings (usually paternal) forms a particularly crucial narrative element, representing a fateful line of cleavage in the society. The paradigm is contained in the Gayo origin-story, versions of which are told throughout the highlands (Bowen 1991:215–41). In this story, Genali, the Gayo founder, has a son in the old Gayo capital of Lingë and then, after death and rebirth, a second son in Aceh. The two meet, and they fight until they realize that they are half-siblings. Their relation remains profoundly ambivalent thereafter: though they share a father, the story emphasizes their opposition. The Lingë son inherits his father's position as Gayo ruler, but the Aceh son inherits his father's spiritual powers, and his new kingdom soon dwarfs that of Lingë.

A second, related theme in Gayo narratives concerns the dangers posed by improper marriages, especially those between close kin. Isak Gayo differ on how close the kin ties may be between potential spouses: some consider second-cousin marriages possible, though dangerous; others consider fifth-cousins (reckoned bilaterally) to be the closest proper partners. Any traceable tie may be cause for some alarm; the drift of one religious teacher's son into the Communist Party was widely blamed on his marriage to a far-distant relative. Gayo find stories about inadvertent brother-sister incest to be particularly moving. In the popular "Green Princess," for example, a girl discovers that her husband-to-be is her long-lost brother and, deeply shamed, throws herself into a nearby lake. Improper marriages also appear in myth as the cause of social differences. One story reports that the first Chinese people came from a set of Adam and Eve's twin children who were banished for their insistence on marrying each other (thus carrying out Cain's original, but unrealized, intent); another that, when a son of the first Gayo ruler could not be circumcised, and thus could neither embrace Islam nor marry under Islamic rules, he became the ancestor of the non-Muslim Karo Batak people (Bowen 1991:232–33).

The story told by Tengku Daud not only resonates with local concerns, it is also part of a general Muslim response to perplexities raised by the Cain and Abel story in the Qur'ān. The Qur'ān adumbrates the story of "the two sons of Adam" as part of an exhortation to repent. The brevity of the passage has led later commentators to offer expansions and explanations (Qur'ān 5:27–31):

> Recite unto them with truth
>   the story of the two sons of Adam;
> How they offered a sacrifice,
>   and it was accepted from the one of them
>   and it was not accepted from the other.
> The one said: "I will surely kill you."
> The other answered: "God accepts only from the Godfearing.
> Even if you stretch out your hand against me to kill me,
>   I shall not stretch out my hand against you to kill you;
>   I fear God, the Lord of the Worlds.

I desire that you should bear the punishment
  of sin against me, and thine own sin,
  and become an inhabitant of the Fire.
  That is the reward of evildoers."
But his soul led him to kill his brother,
  so he slew him and became one of the losers.
Then God sent a raven scratching up the ground,
  to show him how to hide his brother's naked corpse.
He said: "Woe is me! Am I not able to be as this raven
  and so hide my brother's naked corpse?"
And he became repentant.

As in the biblical account (Gen. 4.1–16), the Qur'ān explains the fratricide as the consequence of God's having accepted only one brother's offering. The killing seems undermotivated, however, and Jewish, Christian,
and Muslim historians have all sought to explain how Cain came to commit
his terrible deed.[6] The early Muslim community turned to men knowledgeable in Jewish and Christian lore to expand on these scriptural passages. Beginning in the first Islamic century, narrators (*qāss*) recited tales of the
prophets (qisas al-anbiyā') for popular edification and entertainment; historians and Qur'ānic commentators then drew on these tales to clarify scripture
and enrich their histories (Duri 1983:30–41; Kister 1988; Thackston
1978:xiii–xvi). The early compendia of religious lore became standard
sources for later Muslim historians (Duri 1983; Rosenthal 1989:44–78).

To explain the fratricide, historians have postulated sources of difference
or conflict between the two brothers. One group of accounts focuses on the
circumstances of their birth: perhaps they had different fathers (Cain's
being Satan).[7] Or perhaps they were born in two different epochs—Cain in

[6] The Muslim accounts come from the genre of tales of the prophets (*qisas al-anbiyā'*), the
earliest examples of which are found in papyri from the mid-eighth century; some of these
early works were Qur'ānic commentaries (tafsīr) that had incorporated popular lore (Kister
1988:82). Of particular influence on later historians were the writings of Wahb ibn Munabbih
(d. 728) (Duri 1983:127). The "Tales of the Prophets" written in the eleventh century by al-
Tha'labī (d. 1036) is the source for many later histories (al-Tha'labī n.d.; see Thackston
1978:xxxi n25). One of the most popular tales was written shortly before the year 1200 by a
certain al-Kisā'ī (1978; Thackston 1978:xix). An anonymous Indonesian-language "Tales of
the Prophets" (Qishashul n.d.) is frequently reprinted and may ultimately derive from
Tha'labī's work. Also referred to here is the ninth-century *Great Book of Classes* (*tabaqāt*) by
Ibn Sa'd (1962:189–96) and the tenth-century "History of Prophets and Kings" by the historian and commentator al-Tabarī (1989). I explore the correspondences between Jewish and
Muslim sources in Bowen (1992).

[7] Following standard practice I use the familiar names Eve, Cain, and Abel in place of the
Arabic names Hawwā, Kābīl, and Hābīl (and their variants). Some Muslim commentators
refer to a child born before Cain whom God kills (Sadik quoted by Tha'labī). In al-Kisā'ī's
tale (1978:72–73) the first child's paternity is left vague, but Satan supplies Eve with its name
and God causes it to die shortly after birth.

Paradise, Abel after Adam and Eve's expulsion—and this difference profoundly affected their respective natures.[8]

A second set of explanations focuses on the different livelihoods of the
brothers and on God's rejection of Cain's offering. Cain may have offered
the fruits of his harvest only after he had eaten most of it, leaving but a few
grains of flax seed or grain of poor quality, while Abel offered the best of
his flock.[9]

The commentaries devote the most space, however, to a third kind of account, one which itself raises a separate problem to be resolved: namely,
the identity of the brothers' wives. If Adam and Eve had only the two sons,
then whom did each marry? If the wives were their sisters, did the brothers
not commit incest? Early commentators devised an ingenious answer to this
problem, one that also explained why Cain killed Abel.[10] The answer involves a divinely commanded and intricate marriage rule, which I will let
the influential Muslim historian al-Tabarī explain. His approach to the
marriage problem in his tenth-century *History of Prophets and Kings*
(1989:307–17) illustrates the open, pluralistic attitude of most early Muslim
historians. Tabarī accepted as legitimate each of several distinct narratives
for which a reliable chain of transmission (*isnād*) could be established. He
drew on Jewish scholars, those "knowledgeable in the first Book," as well
as on Muslims. The following is one of several closely related passages in
which the problem of marrying sisters is linked to the fratricide (al-Tabarī
1989:310–11):

AL-TABARĪ ON THE MARRIAGES OF CAIN AND ABEL

Eve reportedly used to carry only twins, one male and one female, and in
twenty pregnancies she bore from Adam's loins forty children, male and female. Each man among them would marry any sister of his that he wanted, except his own twin sister that was born together with him; she was not permitted to marry him. Men could marry sisters at that time, because there were no
women except their sisters and their mother, Eve.

According to Ibn Humayd—Salamah—Muhammad b. Ishaq—some
scholar(s) knowledgeable in the first Book: Adam ordered his son Cain to
marry his twin sister to Abel, and he ordered Abel to marry his twin sister to
Cain. Abel was pleased and agreed, but Cain refused, disliking [the idea], because he considered himself too good for Abel's sister. He desired his [own]
sister and did not want Abel to have her. He said: "We were born in Paradise,

---

[8] al-Thaʿlabī (n.d.:37–41) examines several opinions to this effect; see also al-Tabarī
(1989:310).

[9] This possibility is examined by al-Tabarī (1989:308, 313) and Ibn Saʿd (1962:192).
Thaʿlabī notes that Abel offered "a ram that he loved most" but that no such similarly sincere
sacrifice was made by Cain.

[10] See Ibn Saʿd (1962:192); al-Thaʿlabī (n.d.:37–41); the Indonesian *Qishashul* (n.d.:13–
14); and al-Tabarī (1989:309–11, 314). Shi'ite accounts avoid the problem by having the sons
marry spirits sent by God (Kister 1988:113–14).

and they were born on earth. I am more deserving of my sister." Some scholar(s) of the people of the first Book say(s): Rather, the sister of Cain was one of the most beautiful human beings, and Cain begrudged her to his brother and wanted her for himself. God knows best what it was!

Tabarī then reports that each brother offered a sacrifice to God so that he would decide who was to marry Cain's twin. God accepted only Abel's offering, indicating him as the chosen spouse. Enraged, Cain killed his brother.

Each of these several explanations of Cain's murderous act are based on distinctions between the brothers, whether of birth (in or out of Paradise), in subsistence activity, or in choice of spouse. I suspect that the explanation based on the marriage problem became the most frequently proposed account because it touches on what is, after all, a universal cultural question: How to make spouses out of sisters.[11] This set of distinct yet interconnected explanations constitutes a narrative repertoire rather than a single story. Each new narrator may recombine the elements of this repertoire in a new context.

Gayo tell and sometimes read stories of the prophets' lives. Indonesian-language books of tales of the prophets (inter alia, Qishashul n.d.) circulate in the highlands as they do throughout Indonesia. One also finds direct access to older Arabic-language sources: my primary religious teacher possesses an Arabic translation (printed in Cairo) of the eleventh-century Persian-language "Tales of the Prophet" by Ibn Khalaf al-Nīsābūrī. Other such books may have been in circulation earlier in the century. On the celebration of the birthday of the prophet Muhammad (Maulid), the religious official of each Isak village tells a story from the life of Muhammad, sometimes using a printed text; in Takèngën, scholars are invited to schools and prayer houses to relate these histories. Men and women also frequently tell stories of prophets' lives in informal settings, such as the conversation with Tengku Daud recorded above.

Gayo narrators have managed to bring together Islamic and Indonesian traditions by elaborating on what the two traditions already share: namely, a causal relation between a threatened unsuitable marriage and the death of a close kinsmen. In the Indonesian stories about the origins of rice, sacrificing a daughter resolves the threat of improper marriage that arises from a surplus of daughters, an unsuitable choice of spouse, or a potential act of incest. In the Islamic stories about Adam and Eve's children, killing a brother resolves a threat to the divinely commanded plan of marrying daughters to their non-twin brothers. Some Gayo narrators make the link between the two sets of stories explicit by identifying the rice daughter as a child of Adam and Eve whose death is tied to two brothers' conflict over spouses.

[11] This is, of course, Lévi-Strauss's point in his classic study of marriage rules (1969).

HUNTING, HEALING, AND SPIRITUAL SIBLINGSHIP

Gayo narrators have drawn on another element of the Cain and Abel repertoire to account for the broad distinctions between uplands and lowlands activities: the contrast in modes of subsistence practiced by the two brothers.
Gayo have merged two distinct narrative traditions, changing each in the
process. They have reworked the scripture-based contrast between Cain's
farming and Abel's herding into a locally relevant contrast between lowlands agriculture and uplands hunting. They have also introduced Indonesian ideas about the role of the placenta as a powerful sibling into this narrative framework, through two transformative steps: equating the placenta
with another Indonesian figure, the Old Hunter, and identifying the Old
Hunter with the uplands hunting brother.

In 1979 Aman Méja, a noted hunter and healer, responded to my inqui-
ries into Gayo knowledge about hunting and farming by situating the origins of that knowledge at the beginning of human history:

AMAN MÉJA ON CAIN AND ABEL'S DISPUTE

Adam and Eve had six children in all. Their first child was a boy, but Eve delivered it after she and Adam had only been married for a few months. Adam
said that it was not his child, and Eve, ashamed, took him out into the forest
where he grew up.

They had a second child, also a son, and he grew up in the rice-growing
plains and learned to farm. He cut down trees to expand his farm, then went
home to sleep. When he came back the next day the trees had all been stood
up again and made whole! He cut them down again, but the next day they had
been stood up again. Again a third time, until his father told him to hide there
overnight. He did and he saw his elder brother, although he did not know who
he was, come and replant all the trees.

They started to argue and fight. The elder brother said that the forest and the
trees were his, while the younger said that the fields were his and that he was
enlarging them. The younger brother swore by his father, and the elder brother
said that they had the same father and that the younger brother would have to
recognize him as his true brother. He did, and they parted. The elder brother,
living in the hills, was Abel, and his descendants are Muslimin; the younger
brother, living in the plains, was Cain, and his descendants are Muslihin.[12]

Aman Méja's narrative elaborates on the Cain and Abel theme of a clash
over alternative uses of land. But he portrays that clash as an initial mis-

[12] The assignment of Cain and Abel (Kabil and Habil) to plains and hills varies from one
Gayo account to the next. The similarity of the names has led Gayo to interchange them rather
arbitrarily, a practice that is understandable in light of the Gayo emphasis on the distinction between the two domains rather than, as in the scriptural traditions, on the character of Cain himself. It is reinforced by the use of other similar-sounding names as interchangeable designa-
tions for the two brothers, as with Muslimin/Muslihin and Salih/Salihin.

communication that leads to a complementary relation between the two half-siblings, rather than as the prelude to murder and shame. In so doing he draws on a plot familiar to Gayo: that of a dispute followed by an oath that reveals the combatants to be siblings. These events repeat a sequence from the Gayo origin-story described earlier. The sequence emphasizes the complementarity of hunting and farming, a message highlighted by the use of similar-sounding Arabic derivatives, Muslimin and Muslihin, for the descendants of the two brothers.

This story provided Aman Méja with a narrative framework within which to launch his explanations of farming and hunting rituals. Other themes from the Cain and Abel story also entered the narrative. Aman Méja intimated that the elder brother was fathered by someone other than Adam, echoing an explanation offered by early commentators. This fact accounts for the boy's residence outside the community. Because he stressed the brothers' complementarity, however, Aman Méja drew no implications about the boy's conduct from his distinct parentage.

Aman Méja's focus on resource competition did not prevent him from introducing the problem of marrying siblings in his narrative. After the above story, and as a kind of interlude before launching into the account of rice ritual, Aman Méja leaned back in his chair and took up the story from a totally different starting point:

> Now, Adam and Eve had six children. The two youngest were told to marry each other, as all the children had to do, but they knew that they should be ashamed [kemèl] at such an idea and refused. So Adam sent them away, and they were never buried.

Aman Méja's brief summary of the problem of marrying siblings presents it as a conflict between the children, who possessed the proper sense of shame over incest (the central element in Gayo incest stories such as the "Green Princess"), and their parents. Thus, he shared Tengku Daud's views on incest, but not his view that Adam and Eve's conduct was appropriate to their epoch. Adding that the children were never buried reminds Gayo listeners both of Abel's delayed burial and of Gayo narratives about powerful ancestors who are never buried. After these few sentences Aman Méja paused, and then continued with his description of rice ritual. His mention of the problem of marrying siblings broke up his narrative; I believe he added it because, for him, it formed a narrative set with the other stories of Adam and Eve's children (indeed, he later added a third story about them).

After he had finished talking, and we sat drinking coffee, he added, as an aside, that one of the two brothers in his first story was the ancestor of humans, while the other became the Old Hunter. He then said that he called on the Old Hunter for assistance in healing and hunting, but that he did not wish to discuss the matter more fully.

I understood Aman Méja's reserve later, when I learned that he was often accused of using his association with the Old Hunter to cause illness in others. I also understood his own narrative focus on the complementarity and equal legitimacy of the two brothers and their respective domains. In calling on the Old Hunter, Aman Méja presented himself as invoking his own spiritual sibling.

In fact, others in Isak also call on the Old Hunter for help in hunting or healing and link themselves to the spirit by way of the Cain and Abel tradition. The Old Hunter is generally considered to be the spiritual sibling of each human individual. Humans are linked to the Old Hunter through their placenta, their younger sibling. After its burial and union with the natural elements, the placenta is frequently called on as the link between a human and the natural world. As we saw earlier, the placenta is also the material embodiment of the Old Hunter. The Old Hunter can be asked to perform diverse tasks, from sending or removing harmful spirits to assisting hunters in finding deer or other game. The Old Hunter is ontologically the closest of all spiritual agents to humans in that it lies just across the divide between the visible world (here, the placenta) and the spiritual world. Its abode and activities also signify the boundary between the area of human settlement and cultivation (the realm of Adam, hak Edëm) and the area inhabited by wild creatures (the realm of God, hak Allah). It is thus the spiritual agent most amenable to human bidding, and yet it is also associated with the wild, the untamed, and the malevolent.

Because of its association with the hills, the Old Hunter is invariably appealed to by deer hunters. Deer hunting is a major source of animal food for the people of the community, and every adult male in Isak has probably been on a deer hunt at some time in his life. Expert hunters (*pawang*) ask the Old Hunter to guide their steps and to send the deer in their direction. They leave as offerings the ingredients for betel chewing, or, if the hunt is unusually important or if a member of the party has been injured, a complete ritual meal.

But there is also a dark side to the Old Hunter: for example, an accident may be caused by it at the behest of a third party. Some healers employ the Old Hunter to expel the spirits afflicting a patient, but these same healers are accused by others of sending harmful spirits into healthy people so that they will become clients. The association of the Old Hunter with individual desires and moral ambivalence makes those who claim to use it for good automatically suspected of using it for evil as well. Indeed, some people view both hunting and healing as "hot" activities that, because they involve appeals to spirits, are profitable only in the short run, and inevitably bring misfortune upon their practitioners. Some hunters are said to experience poor yields from their rice crops because God disapproves of their offerings to the Old Hunter.

Among the many spiritual agents with which one deals, the Old Hunter is probably viewed with the greatest ambivalence. It resembles the hunter or healer himself: someone with the power to bring wealth and health but also one to be suspected of doing just the opposite. The Old Hunter's triple identity as hunter, sibling to humans, and agent capable of malevolent acts is redolent of the figure of Cain.

Aman Méja cast his narrative as a Cain and Abel story, and only secondarily, and cautiously, identified one of the brothers as the Old Hunter. Other stories told by expert hunters, however, explicitly concern the Old Hunter's origins. They suggest Cain and Abel only in that they stress the differentiation between two siblings and their modes of subsistence. Abang Das, an avid storyteller and enthusiastic hunter, told such a tale in 1979 in response to my queries about hunting. The story agrees in its main points with most Isak accounts of the Old Hunter's origins. (Parentheses indicate the narrator's asides; square brackets, my own.)

ABANG DAS ON THE OLD HUNTER

This brings us back to birth. . . . At birth come the four companions; [together] they are the younger sibling of the individual, and they are what became the Old Hunter. This younger sibling does not have a soul [nyawa].

The spirit [ruh] of the Old Hunter came from the spirit let loose by the angel Jibra'il. When Jibra'il first carried a spirit [ruh] to place in the prophet Adam at the creation, the first soul he brought escaped. It later entered the buried placenta of a human infant, and it was then reborn as the infant's younger brother. It was now a Muslim spirit and would do good or bad things depending on who gave it sustenance and on what it was asked to do. That is the characteristic of the Old Hunter.

The elder brother was named Salihin and the younger brother, born of the placenta, Salih [the Arabic plural and singular forms of *pious*]. This is because he was *salah* [wrong]; everyone named Salih is salah. Salihin died and Salih, the younger brother, married into our village [Kutë Rayang in Isak] and had a son.

Salih went off to the hills every day to hunt. One day his wife asked him to find her a "deer with antlers and a child inside" [a male pregnant deer]. He went to the hills, but of course could not find one and so, because of his embarrassment, could never return to the plains. His son asked his mother if he had a father, and she said yes, but that he stayed in the hills. His hunting dogs returned to the village every Monday and Thursday to eat, though. One day the boy's mother tied a packet of rice to one dog's tail and said: "Follow the dogs. When the rice runs out, there will be your father." (This is knowledge you can use when hunting [to find the Old Hunter].)

The son followed the trail of spilled rice to where it ran out at a small hill, where a well stood. He bathed there. He then met a boy his own size. Salih had married a spirit [jin] in the hills who bore him a son, Annar [<Ar. *an-nār*, fire, the stuff of jin]. Whenever this son threw his spear into the air it fell onto blood, never onto earth [it would always hit a living thing]. They fought fiercely, to a draw. . . .

[The son returns home and comes again; the boys fight and their father, recognizing his son from the plains, stops them.] The father, Salih, told them that he had never returned to the plains because of his embarrassment at not finding the "deer with antlers and a child inside." Each Molud season he tried to return but his wife hung an old *niyu* [three-cornered woven reed tray used to sift rice and dry meat] above their door. She, too, was embarrassed that he did not return. He feared the rice tray and could not reenter his house. (It is forbidden for any hunt leader to enter a house with a rice tray hung over the door; his knowledge and spells will not be effective if he does so.)

He then told his son from the plains that he was the elder brother when in the plains, and told his son from the hills that he was the elder brother when in the hills. Their statuses were different. The hills brother would always hit blood with his spear, and if he hit the plains brother, he would have to report to his father; only he could remove the spear. Added the father: "And if the hills son journeys to the plains, the plains son may not talk directly to him; the words must pass by way of me."

The two sons traveled to the plains to have a ritual meal together. But when the wife took up her rice tray to sift the husks out of the puffed rice, Annar became smaller in size and was embarrassed to enter the house. So she gave him the meal without completely preparing it: unsifted puffed rice, an unshelled egg, uncut bananas. He returned to his abode in the hills with it. She then told her own son that, because it was the elder wife who had prepared the meal, whatever he requested his father would have to grant.

Abang Das brought together what for other tellers were two different stories: that concerning the role of the placenta as the younger sibling of humans, and that of the resource complementarity between two half-siblings. The first story is the general Indonesian one of the placenta as protector; the second, as told here, does not mention Cain and Abel, but is structurally close to that told by Aman Méja. Abang Das maintains the integrity of each story, and describes two sets of siblings. Salih and Salihin stand for the placenta and its human sibling; the relation between Salih's two unnamed sons is analogous to the sons' contrasting occupations in Aman Méja's narrative. But the two sibling relations are linked. Although the two sons of Salih stand for the hills/plains contrast, it is Salih himself, not his hills son, who is the Old Hunter, and the names Salih and Salihin that underscore sibling (and resource) complementarity. However, in his own remarks on the story and in hunting spells, Abang Das made clear that the Old Hunter stood as sibling to humans.

11. Abang Das Engaged in Telling a Story

The encounter between the second set of brothers closely resembles the Gayo origin-story, as Abang Das or others would tell it (Bowen 1991:215–41). In the story, the Gayo founder's second son, born in Aceh, returns to Lingë and fights with the Gayo-born son until they recognize their sibling-ship. Their complementary relation mirrors that between the Old Hunter and humans, in that each can claim a particular, limited kind of superiority with respect to the other. Abang Das's story thus makes apparent the grounding of his (and Aman Méja's) stories about hunting in the general Gayo mythic proposition that half-sibling relations generate important social differences.

The Old Hunter's quest (in this and many other Isak versions) also dramatizes the tensions between husband and wife that surround deer hunting in Isak. Men who love hunting often spend much time at it with scant results. Even hunts held close to home last most of the night, leaving the hunters too tired for work the next day. In households living close to the margins of subsistence, some women would rather their husbands spent the time clearing a cash-crop garden or raising money in some other way. Hunters feel the pressure to return home with something to show for their efforts, but deer are difficult to find. A hunter sometimes feels he is engaging in an impossible quest. The Old Hunter both exemplifies these tensions and offers assistance to the hunter.

The power of the rice-sifting tray, a symbol of agricultural domesticity, sharpens the depiction of tensions between the two modes of livelihood and between men and women. The tray can nullify hunting spells. It prevents the Old Hunter from reentering his house and causes his son born in the hills to shrink. In the narrative it is also a reminder that the meat that would have been laid upon it to dry (in some versions destined for their son's seventh-day name-giving ritual, the 'aqīqa) was never procured.

In response to these tensions between men and women, the narrative stresses the availability of spiritual assistance for men through the sibling relation of humans to the Old Hunter. In the course of the story, the clash between the two siblings (not strongly motivated) becomes a complementary, reversible relation in which the hunter is the younger brother in the lowlands and the elder in the hills. In the hills, Abang Das and other hunters always include in their spells addressed to the Old Hunter the phrase "You are the elder brother; I am the younger brother." In the plains, the afterbirth that reproduces the generic human tie to the Old Hunter is the younger sibling.

Abang Das's narrative encodes as sibling relations those of child to placenta, outer material form to inner source of power, domestic to wild, agriculture to hunting, and human world to spirit world. As the elder brother in the hills, the Old Hunter expresses the sense of the forest's power and unruliness; as a younger brother who, when offered the right foods, will obey one's directions, he serves as a willing agent of healing or destruction. The reversible relation of elder to younger brother brings the possibilities for cooperation and strength to the human agent, but it also expresses the ambivalence felt toward one who is like oneself and yet profoundly different, cooperative and yet competitive: a sibling.

The figure of the Old Hunter appears elsewhere in the Malay-speaking world, but not, to my knowledge, as a sibling. Malay versions (Skeat

1967:112–20) tell of a hunter, sent to find a pregnant male deer, who becomes the Hunting Ghost and plagues humans with various illnesses. The spirit is an unequivocally negative figure in these tales, with no role to play in hunting and no relation to the division between hills and plains. Moreover, no sibling relation with humans is mentioned (although, as in the Gayo stories, the Hunting Ghost is of human origin). Gayo thus have made what elsewhere is a solitary, negative figure into a potentially helpful spirit sibling by locating the spirit's origins in the human placenta.

The specifically Gayo image of the Old Hunter as sibling makes possible, though not necessary, his identification as Cain. For Aman Méja, viewed with varying degrees of ambivalence by others in the society, adopting an Islamic narrative framework is quite attractive. Aman Méja identifies himself strongly with the Old Hunter, yet is well aware of the disapproval this identification generates. He thus casts the relation of the hills to the plains in explicitly "Cain-and-Abel" terms, emphasizing the difference between the descendants of the two brothers (as in the scriptural repertoire), and not including the Old Hunter (yet bearing him very much in mind). Ironically, Aman Méja's story is closer to the genre of prophetic history (represented by Tengku Daud's story) precisely because of Aman Méja's morally marginal place in the community.

Abang Das, by contrast, delights in talking about hunting ritual and the Old Hunter's role, in part because he is not suspected of malign magic and in part because he sees himself as something of an expert in ritual exegesis. He is also a local healer, and thus emphasizes the importance of the placenta, knowledge of which is central to healing practices. But he is also wary of making the Old Hunter unambiguously legitimate, and resists bringing the narrative under the rubric of Cain and Abel.

Abang Das did include Cain and Abel as actors in his account of the origins of rice, and I asked him about their connection to hunting. He replied: "It is better if you do not take the story in that direction." He argued that invoking the Old Hunter should be strictly limited to hunting, and that appealing to the spirit in healing spells or introducing it into the story of Cain and Abel is to dangerously augment its importance. He saw Aman Méja as compromised by his overuse of the Old Hunter in healing, hunting, and narrative. His objections to stories of the origins of rice such as that told by Aman Méja were based less on truth-value (he admitted that one could construct the story so as to include Cain and Abel) than on the social and moral implications of taking the story in that particular direction.

Both Abang Das and Aman Méja were aware of the strong objections held by Isak religious teachers to any discussion of spirits such as the Old Hunter. Tengku Daud and Tengku Asaluddin, among others, insisted that trafficking with spirits implied polytheism, and that telling stories about such trafficking was little better. This accounts for the caution both men (and others) exercised in discussing such topics. Both narrators crafted their stories around their own social and moral positions, all the while recognizing other ways in which the stories might be told and other values that might be placed on their own versions.

The origin stories of the Old Hunter and those of the rice plant explain human powers and nourishment in formally similar ways, but this formal resemblance is the basis for an important set of contrasts regarding gender and nutritive value. Both the Old Hunter and the rice plant are siblings to humans, but in both cases the ties are mediated by transformations of substance. The Old Hunter is created from Adam's first spirit and a human placenta, thus out of something very close to but substantially distinct from a human child. The rice plant is created from Adam and Eve's daughter (or daughters or granddaughters), but only after she has been sacrificed and transformed into a new substance. In both cases Gayo underscore the lingering substantive connection: rice nourishes because it is of human origin, and the placenta continues to link humans to the natural world and the Old Hunter for the same reason.

But rice and the Old Hunter differ in culturally important ways as well. Rice, a female element, is itself the source of nourishment; it needs only to be coaxed and cared for to produce the basis for subsistence. Its spiritual component is its vital force (semangat), a relatively passive element that does not so much act on its own as translate others' actions (in this case, the actions of farmers) into states of well-being. The Old Hunter, by contrast, is a male element that is as likely to harm as to aid humans. It is a free-floating spirit, not the hunted game itself, and one must use great care in speaking to it. The Old Hunter's spiritual element is its spirit (ruh), to which one makes offerings as one would to a human spirit and which is capable of independent action. These contrasts underscore the greater value of rice and its relatively stable productivity vis-à-vis hunted game, as well as the female origins of nourishment and fertility.

Anthropology has rarely acknowledged the social life of scriptures, attending instead to the internal structure of biblical texts (Douglas 1966; Leach and Aycock 1983).[13] At least in the case of the Gayo, narrators play out broad issues of Muslim identity in relation to distinctive local concerns, in part by elaborating and transforming elements from scripture.

The above narratives illustrate how the Gayo have made scripture their own, even as they have shaped their identities out of its transcendent depictions. The scriptural stories about Adam and Eve's children pose the gen-

---

[13] McKinley's apparently relevant article, "Cain and Abel on the Malay Peninsula," does not in fact concern the Cain and Abel narratives.

eral problem of how to create difference out of unity. The conflict between Cain and Abel frames the problem in terms of marriage (how to turn siblings into spouses) and shows what happens when the solution (let non-twin siblings be considered as marriageable) is disregarded. But written scriptural commentaries already include other explanatory possibilities: that Cain had a different father, making the brothers only half-siblings and thus already of differing natures; that the different economic pursuits generated important social and moral differences between them; that the act of murder itself created basic moral differences.

Gayo narratives add to these stories additional elements: the genesis of nourishment from the sacrifice of Adam and Eve's daughter, and the genesis of hunting prowess from placenta-born spirit siblings. In their relationship of mediated siblingship to humans, both rice and the Old Hunter are like half-siblings and thus continue one theme of the scripture-based commentaries. Gayo narrators have reworked into a sibling framework several pan-Indonesian figures: the sacrificed rice daughter, the Old Hunter, the placenta. The rice daughter appears in Isak as a daughter of Adam and Eve with female and sometimes male siblings. The placenta appears as the source of the Old Hunter, who in turn plays the role of a spiritual sibling to all humans, a role that is not, to my knowledge, found elsewhere in the archipelago. Each of these figures can be (but is not always) depicted as a child of Adam and Eve as well. More specifically, the events in each of these stories can be portrayed as motivated by one or more of the conflicts between Cain and Abel, especially the conflict over the apportionment of sisters as spouses.

The structural convergence between the archipelagic and the Islamic narratives is probably an overdetermined one, in that themes of siblingship and close marriages are prominent in a wide range of Gayo narratives as well as in the Islamic stories. Sibling relations and improper marriages figure importantly in many cultures, but the prominence in Gayo myth of half-sibling differentiation and incest undoubtedly contributes to the cultural attractiveness to Gayo of stories about Adam and Eve's children. Ideas and emotions regarding the sibling relation are powerfully evoked by the emotional and moral ambivalence of the Old Hunter as sibling, the complementary roles of the hills and lowlands, and the sacrifice of the sister to nourish her siblings.

As a result of this convergence, Isak narrators are aware of a broad set of narrative possibilities that have varying degrees of explicitly Islamic content. Although Abang Das chose not to identify the Old Hunter with Cain, he made his choice against the background possibility of such an identification and what were, for him, its negative moral implications. Within this already structured set of possible narratives, individual Gayo have positioned themselves by making careful selections and combinations. When Aman

Méja played up the Cain and Abel connection to hunting, when Abang Das played down the same possible tie, and when Aman Jukri created a strongly Islamic narrative of rice origins, they were constructing their own public identities as well as explaining ritual.

In uttering spells, healing the sick, ensuring a good rice crop, or calling on the Old Hunter for assistance, Gayo in Isak are putting into effect a single set of ideas about human empowerment. They explain human fortune and misfortune in terms of the acts of humans and spirits, and provide ways of countering malevolent actions without requiring that those responsible be publicly identified. By pleading with, threatening, and making offerings to various kinds of spirits, Isak men and women are able to change the outer world by way of the inner. They articulate their understandings of these events and remedies in explicitly Islamic terms, and in particular through narratives about cosmological and human history. But they incorporate into those narratives wider Indonesian codes, among them correspondences across sets of four elements; the figures of the rice daughter, the placenta, and the Old Hunter; and the importance of balance and harmony in healing and in cultivating the soil. Isak discourses about the social and natural worlds are constructed around local imperatives—the importance of communication, exchange, and community—but these local imperatives are already placed in an Islamic setting.

PART THREE

Negotiating Public Rituals

Chapter Ten

TRANSACTING THROUGH FOOD:
THE KENDURI AND ITS CRITICS

GAYO CONSIDER their healing spells or rice rituals to be specific to their society, or at least to their part of Sumatra. Though grounded in Islamic theories of powerful speech, they are not part of a broadly distributed and generally accepted Islamic ritual repertoire. Those who challenge the legitimacy of using spells or requesting aid from an Ancestor are rejecting the very idea of such spells or requests.

In the chapters that follow we turn to a different category of event: rituals that all Gayo consider necessary in some form or other. These generally accepted practices include celebrating the prophet Muhammad's birthday and the Feast of Sacrifice, carrying out rituals of birth and death, and worshiping God on a daily basis. Where Gayo may differ is on how each of these rituals ought to be understood and carried out: Alimin and Asyin, in their exchange at the tailor's kiosk, argued over how to bury the dead and worship God, not whether to do so.

One focus of these debates is the kenduri, the ritual meal marked by special foodstuffs and speech to spirits. In Isak most people hold kenduris to celebrate Islamic holidays as well as many other occasions. In Chapter 8 we saw that kenduris are the central public events in the series of rice rituals but are regarded with ambivalence by some Gayo.

Kenduris are not in themselves "traditionalist" or "modernist"; participants may interpret their actions at a kenduri as saying prayers to God, generating merit for ancestral spirits by reciting scripture, or allowing angels to enjoy ritual foods. Most villagers understand them as events of transaction and communication with spiritual entities, in which participants speak to the inner (batin) world. Precisely because of this possible understanding of nearly any kenduri, some modernists object whenever a kenduri is held to celebrate an Islamic holiday. Setting out foodstuffs, they argue, misleads people into seeing religious events as self-interested spiritual transactions, when in fact they are primarily acts of obedience to God. Muslim holidays, in their view, are primarily about remembering and celebrating events in Islamic history, conforming to the historical example set by the prophet Muhammad and demonstrating obedience to God through sacrifices, fasts, and worship.

People not only argue about kenduris, they often do so when they are gathered at kenduris. On these occasions scholars and community leaders may seek to change others' opinions about ritual matters, and the ensuing discussions show how these specific ritual disputes implicate broad issues of religion, society, and culture.

PRAYERS, FOOD, AND SACRIFICE

In the course of any single week in Isak I would probably be asked to take part in at least one kenduri.[1] At most kenduris someone, often a religiously learned man, says prayers over burning incense, and usually special foods are present. Sometimes the guests recite well-known Qur'ānic verses together, and guests nearly always share the best fare the hosts can provide.

A Gayo person may use the term *kenduri* to refer to nearly any meal that is distinguished in some respect. For example, a host may dignify his invitation to eat by asking his guests to kenduri with him. But people generally reserve the term for meals at which the hosts intend to accomplish something of religious or ritual import. The occasion may be an event in the Islamic or the local agricultural calendar (the prophet Muhammad's birthday, the Feast of Sacrifice, or the beginning of the rice cycle); an event in an individual's lifecycle (birth, circumcision, death); or a sudden, noteworthy happening (an illness or a recovery, a departure or a homecoming). In all these cases the kenduri involves a transaction between the host and a spiritual agent. At a funeral kenduri, reciters generate merit and ask God to direct it to the spirit of the deceased. At an Ancestor's grave a couple might offer a kenduri in return for their child's health. Kenduris held at the annual Feast of Sacrifice ensure that the sacrificed animal will serve as transport on the Day of Judgment. And even modernists hold kenduris to ask God for safety and health on a journey.

The least controversial part of any kenduri is the set of prayers to God recited by a prayer leader, the tengku. The prayer leader recites in Arabic and leads the guests in reciting one or more short Qur'ānic verses. He may also communicate specific requests to a spirit (compare, for Java, Woodward [1988:78–80]).

At some kenduris, such as those held in fulfillment of a vow or on the prophet Muhammad's birthday, the collective recitation will be very short, perhaps consisting only of the opening verse of the Qur'ān, al-Fātiha. On

---

[1] Because the term has a broad range of meanings I leave it in the original. The term and the ritual meal it describes are common in Aceh (Snouck Hurgronje 1906, I:214–16) and in the Malay Peninsula (McAllister 1990), and correspond roughly to the equally important Javanese *slametan*, which can also be called a *kendurèn* (Geertz 1960:11–15; Woodward 1988:64). A similar ritual meal, called the *khatam qur'ān* (sealing the Qur'ān), is performed in South Asia; see Werbner (1990:156–71) on Pakistani reshapings of the ritual in Britain.

these occasions the emphasis of the kenduri is elsewhere: on the animal killed for the occasion, the words of dedication, or the prayers for Muhammad's welfare. But at other kenduris the collective recitations are central to the event. The major task at a funeral kenduri, for example, is to recite sacred words that will ease the torment of the deceased.

Virtually all Isak Gayo would agree that saying prayers and reciting verses before a meal is religiously proper; anything else is controversial. For that reason, the more public and widely attended the kenduri, the greater likelihood that the prayer leader will only recite prayers and verses out loud. If he makes a request to a spirit in such contexts, he will do it sotto voce or pronounce it before the kenduri begins.

At most kenduris in Isak the prayers are said directly over a small bit of benzoin incense (*kemenyèn*) burning in a coconut shell. Some participants say the incense merely provides a pleasant aroma; others, that it calls the angels to partake in the feast and sends the prayers and recitations up to God. (Modernists avoid using incense because of its implied function of transmitting requests to angels and other spirits.) I was told that it acquired its ritual use directly from the prophet Muhammad, who discovered benzoin's powers when emigrating from Mecca to Medina. He and Abu Bakr hid in a deep cave to elude their Meccan pursuers. In the cave, Muhammad picked up a piece of benzoin and, scratching it with his fingernails, released its characteristic smell. He said to the wood: "Just as I am honest and straightforward, so you must carry straight to God whatever is requested by the people who burn you." He added the wish that he not be discovered, upon which a spider quickly spun a web across the entrance to the cave. His pursuers, seeing the large web, passed by without checking inside.[2]

At a small kenduri, with no one of special religious learning present, anyone might choose to lead the prayers, just as anyone who knows the proper prayers may lead a group in worship. Sometimes no one is really qualified, and the result can be embarrassing.

Aman Bani recalled that, during the Darul Islam period in the 1950s, he and other rebel soldiers held a wedding downstream from Isak. At the kenduri they kept passing around the coconut shell with the incense because no one felt capable of saying the prayers. Finally Pang Alim [a famous fighter of the period whose name means "religiously-learned warrior"] felt embarrassed and accepted the shell. He thought for a minute, and then [rather than reciting a long prayer and ending with a collective recitation of Surah al-Fātiha, as is the norm] he called right away for al-Fātiha! Afterward people shook their heads and said: "Darul *Islam*?"

[2] The story of his concealment in the cave is mentioned in Qur'ān 9:40; see also Schimmel (1985:13).

For most Isak people a kenduri must also include one or more ritual foods. Indeed, people indicate the size of a kenduri by mentioning the ritual foods to be included. The most elaborate and complete kenduri has four ritually marked foodstuffs and is called the "kenduri of four elements" (*kenduri opat perkara*). Someone wishing to make a weighty request to a spirit would put on such a kenduri. More modest requests may be transmitted at feasts where only one or two of these foodstuffs are present.

A kenduri of four elements is laid out in a fixed form and sequence. A prayer mat is rolled out on top of brightly colored, woven-reed eating mats. A glass of water and a betel case are set on top, near the man who will preside over the prayers. Each of the four elements, listed below, is then set out on a plate and covered with banana leaves.

1. "A plate of puffed rice, four bananas, one egg." The puffed rice (bertéh) is made from glutinous rice (the thinner skin allows it to cook more evenly). Four bananas (usually of a short, sweet kind) are placed around the circumference of the plate, and a hard-boiled egg is placed in the center.
2. "Seven cup-measures of glutinous rice." The cooked rice (*kunyit*) is heaped up on one plate.
3. "Forty-four rice cakes." These flat cakes, called *apam*, resemble small pancakes. The precise number included in the kenduri varies, but they are stipulated as forty-four in number (cf. Woodward 1988:73).
4. "One plate of cooked rice." The single plate of rice stands for the rest of the rice that will be brought out for the meal. (Some people would include the meat and vegetables as part of the fourth element.)

Isak people interpret the significance of these foods according to their religious orientations. Most consider the first three foods to be offerings to God and other spirits, and the cooked rice to merely signify the meal. Those with modernist leanings hold that such offerings would be improper and that in any case humans cannot transmit enjoyment or blessing from food. Some modernists conclude that setting out these foods is a sign of the hosts' idolatry, and they therefore avoid the kenduri; others conclude that the real meaning of the foods is symbolic, and they therefore attend. No public decoding takes place, and people draw their own semiotic conclusions.

Whatever their convictions about the role of ritual foods in sending blessings, most Isak people would agree that, because all four foods are made from rice and are thus of human origin, they are especially powerful symbols of human qualities. Some villagers would add that for this reason rice is especially effective in transmitting human desires.

The puffed rice is the key element, the "head of the feast." Puffed rice was the food of the prophets, I was told, and is the sole food of men or women who wish to become more spiritual. By including it in the kenduri we bring ourselves closer to God. For this reason, some people argued that it should be present at all kenduris. Some kenduris consist only of a single plate of puffed rice. When a child is weaned from her or his mother, for example, the kenduri functions only to calm and reassure the child's spirit, a relatively minor task that needs but puffed rice to be complete.

The second element, the seven cup-measures of sticky, glutinous rice, tightens and solidifies the ties between the hosts and the spirit world. Abang Das said that the seven measures were destined for the seven guardians of our bodies: God's being (zat), the Light of Muhammad, the four archangels, and Adam. These seven guardians repair the body and keep its elements in their proper balance, so they are rewarded and encouraged by offerings of glutinous rice. Other people spoke of the glutinous rice as cementing the bonds between themselves and their healers. A kenduri given for a healer often consists of just the seven cup-measures followed by an ordinary meal. After a name is chosen for a child, the parents offer glutinous rice to the men presiding over the ritual so that the name will sit well with the child throughout life.

The rice cakes, the third element, are associated with God and with the spirit of a deceased person. Whereas glutinous rice is intended to affect relations among humans, the rice cakes are usually given as offerings. People in Isak often sent a plate of cakes to the mosque on Friday for the worshipers to eat right after the service, with the hope that the donation would reach God and procure merit for the donor. The cakes are nearly always served at kenduris held after a death; their essence is enjoyed by the deceased. They also provide a cover over the grave so that the body will not rise from it. At one burial I witnessed in Isak, three cakes were thrown in after the body "for the food of the deceased."[3]

The modernist teacher Tengku Asaluddin denied that one can send foods to spirits but did value the foods' naturally symbolic qualities:

> The puffed rice is light; it is included so that the object of the feast also will be lightened in some fashion. Thus if a boy was turned over to a teacher but was unreceptive to the teachings, his parents would sponsor a feast that featured puffed rice. The teacher would say some words over it and then have the boy eat it. The glutinous rice, because it is sticky, ensures that some quality will stick to a person. A student who acquires knowledge will sponsor a feast of glutinous rice so that the knowledge will stick to him.
>
> The rice cakes are the fixed places on which things sit. The number forty-four ensures that the object of the feast reaches its final destination: forty-four days after death a person's life finally closes, for example. And the cooked rice stands for life: as long as I still eat rice I am alive.

[3] Compare a similar set of practices in lowlands Aceh (Snouck Hurgronje 1906, I:119–20).

These four elements of the feast remind us of the four natural elements of which we are made, that all things come from these elements and therefore from God. But it is not true that their essences are enjoyed by spirits.

The final disclaimer returns Tengku Asaluddin to his generally held position on kenduris: that food cannot serve as the medium of ritual transactions with spirits. His ambivalence on the legitimacy of these special foods accords with his combination of doctrinal modernism and cultural nostalgia. Quick to condemn the general ideas behind kenduris, he nonetheless is a child of a kenduri-based religious culture.

The elements of a kenduri can be perverted, say Isak Gayo. Preparing them in an incomplete form (raw or partially cooked) sends their value to evil spirits rather than to God and the angels. A person who seeks to harm another prepares a kenduri of "puffed rice that has not been sifted" (i.e., that has been puffed with the husks) and adds uncooked rice and an uncooked chicken, perhaps together with chicken blood. The person also may include four rather than forty-four rice cakes in the kenduri. These offerings are incomplete foods that are appropriate to the spirits that live outside the community, such as the Old Hunter or the jin that carry illness.

Kenduris may release individuals or households from spiritual debts and obligations. A household may make a vow or "intention" (G. niët; Ar. niyya) to a powerful ancestral spirit, asking it to help them in some way in return for the promise of an offering. They fulfill the vow if they judge that the spirit did in fact render some assistance. Some households, especially those who have especially powerful ancestral spirits, make vows regularly to obtain continual protection. At the start of each rice season, for example, several families in Kutë Robel would make vows to one of their ancestors, Datu Gergung, that if nothing befell them during the season they would offer a kenduri of four elements to him.

Other kenduris are made to release the hold of a spirit over an individual's fate. A "kenduri with four legs" (*kenduri opat kiding*) includes the basic four elements and a goat. The host dedicates the goat to a particular spirit before killing it. The dedication, deeply offensive to modernists, is usually made apart from the kenduri, though it is not a secret matter.

One sacrifice made during my residence in Isak fulfilled a vow made in the early 1940s, during the period of Dutch control. The subject of the vow was a baby girl, now called Inën Merkiyah. Her mother's father told her that when she was grown she must hold a kenduri with four legs dedicated to the Ancestor Merah Mëgë. Although he told her mother about it right away, the vow was ignored for many years. When Inën Merkiyah married she was unable to have children. Her mother's brother's son gave her one of his daughters, named Merkiyah, thereby furnishing her with the teknonym (Mother of Merkiyah) that gave her full adult status. But in the community where she lived, north of Takèngën, she was often referred to as a childless woman. She desperately wanted a child of her own; she felt incomplete. The healers she consulted learned of the unfulfilled vow (they said the vow announced itself to them) and concluded that it was the cause of her childlessness.

In September 1979 Inën Merkiyah came to Isak to fulfill the vow. She purchased a goat from a relative in Isak and, accompanied by her husband, her parents, and several other relatives, took the goat and the ingredients for a meal up the hill behind Kramil village to the prayer site of the Ancestor of Isak. There, a relative who often served as intermediary to the Ancestor conveyed Inën Merkiyah's intent to him. The relative, Inën Lukman, entered the Ancestor's shelter with incense and a bowl of water into which a mungkur had been cut. She poured the water over the headstone, lit the incense, and began to speak softly to the Ancestor's spirit. She later told me approximately what she had said: "It was just my own words, in Gayo, nothing fixed":

> So, Ancestor, concerning my child here,
> we consulted this healer and that healer,
> It turned out to be the vow.
> So now what was dark is light;
>   what was overgrown is cleared away.
> It is intended in the heart,
>   and spoken with the tongue.
> Because this child's grandfather made a vow a long time ago to you,
> and [we were] wrong, negligent,
>   forgetful, careless.
> So now it is the time and the moment,
>   the hour and the instant,
> Her grandfather declared the intention;
>   only now do we know of it.
> So here is the body that we bring here, with four legs.
> Keep danger away from my child, Inën Merkiyah,
>   keep sickness distant.
> Here is the object, with four legs.
> May her years be many and her fortune easy, here is the body.

The goat was then sprinkled with purifying water from the citrus fruit and killed. A tray of rice cakes and a plate of glutinous rice were placed on the Ancestor's prayer site.

That afternoon a kenduri was held. It consisted of the recitation of Qur'ānic verses and prayers followed by enjoyment of the food. As the prayer leader told me later, before he began to recite he declared silently

12. Inën Lukman (right) Fulfilling a Vow to the Isak Ancestor, Merah Mëgë

that the kenduri was intended to fulfill the vow made earlier. Neither he
nor anyone else mentioned the sacrifice publicly, however. The intent of
the kenduri, the dedication of the goat, and the placing of ritual foods on
the Ancestor's grave all were anathema to many of the acknowledged religious leaders of the community, some of whom attended the kenduri (and
who, when I asked, were reluctant to discuss its purpose). On this occasion

the prayer leader was a learned man who kept company with Isak's modernists despite his willingness to oversee sacrificial events such as this one. He was able to comfortably attend the kenduri because, aloud, he only recited scripture.

In its two-stage, compartmentalized character, the sacrifice to the Ancestor resembles the ritual with which the Lord of the Fields begins the rice cultivation season. In both cases the specialist speaks to spirits in a secluded place, after which a public kenduri is held at which the only openly acknowledged communication is with God. People were able to ignore one part of the ritual and participate in the other, more widely accepted part.

Kenduris are, for Isak Gayo, the form through which a collectivity (a household, village, or larger community) enters into transactions with spiritual agents (place spirits, Ancestors, God). Gayo have in mind a model, what cognitive scientists would call a "script," for holding kenduris, which includes the elements of offerings and transactions. Gayo have interpreted a wide range of ritual and religious events using this script, much to the consternation of modernists. Most modernists have resisted kenduri-based renderings of Islamic rituals, seeking to substitute alternative forms that emphasize ideas of obedience, worship, and conformity. Because kenduris always include food, and this food is involved in the spiritual transactions they detest, modernists often object particularly strongly to any association between religious ritual and the eating of food. We will now look at the interplay of these two complexes of ideas in both calendrical and life-crisis rituals, and, in the next two chapters, in rituals of death and sacrifice.

CELEBRATING THE PROPHET MUHAMMAD'S BIRTHDAY

The Islamic lunar calendar includes several holidays, a month of fasting, and a month devoted to the pilgrimage to Mecca.[4] Among the holidays is that celebrating the birth of the prophet Muhammad on the twelfth of Rabi'ul-awal, the third month of the year. Muhammad's birth is celebrated in many Muslim societies by the reciting of stories and poems (cf. Knappert 1971; Tapper and Tapper 1987). Gayo celebrate the Prophet's birthday, or *Molut*, on this date, and they also recognize the twelfth day of each of the following three months as secondary Molut days.[5] Several Isak men

---

[4] Optional fasts are sometimes observed, such as that of 'Ashūrā', on the tenth of Muharram, historically occasioned by the martyrdom of Muhammad's grandson Husayn. Isak observers of this fast know the date only as the "sad day" on which Adam left Heaven and human hardship began. Acehnese, however, have recognized the link to Husayn (Snouck Hurgronje 1906, I:194), and some Minangkabau people hold a procession in observance of the event.

[5] The Arabic *maulid* usually refers to the birthday and to its celebrations, while *maulūd* refers to the associated literary genres; see Schimmel (1985:144–58). I use the Gayo *Molut* throughout the following discussion. For Maulid celebrations elsewhere see Tapper and Tapper (1987) on Turkey, and Shinar (1977) on northern Africa.

said that Muhammad's close followers and successors, his first four *khalifa* or deputies, died on these dates.

Although Gayo agree that Molut celebrates the prophet Muhammad's birth, they disagree on the proper way to observe it. Some see it as the occasion for a kenduri and the hosting of one village by another, while others emphasize the importance of lectures and didactic discussions about the prophet's life, and find the kenduri to be at cross-purposes with the holiday's commemorative intent.

In Isak during the 1980s, each village held a kenduri, usually on the first Molut day. The kenduri took place in the village prayer house, with each household contributing one or more plates of food for collective consumption. Some households also held their own kenduris at home to commemorate the day. Any Molut kenduri included a betel case, a plate of *lepat* (cylindrical sweets made of glutinous rice and palm sugar), and a plate of glutinous rice. Although only males attended the prayer house events, at which the village religious official or another learned man told of the prophet's life, everyone enjoyed the sweets and the food.

Everyone with whom I discussed the kenduri agreed that it was held to commemorate the prophet Muhammad. Some people added that the sweets, the glutinous rice, and the betel ingredients were enjoyed by angels who visit each house for this purpose. For them, the central events in the Molut kenduri were setting out betel and sweets rather than listening to the lecture.

In 1979 the first Molut day fell on a Friday, the ninth of February. Isak women had spent much of the previous day preparing the sweets, but on this day men and women turned to the problem of finding a chicken to kill and cook. Everyone wanted to kill a chicken because it was the smallest animal that could be properly dedicated to God (by cutting its throat and pronouncing the basmala). A fish could not be killed in this manner, and a goat would be too expensive for most households. (The frenetic activity meant, ironically, that fewer people than usual attended congregational worship at the mosque.)

Four of the five villages held kenduris at their prayer houses in the afternoon (members of the fifth village, Kutë Rayang, spoke vaguely about holding a kenduri the following month). The kenduri I attended, at Kutë Kramil, happened to be the best-attended in Isak that year. About thirty men, a majority of the village's adult males, came to the prayer house. Each man brought two small plates wrapped in cloth, one with sweets and another with rice and meat or vegetables. Each man placed his plates on the floor by the door as he entered.

In charge of the event was a Kramil man who went by the title Kuakek, the acronym of the local office he had once held (Kantor Urusan Agama Kecamatan, Subdistrict Religious Affairs Office). He was a man of generally modernist leanings who sought to reform village practices by participating in them rather than by openly criticizing them (although, as we will see shortly, he did that too).

By about four in the afternoon, when it appeared that everyone who would come had arrived, the Kuakek began to talk of Muhammad's life. He told of how all living and nonliving things on the earth came from the Light of Muhammad. He then described the succession of miraculous events in Muhammad's life, from his painless birth, to Jibra'il's opening and cleansing of his body, to the many miracles that ensured him victory in battle. He spoke casually, as if making a series of asides, and at one point just stopped at the end of a story and suggested we all eat what we had brought. We each chose a pair of plates at random from the collective pile, ate the sweet rice dish, and then, after several minutes of further conversation among ourselves, the regular food. No prayers were said. After we had finished eating and each man had recovered the plate he had brought, the kenduri was over.

In the following year I chose to attend a Molut kenduri in Kutë Robel. The officiant, Aman Rabu, was a man who had studied religion with Tengku Ubit, the most venerated Isak teacher of the 1920s and 1930s. He and others in Robel saw themselves as traditionalist scholars who upheld older religious standards in an otherwise impious community. The kenduri was held at night, and the men performed their evening salāt worship before beginning the feast. Aman Rabu read from a printed Arabic-script Malay book of the prophet's life.[6] He chose to read a detailed account of Muhammad's genealogy and then a section on major events in his life, including miracles. After recounting the death of Muhammad's first wife, he stopped and said that, because there were not many participants, he did not feel like going any further. We chose plates of sweet dishes and before eating chanted several *shalawat*s, recitations for the prophet's welfare.

The focus on feasting on Molut was even greater in the early colonial period, when each village would host another on one of the four Molut days (the twelfth day of Rabi'ul-awal and of each of the next three months). After all the guests had been served, host-village men would hand special plates, wrapped in brand-new cloths, to men from the guest village with whom they wished to begin or affirm ties of friendship. The guest village would return the invitation, and reciprocate the gifts, on another Molut in that or the following year. (In the 1980s Molut hosting continued to be practiced in the southern Gayo Luës district.)

One traditionalist scholar, Tengku Madin Pas of Takèngën, explained to me in 1989 why there must be a kenduri on Molut. The Prophet's life story should be told over a meal, he said, in order to follow a pattern begun centuries ago. The first commemoration of Muhammad's life was sponsored by

---

[6] Called the *Barzanji*, the book is a Malay version of the *Mawlid al-nabi* of Ja'far ibn Hasan al-Barzanji (d. 1766) of Medina. The book is used throughout the Muslim world.

a ruler who gave 300 dinars to an ulama so that he would write out the
Prophet's life story. He also ordered that 10,000 goats and many cows be
slaughtered for the meal. Religion had fallen into disuse and the meal was
held to attract people back into religious observance. "The modernists
claim that kenduris are not important," Tengku Madin Pas complained,
"though they recognize that the first celebration of Molut was a kenduri."[7]

Modernists do indeed object to the interpretation of Molut as a kenduri.
Public celebrations in Takèngën take the form of didactic lectures at which
a scholar may express a disdain for including food in the event. I attended
one of these celebrations in February 1978 at one of Takèngën's high
schools. Tengku Ali Jaidun, the chief spokesperson for Muhammadiyah,
presided over the event. He began by commenting on Qur'ānic verses that
depicted life in Mecca prior to the revelations. He explained in some detail
the nature of trade routes and economic competition among tribes in the region. He then began to contrast Muhammad's ideal family life with that of
the prophets before him. All suffered by comparison: Adam and Eve because Eve disobeyed, Noah because his wife and children refused to follow
him, Job because his wife abandoned him, and so on. The program ended
with group singing of Indonesian songs, a Gayo didong song, and recitations of prayers for Muhammad.

Tengku Ali Jaidun's chosen texts emphasize the role of Muhammad as exemplary person, whose life is of direct relevance to ours today. The event
had a scholarly tone to it, rather than one of awe at Muhammad's miracles.
Ali Jaidun scowled disapprovingly when a small plate of cakes was passed
around for the students, a modest refreshment that he nonetheless labeled a
"holdover from pre-Islamic [jāhilīya] times." He and other modernist scholars find the inclusion of any food on this occasion to be a dangerous reminder that other Gayo celebrate the event in a different way, as a kenduri.
The presence of even a single plate of cakes serves as a link to the entire
kenduri complex, with its attendant ideas of transmitting benefit to spirits.

THE CHILD'S ENTRY INTO THE WORLD

The same contentions arise with regard to the steps performed to welcome
an infant into the world. Seven days after the birth of a child, Gayo carry
out a series of rituals known either by the phrase "descending, being
bathed" (turun mani) or by the term kikah, from the Arabic 'aqīqa.[8] Most
Isak residents use the former term; most town residents, and virtually all

---

[7] Shinar (1977) traces the development of Maulid feasting; see also Schimmel (1985:
144–49).

[8] The root mani, usually in the form imanèn, "to be bathed," is only used for infants and
corpses; all other humans niri, "bathe," and animals are inirin, "bathed."

modernists, the latter. The two terms refer to different moments in the ritual series, and the choice of terms indicates the choice of a larger ritual context for this act, which I shall call, neutrally, the "child's initiation ritual."

Some elements in the ritual are practiced by nearly all households. Seven days after birth, or at another, equally propitious time, the baby is taken outside the house for the first time.[9] (The same procedures are followed for male and female children.) The infant is bathed, more or less elaborately (the step referred to by the term *turun mani*). At the kenduri that follows a name is selected for the child and a lock of hair is cut, which may be buried afterward. A sheep or goat may be sacrificed on this occasion (the step referred to by the term *kikah*).

As is the case for agricultural rituals and sacrifices after vows, the initiation ritual is segmented into two major events: the bathing of the infant by the edge of the river, and the feast, held immediately afterwards, at which the name is given and the hair cut. And, as with other ritual events, the compartmentalization of the ritual allows people to acknowledge some of its components and ignore others.

The bathing ritual introduces the child to the natural world in two ways: by presenting the child to the elements, and by inoculating her or him against the shocks of cold and noise. I followed one such event in July 1978. Four women played important roles in the ritual. The ritual specialist was, as is ideally the case, a relative and member of the same village as the infant boy. A second woman, the baby's "holder," cradled him in her arms during most of the ritual. A third woman carried the uncooked rice that later would be given to the holder, and a fourth woman carried a tape recorder with a cassette of gong music (instead of the actual gongs that sometimes are used), which announced their passage from the baby's house to the water's edge.

The trip to the river was potentially dangerous to the child. Since his birth, seven days earlier, he had been kept near his mother. He had been protected from possible spiritual dangers by various talismans hung in the house, and by the four walls of the house itself. After the completion of the

---

[9] The ritual may not be held on the dates of the Islamic month that are "human creation dates" (*mengguë ni jema*). Every sixth date is of this category (the creation dates for six objects—humans, buffalo, steel, cloth, rice, gold, in that order—cycle through the month). Thus the ritual may not be held on the 1st, 7th, 13th, 19th, and 25th. Other prohibited days include "nine" dates (the 9th, 19th, and 29th), the last Wednesday in the month (called "unlucky Wednesday" [*Rabu nas*]), and the day of the week on which birth took place. Major holidays also are inappropriate for holding a feast of this sort. If the seventh day after birth coincides with one of these dates, then one must either choose the next appropriate date or wait until the fourteenth or the twenty-first day of the child's life. Isak Gayo also avoid holding weddings on the prohibited dates and days.

ritual he would be stronger and better able to resist evil spirits and the diseases they brought, but in the meantime he would be dangerously exposed. Preparations had to be made. The baby's holder twisted a bit of cotton cloth, picked it up with a steel betel-nut cutter, and set it afire. The steel provided an element of hard resistance to spirits, and the fire helped to scare them off. The gong music also repelled them. A sprig of the first plant ever to exist on the earth, the "tough plant" (batang teguh), was used at many stages in the ritual; its toughness was said to rub off on the baby. Just before stepping from the house, both the ritual specialist and the holder (with the baby) dropped a sprig of tough plant and stepped on it. The holder kept an umbrella over the baby during their procession to the river.

At the river the women spread a colorful reed mat on the rocks, and the holder sat with the child. The specialist arrayed four colored piles of uncooked rice in a circle on a banana leaf. In the center of the circle were four selensungs, betel leaves wrapped around a bit of areca nut and lime.

The specialist then held the leaf over the baby's head, pronounced the names of the spirits in the river, and waved the leaf in a counterclockwise direction over the baby's head, counting from one to seven. This process transferred (seduëi) any illness or bad fortune from the four elements that constitute the baby into the four rice piles on the leaf, just as healers transfer illness into a chicken for diagnosis. As in other cases, the transfer was possible because of the correspondence between the four natural elements and the four rice piles that stood for them. "Inside are the four elements; outside are the four kinds [of rice]," she explained. She then held the leaf over the river and, before letting it drift downstream, counted backward, from seven to one, thereby sending illness and bad fortune away.

Specialists differed in their accounts of the water spirits. Some described four spirits that corresponded to the four elements and rice piles: one upstream, one downstream, and one on either bank. Others mentioned prophets: Yakub who governs the rocks, Yati who rules the river, and Kedemat who governs the earth. But all agreed that the rice told the spirits of a new human in the natural world, just as the colored rice piles sent by Abang Kerna in healing signaled a human presence. As one specialist put it, sending the leaf with the rice and selensungs said to the prophets and spirits: "This is our child; do not hurt him or we will twist your ears off."

The ritual focus then shifted from announcing the birth to inoculating the child. The specialist bathed the child several times with flour, mungkur water, and river water. She split a coconut over his head ("so that he will not be afraid of thunder") and let the milk fall on his face ("so that he will not be afraid of rain"). She then held a mirror up to his head ("to show him his own light," meaning the reflection of the four colors that made up his body). The mirror also permitted the four natural elements in the body to

13. The *Turun Mani*: Inën Mudë Kursi, Healer, Carrying an Infant to the Water's Edge

see that this new being was, indeed, a human being and should be protected. (Before the availability of mirrors, infants were held over the river to see their reflections.)

The bathing ritual was complete when the ritual specialist, acting on behalf of the mother, gave a measure of uncooked rice to the child's holder, "to redeem the child from her." The rice (sometimes, but not in this in-

14. Splitting the Coconut so the Infant Will Not Fear Thunder or Rain

stance, accompanied by money or sugar) compensated her for her trouble
and, more important, freed the baby from any claim that the holder might
have because of her protective role in the ritual.

The second part of the initiation ritual is a kenduri of four elements at
which the child is given a name, a bit of hair is cut from the head, and, in
some cases, a sheep or goat is sacrificed. The sacrifice, kikah, "redeems"
the child from God, as one would redeem mortgaged land. We are in debt
to God for a child, I learned, and this sacrifice cancels that debt. It also creates a tie between the parents and the child.

Most Isak people, however, consider the sacrifice to be recommended (sunna) rather than required (wājib), and many families hold the kenduri without killing a goat. (For that reason most people in Isak refer to the kenduri as a *kenduri turun mani* rather than as a *kikah*.) Some said that they could perform the sacrifice at any time during the child's life or even after death. When my neighbor Sahim discussed the ritual he was about to hold for his infant daughter, he remarked that he hoped to kill a goat for the occasion. His mother interjected that it was not required to do so and that he had better use the precious animal as a gift to his healer, who had cured him of a serious illness two years earlier, to make the cure complete and lasting. Sahim agreed, and served only chicken.

In choosing a name for the infant, the chooser must know the science of names. Names have a direct relation to character and fortune. If a name is too "high," or demanding, the individual may not be able to bear the burden and will fail in life. Conversely, a name that is too "low" could hold a child back. A person's problems later in life may be diagnosed as due to an ill-fitting name, and the name may then be changed. (I witnessed several such rituals.) The person who chooses a name thus must fine-tune it to the child's characteristics, which derive from the time and circumstances of birth.

Because of the importance of a name, the older men who attend the kenduri either suggest names or choose from among several composed by other knowledgeable people. Sahim wanted to name his own daughter, choosing to call her Sugaila Déwi, a contraction of *Suku Gayo Asli Lingë Demi Wanita Islam/Isak* (Gayo People, Original Lingë [Stock], for the sake of Muslim/Isak Women). The name fit her well, he said, because it began with the letter *s*, which figured prominently in the name of her day of birth, *Senin* (Monday), and in her parents' names, Sahim and Asna.[10]

At the feast following the bathing ritual described above, three men stood and spoke about the significance of the overall event. Each understood it in different terms, and their distinct discourses made salient the divergence in Isak views on the relation of older Gayo-ritual institutions to broader Muslim traditions.

The first speaker was Rëjë Hasyim, a man then in his early sixties who was known for his skill at ritual speaking (Bowen 1991:154–62). After the meal he rose to give a welcoming speech on behalf of the hosts. As it turned out he also spoke on behalf of ëdët, Gayo norms and traditions:

> I am going to talk about ëdët. I don't know whether or not what I have to say is in accord with religion [agama], but I'll leave that for the learned men [tengku] to decide. What I know, I learned from the didong singers, not from learned men. There are four debts [*utang opat*] to pay:

[10] Some of the older men later challenged Sahim's interpretation of the name on the grounds that he had conflated different Arabic letters and that he had misread the *mengguë* dates. But he kept the name.

the turun mani;
turning the child over to a teacher;
throwing away the forbidden [haram],
  keeping that which is permitted [halal] [a phrase referring
  to circumcision];
letting go [marrying off the child].

And there are four steps in the turun mani, as I learned it from the didong singers:

carry it [the infant] to the water with a headdress of *urip-urip*,
  because that was the first grass to live on the earth;
then show it a mirror
then split a coconut over its head so that it will not fear thunder;
then take it back to the house and give it a name, chosen
  so as to be in accord with religion.

The name is for the soul (nyawa) of the child. Regarding the other two debts: for circumcision, it is part of ëdët because the holy book does not say that it is the sign of a Muslim. And marrying off the child is only a major debt if it is a girl; she must be married off even if she is thirty years old.

Rëjë Hasyim made a sharp distinction between the domain of Gayo norms, which he learned from maxims transmitted by village rulers and didong experts, and the domain of Islamic norms, especially as interpreted by self-styled tengkus (I detected a sneer at this point). For him, the initiation ritual, and for that matter the rest of the life cycle, were matters of ëdët, not Islam. (Other people had also pointed out to me that circumcision is not mentioned in the Qur'ān and thus was not a matter of religion.) He organized his speech in the manner of Gayo ritual speaking, highlighting the authoritative maxims that carry Gayo culture (Bowen 1991:139–51).

Rëjë Hasyim was followed by Guru Manap, the head of the local public school, speaking on behalf of the guests. Whereas Rëjë Hasyim had spoken in Gayo, Guru Manap used Indonesian. He spoke less about the significance of the feast than of the duties of the child to his religion and to the nation. He did not, however, comment on Rëjë Hasyim's words.

The mother then brought her child into the room and handed him to the Kuakek (the subdistrict religious official). The Kuakek brought some sweet tea to the baby's lips, so his speech would be sweet, and cut off a lock of his hair. The hair, he explained as he cut, could be thrown into the river or buried; in either case it would take with it any diseases or dirt that accompanied the child at birth. The baby was then handed to Rëjë Hasyim, as the elder among the hosting party. Rëjë Hasyim arranged two betel leaves to cover the three slips of paper onto which names for the child had been written. The baby's mother then chose blindly one of the three.

Having completed this work, the Kuakek rose and met Rëjë Hasyim's outspoken challenge to the authority of Islam. He spoke in Gayo, though he included many Indonesian expressions. "Sometimes traditions conflict with religion," he began, "and when they do they have to be abandoned." He continued:

Three special dispensations were granted to the province of Aceh [in 1962, after the Darul Islam rebellion]. They are education, *adat-istiadat* [rules and customs], and religion. But only the adat that is not in conflict with religion can be retained.

Furthermore, the "four debts" [to children] are really commands from the prophet Muhammad to us. The benefit of the turun mani initiation ritual occurs when the parents say the Islamic confession of faith in the infant's ear, so that he or she knows who God and his prophet are. And it was the prophet Muhammad who first put the sweet taste in the child's mouth as I just did. The kikah is obligatory [wājib] for all those who can afford it; the child is still mortgaged from God and must be redeemed. The prophet Muhammad also ordered the name giving and hair cutting that we do here, down to specifying certain proscribed names and the way of disposing of the lock of hair: it must be thrown into a river, not just thrown away.

On the other debts held by parents to the children [responding directly to Rëjë Hasyim's remarks]: *chatan* [circumcision] is performed following the example of the Prophet, who himself was circumcised. Thus we should say "sunna Rasul," which means following the example of the Prophet, and not "sunët Rasul," which we often say here to mean just circumcision. All religions command their followers to be circumcised, for health reasons. On the fourth debt: as Rëjë Hasyim said, it is more important to marry off a daughter.

The Kuakek undercut Rëjë Hasyim's rhetoric in several ways. He began by broadening the context from Gayo traditions to adat and religion in Aceh as a whole. Whereas reciting Gayo proverbs is highly persuasive to an Isak audience, those same individuals, if forced to consider the issue abstractly, will agree that adat must be made consistent with the higher claims of religion.

The Kuakek's brilliant move was to then encompass Gayo norms in the broader field of actions commanded by the prophet Muhammad. He did so by ignoring the bathing ritual entirely and extracting as the essence of the total ritual sequence the moment when the confession of faith is spoken into the baby's ear. He asserted the importance of the kikah, not mentioned by Rëjë Hasyim. He then returned Rëjë Hasyim's sneer at tengkus by correcting the way "we," by which he meant the less-learned in religious matters (a category meant to include Rëjë Hasyim), mispronounced the Arabic names for ritual events.[11]

---

[11] He used an inclusive "we" (*kitë*); but this form is obligatory in polite, formal discourse, and is often used as a polite second-person plural.

These two conceptions of the event hardly overlap at all. For Rëjë Hasyim the event is part of Gayo ëdët, inscribed in Gayo maxims, and features bathing and naming the child. For the Kuakek it is part of religion, inscribed in the hadīth, and features the kikah and other actions first carried out by the Prophet. In both views the ritual accomplishes certain practical ends, but for Rëjë Hasyim (and most others in Isak) it is basically about introducing the infant to the world, whereas for the Kuakek it is basically about conforming to the historical example of the prophet Muhammad. This discrepancy in interpretation is supported by the compartmentalization of the overall ritual, in that the Kuakek and like-minded others need not acknowledge the initial activities held at the water's edge.

The dispute continued in an informal way after the kenduri. Several of the men walked over to a nearby prayer house to relax and chat. I asked Rëjë Hasyim about the meaning of the bathing ritual. Usually reticent in talking with me, he spoke at length of the ritual's significance. He did so in part to take a little cultural revenge on the Kuakek by means of my presence. As he told me why the women had carried a burning cloth to the river and set adrift the colored piles of rice, the Kuakek, standing nearby, kept up a nervous laugh punctuated by remarks that "people used to do this, they don't anymore" (pretending that the bathing ritual had not taken place). Rëjë Hasyim's discourse effectively isolated the Kuakek from the others present, because the others found the description interesting and true.

Debates about the kikah are at least half a century old. At the beginning of this century, most people in Isak delayed the kikah until after the death of the individual (Snouck Hurgronje 1903:314). It was nearly undistinguishable in purpose from the sacrifice carried out at the Feast of Sacrifice, in that both were intended to transmit benefit to the spirit of a deceased person (see Chapter 12).

By the late 1920s, however, modernist Muslim teachers had begun to criticize the practice of delaying the kikah. They did so on two grounds: that the prophet Muhammad had clearly ordered that it be done shortly after birth, and that delaying it showed that it was done for the wrong reasons: not to obey God but to send benefit to the deceased. The practice was strongly criticized by the scholar-poet Tengku Mudë Kala in the late 1940s (Daudy 1950:4–5). After describing the proper way to perform the kikah (for which he uses a term, akikah, partway between the Gayo kikah and the Arabic 'aqīqa), Mudë Kala warns his listeners not to err by sacrificing on behalf of an adult or a dead person:

kë jema kaul akikah a enti ibubuh	For adults, don't perform the akikah;
gërë ara isuruh	it is not commanded,
akikah a géh kené agama	the akikah, according to religion.

lebih-lebih sesat	More than that is in error;
gërë sunët ku jema si matë	it is not sunna, [sacrificing] for a dead person,
iperbuët ahlié	done by the relatives,
akikah a iatan ni donya	the akikah, in this world.

oya perbuëtën akikah a nggëh iperintah	Doing the akikah like that is not ordered;
oya buët salah	that is wrongdoing:
bid'a ipanang agama	bid'a in the eyes of religion.

Ibu Inën Muhammad, my mother in Takëngën, was among the many modernists in town who strongly agreed with Tengku Mudë Kala (whose poetry she remembered, admired, and sometimes sang to herself). As we sat one evening after a meal, she asked me whether I had seen the women in Isak carry the burning cloth for a turun mani. I had, I answered, to which she grunted and shook her head in deep disapproval: "How could people do such things. Whereas the Messenger of God said that you should hold a feast seven days after the birth of a child, and kill two goats for a boy and one for a girl, he said nothing about the rest, so they should not do it." I asked if it were not ëdët and thus permissible. "But you cannot just add things any which way," she replied. She meant that the Prophet's command placed the entire ritual in the domain of religious worship, where one may not add new elements but must do just as he did.

She began to talk about the kikahs held for her grandchildren. For each of them she recalled how she had insisted that the parents sacrifice a goat precisely on the seventh day after birth, no matter how inconvenient that might be. "When Gemboyah was born [in Jakarta] the seventh day was a Sunday and all the office workers wanted it put off, but I said no, the Messenger of God said seven days and I won't budge from that; you can hold another feast later on if you want to." She had her way on these and other occasions. (On each occasion only one goat was sacrificed, regardless of the child's sex.) Even when the parents had little money, she said that all they needed to do was kill the goat and give the meat to the orphans; inviting large numbers of people was not important.

Ibu Inën Muhammad shares the disapproving opinions held by the Kuakek (and by Tengku Asaluddin, a close family friend) about the way a child's initiation ritual is performed in Isak. Rejecting the framework of the kenduri and the justification of ëdët, they refuse to acknowledge the legitimacy of any practice not ordered by God through the prophet Muhammad. Ibu Inën Muhammad lives among people of roughly the same opinions, and need not confront those practices in village settings. Indeed, she often relegates them to the pre-Islamic past, as did Tengku Ali Jaidun in commenting on the cakes eaten at the Takëngën Molut observance. By contrast, the

Kuakek and other modernists in Isak face contrary practices and opinions at such public events as Molut and the child's initiation ritual. There, they seek to resituate the ground for ritual commentary onto a scriptural plane. They do so in a relatively moderate rhetoric, one that ignores and avoids certain confrontations, just as, whenever possible, Isak modernists avoid kenduris of questionable intent rather than confronting the hosts.

The rare confrontations that do occur, such as that between Rëjë Hasyim and the Kuakek, point out the radically diverse frameworks that different members of the same community bring, time after time, to the same ritualized occasions. Though sitting down together at the child's initiation ritual, some see it as primarily a reenactment of the prophet Muhammad's actions in the seventh century, while others see it as a fulfillment of Gayo norms that preserves relations of exchange and communication across generations and between people and spirits.

Chapter Eleven

SPEAKING FOR THE DEAD

PERHAPS NO ISSUE strikes as profoundly into the hearts of ordinary people in the highlands as does caring for the dead. Death shakes the survivors and sharpens religious disputes. A contrast in ritual understanding becomes a clash of moralities.

In Isak, as death approaches, arrives, and moves on, men and women pray, carry, dig, chant, and settle their debts. All this work, alongside near-continual hosting, cooking, and cleaning, is morally incumbent, emotionally draining, and physically exhausting. But work it is, and work that has a moral purpose to it may be the best thing for the bereaved family.

Much of this labor is religious. At the grave people remind the deceased, in Arabic, of the tents of Islam. In the evenings they gather to chant verses of the Qur'ān. They also direct special prayers of petition to God, asking his intercession on behalf of the deceased. Despite the scriptural content of these speeches, modernists have attacked each of them—the reminder at the grave, the Qur'ānic recitations, the petitionary prayers. The issue is not the choice of texts but their communicative and salvationist intent. Modernists ask rhetorically: How can the dead hear? How can chanting help them? How can one person make up for the sins of another, even by way of God?

The two positions involve sharply divergent ideas about the temporality of death and its social consequences. For most people in Isak, the living and the dead continue to have a lot to say to each other and do for each other after death. Funeral rituals demonstrate this continued relationship through their acts of exchange and offering. Ritual also structures time for the bereaved into long stretches of work on behalf of the dead, alternating with moments of closure and catharsis. These stages ease the torment of the deceased, and gradually relax his or her ties to the community of the living.

Modernists portray death's temporality very differently, as a sharp break between one state and the next, across which very little communication can or should take place. Because they reject the possibility of the living aiding the dead, modernists also reject the validity of gradually phasing out ties to the dead. Through everyday discussions and religious poetry, they have interjected into Isak life an emphasis on the finality of death that runs against the gradualist grain of older ritual practice.

The Gayo controversies recall a continuing debate among anthropologists over the social significance of funeral rituals. Some anthropologists have argued that funeral ritual supports the social order (Bloch 1982). Others have responded that sometimes it challenges that order, but that funeral ritual generally embodies central cultural values (Metcalf and Huntington 1991). Both positions follow Emile Durkheim (1965) in emphasizing the social and cultural importance of the prescribed form taken on by mourning practices in any society. A third position questions the extent to which ritual form shapes the experience of others' deaths (R. Rosaldo 1984), but common to these and most ethnographic accounts of funeral ritual is the Durkheimian assumption that the members of each society follow, with little reflection and even less doubt, a single set of prescribed rituals. Rare is the ethnographic glimpse into hesitations or quarrels over the moral and social propriety of alternative ritual forms (M. Rosaldo 1984). In Indonesia, as we saw earlier, anthropologists have largely avoided looking closely at Islamic rituals, where such quarrels are common.

Gayo certainly do engage in lengthy discussions on such questions, as we saw in the exchange between Alimin and Asyin in Takèngën. For the Gayo people I know, the form taken by funerals is of vital moral and emotional importance. Though they all see it as channeling the way people think and feel about death as well as directly affecting the welfare of the deceased, they disagree about which ideas and emotions people ought to hold, and which ritual actions can, and ought to, be effective.

Speaking to the Dead at the Grave

For most Isak people, death is a long process that requires much from the living. Relatives and friends speak to the dying person, and then to the spirit of deceased, to ensure a peaceful death and to ease the torment of the grave.

In late February 1979, Inën Selamah, the wife of Abang Das's father Aman Selamah, began to suffer a series of ailments: raspy coughing, swelling in the legs, and fever.[1] Accomplished healer that he was, Abang Das tried a number of remedies. By early April, however, "her sickness would not listen to the rajah anymore" because her moment to depart had arrived. On the fifth of April, at about two o'clock in the morning, she woke up and began to complain of pains. Death had begun.

Abang Das now shifted from trying to cure her to ensuring that she die peacefully, untroubled by bothersome jin. He asked God to ease her gently out of life. He asked her to repeat the confession of faith after him "so that she would remember that there was only one tie to God and to the

---

[1] This account is taken from my field notes, with minimal editing, and is based on my observations and Abang Das's explanations unless otherwise noted. Inën Selamah was Aman Selamah's second wife; his first, Abang Das's mother, had died years earlier.

Prophet." He was pleased that she was able to repeat it, because she would probably be able to say it in the grave as well and would avoid torment. He also read the whole of the Surah Yā Sīn (Qur'ān 36), which says that God will protect you from jin. Reading this chapter aloud keeps the jin away, he explained to me.

By the time she died, about four o'clock that morning, about a dozen women had gathered at her house. He asked them not to cry over her, because if one cries then one is punished later. The Prophet said that people could cry over him while he was alive but not once he had died. There was little weeping, in fact, and none at all after sunrise, when others began to arrive at the house.

By noon the younger men had dug the grave and had built the bamboo platform used to carry the body. Her female relatives then bathed her, wrapped her in cloth, and carried her to the front room.[2] As they walked they chanted a shalawat prayer:

Allāhumma shalli 'alā saiyidinā Muhammadin nabi al-ummi wa 'alā ālihi wa ashābihi wa salam.

[God, call down blessing on our master Muhammad, the illiterate prophet, and on his family and companions, and greet them with peace.]

The shalawat "brings you closer to the prophet Muhammad," explained Abang Das; "you say it because you are following his orders for washing and carrying the corpse."[3] In the front room the women dressed the corpse in white cloth. They ripped the edge of it so that when she awakened momentarily in the grave she would realize that she had died. Her children came and each asked forgiveness of her for ill-considered things they may have done or said during her life. Abang Das and his eldest daughter, Itěm, then sprinkled uncooked rice from her head to her feet. Abang Das spoke softly for several minutes; I learned later that he spoke to the spirits of his own former teachers (including the famed Aman Mok, his father-in-law), returning a vow made during her illness in which he had promised to sacrifice a goat or sheep if she recovered. Because she had died he could release himself from the obligation. Tengku Daud then made a brief speech in which he asked that anyone who owed her a debt or to whom she had owed one come forth so that the debts could be forgiven or paid.

The procession continued to the Isak mosque, where the men and women

---

[2] The body was washed four times, with three, five, seven, and then nine cupfuls of water. Each washing was accompanied by a distinct prayer.

[3] The prophet's illiteracy is considered proof of the divine origin of the finely poetic Qur'ān. Reciting a shalawat at this moment is recommended in a prayer manual that Isak people sometimes consult, the *Majmu' Syarif* (Suhaimi n.d.:238). Such blessings are elsewhere called *tashliya* and are subject to many variations. Among the benefits of reciting these blessings is relief for the deceased from torment in the grave (Padwick 1961:152–66).

performed the special salāt worship required for a corpse (G. *semiyang mèt*). The worship took only a few minutes. I was told that the spirit of the deceased followed along with the living for this final act of worship. The men then carried the corpse to the grave site where her family was buried, on the hill above Kutë Baru. The women remained below. All the graves lay on a north-south axis, so that the heads, facing to the right, also face Mecca. The body, dressed only in the white cloths, was placed in the grave and covered by the plank on which it had been carried. Pieces of the bamboo frame and a mat were used to protect the body as the grave was filled.

When the earth had been mounded over the grave, Imëm Caya, the religious official for Kutë Robel (Inën Selamah's natal village), took an earthenware pot filled with water and sprinkled it from the head to the foot of the grave, where he upended it and thrust it into the grave. ("As one waters a tree; the water is drawn upward," explained Abang Das later. "Just as water is cooling, so will she be cooled and refreshed.") He also pushed one stick into the dirt at the head of the grave and another at the foot.

Imëm Caya then sat by the head of the grave and read the *telkin* catechism to the woman's spirit. The text took up three pages of small, printed Arabic script. The religious official from Kutë Rayang (Abang Das's father's village) sat by him and from time to time helped him interpret a letter or word in the text. During part of the reading, when he reminded the spirit of the tenets of Islam, he held the stick with his right hand so that the reading would reach the spirit. All the men then joined in reciting several Qur'ānic verses, beginning with al-Fātiha. During the recitation a member of Abang Das's kin group gave some money to the two religious officials and then to those who had helped with the work but were not close relatives of the deceased. Abang Das made a short speech in which he thanked everyone, and said that he was very satisfied with the turnout at the grave and that he hoped everyone would come back to the house for a kenduri.

When Imëm Caya knelt by Inën Selamah's grave and recited to her the fixed text of the telkin, he was performing an act that most Gayo still consider morally incumbent. The telkin (<Ar. talqīn) is an Arabic-language catechism that reminds the deceased of the main tenets of Islam. It is read aloud in order to prepare the deceased for the impending and rather rough interrogation at the hands of two angels, Mungkar and Nakīr. Along with Muslims elsewhere, Isak people hold that God returns the soul of the dead person to the body for a few moments after burial. For Isak Gayo, this moment comes when the telkin reader reaches the Qur'ānic phrase (Qur'ān 3:185)

Kul un-nafsin dza'iqatul mauti   Every soul will experience death.

The spirit of the deceased has remained near the body since the moment of death, and at this moment reunites with the soul to revive the person.

The spirit feels the edge of the burial cloth, perceives that it has been ripped, not hemmed, and thus realizes that he or she is dead. (It is here that the reciter of the telkin grasps hold of the stick leading down to the corpse.) The spirit listens to the catechism, after which the soul leaves the body and only the spirit remains in the vicinity of the grave.[4]

The catechism is always read from a written Arabic text (as was the case in lowlands Aceh; Snouck Hurgronje [1906, I:427]). Unlike virtually all other important recitations, it is never memorized. Gayo say that its contents must be transmitted accurately to the deceased. "If you make even one mistake," one of the officials told me, "it would be a very great sin." Indeed, the officials have seemed to me to be a bit nervous when they kneel to read. Abang Das suggested another reason for not memorizing the passage. "Memorizing it would be 'asking for it' (*muteniron*), as when people memorize spells for invulnerability or power, and then God tests them by involving them in fights." It happened in the past, he added, that a religious official would memorize the text, "and suddenly he had a lot of work to do" because more people would then begin to die. Refraining from memorizing the telkin emphasizes that its function is purely instructional and does not empower the speaker in the manner of a spell.

The telkin reader may choose among several available texts. The religious official in Kutë Kramil village, Aman Bani, reads the talqīn printed in an Indonesian-language book (Qusyairi n.d.:146–51) available from Takèngën book sellers. The book provides the text in Arabic, in Latin transliteration (so that it will be pronounced correctly), and finally in Indonesian. The Indonesian translation occupies two pages of fine print. He showed me six other printed books from which he took prayers for the dead, and also sheets of paper on which he had copied prayers learned from others.

In an effort to standardize village practice, the Takèngën branch of the traditionalist al-Washliyah organization issued a version of the talqīn in late 1989. The text describes why it is important, thus justifying itself to the listeners, alive and dead:

Hai [Name]! You now have left the world and all its attractions and are entering the next world, the realm of Barzakh [the transitional realm between this world and the world of the final judgment]. Do not forget the agreements that separate this world from the next. Now bear witness that there is no deity but God and that Muhammad is his Messenger. Soon two angels will come,

---

[4] The idea that the soul rejoins the body at this point is widely held by Muslims, but precisely how this happens, a tricky business, is passed over "rather lightly" in the popular Middle Eastern manuals on death (Smith and Haddad 1981:40). On the questioning by the two angels see, for Egypt, Lane (1860:522–25); for Morocco, Westermark (1926, II:464–65); and, for the range of scholarly opinions, Smith and Haddad (1981:41–50). Skeat (1967:406–7) describes the talqīn in Malaysia.

Mungkar and Nakīr. Know that these two angels also are creations of God, and do not fear them. If they ask you questions, answer them in a clear voice. The questions will be:

1. Who is your God? Answer: My God is Allah.
2. Who is your prophet? Answer: My prophet is Muhammad s.a.w.
3. What is your book? Answer: My book is the Qur'ān al-Karīm.
4. What is your kiblat? Answer: My kiblat is the Kabatullah [Mecca].
5. Who are your people? Answer: All Muslim men and women

Answer these questions with a clear voice.

This text is supplied in Arabic and Indonesian so that, as Tengku Ali Salwany, the al-Washliyah leader, put it, "it can benefit the living as well as the dead." The dead can understand Arabic, he explained, whereas the living need an Indonesian translation.[5]

Most people in Isak consider it their moral duty to have the telkin recited for a deceased relative. The reading readies the deceased for the interrogation by the angels, and thus lessens the likelihood of severe beatings. The "torment of the grave" is thought of as physically real, such that we could hear the screams of agony from the spirits if only we heard well enough.

Modernists have roundly attacked the telkin and the ideas behind it. In popular discussions they criticize it from a commonsense perspective, stating flatly that the practice is absurd. They ask: How can the dead hear? They quote a verse from the Qur'ān (27:80) to support their claim that the telkin violates a basic assumption of Islam. The verse reads:

> Thou shalt not make the dead to hear
>   neither shalt thou make the deaf to hear the call
>   when they turn about, retreating.
> Thou shalt not guide the blind out of their error
>   neither shalt thou make any to hear, save
>   such as believe in Our signs, and so surrender.

Nor, continue the modernists, is it clear why one should need the telkin at all. After all, does not everyone know the basic facts it repeats? My own "elder brother" Abang Evi, returning from a funeral where a telkin had been read, joked with his companions: "I'll just take a notebook with me when I die and whip it out in the grave for a review: 'prophet is Muhammad,' 'God is God,' and so forth." His pro-telkin companions laughed nervously.

In their attacks on the telkin Takèngën modernists have drawn heavily on

---

[5] Geertz (1960:71) reports that in East Java the talqīn sometimes is read in Arabic and then in Javanese. A Malay text from the turn of the century is found in Skeat (1900:406–7).

a series of articles written in the 1930s by Ahmad Hassan (1968, 1:210–14; 1979:365–67), the reformist Hassan Bandung discussed in Chapter 3. Hassan labeled the talqīn "the work of fools" (1968, 1:211). "Let corpses teach corpses," he mocked; "let them open schools for corpses" (ibid.). Hassan's rhetoric is echoed by Gayo modernists such as Tengku Joharsyah, who, as subdistrict official for Isak in the 1950s, tried to extirpate what he saw as idolatrous practices. "People were teaching corpses 'there is no deity but God,'" he complained. "Can a stone hear? Of course not. In what book did they read that? It is because of influence from India, which is even worse on Java than here."

Modernist sneers are not well received in Isak. Villagers resent what they see as the cold attitude of those who would not have the telkin read. Speaking of one local modernist teacher, Aman Bani said that "for him a dead person is just an animal or a piece of wood, to be tossed away. But in fact the soul returns for a bit; that is why we must read the telkin."

Alongside the popular name-calling, the talqīn is also the subject of a debate among religious scholars. Discussions about its religious validity invariably come around to the interpretation of a single hadīth:

Recite to those who are dead/dying: "There is no deity but God."[6]

People argue over the correct reading of the Arabic term *mauta*, "the dead," in the above hadith. Does it refer to those who are already dead, or those about to die? The modernist Aman Murni accepted the hadīth as valid but argued that to make any sense it could only refer to the dying. Others pointed out that the word *talqīn* simply means "teaching," and that teaching is best done while alive. Furthermore (and this argument is, for the modernists, conclusive) no sound hadīths report that the prophet Muhammad ever recited the talqīn. Because mortuary ritual lies squarely in the domain of religious matters, they argue, it must only include that which is commanded by the Qur'ān or was practiced by the prophet Muhammad. The talqīn fits neither criteria, and therefore must not be practiced.[7] For the modernists, what is at stake here is the willingness of Muslims to follow the dictates of scripture and to teach when it can really do some good, namely, during life.

Traditionalists respond that, first, they do teach the living as well as the dead, and, second, that the practice of reciting the talqīn can be justified on hadīth grounds. Tengku Ali Salwany had developed a brief for the talqīn

---

[6] The hadīth is attributed to Muslim. It is in the *Mishkat al-Masabih* (Robson 1963–1965:337) and also in the al-Washliyah collection used by Tengku Ali Salwany (Anon. 1969–1970:69).

[7] This argument is made by Ahmad Hassan (1968, 1:210–14; 1979:365–67) and by the Acehnese religious scholar Ash-Shiddieqy (1952, 2:247–48). In the 1980s Takèngën modernists still kept works by these two writers close at hand.

for al-Washliyah. He began with what he admitted to be a weak (*da'if*) hadīth in which Muhammad orders his followers to remind those who have just been buried of their God, their prophet, their religion, and their sacred book. The weakness of this hadīth, he explained, was not due to its content but to the unreliability of one of its transmitters. One of the people in the chain of transmission (isnād) was a man named 'Ashim who had a poor memory. If a hadīth is weak for this sort of reason (rather than, for example, because the person had little faith), it can be raised to the level of an acceptable (*hasan*) hadīth if it can be supported by another hadīth of undisputed merit.

Such supporting hadīth do exist, continued Ali Salwany, in the form of reports that the prophet Muhammad assumed that the dead could hear the words of the living. These hadīth, all considered reliable (sahīh), thus support the findings of the disputed hadīth, because they indicate that Muhammad very well could have urged his followers to speak to the dead after burial. In one of these reliable hadīth Muhammad stated that a dead person hears the footsteps of the people who have buried the corpse as they leave the grave site. In another hadīth he instructed his followers to greet the inhabitants of the grave as they pass by a graveyard. Modernists also greet the dead, added Ali Salwany, proving that even they accept the idea that the dead can hear.[8]

Even stronger in its support for the talqīn is a second reliable hadīth, in which Muhammad is reported to have passed by a graveyard in Medina, stopped, and placed a leaf over a grave. He then began to pray over the grave. When he had finished, his companion, Abu Bakar, asked him why he had done it. Muhammad replied that he had heard the person in the grave screaming in pain, so he asked God to please forgive the person's sins. Abu Bakar then asked Muhammad if the dead person had heard Muhammad. Muhammad replied that he heard better than would persons living on the earth.

Five generations after Muhammad, continued Ali Salwany, scholars were sifting through the collection of hadīth and came upon these reports. On the basis of these they decided that it would be proper to remind the deceased of the bases of their religion. Thus people began to recite the talqīn. But they also recited *lā ilāha illā Allāh* (there is no deity but God) before a person died to remind him of God.

The debate over the telkin takes place in several distinct yet interpenetrating spheres of discourse. Most Isak people carry out the telkin (or any other mortuary activity) in order to aid the deceased, not to follow scripture. From their perspective the issue is not how to read the hadīth but how

---

[8] Ali Salwany's major source on this and other issues is the set of semi-official al-Washliyah opinions published in Medan (Anon. 1969–1970).

to respond to the needs of fellow humans undergoing the "torment of the grave." But they do know about the relevant hadīth, especially that which reads: "Recite to those who are dead/dying: 'There is no deity but God.'" They probably are more likely to know it today than a half-century ago because of the debates among scholars that have taken place in Takèngën since the 1930s. These debates do turn on the interpretation of scripture, but they also take some of their moral charge from the village practices those scriptural interpretations confirm or deny.

NEGOTIATING THE PASSAGE OF THE DEAD

The seven days after Inën Selamah's death were a period of feverish activity for her relatives. They were times of torment for her spirit, and people worked hard to reduce her pain. Friends and family gathered in the evenings to hold kenduris and recite scripture for her benefit. During the days they cooked and cleaned, and also worked to pay off any outstanding debts. These activities were intended to help her through the transition between the moment of death and her release from the community.[9] But they also are severely attacked by some of the community's religious leaders, for whom kenduris are a burden on the living and useless for the dead.

Every morning and evening for the first seven days after his wife's death, Aman Selamah held a small kenduri for her spirit. He would light incense next to a plate of the small, flat *apam* cakes and a bowl of rice. He would sit by the incense, uttering a few prayers to himself, and after awhile would eat his meal. Inën Selamah's spirit remained near the household during these days, he told me, and would come to each kenduri. He smiled when he added: "She comes when the rice is cooked." The apam cakes lessen the torment she is receiving in the grave. "The stories of older people said that the cakes hold back the staff of the angel about to strike her."

Abang Das was particularly busy. Not only did he organize and lead many of the nighttime rituals, he also performed the salāt regularly—not his usual practice in those years—and said additional prayers of forgiveness for her sins. "The prayers are like depositing money in a bank," said Abang Das. "God repays them by sending enjoyment to her spirit."

The first of several mortuary kenduris was held right after burial. It was brief but elaborate, with all four ritual foods. During the burial process, Akan Das (Abang Das's wife), aided by several close relatives, had swiftly put their household into a kenduri mode of operation. They had taken the boards off the back of the kitchen and set up several large cooking pots out-

---

[9] The sequence of events after her death was typical for Isak in the 1970s and 1980s. The major exceptions to the ritual occur for children who die within a few days of birth, before an initiation ritual has been held for them. Because they have no sins, they do not need to be given kenduris.

side. Relatives and friends stopped by with contributions; some stayed to help cook. For the next week the household would be busy with cooking and hosting, with many relatives and friends cooking and eating together, keeping the bereaved occupied and their spirits up.[10]

That night about sixty men and women gathered at the house to take turns reciting Qur'ān (ngaji). The women sat in the kitchen, listening, talking, and cooking, while the men recited in the living room. Two or three men alternated reading verses, and then passed the Qur'ān to another group, and so on, until everyone had taken a turn, no matter how unsuited his voice might be. (Some had difficulty suppressing giggles when one older man read.) The session lasted until about midnight. Abang Das explained: each word of the Qur'ān that we recited contained merit (pahla). God received the merit and lightened the deceased's suffering accordingly. The words were our gift (sedekah; Ar. sadaqa) to the spirit. The spirit also enjoys the nourishment (berkat) of the food included in the kenduri. We recited in the capacity of Inën Selamah's children, her "children of pious deeds" (anak amal saléh).

The passage of seven days marked changes in the state of the body and spirit of Inën Selamah. Initially the spirit remained near the house. But as her body decomposed (beginning on the third day and continuing through the seventh), the spirit was gradually freed of its ties to the village and could roam in the hills and fields.[11] Kenduris held on the first, third, and seventh days helped to move the spirit along as well as relieve its suffering. Relatives and friends sent supplies for the kenduri on the first day (called the "lowering of the corpse," turun mèt) and the most elaborate kenduri on the seventh day (called the "sevening," Malay nujuh). The third-day kenduri (the negari or nenggari, from Malay tiga hari, thus "three-daying") was much smaller, with only about ten close families attending, and was followed by an evening of Qur'ān recitation.

---

[10] Inën Rat, Abang Das's cousin and the owner of the store from where he obtained his supplies, estimated that the net cost for the first kenduri was only about Rp 500, the cost of six cartons of cigarettes. By the time people arrived to eat, relatives had contributed enough rice for about three such meals (over three tèm measures of rice), six kilograms of sugar, eleven coconuts, the materials for betel chewing, and a chicken. Vegetables came from Abang Das's garden and from nearby trees. More would be donated before each subsequent kenduri. Who bears these costs has been a matter for some debate, as we shall see.

[11] Without practicing secondary burial, and thus witnessing the process of decomposition, Gayo nonetheless associate the ritual process and the spirit's passage with these physical changes. Hertz (1960) first noticed this association as the basis for a general model of death as passage; elsewhere (Bowen 1984) I have discussed the limitations of Hertz's model for understanding the Gayo and other Indonesian conceptions of death.

The periods of three, seven, and forty-four days also mark transitions after death in some Middle Eastern Muslim societies; see, for example, Westermarck (1926, II:438–510) on Moroccan mortuary sequences. Gayo do not, however, mention such resemblances.

The events of the seventh day signaled the end of Inën Selamah's torment and transition. The women worked well into the night of the sixth day to make special sweets and prepare the ritual foods for the kenduri held the following afternoon. Relatives came from villages north of Takèngën to attend, and stayed for a *samadiyah*, a nighttime chanting session (discussed below).

The next morning (because days begin in the evening, it remained the seventh day) about twenty of Inën Selamah's closest relatives walked to her grave. They carried several large stones, jugs of water, and some uncooked rice. The men broke up the bamboo that had been used to carry the body, and used the pieces to build a fence around the grave, "to keep away the pigs." Two men placed small, white cloths underneath two of the stones and then placed them at the head and foot of the grave. As they did so they pronounced softly a tasbīh, a prayer to the glory of God.[12] The women began to place more stones at the head and foot of the grave, saying the tasbīh under their breath as they worked. "The stones continue to say the tasbīh after we have left the grave," said Abang Das; "jin will not dare approach the grave because of the tasbīhs." "They follow us to heaven," added Aman Rabu, the man who said the prayers at the three-day kenduri, "and they keep on saying the tasbīh until the day of judgment, giving her merit." One woman then poured the contents of three jugs onto the grave: one of water mixed with uncooked rice, a second of water mixed with mungkur juice, and a third of plain, fresh water. The first two jugs were emptied onto the head and then the foot of the grave; the fresh water was poured over the entire grave from head to foot and the remainder was poured onto nearby graves. A senior relative of the deceased then said that the prophet Muhammad commanded his followers to say the "Qul hu wallah" (Qur'ān 112, Sūra al-Ikhlās) to themselves eleven times. After everyone had done so, he said a prayer and we collectively recited al-Fātiha.

At the kenduri that followed (which featured the apam cakes) we discussed the outstanding debts of Inën and Aman Selamah. Although Aman Selamah was still alive, their individual debts were considered the collective debts of the household and must therefore be settled for her spirit to rest in peace. Abang Das spoke of the urgency of settling the debts quickly, and expressed anger that his father had not told him of several substantial debts that would take time to repay.[13] After his speech he sat down, and

---

[12] The basic tasbīh prayer is *subhāna 'illāhi*, "[I proclaim] the glory of God," and Gayo (and other) Muslims sometimes say longer versions. Abang Das explained that saying the tasbīh ensures that the stones will follow the deceased to Heaven; otherwise they will be our firewood in Hell. For comparative materials see Padwick (1961:65–74).

[13] Inën Rat explained to me later that it was important to repay debts right after the seventh-day kenduri, and that the prophet Muhammad even said that debts should be paid before the deceased is buried.

then quickly moved across the circle of men to where his father was sitting. Without looking directly at him, he crouched low, bent his head down into his father's hands in the movement of obeisance (*semah*), and asked forgiveness for any mistakes and missteps he may have made during the past days. He proceeded to his father's right and either shook hands with or (for close elder kinsmen) showed obeisance to everyone in the room. Then all the other "children" (including his brothers' children) came to crouch before Aman Selamah in the same manner. Everyone but Abang Das was crying afterwards, and even he was on the verge of tears. His cousin Inën Ipol began to "wail over" (*pongoti*) Aman Selamah, sobbing out words of regret and sadness.

This moment was the emotional climax of the funeral days, the only time when everyone released their feelings of sadness, loss, and frustration. Seven days after the death, the crying was no longer in regret of the death or in defiance of God's will, but in sadness over the eventual loss of everyone's parents (Aman Selamah's own advanced age was frequently mentioned in the speeches and in Inën Ipol's wailing). It was the loss, not the body, that was bemoaned.

With this moment of apologies, obeisance, and emotional release the spirit of the deceased woman left the house and the community, her period of torment over and her ties to the social world loosened. The spirit would return from time to time until the kenduri marking the forty-fourth day, the *nyawah lo* (arriving at the [final] day). By that day the debts would be paid, and the spirit would be given a final send-off with another nighttime samadiyah session. From then on the spirit will have left the community to reside "up in the clouds" (*i awang-awang*), no longer free to roam in the community. Yet it would also become accessible at the grave, as an object of attention and possibly a source of aid to the living. Abang Das and others in the family would visit the grave at least in the first days after the fasting month, and at times of personal stress they might offer a kenduri in hope of aid. Inherently bilocal, in Peter Metcalf's apt phrase (1982:235), the free-ranging spirit of the dead person would have completed its passage out of the household and community to become reconfigured as a fixed interlocutor at the grave.

CHANTING FOR THE DECEASED

The heart of the funeral kenduris are the nighttime recitations, the samadiyah. Samadiyah sessions are held in the home of the bereaved on the first, third, seventh, or forty-fourth evenings after death. The chants are entirely in Arabic, and include repetitions of Qur'ānic verses and the phrase "there is no deity but God," as well as long invocations. Most villagers hold that the recitations generate merit for the deceased. A prayer leader sings long petitionary prayers and channels the merit of the recitations to the spirit of the deceased (or, say some, to God for the deceased's benefit). Food is served throughout the evening, and, according to some, the deceased's spirit enjoys the essence of the food.

The name *samadiyah* derives from the Arabic word *shamad*, "eternal, everlasting." The word appears in the second line of Sūra al-Ikhlās (Qur'ān 112), the sūra that is central to the samadiyah session:

Qul hu wallāhu ahad	Say: He is God, One,
allāhhu shamad	God, the Everlasting Refuge,
lam yalid wa lam yūlad	who has not begotten, and has not been begotten,
wa lam yakul lahu kufuwan ahad	and equal to Him is not any one.

Samadiyah can be very moving to all present, but for the close relatives it may also provide contact with the spirit. Aman Bani, the religious official of Kutë Kramil village, remembered the evenings after his father's death in 1982. Aman Bani himself led the prayers and chants. (A child of the deceased can be especially effective in transmitting the benefit of the recitations to the spirit.) He could feel his father enter the room to receive the merit. He had difficulty forcing the words out of his mouth, so heavily did the presence of his father weigh upon him. By concentrating his imagination through maripët he could see his father's spirit, his face. His vision told him that the chants were reaching their destination, that his father's life in the grave would be eased.

The most recent samadiyah session I attended was held in July 1989 to observe the forty-fourth day after the death of a young mother of two. About fifty men and fifty women, plus their children, gathered in the upper story of the deceased woman's house. The large room had been cleared of furniture, and brightly colored embroidered mats covered the floors and walls. People started to gather shortly after the evening meal, and the session began at 8:30. Glasses of coffee were handed around.

Abang Irmas, known for his melodious voice and ritual skills (he had been the Isak Lord of the Fields), led the first part of the session; Aman Mudë Pelëdë, an older man who often presides at kenduris, led the second part. In both cases the prayer leader was flanked by two other men who joined him in leading the group through the chanting. The styles of the two men are very different: Abang Irmas modulates his voice in a highly pleasing way through long solo prayers, whereas Aman Mudë Pelëdë, whose knowledge of the prayers may be more extensive, recites in a straightforward manner. Men and women joined in to chant verses and well-known prayers, and punctuated the solo prayers at the appropriate moments with *amīn*. Some were only able to follow a portion of the chanting, and fell silent from time to time before they found a familiar spot to rejoin the group. The men swayed back and forth in the longer collective chants, eyes shut; women, gathered in the back, divided their attention between the chanting and the duties of looking after the children and cooking the meal and snacks. The intent of the prayers and chants, to send requests to God for the well-being of the deceased, was on everyone's mind, and many were visibly moved. The session lasted until about eleven o'clock, but some remained, talking, for most of the night.

This and other similar samadiyah sessions consisted of two distinct parts separated by a break for refreshments. The first part is the samadiyah in the restricted sense and has at its center the Sūra al-Ikhlās from which its name derives. The second part is the tahlīl, during which people chant a zikr (<Ar. *dhikr*, mentioning, remembering), a repetition of *lā ilāha illā Allāh* (there is no deity but God). A long prayer toward the end of the tahlīl section directs the merit of the entire session to the spirit of the deceased. Often a homily or *ta'zīyah* follows the chanting.[14]

The Samadiyah: "God, the Everlasting Refuge"

The opening chants in the first part of the session are requests to God for pardon, known as the *istighfār* from the opening phrase: "Astaghfirullah . . ." ("I ask God for pardon . . ."). The prayer leader and his two assistants recite the phrase, then the others join them for three repetitions. These are short prayers and widely known. The leader may then switch to a slightly different "pardon prayer," again followed by the guests for three repetitions, and then to a third prayer.[15]

"Only after God has been asked for forgiveness may the chanters ask that merit be sent to the deceased," said one leader. "Our chants are only effective if God judges us to be proper Muslims," he added. Those who participate should worship regularly and should have performed ablutions prior to the session, just as they would have done before worshiping God. (Because some people will not have done so, the leaders usually add prayers of their own asking God to forgive their lapses.)

After the opening pardon comes a single *shalawat*, a prayer in praise of the prophet Muhammad. This, too, is sung first by the leader and his two assistants and then by everyone together. (It was chanted ten times at the samadiyah in 1989.) "After all," said Tengku Ali Salwany, "even God and the angels say words of blessing for the prophet Muhammad, so we should, too."

Then come the repetitions of the Sūra al-Ikhlās, the "Qul hu." When Tengku Ali Salwany leads a session he decides on the number of repetitions based on the number of people present: if many people are present he may

---

[14] Tengku Asaluddin told me that before the 1930s people usually referred to these sessions as *tahlīl* rather than as *samadiyah*.

[15] On the general importance of the istighfār to Muslims see Padwick (1961:198–208).

15. Men Reciting Prayers

stop after forty repetitions, but if fewer people are present he may continue to sixty, "so that the merit is more or less the same for all." Several prayer leaders told me that if the sūra were read one thousand times the deceased would be totally freed of torment. At the 1989 samadiyah Abang Irmas led the group in twenty repetitions to a slow beat, and then he changed melodies and adopted a faster beat for an additional twenty.[16]

Many people in Isak told me that the "Qul hu" was equivalent in merit to one-third of the Qur'ān, and that reciting it three times constituted "completing the Qur'ān." From most of those whom I asked about the samadiyah I heard the story of how 'Ali, the son-in-law of the prophet Muhammad and the fourth caliph, first impressed Muhammad by his grasp of this idea. Muhammad had asked his students to recite their way through the Qur'ān. As the others were just making their way through the second sūra, 'Ali closed the book and said that he had finished. To Muhammad's query, "How could this be?" he replied that he had simply read the "Qul hu" three times and thus completed the book. Muhammad, according to those who told me the story, was pleased by this reply.

---

[16] This sūra is efficacious in other ways as well. The man who presides over kenduris at Kutë Robel village said that those who fought in the Medan Front Area against the returning Dutch in the late 1940s would activate the sūra as a spell and would not be touched by bullets.

The Tahlīl: "There Is No Deity but God"

"The samadiyah protects us; the tahlīl transmits merit," said one frequent prayer leader. The essence of the tahlīl is a zikr, the repetition of *lā ilāha illā Allāh*, but it begins with a series of recitations. At the 1989 session these consisted of three more recitations of the "Qul hu," a single zikr chant, and then two additional short sūras of the Qur'ān: Sūra 113, al-Falaq, and Sūra 114, an-Nās. Both sūras are usually identified in such discussions by their first lines rather than by their titles. "The prophet Muhammad said that these three sūras should not be separated," said Tengku Ali Salwany, "and each has a different point: the 'Qul hu' states that God is one; the 'Qul a'ūdzu birabbil falaq' [Qur'ān 113] asks God to save us from the hatred of other people; the 'Qul a'ūdzu birabbin nās' [Qur'ān 114] asks God to ward off devils and also people who are envious."

The prayer leader then begins to recite from Sūra al-Baqarah and Sūra al-Imran, the second and third sūras of the Qur'ān. (Sūra al-Baqarah is usually referred to as *alip lām mīm*, from the three letters with which it begins.)[17] These recitations always include verse 255 of al-Baqarah, called the "Throne Verse" (*āyat al-kursi*):

> God! There is no deity but He, the Everliving, the Eternal Sovereign. Neither slumber nor sleep seizes Him. To Him belongs all that is in the heavens and in the earth. Who is there that shall intercede with Him, save by His leave? He knows all that is present with them and that which is to come upon them, but they comprehend nothing of His knowledge save but what He wills. His Throne encompasses the heavens and the earth, and the preservation of them does not burden Him. He is the Most High, the Most Great.

This verse has retained a special place in the writing and speech of many Muslims for the images of majesty it evokes. Several hadīth promise a quick entry to Paradise for those who recite them (Ayoub 1984:248). Most Gayo prayer leaders also include the first five and final two verses of Sūra al-Baqarah in their recitations. Muslim commentators have often linked the last two verses of this sūra (numbers 285 and 286) together with the Throne Verse as conveying special grace from God (Ayoub 1984:277–78). According to one hadīth, the prophet Muhammad said that these three verses were "in themselves a qur'ān" (ibid.).

The leaders perfect their pronunciation through considerable practice and by learning from others' criticism of their performance. Abang Irmas, for example, had just been told by one of the older men better-versed in Arabic

---

[17] Tengku Ali Salwany used the term *wirid* for the recitation of these passages from al-Baqarah, a usage common to Sufi descriptions of dhikr sessions (Macdonald 1953).

that he had been mispronouncing vowels in his long solo prayer, and he corrected his vocalization on the following night.

Men who wish to become leaders or simply to follow the chants study the verses, not directly from the Qur'ān, but from handwritten notebooks kept by those who are already proficient or from the many printed manuals of tahlīl prayers sold in Takèngën.[18] Most of these manuals are published in Medan or Jakarta; thus the Gayo samadiyah recitations are probably very like those heard elsewhere in Indonesia. Only a minority of the men present at samadiyahs I attended were able to follow all of the recitations. Certain passages are recited by most leaders and are familiar to most guests; others vary from one leader to another.

The recitations are followed by the zikr, usually fifty or one hundred repetitions of lā ilāha illā Allāh. The leader then recites a prayer, which may be very short or last as long as twenty minutes. The prayer asks God to send the blessings of the samadiyah, the tahlīl, and the doa to the spirit of the deceased (at this point he says her or his name, softly) and to keep away the torment of the grave. The leader may add more prayers (at the 1989 samadiyah the leader ended with a well-known prayer which everyone recited with him) before closing the session with a collective chanting of Sūra al-Fātiha.

The prayer leader does more than just coordinate and guide the others in reciting prayers and verses. He also is responsible for transmitting the words and their merit to God. The prayer "will only be accepted if the intent of the prayer leader is proper," explained Tengku Ali Salwany, "only if he says the prayers for the benefit of the deceased, not so people will notice him or because he is a proud person." The prayer leader can also make up for deficiencies on the part of the others, helping prayers reach God that otherwise might not have done so. "That is why he must have a strong maripët," said Aman Bani. (Similarly, an imām can transmit a person's worship to God even if he or she has a lapse of attention or of memory.) Conversely, as another prayer leader explained, if someone dies who never worshiped, a prayer leader will recite as for anyone else, so that the relatives will not be ashamed, "but he will think to himself 'he never worshiped; how can we ask for his redemption? He was the one who decided not to worship' and the prayers will not hit the mark." The prayers will be

---

[18] These books often combine the text of the Sūra Yā Sīn, other verses (sometimes collectively called taktīm), and versions of tahlīl, containing dhikr and associated prayers. Each text is usually given in Arabic and Latin script, and then in Indonesian translation. The selection of recitations in several such books (e.g., Asy'ari [n.d.; published in Jakarta]; Zulfa [1988; published in Medan]) correspond closely to the recitations I have recorded in Isak; the most widely distributed manual is probably Ya'cub's Takhtim tahlil dan do'a (n.d.).

seriët berulës, hakikët beropoh (conduct draped in a ceremonial cloth, inner reality wrapped in a plain cloth); the leader's intent will be concealed by his actions.

Chanting verses for the sake of the deceased is a widespread practice in Muslim societies. Sequences of verses similar to those recited by Gayo have been described for funeral ritual in lowlands Aceh (Snouck Hurgronje 1906, I:428–29), Malaysia (Skeat 1967:407), Egypt (Lane 1860:526–27), Pakistan (Kurin 1984:204–5; Werbner 1990:168), and Morocco (Wester-marck 1926, II:461). Even the reformist guide for women written in northern India in the early 1900s, the *Bihishti Zewar*, approves of the practice of transferring merit to the dead through reciting Qur'ānic verse (Metcalf 1990:145–51).

Whether despite or because of the wide distribution of these practices, Gayo modernists (and most Indonesian modernist scholars) have opposed the funeral kenduris and chanting more strongly than they have any other set of religious practices in the highlands.[19] Public debates on these practices began with the 1941 confrontation between the modernist Tengku Jali and the traditionalist Tengku Silang near Takèngën, and both before and after these debates modernist teachers urged villagers to abandon the samadiyahs. When Tengku Joharsyah returned to Isak in 1945 from his schooling in West Sumatra, for example, he and Tengku Asaluddin attended all mortuary kenduris in order to disrupt them. They would stand shortly after the kenduri began, and ask everyone to worship with them rather than conduct a samadiyah. Some villages developed internal social rifts on this issue. I heard of cases where, at a wedding kenduri put on by a pro-samadiyah party, those who opposed the samadiyah would be served after the others on the grounds that they did not like to work (by praying for the dead) and thus should not eat. These fissures never became open conflicts, but in 1948 fears that they might enlarge led the 'ulamā' of Aceh to publicly condemn a number of funeral practices.

For modernists the samadiyah is the quintessence of misguided religious ritual. They base their conclusion on three arguments. The first is an application of a general principle: in religious matters Muslims must only do what the prophet Muhammad did. We know that he never engaged in chanting, and therefore neither should we. Aman Murni, the former head of the modernist school Islamic Education, explained this principle as follows:

> The prophet Muhammad never recited samadiyah at the house of a bereaved family, and all religious acts have to be based on the prophet Muhammad's

[19] For a detailed description of similar controversies in South Sumatra see Abdullah (1979–80).

example. Thus: When we worship, why don't we recite the Sūra al-Fātiha when we are kneeling or prostrating? [It is said while standing.] Because the way to worship has been strictly set for us, and we cannot just do as we like because we think it is good. That is why the Prophet was sent here: to serve as an example. That is why he said: do what I do. The Messenger of God did say the tasbīh prayer, but we cannot just keep adding onto that; that is bid'a; that is confused.

The second reason against attending funeral kenduris is social in content, but is also based on the prophet Muhammad's example. If we visit the bereaved family and eat and drink at their expense, we are robbing them of their wealth when they are their weakest. We "eat the food of orphans," as some modernists like to put it (especially when in a confrontational mood). "The Prophet forbade us from gathering at a house where someone has died," stated Aman Murni, "because if we do we will eat and drink. What he did command is that we bring food to that house. Eating up the wealth of the deceased is the same as eating fire. And if we start reciting Qur'ān we really burden the household; sometimes they have to sell buffalo or mortage their fields to bear the costs."

The third argument against the samadiyah is in fact a general argument against the possibility that the living can aid the dead. Samadiyah implies that one can produce merit for someone else; this idea would radically undermine the moral accountability of the individual to God. "You cannot redeem the sins of others," said Tengku Asaluddin; "you can only earn merit for what you do in your own lifetime." He then quoted a hadīth (collected by Abu Daud) quoted by virtually anyone who made this point:

When a child of Adam dies, all but three of his deeds are discontinued: alms given while alive, useful knowledge, or a pious child who invokes God in his favor.

"Your own children can, and indeed should, pray for your soul," explained Tengku Asaluddin, "and God may indeed hear those prayers and act on them. Not even your own children, however, can erase your sins or give you merit, and thus the samadiyah cannot help the deceased." For Tengku Asaluddin, the elements of the samadiyah were legitimate religious practices, but participants misunderstood their real nature. "The tahlīl is not a *dowa* [here indicating, approximately, "prayers said for their spell-like efficacy"]," he said; "it is each person's statement of belief in the oneness of God, because it reads: *lā ilāha illā Allāh*." To believe otherwise, as most village people do, is to deny the central idea of individual responsibility. If a quick catechism can substitute for religious study while alive, and chanting can compensate for the failure to observe God's commandments, then it is no longer true that one is judged according to his or her deeds. "It would be easy, wouldn't it," remarked Tengku Asaluddin, "to just wait and let our children substitute prayer for our own deeds during life."

Traditionalists have objected to this last modernist argument on the basis of the same hadīth quoted by modernists: that children may continue to affect the welfare of deceased parents by praying for them. Traditionalists have argued that children might need help, and also that "child" is not to be taken in a strict biological (or Islamic legal) sense, but in the broader sense of those left behind by the deceased. As a prayer leader in Kutë Robel village remarked: "When people die, their own actions can no longer help them, only those of their pious children, and that is why they need food and verses to help them."

In Isak people sometimes make this argument in the course of the samadiyah itself, as part of the ta'zīyah speech intended to remind participants of the evening's purpose. At the samadiyah I attended in 1989, the speech was given by Aman Jelimah, who included the following comments:

> As long as there are people left on the earth, they have to help the dead. If not why would we say the hadīth [here he recited the above hadīth]? Take the pious child [anak amal saléh]: What good is he? A child becomes a pious child to the extent that he helps the parents; someone else becomes a "pious sibling" [saudërë saléh] because he wants to help say the prayers. We just recited prayers for the deceased. But all our fellow Muslims in Istanbul, Damascus, Syria, Baghdad, Egypt, Jerusalem, America, and Babylon: all their prayers reach us, and all ours, them. You do not have to be close by. Islam requires everyone to help each other. As long as there is Islam everyone is required to help those who are dead.

Aman Jelimah not only reinforced the convictions of those who had gathered to relieve the torment of the deceased, he also depicted the gathering as but one component of a universal network of mutually assisting Muslims. The image was powerful, and people remarked on it favorably over the next few days.

Because the above hadīth can be turned against them, modernists sometimes prefer to rely on a second, related by Bokhari and Muslīm, which emphasizes the moral boundedness of the individual after death:

> Three things accompany the deceased: his family, his wealth, and his deeds. Two return and one remains: his family and his wealth return; his deeds remain.

This hadīth, more directly than the first, emphasizes the individual nature of moral accountability and the impossibility of producing merit for someone else. It leaves pious children out of the picture entirely. It was the basis for an influential poem written by Tengku Mudë Kala in the late 1940s (Daudy 1950:11). The poem began with the above hadīth, developed its message, and then drew the following conclusion:

sengkirën ko maté ahlimu	If you die and your relatives give
bersedekah	alms;
oya gërë sawah	that doesn't reach
kin ningko pahala	you, the merit.
gërë-kë ipengé ko peri ni tuhën	Did you not hear the words of God:
"laisa lil insan	"A person shall have
ila masaha"	only as he/she has labored"?

The poem, performed in villages, was particularly persuasive because it begins as an interpretation of a hadīth and ends with a quote from the Qur'ān, all to the effect that you only reap what you have sown.

The result of decades of debate over this issue is that many in Isak today feel unsettled about what is proper and what is not. The day after the ta'zīyah discussed above was delivered, Abang Kerna (whose doubts about healing are discussed in Chapter 6) and Tengku Daud (who has tended to take a generally modernist approach) pondered Aman Jelimah's claims.

Tengku Daud objected to the idea that anyone could pray for the deceased. "Only those pious children, real children, who meet ten criteria count; they cannot be proud, haughty, and so forth; there is a Qur'ānic verse on that."

ABANG KERNA: Other ulama see it differently. If you have, say, fifty people in a room, and some of them never worship, they don't count for anything, but we leave the matter up to God. For them, it's like pouring water into a basket; they say the prayers but it is just didong to them.

· TENGKU DAUD: For those people it is like winnowing rice: the empty grains just drift away. But I've heard of people who carefully selected those they wanted to have say prayers, and invited the others just to eat. But a hadīth reported by Ja'far stated that the Prophet would bring food to the bereaved, never just go to eat. Look how they do it in Baléatu: people bring food they have cooked at home.

ABANG KERNA: But look, what harm does it do to make merry, to comfort the bereaved? Take last night: I was just over there and they have two huge sacks of uncooked rice left over, at least ten coconuts, and lots of sugar, so it was not a burden on them.

TENGKU DAUD: But maybe the cooks were short on something, say salt, and so the people in the house had to provide it. And they had to do the cooking. It's best when "if there is a coconut, they don't need to split it." There

were ulama who told a poor man to sell his buffalo cart and give them the
money to pray for his dead father. "You will always be able to eat," they
said, "but who will help your father?"

ABANG KERNA: Of course that's true, but what about the rich man who wants
to help his parents by putting on a kenduri? I once asked Tengku Jali [the
Takèngën modernist teacher] this question. I stood as brother-in-law to him
and we were neighbors when I lived in Balé. He could not answer the question; he was entirely speechless. [I cannot imagine Tengku Jali having been
speechless, but people often speak of their own cleverness in this way.]

TENGKU DAUD: The problem is that there are two verses [in fact, hadīth]: one
says that only pious children can help us, and the other that we should help
each other. In the end there are many things that we do not know that God
will have to decide.

Abang Kerna and Tengku Daud negotiated among the competing imperatives of helping the deceased and pitying the living, each of which can be
given a scriptural foundation. For them, as for others in the highlands,
the relation of ritual form to society and culture (that stock-in-trade of anthropological discussions) is very much a live issue. Indeed, the very ideas
of society and ritual are up for grabs here. Gayo have argued vehemently
about the telkin and the kenduri because they see each as directly implying
particular ideas about death, communication, and exchange. At least in
Gayo society, debates about ritual form are also debates about individual
responsibility and about moral obligations, about who each person is as a
religious individual and what each person can do as a member of a larger
community.

Chapter Twelve

SACRIFICE, MERIT, AND SELF-INTEREST

ONE OF THE INSIGHTS of social anthropology concerns the power of sacrifice to bring together specific images of society, divinity, and subjectivity.[1] When individuals come together to sacrifice something to spirits or gods, they also say something about who they are and what kind of moral bonds unite them: "Every sacrificial rite involves much more than the offering" (Valeri 1985:67).

Virtually all Gayo observe the Islamic command to perform an annual sacrifice, but they interpret that command in markedly divergent ways, thus making particularly clear how different religious conceptions generate contrasting ritual forms. Most villagers (in Isak and elsewhere) interpret the event as an occasion to generate spiritual benefits for themselves and their ancestors. They see it as primarily a transaction. Modernists, finding such a notion aberrant, try to distinguish their own observances of the sacrifice as sharply as possible from Isak practices. They emphasize their attitude of selfless sacrifice, and in doing so provide a link to Indonesian state ideas about sacrifice for the common good.

GENERATING MERIT IN ISAK

The annual Islamic Feast of Sacrifice commemorates the willingness of Ibrāhīm to sacrifice his son at God's command. The Feast takes place on the tenth day of the twelfth Islamic month, Dhū 'l-Hijja, the month of pilgrimage. God's command to sacrifice to him and to him alone is contained in the Qur'ān in chapter 22 (verses 34–38) and again in chapter 108. The major collections of hadīth specify how Muhammad carried out this command during the month of pilgrimage. These reports are important sources for Muslims' ideas and practices regarding, among other things, which animal is the best victim, what to say when killing the chosen animal, and who benefits from the sacrifice.[2]

---

[1] The classic statements of this position in the anthropology of sacrifice include the 1898 comparativist essay by Hubert and Mauss (1964), Durkheim's remarks in his study of religion (1915:385–89), and the ethnography of Nuer religion by Evans-Pritchard (1956). Among many recent studies are Valeri (1985) on sacrifice in ancient Hawaii, and Combs-Schilling (1989) on Islamic sacrifice in Moroccan political history.

[2] Among the most widely accepted of these hadīth collections is that by Imām Muslim; the section on sacrifice, entitled Kitāb al-Adhāhī, is Book 20 of this collection (Muslim n.d. 3:1080–94).

Gayo refer to the Feast of Sacrifice in diverse ways. It is the "holiday of sacrifice" (G. *reraya qurbën*) or the "great holiday" (G. *reraya kul*), in explicit contrast to the holiday celebrating the end of the fasting month of Ramadan, which is called simply "holiday" (G. *reraya*) or, in Indonesianized Arabic, Idul Fitri (Ar. 'īd al-fitr). Upward of one hundred Gayo undertake the pilgrimage each year, and in the highlands during the holiday period, Gayo often talk about the sacrifices the pilgrims are carrying out in the city of Mina simultaneously with their own. In these contexts Gayo also may refer even to the local event as the "pilgrimage holiday" (G. *reraya haji*). Some Gayo, usually of modernist leanings, seek to emphasize the scriptural commandments regarding the sacrifice and to downplay local traditions, and these men and women might use the Arabic designation "Great Feast" ('īd al-adhā). These different labels suggest contrasting conceptions of the event itself.

In Isak, most married residents attend the congregational worship service on the morning of the feast day, but the main focus of attention is on the sacrifice and the meals that will follow. In 1989, Isak seemed nearly deserted the week before the feast as men and women went to Takèngën to sell sugar to raise money, or to the Javanese-populated transmigration area in the hills to buy a sheep, or to the downstream buffalo pens to choose an animal.

Nearly all Isak households sacrifice on the prescribed day. At the very least a household will kill one of its chickens or ducks or buy one from another household to sacrifice. If times are very bad, two households might jointly hold a feast and share a chicken or duck; several of my friends did this during my stay. As long as the throat can be cut and the meat eaten, I was told, the sacrifice meets the demands of God. (In principle, said some, half-jokingly, even a grasshopper would do as a sacrifice.)

But a meal with only a chicken or duck, although acceptable to God, is hardly ideal. If possible, households sacrifice a sheep, goat, or water buffalo.[3] These larger sacrificial victims do more than fulfill the minimal religious obligation; they also create ties between the living and the dead, and serve to unite the living in their future state of resurrection.

The largest and most public sacrifice is of a water buffalo. Whereas on other occasions one might kill a buffalo in a relatively isolated spot, a sacrificial killing on this day often is done in the middle of the main residential area, with the active participation of many individuals. The sacrifice is a testimony to the resources and the piety of the sacrificing household. Several

---

[3] Isak residents strongly prefer sheep to goats (although the latter are somewhat more plentiful) on the grounds that goats scavenge and dislike water, and thus are relatively unclean. One man said that if you penned a goat for forty-four days its "stolen food" would pass through its system and then it would be clean and good to sacrifice. Takèngën Gayo often choose goats, perhaps in deliberate rejection of village preferences, or perhaps with the horns of the ram sacrificed by Muhammad in mind.

16. Isak Men Preparing to Kill a Buffalo at the Feast of Sacrifice

men tie the buffalo's legs together with rope and then topple it on its side. They can receive nasty bruises when the buffalo, sensing its danger, kicks out at the men. One man (not necessarily the sacrifier) then spiritually cleanses the buffalo by sprinkling it with healing water and dusting it with puffed rice (which by its lightness is a highly spiritual food). These cleansings prepare the buffalo to meet God; the men give it a spiritual benefit in return for its past gifts of milk, and for its future gifts of meat and its spirit.

Who actually cuts the throat is not of great importance, and people often delegate the job of killing the buffalo to someone else. In their social practice, Gayo thus distinguish between the knife wielder (Hubert and Mauss's "sacrificer" [1964:9–28]) and the person in whose name the sacrifice is performed (the "sacrifier")[4] Just prior to cutting the victim's throat, the sacrificer dedicates the animal to one or more relatives. In 1978 my neighbor Abang Das sacrificed a buffalo for the benefit of his parents and grandpar-

---

[4] The distinction is also reported for the coasts of Aceh in the late nineteenth century, where the sacrifier often handed the victim over to a man of religious learning (an ulama) and asked that he carry out the sacrifice (Snouck Hurgronje 1906, I:243).

ents. Just prior to cutting the animal's throat he pronounced the basmala ("in the name of God, the Merciful, the Compassionate") and the confession of faith ("I attest that there is no deity but God and that Muhammad is his Messenger"), and then dedicated the buffalo as follows: "This is the sacrifice for my father [Name], for my mother [Name] and their families." He then said his own name followed by "In the name of God; God is Great" (*bismillāh Allāh Akbar*) three times. At the completion of the dedication he slit the buffalo's throat.

Some people say they know the victim will reach its spiritual destination from the conduct of the sheep or buffalo itself. When Aman Bani, the religious official for Kutë Kramil village, sacrificed two sheep in 1989, he found both ready and willing for the knife. Just before their death, he said, they suddenly became tame, and he could "see in their eyes" that they were willing.

People differ as to whether further conditions apply to the sacrifice. Some hold that the animal, once sacrificed, is automatically readied for use on the day of judgment. For others, however, the sacrifice is only effective if the sacrifier (rather than the beneficiaries) observes the commands of Islam. I have heard wives remind their husbands that unless they both perform salāt worship regularly the sacrifice will have been in vain. All sacrifiers understand their act as part of Islamic history; indeed, the rich imagery of eschatology assures many people of the ritual's ultimate efficacy.

The sacrifice is carried out for the household as a unit: women as well as men speak of "their" sacrifice, and couples decide jointly on a list of people who will receive its spiritual benefit. In the case of a buffalo, the beneficiaries usually include parents on both sides, and daughters as well as sons. Widows also carry out sacrifice (without being socially redefined as men), and when a wealthy female trader sacrificed a buffalo everyone spoke of it as *her* sacrifice, not that of her husband (who was also part of the household).

The distribution and consumption of the victim form an important part of the total ritual. If a sheep or buffalo is killed, the animal's meat must be divided and shared in a fixed fashion for the sacrifice to be complete. In principle, one-third of the meat should be given away to the poor (*fakir-miskin*) (each sacrifier decides who could be considered "poor" in his village or among his relatives).[5] An additional one-third of the meat is to be given

---

[5] Declaring someone "poor" in the sense of "without sufficient resources or income" is tricky in a society that values helping one's kin. Isak people include as poor, for Islamic purposes, those too old to work for themselves and without sufficient assets, even if they are well supported by their children. In 1978, when Abang Das sacrificed a buffalo, he gave a share to Inën Rat's father, a very old man who kept his own household and was considered poor even though Inën Rat supplied him amply with his everyday needs. In all, Abang Das gave away hunks of about one kilogram each to each of eight people considered to be poor. The sum was less than one-third of the total, but there were no more local poor, he said.

to people who come and ask for a piece, usually in exchange for other foods.[6]

Sharing of meat is an important part of the experience of the Feast of Sacrifice (an element that is amplified in Takèngën ritual, as we shall see). The one-third of the meat that remains should be eaten at a kenduri. The kenduris vary considerably in their size. A household in which only a chicken or duck was killed consumes the cooked animal with a minimum of ritual: at most, the household head or a learned relative recites a short prayer. A household that sacrificed a sheep invites guests from among neighbors and relatives. If a buffalo was killed, the entire village is automatically invited, and the guests bring raw foods (milled rice, coconuts, and sugar), which the hosting household and their close relatives prepare for eating. Contributing guests also receive a bit of the raw meat from the sacrificed animal.

Giving meat to the poor brings benefit to the sacrifiers; sharing meat among neighbors and relatives highlights the importance of eating together on this religious holiday. (This social aspect of sacrifice is important for Muslims elsewhere, too; cf. Werbner [1990].)

At feasts where a buffalo or sheep is eaten, a religiously learned man leads a group recitation of short Qur'ānic verses, recites a long petitionary prayer (punctuated by choruses of *amīn*), and repeats, for God's hearing, the names of the beneficiaries of the just-completed sacrifice. These recitations play an instrumental role in securing the benefit of the sacrifice; they also reaffirm relations of sociability among the participants (see Robertson Smith 1972:265). The guests then recite *takbīr*s, proclamations of God's greatness: "Allāhu akbar."[7] The evenings before and after the sacrifice people may also gather at the sacrifier's house to read from the Qur'ān together, adding to the total merit created by the event.

By placing the Feast of Sacrifice in the framework of the kenduri, Isak Gayo highlight the transactional aspect of the holiday over other aspects (such as the commemoration of Ibrāhīm's selflessness). This particular emphasis is further accentuated by the samadiyah sessions held to accompany most buffalo sacrifices. These sessions are identical to those held for the recently deceased. At each such session a prayer leader is given the names of those to whom the buffalo has been dedicated. He then directs the merit of the chants to these (usually seven) spirits. He may mention their names in his long prayer, or, more often, simply "send [the merit] through intent" (*niëtën*) in their direction. (Merit from the Qur'ān reading evenings was sent in the same way.)

In each of the four years I was present for the Feast of Sacrifice in Isak, three or four households each sacrificed a buffalo, sponsored a villagewide

---

[6] Abang Das received a total of six tèm measures of rice, thirty coconuts, and five kilograms of sugar in exchange for the meat he gave out in this way.

[7] On the takbīr in the context of worship, see Padwick (1961:29–36).

feast, and held an all-night recitation session. They held the feasts at different times so that men or women with ties to more than one village would be able to satisfy their multiple obligations. These major feasts were occasions for relatives who had moved away from Isak to return and to join with others in helping the spirits of those who had died before them. The sponsors whom I knew well spoke to me about the dead who were to benefit from the night's sessions; these days were times for reflection and remembrance as well as for contributing to the welfare of relatives and neighbors.

These events of transmission (at the moment of killing, the afternoon kenduris, and the nighttime samadiyah) are the most important aspect of sacrifice to most Isak Gayo. Indeed, they generally reserve the phrase "to sacrifice" (G. gelé qurbën, lit., "to cut the throat of a sacrificial animal") for occasions when a goat or buffalo is killed and served at a kenduri. By making the Feast of Sacrifice into a kind of kenduri, Isak Gayo have configured it as an event of transaction and communication.

This process of configuring is relatively recent, however. Around 1900, Gayo sacrifice had an entirely different relation to the broader Muslim tradition than it does today. The Feast of Sacrifice was not celebrated (Snouck Hurgronje 1903:327),[8] and one sent benefit to the dead by means of the kikah sacrifice, which at that time was performed after an individual's death (Snouck Hurgronje 1903:314). Only in the 1930s, and at the insistence of modernist teachers, did Isak people begin to offer the kikah sacrifice as part of the child's initiation ritual. At about the same time they began to observe the Feast of Sacrifice, which they interpreted in the transactional terms with which they were familiar. Even in the 1980s, some Isak people would omit the kikah from the child's seventh-day ritual, reasoning that they could always make a sacrifice at the Feast of Sacrifice in its place.[9]

Not only do the words sent to God generate spiritual benefit for deceased relatives, but the sheep or buffalo that has been sacrificed also provides a future material benefit. On judgment day (G. kiamat; <Ar. al-qiyāma) the persons named as sacrificial beneficiaries will be able to ride on the animal to the place of judgment, the Meraksa field (Ar. al-mahshar). Only one person can ride a goat or sheep to the Meraksa field, but seven can ride on a buffalo. A buffalo sacrifice thus provides the opportunity to bring together parents, children, and grandchildren on the back of the afterlife vehicle.

If they had the resources, most Isak people would stage a buffalo feast at

---

[8] In lowlands Aceh, however, the Feast of Sacrifice was observed (Snouck Hurgronje 1906, I:243), and in the seventeenth-century realm of Sultan Iskandar Muka it had been a lavish royal ritual (Reid 1988:175–77).

[9] On the historical connections in the Arab world among the Feast of Sacrifice, the 'aqīqa, and other sacrificial events, see Chelhod (1955); on these links among Pakistanis, see Werbner (1988).

some time during their life.[10] Aman Bani remarked that ideally everyone would be included in the dedication of seven animals, so that they could change from one to the other on their way to Mecca. "But the very best thing to sacrifice would be a camel," he added wistfully.

Isak couples shape their sacrificial strategies with afterlife sociability in mind. Each couple tries to provide a vehicle for themselves, their children, and, if possible, their parents and grandparents. Parents feel a particularly strong obligation to provide a vehicle for a child who died young, as do children for those parents and grandparents who did not have the resources to make a sacrifice in their own name. I heard stories about children who would not acknowledge their parents on the day of judgment because they had not bothered to sacrifice for them. "Without a sacrifice there is no tie between parents and children," said one woman. The prospect of future abandonment by one's children horrifies most people and provides further encouragement to perform the sacrifice. It also leads people to include in their dedications even those parents or children who already have a vehicle provided for them, in order to ensure that family ties will be preserved during the harsh times of judgment.

In 1979 Sahim's son died three days after birth, and he and his wife decided to sacrifice a sheep for him on the next Feast of Sacrifice. "This means there will be a connection [*tali*, lit., "rope"] between us and him in the afterlife." He remembered that when he was little his grandfather had sacrificed on this day and told Sahim to grab on to the rope around the sheep's neck "so we will meet in Heaven."

The sacrificial victim is clearly something more than the sign of the household's obedience to God. The ritual is framed as a kenduri, at which spiritual and future material benefits are produced by sacrificing in the name of God and by chanting his words. The ritual also connects the men and women of one generation with those of another through the shared sacrificial animal. The ritual projects this cross-generational, bilateral continuity onto the eschatological plane through images of families riding together toward the place of judgment.

"Selfless Sacrifice" in Takèngën

Takèngën modernists have developed their own form of the Feast of Sacrifice against the background of village practices. Precisely because most Gayo historically came to understand the Feast of Sacrifice in terms of feasting and transaction, modernists have worked to rid the feast day of those el-

---

[10] Similar ideas about the use of the animals as vehicles on judgment day are reported for Aceh in the nineteenth century (Snouck Hurgronje 1906, I:243) and for contemporary Java (Woodward 1989:86). For Arabia, the equivalence of seven sheep to one larger animal (in this case, a camel) is reported by Goldziher (1967:218).

ements. They do not hold kenduris on the Feast of Sacrifice (although they do on other occasions), and they emphasize the sharp distinction between the living and the dead.

In 1989 I observed the celebration of the Feast of Sacrifice in the Baléatu neighborhood of Takèngën. Baléatu residents are strongly associated with the modernist Muslim organization Muhammadiyah, whose school is located next to the neighborhood prayer house. When asked about the purpose of the ritual, Baléatu residents invariably referred to God's command in the Qur'ān to follow the example of Ibrāhīm. (Isak residents, by contrast, usually mentioned the importance of providing a vehicle for the afterlife.) In recounting the story of Ibrāhīm, they emphasized his prior decision to give something away in devotion to God, not the moment of sacrifice itself. "Prophets had always sacrificed," explained one scholar, by which he meant they had always been willing to surrender something, "but the prophet Ibrāhīm said that he would sacrifice his child if one were born to him; the idea came to him in a dream." This account emphasizes Ibrāhīm's proper attitude of abnegation rather than the command to kill his child.[11]

To follow the example of Ibrāhīm thus means to adopt his attitude of selfless and sincere devotion, *ikhlās*. God has ordered us to sacrifice as an act of worship of him, explained Tengku Asaluddin. We receive merit only in accord with our intention at the moment of action, and the intention appropriate to any positive religious act, including sacrifice, is to act in order to obey God's commands, not in order to obtain a future material return. "God loves to see blood flowing," explained Tengku Asaluddin, "so the sacrifice of any animal to him can give us merit, but only if done for the sake of God and not for a worldly reason; it depends entirely on our intention." From this perspective, if you sacrifice on the Feast of Sacrifice in order to create a vehicle for the day of judgment (an idea Tengku Asaluddin called "just something said for amusement") or for the benefit of a departed spirit, then you will not receive the full merit of having carried out God's command. (You will not receive what you intended either, as your intention rests on the faulty theory that you can transmit spiritual benefit to others.)

Modernists take care to provide explicit counterrepresentations to the prevailing village ideas. Thus, Ibu Inën Muhammad in Baléatu acknowledged that one could dedicate a buffalo to seven people, but added that these people would be seven living heads of household who each contribute to the buffalo's cost and thereby receive merit from the sacrifice. "Dead ancestors

---

[11] The emphasis on ikhlās, on the correct attitude of selfless devotion, is found elsewhere in Indonesia as well; for example, in influential Javanese commentaries on the Feast of Sacrifice (Woodward 1989:84–87). Nakamura (1983:173–74) paraphrases a sermon given by a modernist preacher on Java in 1965, who stressed that sacrifice is worthy because of the ikhlās with which it is made, again on the model of Ibrāhīm.

are not involved at all in this; they only receive merit from prayer uttered as part of their descendants' daily worship," she said. "Sacrifice is to free us [the sacrifiers] from torment after we die by increasing our merit; prayers in worship are for the dead; that's all there is to it."

Yet, although on a popular level town residents explicitly condemn village ways of carrying out the sacrifice, sacrifice never became a topic of scholarly dispute in the Gayo highlands. By now it will have become clear that Gayo are not reticent in debating such issues; the reason for the general scholarly silence on this topic may be that the Qur'ān does not explicitly condemn the idea that a sacrifier benefits from the sacrifice. Rather, it is critical of two practices, neither of which is characteristic of Isak observations of 'īd al-adhā: sacrificing to a being other than God, and claiming that the flesh and blood of the victim reach God (Qur'ān 22:34–38).

It has therefore been possible for some modernist scholars to support the claim that sacrifice generates merit for the sacrifiers. The influential modernist scholar Hasbi ash-Shiddieqy, for example, argues that, because the prophet Muhammad stated that the sacrifice was for him, his relatives, and his followers, we (his followers) do indeed benefit from it (1950:24).[12] Although this interpretation by a modernist scholar does not sanction the idea of transmitting benefit to specified others, it does introduce into respectable religious discourse the notion that the sacrifice confers a spiritual benefit.

The general town sequence of the Feast of Sacrifice resembles that followed in Isak—public worship followed by the killing of the sacrificial animal followed by meals—but the form and meanings of each stage are quite different. In Isak each household approaches the event as an opportunity to transmit spiritual and material benefits to their relatives and themselves. The key events are the act of dedicating the victim and the several kenduris which one might attend, both in the day and at night. For Baléatu residents the congregational worship is the most important element in the ritual, the killing of the victim is strongly played down, and the meals consist of casual home meals and communal enjoyment of food in a nonritualized setting.

This shift in emphasis is social and political as well as religious. In Isak the events considered to be of the greatest ritual importance took place in homes (feasting and reciting); in Baléatu greater religious significance was attached to events taking place in the streets, at the open-air site for congregational worship, and in the neighborhood prayer house. The spatial contrast indicates a shift in the social focus of the key ritual event, from the private, if shared, interests of the household, to the general interests of the community as a whole.

---

[12] He quotes a hadīth that is included as number 4845 in the collection by Muslim (n.d., 3:1087–88).

17. Ibu Inën Muhammad Ready to Depart for Worship at the Takèngën Feast of Sacrifice

The congregational worship service on the morning of the feast day, relatively unimportant in Isak, was the culmination of several days of activity in Baléatu. Although many Baléatu people did take time to obtain a goat for sacrifice, they were more concerned with their preparations for the morning worship service (for which some purchased new clothes) and the visiting of neighbors and graveyards that would occur afterward. The feast day was preceded by a night of takbīr, of proclaiming God's greatness. A convoy of cars drove around and around the town, led by a car with a loudspeaker from which the takbīr was called out over and over again. The evening's amplified proclamations, following a day of recommended fasting, built up a sense of expectancy for the next morning's worship activities.

By about six o'clock on the following morning several of the best Qur'ān reciters had arrived at the site for the congregational worship, a broad field next to the Takèngën town mosque with a stage at one end. The reciters began to chant the takbīr over loudspeakers, and continued to do so for over an hour, while men, women, and children gradually filled up the worship space in front of the stage. The district finals of the national Qur'ān recitation contest had just ended and had created a particularly receptive atmosphere for this part of the service. The reciters on the stage were all winners of past contests, and the crowd of worshipers clearly enjoyed their skills. Men and boys filled the space closest to the stage; women and girls in an area behind them. Men, women, and children were dressed in their finest: men in fine sarungs, often of silk, and some wearing sport coats; women in brightly colored blouses and sarungs. On two worship occasions, 'īd al-adhā and 'īd al-fitr, women in the town dress in their most splendid clothes (following a command of the prophet Muhammad, they say); for other worship services they wear a white garment that leaves only their faces visible.

The worship service was preceded by a welcoming address from the district military commander, setting the event in a governmental frame. The sermon, which follows worship, generally takes as its topic the willingness of the prophet Ibrāhīm to sacrifice his son to God. On this particular occasion the sermon giver talked about the importance of sacrifice in all areas of life, and specifically for the successful development of the country. He stressed the value of ikhlās (sincere devotion) in such sacrifices, likening our efforts in infrastructural development to the obedience displayed by the prophet Ibrāhīm.

Baléatu celebrants, in the way they killed the victim and consumed the meat, stressed the attitude of ikhlās and explicitly contrasted their practices with the Isak-type forms they consider un-Islamic. They have played down the instrumental religious significance of the killing and the meals, emphasizing instead the general values of family and community.

Whereas in Isak the morning worship was followed by sacrifice and ritual meals, Baléatu residents returned home to express the depth of family ties. In Abang Evi's household (my own when I live in Baléatu) the parents seated themselves on a couch in the living room. In descending order of seniority, each family member, and then several close family friends, kneeled in front of the parents, burying his or her head in the parents' hands and re-

18. Waiting to Worship in Takèngën

ceiving their blessings, wishes, and outpourings of emotion. My "mother" in particular found herself moved to tears and to long plaints over the bowed heads of her grandchildren: "You have to learn to behave better"; "You are the youngest and so you always catch it; do not take it to heart, little one." Each member of the family kneeled in the same fashion before all those senior to him or her, sometimes just for a moment, and sometimes with longer exchanges of caresses and tears.[13]

On this day and the next, men and women in the neighborhood celebrated the holiday in the Baléatu prayer house and the adjacent Muhammadiyah school. Cassette recordings of the takbīr were played through the prayer house loudspeaker, and children lined up at the school to take their turns at an amplified takbīr. Town scholars spoke to the schoolchildren about Ibrāhīm's sacrifice. At the prayer house, several men gathered to slaughter a cow and several goats that had been donated for the occasion. (The men included Alimin, the son of Tengku Mudë Kala with whom I had been transcribing religious poetry.) Neighborhood women prepared two large meals: one for the neighborhood children and all the children living in the Takèngën town orphanage, and a second for the neighborhood adults.

---

[13] Although this family ceremony is not held in Isak, a similar ceremony held on 'īd al-fitr, in which individuals ask forgiveness from their elders (and, on an equal basis, from other people), is observed by all Gayo and by most Muslims in Indonesia.

Both meals were held in the prayer house. Most residents of the neighborhood had contributed money and a portion of their own sacrificial meat toward the meals. A few better-off residents had given goats. About sixty men and thirty women attended the second, neighborhood meal. After everyone had eaten they began to chant the takbīr. Women began to pound out a slow rhythm on gongs. Two men rose and danced the Gayo *tari guël* dance once performed by new bridegrooms. No prayers or dedications were uttered; the mood of the occasion was social celebration rather than ritual action.

The prayer house leaders first organized the meals in 1974, continuing a tradition begun by the modernist school Islamic Education in the late 1930s. They revived the meals in part to dislodge the celebration of 'īd al-adhā from its village context of feasting and transaction. Baléatu people referred to the meals as "eating together" (Ind. *makan bersama*) and never as kenduris. They underlined the importance of giving away food without hope of a return as truly selfless sacrifice, and mentioned prominently the invitation given to the orphans as proof of the event's real character.[14] Indeed, in some years Abang Evi's household and several others in the neighborhood invited orphans to their holiday household meal.

The ethic of avoiding self-interest also shaped the way that individuals carried out their obligation to sacrifice. Abang Evi's brother, Abang Gemboyah, who had returned from Jakarta for the holiday, had enjoyed spending much of the day before the sacrifice buying two goats, one for his own household's sacrifice and one for the meal at the prayer house. Once he had purchased the goats he turned them over to a family friend. The next day the friend killed them at his own house, without Abang Gemboyah being present, and cooked one of the goats for the family's evening meal. The meal, eaten outdoors at their patchouli-oil plant just out of town, included no prayers, merely the enjoyment of the meat that, by virtue of its purchase, had already been consecrated to God.

Both brothers downplayed the roles of sacrifier and sacrificer. They were not present for the killing and made no specific dedication (although, of course, the sacrificer uttered the obligatory basmala when cutting the throat). For Abang Gemboyah the religiously important moment was when he purchased the goats, a purchase that was of additional religious value because of the gift of the second goat. He explained that the sacrifices had to be done without any self-interest (*pamrih*), precisely the opposite of the predominant view in Isak.

---

[14] See the similar situation reported by Clifford Geertz (1960:173–74) for Muhammadiyah members in Java in the early 1950s. There, the focus of activity on the Feast of Sacrifice was on soliciting donations of oxen, goats, or money from members and friends of the organization, and distributing the meat to the poor.

Baléatu religious modernists see sacrifice as proof of a sincere and self-less willingness to obey God. The prominence of the takbīrs, the morning worship, and the historical sacrifice by Ibrāhīm all support this central theme. But town modernists also characterize what they do in explicit contrast to village ways of celebrating. Baléatu people emphasize the sharp divide between the world of the living and the world of the dead, and recognize only a thin strand of communication across it, mainly through prayer to God. Practices that in Isak involve transactions with spiritual agents are located exclusively among the living in Baléatu. (Isak-born town modernists often remember such spirit transactions with a shudder, and pretend that they belong to the pre-Islamic past of the highlands.) Celebrating the relations among family members is done in the home through cathartic obeisances and not by way of the sacrificial victim. Eating together (lexically distinguished from holding a ritual meal) is purely and simply that, with no suggestion that the meal or accompanying prayers are directed toward a spirit. Food is given away to orphans as a social demonstration of the sincere devotion to God that should be the sole animating force of religious actions taken during the holiday.

Although Isak and Baléatu residents differ in their ideas about transaction and interest with regard to sacrifice, they converge in their images of family and gender. In both cases women and men alike benefit from the ritual and contribute to it. In Isak sacrifiers bind together the family, its ancestors, and its descendants through sacrifice, and give to this binding the concrete imagery of the journey to the place of judgment. In Baléatu, the selfless sacrifice is performed in the name of the household, and the most intense events are the public worship attended by women and men, community meals, and the cathartic domestic confessions in which women and men play identical roles.

A prominent position for women is indeed more generally characteristic of Indonesian ideas about the Feast of Sacrifice. Indonesian ulama have even argued that women may carry out the sacrifice themselves, as both sacrifier (a practice observed in Isak) and even as sacrificer, the wielder of the knife. The influential modernist scholar Hasbi ash-Shiddieqy, for example, argues that a woman who owns an animal to be sacrificed ought to kill it herself, or at least act as formal witness to the killing (1950:26).

Because the Feast of Sacrifice is accepted by village and town alike, it provides a clear-cut case of how transactional and commemorative viewpoints lead to markedly divergent ritual forms. People in Isak and Baléatu are well aware of the differences between their conceptions of the ritual, and each group has shaped the ritual with those differences in mind.

The case of sacrifice also indicates the political significance of changes in ritual form. As town forms of ritual have moved it into a public sphere, it has also become more closely integrated into the ideology and control apparatus of the Indonesian state. The relationship of state and religion is never a direct one in Indonesia. Unlike the Islamic states of the Middle East and South Asia, Indonesia proclaims itself nonconfessional, welcoming all monotheisms. Indonesian rulers therefore neither can nor wish to make any particular Islamic ritual into an explicit rite of political legitimacy. But two emphases within modernism open it up to political uses and interpretations: that on proper attitudes (such as ikhlās), and that on public worship ritual.

Recall the worship event itself, and the efforts by the preacher to link the event to the necessity of sacrifice for development. The idea of ikhlās provides the conceptual transition and indicates a more general quality of Indonesian modernism, what we might call the intransitive quality of its discourse. Modernist speeches and sermons emphasize proper piety—one should sacrifice, be devoted, worship—to God, of course, but more importantly as an intrinsically valued set of actions ("value-rational" rather than "ends-rational," in Weber's terms).

The intransitive quality is another aspect of the modernist focus on commemoration and having the correct intent (in its contrast with the village emphasis on instrumental transactions). This form of discourse renders modernism particularly open to political interpretations and exploitation. The purpose of a ritual can easily be claimed by the state as its own, when a request for everyone to sacrifice (meaning: give something up) can sound vaguely religious even when the goals are clearly secular. And in Indonesia an emphasis on proper attitudes or states of mind has been central to the creation of state ideology.[15]

If the intransitivity of modernist discourse has provided the content for this link between religion and state, the increasingly public character of ritual in the town has provided the opportunity. Beginning in the 1930s and 1940s, modernist leaders urged people to practice public, congregational worship instead of older transactional forms—mortuary kenduris, for example, or kenduris at the Feast of Sacrifice.

Once established as ritually central, public worship and other public religious gatherings were rather easily put to the service of particular political agents and parties. In the late 1930s the newly powerful Gayo ruler of the Bukit domain in Takèngën, the largest political domain in the town area, ordered that the worship at the Feast of Sacrifice take place in front of his residence, with the worshipers prostrating themselves in its direction (Bowen

---

[15] One thinks of the importance to Javanese of the state of peace known as *slamet* and the use made of this category (along with similar notions of social harmony, e.g., *rukun*) in encouraging political inactivity. Elsewhere (1986) I have examined the political history of the state-created theory that Indonesians ought to be ready to work for the general good because of the cultural importance ascribed to "mutual assistance" (*gotong-royong*).

1991:87). Anticolonial leaders could also avail themselves of modernist-led events to advance the cause of nationalism: recall how public gatherings to plan the celebrations of 'īd al-adhā and 'īd al-fitr were transformed into celebrations of a new nationalist spirit.

Religion in its new public form provided the perfect forum and cover for anticolonial politics, and has continued to provide the opportunity for Indonesian state interventions. Congregational performance of worship indeed forces out issues of religion and politics because of its obligatory and public character, which we will examine further in the following chapter.

Chapter Thirteen

WORSHIP AND PUBLIC LIFE

"WORSHIP IS LIKE WAR," declared Tengku Asaluddin. "The enemy is the Devil, who comes to distract and trouble us while we worship. As is stated in the Qur'ān: 'worship is very difficult, except for those who lose themselves in worship of God.'"[1]

Abang Kerna used quite a different metaphor to describe how he approaches worship. "Worship is like writing," he said; "you have to shut down all your senses—hearing, smell, and sight—and focus on the thought that God is one. If you understand the meaning of the words you recite that is fine, but even if you do not know them God understands what you mean, and that is all right."

The two men agreed that worship is a time when you must shut out all other cares and thoughts from your mind and heart, for worship brings you into contact with God. But they conceive of that contact through very different images. We have already seen something of these two men's lives. Tengku Asaluddin has been doing battle with the enemies of correct worship since the 1940s. Although a generous and usually mild-mannered man, he readily assumed the posture of the preacher scolding his flock. In the 1980s he often served as the sermon giver for the Friday congregational prayers at the Isak mosque. In the mosque, where he roundly chided the assembled worshipers, as well as at home, where he sighed over their foibles and stubborness, he bemoaned the failure of Isak men and women to read the scriptures and act accordingly. Their sporadic and incorrect ways of worshiping, he complained, came from their unwillingness to study the scripture.

Abang Kerna has molded his life around a different set of practices and motivations. Trained as a healer, he has sought power over the unseen world by engaging in communication with spirits. For him, worship is like using spells for protection, healing the sick, or chanting for the deceased: in each practice he uses language to speak with spiritual agents. By drawing nearer to God through worship, he also draws nearer to inner sources of power that can be used for beneficial or malevolent ends. He worships because God has told him to do so, but worship's essence is less the sheer fact of obedience than the occasion it gives for him to speak to God.

---

[1] Qur'ān 2:45. Here Tengku Asaluddin quoted the Arabic and then translated into Indonesian. The standard translation of the second part of the verse is: "except for those who are humble." Tengku Asaluddin used the Indonesian word *khusyuk*, which here refers to the humility that accompanies deep absorption in worship, hence my translation.

FORM AND FEELING IN WORSHIP

Worship can provide the texts both for interior spiritual journeys and for public social and political discourse. Within the constraints posed by a commonly accepted and scripturally mandated form, individuals create their own worlds of worship. But, as with sacrifice, worship also may express and represent society in its ideal form. When religious scholars enter into debate over ritual details, their disputes are as much about social order and authority as they are over scriptural interpretation and personal salvation.

Words for worship can themselves become indexes of a socioreligious stance. The ritual of worship is called *salāt* in Arabic and *semiyang* in Gayo. Like the Arabic term (and the Persian equivalent, *namāz*), *semiyang* and its Indonesian counterpart, *sembahyang*, refer to worship, but carry the specific connotation of submission through prostration before God. In the multireligious contexts of Indonesian national discourse (for example, on national television), *sembahyang* is used to refer to the worship rituals of Muslims, Christians, Hindus, and Buddhists. In such contexts, and in comparativist discussions in general, the term approximates "liturgy." Reacting against this ecumenical sense of the term (and against its perceived Hindu [Sanskrit] origins), many urban Indonesian modernists insist on using only the term *salāt* to refer to Islamic worship. In the Gayo highlands the salient issues concern correct ritual practice within Islam, and not the position of Islam relative to other religions, so the use of *semiyang* worries very few people. However, some modernist-leaning Gayo will say *salāt* exclusively in order to stress their own ritual correctness.

All Gayo would agree that they are required, as part of their submission to God within Islam, to perform the worship ritual on a regular basis. The basic outlines of the ritual are agreed on by all Gayo (and most other Muslims).[2] Its structure is derived from hadīth on how the prophet Muhammad worshiped, and disputes over ritual procedure usually turn on differing interpretations of these hadīth.[3] The ritual begins with ablutions, after which the

---

[2] Differences among Muslims regarding the ritual come from, among others, the existence of four distinct schools of law (madhhab), Sunni/Shi'ite contrasts, individual interpretations of ritual norms, and sociocultural variation (e.g., in the roles of hierarchy, gender distinctions, and self-styled orthopraxy in constituting local identity). Wensinck (1953c) surveys the forms and history of *salāt*; further descriptions are to be found in Lane (1860:72–91) for Egypt, and Juynboll (1930:52–77) for Indonesia. Beyond the orthoprax consensus are interpretations, particularly by Sufi thinkers, of 'ibādāt as merely external activities that may be discarded once a level of gnosis is reached.

[3] Wensinck (1953c) lists several such disputes and their corresponding hadīth. In Indonesia as in other Islamic countries, the authors of worship manuals compile and translate hadīth that support their particular positions. Among frequently consulted manuals in the Gayo regions are those by Abbas (1976), who follows the Shafi'i law school, and by the modernist Hassan (1979).

worshiper, either alone or in congregation, performs two, three, or four rak'a or worship cycles (the number depending on the time of day) in the direction of Mecca. In each cycle the worshiper executes a fixed sequence of movements (standing, prostrating, kneeling, sitting), each accompanied by a fixed Arabic recitation. The recitations include praises of God, affirmations of his oneness, a general request for divine guidance, and, at the beginning of each cycle, two or more verses from the Qur'ān. Worshipers may also add petitionary prayers (du'ā') to their recitations. Worship should be performed five times daily (at first light, noon, mid-afternoon, sunset, and night), although travelers may perform four of the rituals as two pairs. The Friday noon worship consists of a sermon and two (rather than the usual noontime four) worship cycles, and should be performed in congregation (jamā'a), with a prayer leader and a sermon giver. Women and men carry out special worship together during the fasting month of Ramadan, at the feast that celebrates the month's close, and at the feast of sacrifice held during the pilgrimage month. They also perform special worship after burial and as part of other rituals of supplication.

Within the fixed contours of periodicity, postures, gestures, and prescribed recitations, individuals may shape their worship according to knowledge and vocal expertise, the constraints of time, place, and (in the case of congregational worship) audience, and the emotional and cognitive needs of the moment.

In each of the the first two cycles, the worshiper recites al-Fātiha and then another entire or partial sūra of her or his choosing. The beginner, or someone who must complete worship quickly, might choose one or more of the shorter sūras, especially one of the final, shortest three sūras (al-Ikhlās, al-Falaq, an-Nās). Those with a greater command of the Qur'ān may choose verses to match their personal needs or emotions. Tengku Asaluddin explained that sometimes he selected verses before he began to worship, but at other times the choice of a recitation would come to him after he had begun. If he had been in danger he might recite the Seven Verses, each of which reminds him that everything comes from God, including afflictions, and that God has the power to withdraw all that he has sent. Verse 107 from Sūra Yunus (Qur'ān 10), for example, reassures him with its words:

> If God do touch thee with hurt, there is none can remove it but He:
> If He do design some benefit for thee, there is none can keep back His favor:
> He causeth it to reach whomsoever of His servants he pleaseth.
> And He is the Oft-Forgiving, Most Merciful.

If he had been worrying over a problem, he often would recite an-Nabā (Qur'ān 78), especially the first part, which "reminds us that we should not worry, that God made the mountains, and the nights for sleeping, and the sun like a huge lamp, that he is all-powerful." If he was sad, he would recite one of the stories in the Qur'ān: that of Yusup (Joseph), for example (Qur'ān 12), or that of Suleiman and Balkis (Solomon and the Queen of Sheba, Qur'ān 27:15–44). "The Qur'ān is medicine for the soul," he concluded.

Ideally, the worshiper enters into a state of concentration in which every-day thoughts are replaced by thoughts of God. Some Gayo (such as Tengku Asaluddin) also stress the importance of understanding the verses recited, while others (such as Abang Kerna) emphasize the overwhelming impor-tance of communicating with God.

Most Gayo would agree that one should eliminate everyday thoughts when worshiping. People often said that they tried to apply the hadīth "kill yourself before you die," meaning that during worship one should shut down the senses, become as if dead to the world. Tengku Asaluddin de-scribed worship as entering the house of God and leaving all else outside. He quoted an Arabic saying: "The heart of the believer is the house of God." These comments recall the musings of the early mystic writers, for example the thirteenth-century poet Rūmī (Schimmel 1975:151–52):

> While performing salāt [they were] drawn up in ranks before God as
>   at Resurrection, and engaged in self-examination and prayer.
> Standing in God's presence and shedding tears, like one who rises erect
>   on [the day of] rising from the dead.

Even the most devout of Muslims have difficulty maintaining this state of concentration. Often I heard the following story about 'Ali, the fourth caliph, who of all Muhammad's followers was best able to concentrate on his worship. During a battle an arrow lodged itself in 'Ali's leg, and only when he absorbed himself in worship could it be pulled out without causing him great pain. Yet even his concentration was not perfect. Once the prophet Muhammad offered a new set of clothes to whomever among his followers could worship perfectly. 'Ali had almost finished his worship when, despite his intentions, a thought flashed through his mind. "I wonder what clothes Muhammad will give me?" he pondered, whereupon his con-centration, and thus the exemplary character of his worship, was lost.

Gayo face this challenge of concentration at regular intervals every day (as do Muslims everywhere). Abang Evi, my "brother" in Takèngën, finds concentration to be the greatest challenge of worship. "I know right from the opening recitation whether I will be able to concentrate on the wor-ship," he said. "The mind is like a computer; thousands of thoughts drift around and can enter your mind while at worship. Sometimes I find myself saying 'amīn,' and I think to myself: 'I've just run right through the chapter and now I am saying 'amīn' but for what purpose?'" For him, concentra-tion was especially difficult at noon and midafternoon, when his mind was full of business problems. At those times he tried to worship with others, because the atmosphere made concentration easier.

Abang Evi also tried to focus on the meaning of the words he recited, although this was difficult in congregational worship if the leader chose a long chapter to recite. He was troubled when he found himself unfamiliar with the verse being recited: "'Why haven't I learned that one yet?' I ask myself." He could achieve the best state of concentration at the final stage of worship when, seated, he would point his finger upward toward God while reciting the confession of faith. "I really become absorbed here," he said, "and then I am ready to say prayers for the well-being of my grandparents."

Whereas Tengku Asaluddin, Abang Evi, and others of modernist orientation underlined the importance of understanding the meaning of the verses they recited, many in Isak emphasized another aspect of worship; namely, its creation of a path to God. Aman Bani, the religious official for Kutë Kramil village in 1989, summoned up his powers of depictive concentration (maripët) to truly enter into God's presence. He would excercise maripët at two points in worship: the very beginning, when he says "God is great" and enters into worship, and again near the end, at the same point mentioned by Abang Evi, when he proclaims the Oneness of God. Here he is sometimes able to reach God, to attain the goal of mystics everywhere (cf. Schimmel 1975:148–55). He explained what would transpire:

> If I am concentrating fully at these two moments I will see a flash of light, like a camera flashbulb when someone takes a picture. This light is the Light of God, the same light we see in the sky; it is all his light. Then we know we are in contact with him. You cannot, of course, see his face, as you can when you imagine a person.

For some, worship is an act of great emotional potential. "Sometimes I find myself in tears in the middle of worship," said Tengku Asaluddin, "because I have been thinking about how, in the end, I will be left only with God. God is the source of all our love for others, and in the end only he remains for us to love." Asyin, the poet we first encountered in Chapter 2, began each worship by thinking himself dead: "It is for me as if I were dead and buried, lying on my side in the grave with the earth over me."

Indeed, proper concentration is emotional, attitudinal, cognitive, and physical. "If you think of God, and are in full concentration, and sincerely surrender yourself to him," explained Asyin, "then, and only then, do you make contact with God in worship and your words and feelings reach him. Otherwise your words will reach him all right, but he will only listen; he will not respond and act on your words." Asyin illustrated this coming together of thoughts, emotions, and recitation by showing me how he feels and thinks about his recitation of the al-Fātiha, the first chapter of the

Qur'ān with which one opens each worship cycle. He recited, translated, and commented on each of the seven verses of the chapter in order to show me their full range of meaning. For the first verse he spoke as follows:

> "Bismillāh irrahmān irrahīm."
> "In the name of God the merciful, the compassionate."
> "God has mercy on all beings, but he only adds compassion for those close to him, the Muslims."
> At this point I try to concentrate fully, and then, "thwap," I come into contact with him.

Each of the five daily times for worship has its own distinctive character. In Takèngën, all five are signaled by calls to prayer, azan (<Ar. adhān), sung through amplified microphones. The daybreak call, cutting through the thin, cold air, rouses nearly everyone out of their sleep; indeed, the call to prayer for this time alone contains the extra line: "prayer is better than sleep." Those who perform worship at the Takèngën mosque may stay afterward for study sessions at which a teacher lectures on a religious topic. These "daybreak lectures" are popular throughout Indonesia, and those given by the more popular scholars are available in cassette form (which some Takèngën families buy and play). Most people prefer to perform the daybreak worship at home, however.

The noon and midafternoon worship times come during working hours and are carried out wherever and whenever the worshiper has the opportunity. Farmers often worship in the huts they have erected in their fields; others stop by convenient prayer houses or worship at home or in their place of employment. Some prayer houses engage religious teachers to lead scriptural study sessions for the half hour prior to the midafternoon worship.

The dusk worship is the most popular time for worshiping at a neighborhood prayer house. Most people will have returned home and begun preparations for the evening meal. The prayer house in Baléatu is often nearly full for this session. Some men, but fewer women, remain at the prayer house for the hour or so between the dusk and evening prayer times. For some of the older men in Baléatu this hour is a prime occasion for conversing with friends who have been away at work during the day. In Isak as well the dusk worship is the most popular time for worship in congregation at the mosque or at one of the five prayer houses. It is the only session for which the call to prayer is sounded from the mosque. In the 1980s even this worship was not well attended, though, with usually no more than ten men and one or two women present.

Some may remain at the prayer house or mosque until it is time for the evening worship; most, however, return home and perform that worship after the evening meal. It is at evening worship, and often during supererogatory prayers late at night, that intent worshipers say they most successfully attain a vision of God's light.

Although worship is primarily performed in fulfillment of one's ritual obligations, men and women also may perform it as part of other activities or in response to personal needs or experiences. One may carry out two worship cycles in thanks to God that a danger has passed or that a wish has come true. Worship in the middle of the night may be designed to make a special plea to God: that a crop be saved, or that whoever stole your chickens come down with a dreadful disease. As we have seen, rice ritual specialists and healers often worship just before asking God for assistance.

Worship changes in its frequency and importance for many Gayo during their life course. Some Gayo men and women speak about their life in terms of their changing relation to worship. Several of my Isak friends who had been rather negligent of worship near the beginning of my fieldwork became much more concerned to perform it regularly as they passed certain milestones. For some, the appearance of grandchildren was the explicit reason for "changing my ways," renouncing conduct that would be seen as unseemly in a grandparent (such as quarreling), and adopting a somewhat more pious attitude. But many of these people also began to weigh seriously the implications of what they did to influence their fates after death, and then took steps to improve the fit between their daily conduct and the prescriptions of religion. Worship was a major realm in which to bring about such improvement.

Abang Das worshiped only sporadically during the two years when he was my neighbor and companion in Isak (1978–1980). He only began to worship fairly regularly in the early 1980s, after a series of conflicts within his village led him to change his affiliation to the natal village of his mother. He began to withdraw from Isak life and to worship even more assiduously. By mid-1989 he said he performed the optional worship cycles (two cycles after the required number) as well, saying that he did not feel right if he stopped after just the required worship. During worship he strives to achieve a feeling of self-extinction, *fana* (Ar. *fanā*), imagining himself in the process of dying as he raises his hands up for the takbīr, "Allāhu akbar" ("God is great"). If one begins to think of one's family or work, he said, "the prophet Hilir [al-Khidr] knows our thoughts and laughs to himself. Sometimes he is worshiping right next to us." Despite his efforts he finds "it is hard to worship correctly. Only 'one out of a hundred, two out of a thousand' can, as the Acehnese say."

By contrast, another of my frequent companions, Aman Déwi, still rarely worshiped by 1989. "I find it difficult to concentrate because I am always thinking about where that evening's meal will come from. When that happens I lose concentration. You should be able to enter worship and see God right in front of you [he pointed about one meter away]. Some teachers say there is no merit in worship without concentration; others say there is some. But I would rather wait until my situation is better so that I can concentrate."

WORSHIPING TOGETHER

Students of Muslim societies generally recognize the social importance of congregational worship. It is here that men (and sometimes women) come together to worship and to hear a sermon, usually delivered by a man of learning from the community. Most discussions of Friday congregational worship (Antoun 1989; Fischer 1980; Gaffney 1987) have focused on the capacity of the preacher to interweave social and political messages together with religious texts and advice in his sermon. The sermon is, however, but one part of an event that includes listening to a melodious cantillation of scripture, speaking to God during worship, and standing together with one's fellow villagers or townspeople. Worshiping together can bring to the fore one's relation to God and to other people. It can be aesthetically and emotionally satisfying, and also embody certain ideas of religious communication and social relations.

More than any other single event, the Friday service in the Takèngën mosque structures the week's activities for men and women living in nearby villages. Many people come to town to shop or conduct business on Friday mornings before attending the mosque. In Isak, too, people come from surrounding garden areas and downstream villages to shop, socialize, and worship on Fridays. To work in the fields in the morning before the service is discouraged, but commerce is in full swing.

Women and especially men begin to drift into the Takèngën mosque during the morning. Men sit in the front portion of the mosque; women gather halfway back, behind a light sheet draped over a rope. Arriving early allows a man to claim a place in the first row, a position that confers religious merit and also places one next to town notables (the highest local-government officials have places reserved for them in the front row). As people enter they perform the recommended worship ritual of two cycles.

The mosque attracts about fifteen hundred men and about two hundred women on most Fridays. It could hold about twice that number. It is spacious, painted white, and open on three sides. The sound of the sermon echoes around the inside of the mosque and is often difficult to hear. By noon most worshipers have arrived, though people continue to enter up to the moment of salāt.

The service begins when the preacher (*khatīb*) mounts the mimbar from which he will deliver his sermon (*khutba*) and greets all those present with the words

> *as-salām 'alaikum wa rahmatullah wa barakhatu*
> [Peace be to you and the mercy and blessing of God].

He then sits, and the *imām*, the man who will lead the congregation in worship, stands. He slowly, deliberately, recites the first call to worship, the azan. As the call begins to sound, those who have just entered remain standing; they must wait to perform the recommended worship cycles until after the azan has been completed. Those seated remain so. All softly pronounce the set responses to the call.

At the conclusion of the first call to worship the preacher rises and begins his sermon. The sermon constitutes the first half of the service, the equivalent of two worship cycles, and thus is followed by a worship of only two cycles rather than the ordinary noontime four cycles. (Those who arrive while the sermon is preached do not, however, consider their worship to have been invalidated because of their late arrival.)

There are in fact two sermons, a long sermon followed by a shorter one. Each begins with fixed Arabic recitations: a formula in praise of God, followed by a shalawat prayer for the welfare of the prophet Muhammad and his family, further prayers, and then one or more Qur'ānic verses. Each sermon concludes with a second prayer for Muhammad, and then a prayer wishing peace on all those in attendance. The first sermon includes a long central segment in Indonesian. This segment ideally is in the form of an expansion of and commentary on the Qur'ānic verses just recited. The second, shorter sermon consists of Arabic prayers, often read from books compiled for this purpose.

Until the early colonial era both sermons were entirely in Arabic. Indeed, some ulama still consider the sermon to be valid (i.e., to count as two worship cycles) only if it is entirely in Arabic; these ulama always perform the noontime worship immediately after the Friday worship to make up for this deficit. The shift to Indonesian was accepted relatively widely and early in Takèngën, however. It predates the establishment of Muhammadiyah in 1928 and the debates between modernists and traditionalists in the 1930s, and thus did not become a major issue of contention, at least in the memory of those ulama still alive in the 1980s. (Nor have I encountered references in colonial records to disputes over the language of sermons.)

The sermon topics range from general commentary on religious matters (the importance of faith, the inevitability of death) to specific criticisms of immediate local relevance, such as the failure of a few to pay their zakāt alms or the errors in recent television broadcasts. General or specific in their targets, many, perhaps most, sermons are delivered as warnings, reminders, or criticisms of some sort. This attitude of the preacher is expected, although too critical a sermon may elicit hostility in the audience (I often heard resentful remarks made in Isak). The Qur'ān itself is to a great extent couched in this mode of warning. But the religious issues that have most divided the community in the recent past are not touched on, under the terms of a general agreement arrived at in 1948 after the Acehnese ulama issued their proclamation on funeral ritual (see Chapter 2).

When the sermon is over, shortly after noon, the worship leader stands to deliver the second call to worship, the qamat, and everyone rises to prepare for the salāt. Worshipers must form straight, unbroken rows, and people move up to fill gaps in the rows ahead of them during these moments. Everyone looks left and right to make sure that the rows are straight and the worship can begin. Sometimes the leader will call out "Rows [syaf]?" and if the rows have not been formed, members of the congregation will reply "Not yet."

In the late 1980s the regular worship leader in Takèngën was a young man named Mukhlis. Mukhlis has a beautiful, lilting voice, and he lifts the verses up to the high roof of the mosque as he sings, then lets them slowly descend to a pause. Although some traditionalist scholars expressed reservations over Mukhlis's Arabic pronunciation (reservations motivated in part by Mukhlis's modernist leanings), they also enjoyed his singing of the verses. (It may be that the difficulty of learning Arabic grammar leads some Gayo and other Indonesians to especially appreciate tone and melody, as further suggested by the popularity of the cantillation contests.)

The worship leader recites on behalf of the congregation as a whole. The men and women who worship behind him follow along silently as best they can, and if they are familiar with the verse they might meditate on its content, but their worship is valid even if they simply listen and wait. On informal occasions, when a family worships at home or several people meet at a prayer house, the leader may simply recite one or more of the shortest verses. The occasion is a casual one, and the choice of verses not socially important.[4] At a Friday service, however, the worship leader usually selects his verses carefully.

The worship leader may choose verses so as to make a connection to the content of the sermon. (The preacher is generally a different person from the worship leader, although I have seen occasions where the same individual performed both functions.) These connections may extend between the

---

[4] In the noon and midafternoon worships the leader recites verses silently, so the followers must choose their own verses to recite to themselves separately. Worshipers usually choose short verses on such occasions so as not to risk falling behind the leader. A woman would be the worship leader of an all-female congregation; a man of a male or mixed group.

two texts (sermon and worship) and between the chosen texts and features of the worshipers' social world.

Let me illustrate how this works with one example from Isak. The sermon preached on 3 July 1989 in the Isak mosque concerned what happens to those who neglect their religious duties, especially their failure to pay the zakāt, the tithe on wealth. The preacher, the son of an Isak woman, had not lived in the community for some years. On his return, I was told, he had learned of several well-off people in the community who had not paid their alms in recent years, and he decided to make them the target of his sermon (no names were mentioned, but the targets were clear to all present). He began his sermon with two Qur'ānic verses: one that excoriates those who think of God only when they are in trouble, and a second that excoriates those who "have eyes but do not see, ears but do not hear" for being no better than animals.

In the course of his Indonesian-language sermon he explained the meaning of both verses, and then described what had happened to clove farmers in West Aceh. The farmers had refused to pay zakāt on their cloves. They claimed that their riches were the fruit of their own labor and not of the productivity of the ground. (In fact there had been considerable dispute among religious scholars as to whether cloves were subject to zakāt.) Shortly after they had refused to pay, disease devastated their crops, and storms took much of what remained. By now, he said, many had been reduced to poverty. The point was clear, and he left it implicit.

As Tengku Asaluddin listened to the preacher, he thought about which verses he should recite for the two worship cycles that were to follow. He settled on al-A'la (Qur'ān 87) for the first cycle and al-Ghashiya (Qur'ān 88) for the second. The first selection (as he described it to me afterward) warns people to think not only of this world, and reminds those who do so of the torments of Hell that await them. The second sūra elaborates on the different fates of those who reach Heaven and those who are destined for Hell. By reciting these sūras he was able to reinforce the message of the sermon without repeating the verses recited by the preacher.[5]

Through the course of the worship, everyone in the mosque moves in unison through the successive movements and recitations of the service. They conclude by greeting those to the right and left of them, and then, usually, shaking their neighbors' hand. The few moments after the conclusion of worship may be used by one or more officials for announcements. In July 1989 in Takèngën, for example, the chief of police stood on several successive Fridays to urge all local Muslims to donate to a fund for victims of a re-

---

[5] I do not know how many worshipers would have made these intertextual connections. A few would have known the sūras in question; most would at best have caught references to Heaven, Hell, and the day of judgment in the imām's recitations.

cent fire in town. The army commander, a man quite adept at delivering speeches in a religious framework, often used the occasion to make an announcement. In addition, the worship ritual for a recently deceased member of the community would be held during these brief moments. After the announcements, the men and women leave the mosque by separate entrances, greeting friends as they slowly walk back to their houses or to the restaurants for the noon meal.

DISPUTATIONS

Accompanying these widely shared experiences of worship are divergent understandings of the ritual and its relation to other social and religious activities. Most villagers, supported on this issue by traditionalist scholars, see worship as an act of communication with God. Because they hold communication to be primary, they tend to accept a diversity of ways of carrying out worship. This attitude leads to what I earlier called the optative view of scriptural prescription: that God, through the prophet Muhammad, sometimes provided the Islamic community with two or more equally legitimate ways of carrying out a particular religious duty.

Modernists, by contrast, argue that there is only one legitimate way to perform each religious obligation, and that one discovers this correct ritual procedure by carefully reading scripture and not by reasoning from a general idea about ritual as communication. Modernists accept that God's reasons for ritual may be opaque, but that we can only follow his demands.

This part of the debate between modernists and traditionalists thus concerns primarily what forms of evidence are sufficient to accept a certain act as religious, as part of the divine norms of worship. The disputes over worship perhaps illustrate these epistemological debates better than those over other areas of ritual conduct because here the two sides can agree on so much. Disputes over sacrifices or recitations for the dead implicate general theological issues such as idolatry or transmitting merit, and modernists therefore challenge the legitimacy of the entire ritual complex. Such is not the case for worship: everyone accepts the salāt as proper and obligatory, so controversies have focused on how one ought to reason from scripture. As a result, the substantive content of the debates may appear trivial; what is at issue, however, is the general and weighty issue of how one is to resolve issues of religion and ritual.

Two worship issues have animated Gayo and illustrate different aspects of these disputes. One issue concerns declaring one's intent to worship, the other involves pronouncing the basmala. Both cases pit a commitment to worship as communication against a commitment to a strict conformity to the example of the prophet Muhammad. In both cases advocates of competing positions feel that the legitimacy of their entire approach to religious interpretation and ritual is at stake.

Pronouncing Intent: The Ushalli

The worshiper enters into worship by standing straight, facing the direction of Mecca, and saying "God is great" ("Allāhu akbar") while raising the hands to the ears. During the time needed to say this phrase one also forms an intent to worship in one's heart. Some also pronounce this intent to themselves in a vernacular (in our case, Gayo or Indonesian) or in Arabic. A standard phrase for worship at daybreak, for example, would be: "I worship at daybreak with two cycles on account of God the Highest." Many Indonesian worship manuals are studiously ambiguous as to whether intent should be pronounced.[6] The advocates of declaring one's intent see it as an aid to proper worship; opponents see it as an illegitimate addition to worship. The opening pronouncement "I worship" is *'usallī* in Arabic, and the dispute has thus been called the "ushalli controversy."

Most Isak people do declare intent when beginning worship. Whatever the historical reasons for adopting the practice locally, many see it as a way of facilitating one's pathway to God. The declarations of intent, along with prayers and recitations, make worship more like speaking with God (or, as in Abang Kerna's image, more like writing to God) and less like automatic performance of a preset routine. Some Isak people personalize their statements of intent. Aman Déwi learned one such statement, which he called a "personal confession of faith," from his wife's grandfather. It has been handed down in Kutë Robel village much as are spells or healing formulas. The statement is in a mixture of Gayoized Malay and Arabic (in that respect resembling spells) and conveys the speaker's total surrender of self to God. "It is better to say it before you begin to worship," he explained, "because that way you start off by exchanging words with God, surrendering your soul [to him]."

As the leader of Takèngën traditionalist scholars, Tengku Ali Salwany has attempted to defend the practice of declaring intent (though not "personal confessions of faith" such as Aman Déwi's) on the grounds of scripture and the consensus of scholars. He explained that the practice was recommended (sunna) because it helped to focus the worshiper's concentration. He admitted that Muhammad did not command us to do it, but neither did he forbid it. It is an innovation, but there are good and bad innovations. Some help us in worship. There are many things we do that Muhammad did not. We wear watches to tell the time for worship and hats during the wor-

---

[6] Thus, early in one very popular pamphlet (Ya'cub 1978:21–23) the author provides an Arabic declaration of intent along with its Indonesian translation, implying that one is to recite the Arabic phrase. But in the detailed ritual instructions (1978:25) he supplies only an italicized Indonesian phrase that one is to "let fall" while reciting Allāhu akbar. The italics imply that the phrase is a formula to be somehow conveyed or expressed, but the instructions and use of Indonesian rather than the Arabic used for all recited passages imply that it is to remain an inner, felt intention.

ship, and we use a microphone to spread the call to worship as far as possible. And we may declare our intent to worship as well. He himself does not pronounce it, but villagers need it to focus their thoughts. The great religious scholars of the past decided that these reasons warranted making the declaration a legitimate option for worship, he concluded, and "who are we to question their judgment?"

Let us look more deeply into this argument to better understand the logic of traditionalist scholarship. Tengku Ali Salwany relied on the writings of his former teacher in West Sumatra, Kiyai Sirajuddin Abbas. Abbas's four-volume *Forty Religious Issues* (1976) is frequently reprinted, and it is sold by Takèngën booksellers. It is the most prominent Indonesian language sourcebook for traditionalist scholars in Takèngën.

Abbas argues for pronouncing the intent to worship by constructing an analogy from a reliable hadīth and then buttressing his argument with the pronouncements of distinguished religious scholars (1976:218–44). He begins with the report that the prophet Muhammad did indeed pronounce an intent when making the pilgrimage to Mecca, in order to distinguish it from a mere casual visit to Mecca. He argues that one may transfer, by analogy, the recommended quality of this statement of intent from the pilgrimage to worship (1976:236–39).

Abbas then makes the general claim, supported by statements from scholars within the Shafi'i legal tradition, that having the correct intent is a required (wājib) portion of any ritual act. How else but through the appropriate intent could one distinguish worship from mere bodily exercise, a religious fast from dieting, or one temporally fixed worship event from another (noon from midafternoon, for example)? Intent divides a mere going-through-the-motions from a religious action. As the prophet Muhammad said, in a generally accepted hadīth, "deeds are judged according to their intent" (1976:239).

Abbas then states that strengthening this intent is recommended (sunna), and that the consensus of Shafi'i scholars is that expressing one's intent to worship in words does indeed strengthen it. In this way "the tongue may help the heart," in the words of the tenth-century scholar Imam Ramli (1976:230–31). It is a "principle of law" in the Shafi'i school, he further claims, that the path to a goal has the same merit as the goal itself. Because verbalizing one's intent strengthens it (and also drives out improper thoughts), and because strengthening intent is itself a recommended act, verbalizing intent is also recommended (1976:240).

Such recourse to extrascriptural principles of law is anathema to many modernists. Indeed, the debates over the ushalli in Takèngën and elsewhere in Indonesia have been about proper modes of legal reasoning, not about doctrine. In Takèngën modernists began to openly criticize pronouncing the ushalli early in the 1930s. Tengku Madin Pas, a cofounder of the traditionalist al-Washliyah organization, recalled the disputes of that period. "They kept telling us we were wrong, and the disputes led to some divorces. Some people moved from Takèngën to Bireuën [on the northern coast] because they were ashamed at all the disputes." These early debates over the ushalli made it emblematic of the traditionalist position. Madin Pas stated the essence of that position in the form of a couplet:

semiyang berushalli	At worship, say the "ushalli";
Molut berkenduri	On the Prophet's birthday, hold a kenduri.

Of all the issues that increasingly embroiled traditionalists and modernists in Takèngën, "it was the ushalli that caused the most turmoil," Madin Pas said. Such was the degree of local antagonism that the principal imām of the mosque in Kota Raja (today Banda Aceh) intervened in the mid-1930s and instructed teachers on both sides to quell the contoversy. But the disputes continued, and the ushalli question was central to the 1941 public debate between Tengku Jali and Tengku Silang.

The radical reformist camp, represented nationally by Persis and locally by Tengku Jali and his Islamic Education school, saw in the ushalli an important issue of principle. Ahmad Hassan, the chief exponent of the Persis position, attacked the practice in a 1931 article (1968:91–95) that continues to be cited by Takèngën modernists today. (It is included in his frequently reprinted collection of columns [1968].) Hassan begins by reminding his readers that Muhammad strictly distinguished between religious and worldly matters. In the latter we are free to innovate as we wish; indeed Muhammad said: "You know better your worldly affairs [than I]." But in religious matters we must do precisely what the prophet Muhammad did and no more. We may not understand why the rules are as they are, continued Hassan. We may not see why we perform only two worship cycles at daybreak but four at noon, even though we have more free time at daybreak. But we must obey these rules and not add to them. After all, as the Prophet said: "Every innovation is error, and every error leads to Hell" (cf. Metcalf 1990:152).

Specifically, states Hassan, we may not add to worship a declaration of intent that is not part of the model we inherit from Muhammad. Such a practice improperly adds to Religion what is not already there (Hassan uses the capitalized Indonesian word *Agama* to emphasize the codified, fixed nature of religion). Nor is it convincing to say that "the tongue helps the heart," as what is on the tongue must first have been in the heart.

Equally improper in Hassan's view (1968:93) is reasoning by analogy (qiyās) in religious matters. The founder of the Shafi'i school himself, the Imam Shafi'i, said so, and also said that such reasoning makes one an unbeliever. One may not, therefore, declare an intent to worship on the grounds the Muhammad declared an intent to perform the pilgrimage. "If you wish to play around with analogies in worship," mocks Hassan (1968:94), "then why don't we add a call to prayer at the worship over the dead [as there is for Friday worship]." Hassan adds insult to injury by quoting two of the Shafi'i teachers to the effect that "he who makes up Religion is an unbeliever" (1968:93).[7]

In the 1980s, modernists in Takèngën continued to consult Hassan's articles. Even teachers who found them to be too extreme nonetheless recommended them to me as the clearest and most authoritative statements of law. Tengku Asaluddin was one such scholar. "Intent is in the heart alone," he said, "and we fear that 'adding to the Messenger's example is bid'a, and each bid'a is in error, and each error means you go to Hell' [quoting Hassan]." For Tengku Asaluddin, getting worship right is indeed like warfare.

Why was, and is, the issue so important to modernists? Part of the answer is that the ushalli issue brought out very clearly what they saw as a major error of the traditionalists, namely, their recourse to general principles and to analogy. Modernists saw the ushalli as a good place to take a firm stand on the limits of interpretation on religious matters, in part because there was no direct, positive support in the hadīth literature for saying the ushalli (as there was for some other issues).

Furthermore, behind the ushalli some modernists see a whole raft of other, highly objectionable speech acts: the spells, formulas, and exorcisms that they consider part of the "Hindu" baggage of their history. Here converge the opinions of some modernists (such as Tengku Asaluddin) and some traditionalists (such as Tengku Ali Salwany), who agree that practices such as setting out colored rice piles at kenduris are non-Islamic and ought to be abandoned. But while Tengku Ali Salwany addresses the problem on a case by case basis, hoping to allow for as much variation as possible in ritual practice, Tengku Asaluddin and other modernists draw a firm boundary between prescribed acts of worship and all other actions.

Finally, modernists did and do consider the issue of intent to be of general importance. Religious modernism's conception of subjectivity makes intent central. The individual who stands before God to be judged is responsible for thoughts, attitudes, and intents as well as for outer acts. Therefore all religious acts must be performed with the correct intent: one must worship or fast in order to serve God, not to impress neighbors, find a spouse, or drum up business. Both Aman Murni, Tengku Jali's successor at Islamic Education, and Tengku Ali Jaidun, the Muhammadiyah spokesman, explained the intent to worship in the same way to me. We express the intent to worship, they said, by preparing for worship: by walking to the mosque,

---

[7] The virulence of Hassan's critiques led Abbas to suggest that anyone who would write in such a way "is not in a normal condition" and that it would be "better to pay no heed" to him (1976:242).

performing ablutions, and so forth, even before we begin to worship. Intent suffuses all that we do before and during worship itself.

Because the right intent should accompany any religious action, there is no need to have a separate statement of intent (the ushalli). Indeed, to have such a statement may dangerously weaken the principle that actions have built-in intentions, because it implies that such a statement is needed.

In the religious poetry written in the mid-1930s and associated with the Islamic Education school, modernist poets stressed the importance of having the correct intent when at worship. In the collection of poems published in 1938, the *al-Tafsīr al-Gayo* (Daudy 1938:72), Tengku Mudë Kala depicts the mere mouthing of prayer as

imën ibibir	Faith on the lips,
nggéh sawah ku até	not reaching the heart.

To carry out acts of worship for reasons other than their intrinsic religious importance is tantamount to having no faith at all (Daudy 1938:7):

oya-lë palisé jema nggéh berimën	Such is the misfortune of the person without faith,
nggéh mera bertuhën ku allah ta'ala	who does not believe in God the Highest.
baring sana buët plèn karna ëdët	Anything done is done only because of ëdët;
berbuët ibëdët plèn karna jema	religious duties are done only to impress others.

Elsewhere the poet lambasts those who perform religious duties for specific reasons of self-interest. One long poem concerns those with profane intentions, such as finding a wife or setting up a profitable trade, who followed the prophet Muhammad in his emigration from Mecca to Medina. To them went only the benefit of their intent (a wife, or a profit), but not the religious merit of the pilgrimage (Daudy 1950:50):

keta tentu oya nieté idemué	So of course they received that which was intended;
lain ari soné tentu gërë dëpët	Anything else of course they did not get.

The ushalli controversy provided the Takèngën modernists a chance to emphasize that intent is an inner quality, not an outer act comparable to the gestures and recitations of worship. They preserved intent as a property that accompanies all actions and renders them valid or invalid.

We might then ask why traditionalists felt compelled to defend the ushalli. At first glance it seems odd that the couplet quoted by Tengku Madin Pas included the ushalli as one of two practices that define the traditionalist position. Part of the answer is undoubtedly historical. Because modernists criticized traditionalists for the ushalli relatively early in the history of highlands debates, the practice became a traditionalist emblem. But the ushalli also represents in rather clear fashion the central idea that worship is communication with God. Listen to how Tengku Ali Salwany ridicules (and interestingly misrepresents) the position taken by the modernist teacher Tengku Ali Jaidun:

> He [Ali Jaidun] even says that he does not express an intent when he is about to worship; that it is enough to have performed the ablutions, because doing this itself involves expressing intent to worship. But that would be as if tonight I said that I was going to write something tomorrow, and then tomorrow I wrote it without thinking of what I was about to write. That would be impossible.

What appears ridiculous to Tengku Ali Salwany is the idea that intent can be expressed at any time other than the moment of the act itself. Tengku Ali Jaidun's point, of course, was that he already is formulating his general intent as he prepares to worship and that intent is always there, "inside" action, so he does not need to declare it. But Tengku Ali Salwany (and most Isak people) see worship as an act of communication, not as a state of mind. Communication needs to have a channel opened for it, and the ushalli does just that by directing worship to God. In the traditionalist view, modernists seek to deny them a way of creating a personal pathway to him.

"In the Name of God": The Basmala

The case of pronouncing the basmala has raised similar issues on both sides, though in a less divisive but more public fashion. The dispute concerns the audible recitation of the opening chapter of the Qur'ān, al-Fātiha, during congregational worship. Al-Fātiha is the most frequently recited sūra in Gayo life. Worshipers recite it at every worship cycle; children learn it by heart very early on; celebrants recite it together at most kenduris. It begins with a basmala: *Bismillāh irrahmān irrahīm* ("In the name of God, the Merciful, the Compassionate"). The sense of the rest of the chapter is

> Praise be to God, Lord of the Worlds,
> The Merciful, the Compassionate,
> The Master of the Day of Judgment.
> Thee alone we serve; Thee alone we ask for help.
> Guide us on the straight path,
> The path of those whom Thou hast blessed,
> Not [the path] of those who earn Thy anger,
>   nor of those who go astray.

The sūra is always followed by an *amīn*. Gayo and other Muslims regard al-Fātiha with special familiarity and reverence. Gayo often say that it (along with Sūra 112, al-Ikhlās) "contains the whole of the Qur'ān." A similar idea is found in devotional manuals elsewhere in the Muslim world: compare the statement by ash-Sha'rānī (Padwick 1961:109) that "all the meanings of the Qur'ān are gathered together in the Fātiha." For its ubiquity, familiarity, and collective recitation it has been compared to the Christian Lord's Prayer (ibid.). Worship leaders are particularly proficient in singing it, and worshipers notice even the slightest inaccuracy in pronunciation.

Notice my ambiguity as to whether the basmala is part of al-Fātiha itself. Indeed, Muslim scholars have long disagreed as to whether it is the first line of al-Fātiha or prefatory to it, as in the case of all the other chapters (where the basmala is considered only an introductory reminder that one begins all tasks, especially the task of reciting from the Qur'ān, in the name of God).

But al-Fātiha is different from all other chapters of the Qur'ān. Its place in the overall work is like that of a preamble or an epigraph. The Qur'ān is generally arranged from the longest verse to the shortest, but al-Fātiha, though very short, appears at the very beginning. It has therefore been assessed differently. There are two well known English versions of the Qur'ān: Yusuf Ali's counts the basmala as a verse; Pickthall's does not (the two translators parse differently, and thus each depicts the chapter as having seven verses, a highly valued number.) Tabarī, in his commentary, treats this first basmala separately, and then remarks that, were it to be considered part of al-Fātiha, the names of God in it ("the Merciful, the Compassionate") would be repeated in line 3 and such repetition "does not exist in the Book of God" (1987:65).

Scholars also differ as to whether or not the basmala of al-Fātiha should be recited aloud at worship. Hadīth can be mustered for each side (Ayoub 1984:46–47). When reciting any other chapter, Gayo say the basmala silently and then begin aloud with the first verse proper. But until the late 1930s, anyone in the Gayo highlands who recited al-Fātiha aloud began with an audible basmala, as do most villagers today.[8]

Here, as for the ushalli, Tengku Ali Salwany provided an optative view, reading the hadīths to the effect that individuals may choose to recite the basmala aloud if they consider it part of the chapter, or silently if they prefer. The prophet Muhammad worshiped in both ways, he explained, thereby signaling to his followers that they had a choice. But the Qur'ān

---

[8] All reciters, Gayo and other Muslims, preface the basmala with a "refuge taking": *Aūzbillah min al-syaitān il-rajīm* ("I take refuge in God from cursed Satan"); see Padwick (1961:83–93) for an analysis of the phrase.

does say that when reciting from it it should be heard, and therefore, concluded Ali Salwany, one ought to recite the basmala aloud, along with the remainder of the chapter.

The modernist line on the basmala has been a relatively soft one. Even the usually vituperative Ahmad Hassan was positively latitudinarian on this issue (1968:103), saying that worshipers did have a choice. But Takèngèn modernists adopted the "silent basmala" position and put it into practice in the mosques where they became imāms, despite considerable protest from among their congregations.

The choice of silent or audible basmala is the major difference in form of congregational worship in the highlands today, and thus is the most salient indicator of the religious orientation followed at a particular mosque and, by implication, in the community it serves. The choice is a major issue to be decided for each mosque community as a whole. However, in some communities the mosque has been captured by a politically influential group of modernists, while the majority of worshipers remain traditionalist in their approach to worship.

Such is the case in Isak, where a large portion of the community avoids the mosque because worship is invariably held in the modernist manner, with a silent basmala. Many Isak religious leaders hold that a congregational worship service is only acceptable to God if the worshipers hear the leader recite al-Fātiha completely, including what they consider to be its first verse. When these men and women worship in the mosque they will recite the basmala aloud if the imām does not, in order to ensure that their worship is valid.

Some in Isak consider the failure to speak the basmala aloud to be disrespectful to God. "After all," said a Robel man, "'bismillāh' means 'in the name of God.'" They also consider the refusal to pronounce the basmala to be part of a general laxity in pronouncing the words of the worship service, as if clear pronunciation—and thus clear communication with God—has been devalued. One of the teachers in Kutë Robel village explained the difference in orientation as follows:

> The modernists, as I understand them, simply do not pronounce the words for much of the worship; the worship leader does not say the bismillāh, for example. When they repeat "Subhānallāh" ["(I proclaim) the glory of God"] at the end of the worship they really just run through the phrase in their minds, saying it much faster than one could say it. They really are saying "semelah" ["one-half"]; they don't pronounce it clearly.
>
> They are wrong to worship in this way. The prophet Muhammad said that the tongue should work with the heart, not just the heart alone. For example, if I say something to you without making a sound, can you hear me? Of course not. You have to speak out loud in order for anyone to understand you.

The problem of basmala is one more indication for the traditionalists that modernists devalue communication.

MOSQUE POLITICS

At times these issues of the form of worship have become highly divisive in the Gayo Muslim community. An earlier controversy, over whether regular noon worship should be carried out after the Friday worship, led people to build new mosques and settle new parts of the highlands. The capacity of these and other elements of worship to carry political weight is due to their highly charged nature as indicators of general, divergent religious orientations with high local significance. But their emergence as signs of sociopolitical allegiance has been motivated by other developments, some of them not particularly religious in nature.

The control of a mosque has great political significance in any Muslim society. Worship in the mosque is obligatory for all Muslims. Decisions about the form of that worship—the nature of the recitations, the content and indeed the language of the sermons, the selection of worship leader— impose upon each worshiper a particular set of religious and often political views. A struggle over mosque control may have as its explicit object a relatively minor liturgical issue (although we have seen how such issues index a wider array of religious issues), but it may also involve a much broader set of sociopolitical divisions (cf. Antoun 1976; Fischer and Abedi 1990:293–94; Gaffney 1987; el-Zein 1977).

Such was the case in Isak in the late 1930s, when a group of modernists began work on a new mosque. The modernists were led by Aman Unan, the uncle of my own "mother," Ibu Inën Muhammad. They had argued that worship in the old mosque was improper, because after the Friday congregational worship another noon worship service was held. (This practice is still followed by some people in Isak and elsewhere in Indonesia.) The prophet Muhammad did not worship in that way, they claimed, citing what they saw as reliable hadīth (see Hassan 1968:162).

The highest indigenous official in Isak, the domain lord or Kejurun Lingë, saw this religious critique as a direct attack on his authority, and he was right to do so. The Kejurun had maintained that he had the right to establish norms of religious ritual in Isak as he saw fit, and that he favored the old way. As Tengku Asaluddin recalled the dispute:

> The Kejurun's political view was that he was the sultan. He said "The Prophet is the representative of God and the ruler is the representative of the Prophet." People who did not obey the *amīr* [commander] thus did not obey the Prophet, he said. People paid obeisance to the ruler back then, but those who had studied said you should kneel before no one but God, and the Kejurun was angered by that sort of remark.

The modernists did indeed intend their ritual critique as an attack on the ruler's authority. To them, the prophet Muhammad had laid down a strict division between religious affairs and worldly affairs, and the claims of a secular leader to set religious policy was anathema. But this controversy was overdetermined in that it was also a clash between two long-standing political blocs in Isak, one of which supported the Kejurun and his Dutch overseers, while the other channeled its most promising children along other avenues, especially that of religious learning. Aman Unan and, in the next generation, Tengku Asaluddin and Tengku Joharsyah were sons of leaders in the bloc that opposed the Kejurun (Bowen 1991:70–76). Thus religious, social, and political divisions overlaid and intensified each other.

By about 1938 the divisions had led a group of Isak people to leave the community. Ibu Inën Muhammad told me the story:

Aman Unan, my mother's younger brother, learned religion from my father, who had studied in West Aceh [where he was born] long before he moved to Isak. Aman Unan was ordered out of Isak because of [the dispute between] modernists and traditionalists. My father was not a modernist or a traditionalist, but he told the people who performed noon worship after Friday worship that they did not need to do so, that the one was already included in the other. But Tengku Ubit did the extra worship in Kutë Robel [where he was imām]. The older people sided with him, the younger people with my father.

Everyone in Isak gathered at a shack downstream to discuss the matter. The Kejurun, Sasa, said of Aman Unan, "You are a troublemaker. I will not allow the modernist ideas here; 'if to the sky, to the red cloth; if to the earth, to the spread-out stones.'"[9] No one spoke, but Aman Unan said, "I'm leaving," and then others said, "If the Tengku goes, we go too."

About ten men left at once for Takèngën, leaving their families behind. Most of the people in the village of Kutë Kramil Bur [today part of Kutë Ryëm village] left. The Bukit domain lord, Rëjë Ilang [who had sponsored the Muhammadiyah organization in Takèngën in 1928], took them under his protection and gave them land to settle north of Takèngën, at Simpang Tigë. The Kejurun Lingë came after them, complaining to the Dutch Controleur that they were his subjects and he wanted them back, but if they were to leave then he wanted their lands! Aman Unan, backed by the Bukit ruler, replied that they owned the lands, and they won the right to sell them or retain them and rent them out.

The explicit issue here was the form of worship, but it brought to the surface a whole range of issues: long-term hostilities between the two blocs, the frustrations felt by newly educated religious teachers at the old prac-

---

[9] An expression meaning: "nowhere in my domain, from the sky to the earth." The expression was common in the older-style didong at which Sasa was proficient (Bowen 1991:177).

tices, nationalist opposition to the Dutch-supported Kejurun, and even the legal status of village land. The liturgical issues (the extra salāt on Friday, the spoken basmala) were deeply felt in their own right, but they also served as indexes of these mutually reinforcing cleavages within the society and were issues over which those out of power could safely express in the open their broad hostility to the ruling officials.

The Japanese invasion gave control of Isak religious affairs to the modernist teachers Tengku Asaluddin and Tengku Joharsyah (Bowen 1991: 106), and thereafter mosque worship was in modernist hands. Kutë Robel village, the home of Tengku Ubit and the foremost religious teachers in Isak, became the locus of the traditionalist alternative. This division has continued through the 1980s. In 1989, Tengku Asaluddin and Aman Hariani, the new, modernist-leaning subdistrict religious official, were the principal preachers at the mosque. Other men have been invited to give sermons from time to time, but the alternative perspective, embodied in the Kutë Robel leaders, is not openly heard.

In Takèngën, disputes over liturgical form have been overlaid by disputes over the relationship of Gayo society to the Indonesian nation-state. In 1946 leaders of both the modernist and the traditionalist camps joined the Islamic party Masyumi. Masyumi leaders engaged in a series of uneasy, temporary alliances with the Takèngën district officials, members of the Indonesian Nationalist Party (Partai Nasionalis Indonesia, PNI).

Initially modernists and nationalists joined in rejecting the older, procolonial political structure. In a meeting held in 1946, Tengku Jali, the head of the radical reformist camp, and Abdul Wahab, the principal figure in the nationalist movement and the first district ruler, agreed on a program of rejecting Gayo norms (ëdët) without agreeing on what was to take their place (Bowen 1991:110–14).

But dissatisfaction with the central government led most of the religious leaders to join, or at least sympathize with, the Darul Islam rebellion of 1953–1962. The Gayo leaders in the rebellion were primarily traditionalist ulama from villages around Lake Tawar, many of whom had been active in the war for independence but had not been given a place in district government affairs. Many were concerned with the threat to religious propriety represented by "modern" tendencies in dress, education, and comportment. Most of the leading modernist teachers in the town remained officially neutral.

Thus postwar developments meant that liturgical disputes, which had taken on a pronationalist and anticolonial aura in the 1930s and early 1940s, no longer carried a direct political meaning in the 1950s and 1960s. The Masyumi party was not particularly identified with the modernist position; if anything, more leaders from the traditionalist camp were involved. Modernists such as Tengku Jali, Aman Murni, and Tengku Asaluddin remained relatively removed from political disputes; many welcomed government support for their activities.

In the post-1965 New Order as well, many leading modernists have refrained from actively supporting Islamic political parties. The focus on education that served as common ground for the nationalists and modernists from the mid-1930s through the 1950s became, in the 1970s and 1980s, the basis for selective alliances between the district government and certain modernist leaders. State assistance to religious schools (including Aman Murni's successor school to Islamic Education), state sponsorship of new mosques, and threats against those religious leaders who remained outside the state party, Golkar, have forced many religious leaders into line with government policy.

One of the district government's means of inducing ulama to join Golkar has been their control of the Takèngën mosque. Friday congregational worship in the Takèngën area once was distributed among several mosques. The mosque in the village of Balé, just across the Peusangan river from the town proper, was a stronghold of Islamic Education and thus highly modernist in its liturgy and its teaching. The mosque located in the town itself, just across the river from Balé, had been built by Minangkabau traders and long was called the "Padang prayer house." It was generally Muhammadiyah and thus moderately modernist in approach. Just downstream from Balé was a mosque in Asir-Asir that was as resolutely traditionalist as Balé's was modernist. These three mosques were within five hundred yards of each other, and even before the advent of microphones worshipers could hear each other's calls to prayer.

Two other mosques were in the general vicinity of town. In Kebayakan and in Bëbësën, traditionalists continued to control mosque affairs despite the presence of modernist leaders, especially in Kebayakan. By the mid-1980s those two mosques continued to operate as mosques, holding Friday services, but those in Balé and Asir-Asir, along with the older mosque in Takèngën proper, had been demoted to the status of prayer house, without the right to hold Friday congregational services. The greater Takèngën area was consolidated into one large mosque district, with everyone expected to worship in the new, central town mosque.

Unlike any of the older mosques, the new mosque is closely associated with the district government. It is located near the government offices and it is run by a government-appointed mosque committee. The government has used that channel of control to keep independent preachers from having access to the mosque. Thus the presence of a particular preacher at a mosque takes on political significance regardless of the content of his sermons.

The effect of the consolidation has been to remove possible sources of antigovernment publicity. No sermons may be preached anywhere in the town (or across the river) except in the government mosque. Furthermore, be-

19. Takèngën and the Town Mosque

cause preaching in the one, large mosque now has become quite a prize for any aspiring religious teacher, men are more likely to make themselves acceptable to the government in order to be given the opportunity to preach.

These rules for mosque worship mirror the self-image of Golkar as an entity that stays above internecine disputes. In principle, imāms who practice the "loud" and the "soft" basmala alternate weeks (in practice the traditionalists have had difficulty finding a competent representative) and compromise on several other minor issues. Liturgical compromises and state direction combine to construct an image of state-and-religion as the umbrellalike beringin tree (the emblem of Golkar) under which all can sit.

I noted in the previous chapter that modernism's stress on public events has created an opening for the state to capture religion for political purposes. Public worship is also the most suitable way for the state to mediate between religious positions. Issues such as the basmala or the ushalli can be portrayed as technical ones, on which compromise surely is possible, rather than as fundamental differences, on which the state might be required to take a position, as did the Acehnese ulama on funeral kenduris. The essence of New Order politics is not taking such stands but rather appearing to encompass the differences.

Of all Islamic rituals, it is probably in worship that the personal, social, and political aspects of religion most closely coalesce. Muslims can design their own styles of worship to suit individual needs and emotions, but when they gather for the obligatory, weekly congregational worship they must worship as a single body. Styles of worship then may become both declarations of particular religious orientations and also part of struggles for control of public space.

On the religious plane, styles of worship embody specific opinions on ritual form (for example, whether or not to audibly pronounce the basmala). They also implicate questions of religious epistemology, or how to arrive at valid religious knowledge: for example, whether a general appeal to the importance of strengthening intent (as in the ushalli case) or communicating clearly with God (as in the basmala case) is a valid consideration in weighing different interpretations of the available hadīth. Methods of worship also have broad implications for the shape of religion and society, for it matters a great deal whether one rejects all practices not clearly sanctioned by reliable hadīth (as do many modernists, at least in principle) or accepts certain practices because they fit a general model of transaction and communication (as do most traditionalists, at least in practice). Even apparently small details of worship style reverberate throughout the Gayo socioreligious network.

Of course, other rituals also have broad social implications. But the public, obligatory nature of congregational worship makes it a particularly salient index of one's social and religious stance. In Gayo as in other Muslim societies it is the form of public worship that is likely to be fought over with particular vehemence. Worship styles that had been developed for reasons of religious conviction or cultural tradition can thereafter become emblems or indexes of group membership. Even the position of a finger or a hand during worship can become the basis for political differentiation and, in some societies, open conflict.[10]

Centralizing control over worship, as has happened in Takèngën, thus has the potential to sharpen the politics of Islam. It can also, however, give the state a powerful tool for control, not only because critics can be silenced, but because the fact of power can be given a public, benign, religious face.

---

[10] Such is especially the case in those societies where groups are in the process of establishing religious and social identities. For descriptions of these processes, see Gladney (1991: 193), Metcalf (1982:274–94), and my general discussion (Bowen 1989).

Chapter Fourteen

THE SOCIAL FORMS OF RELIGIOUS CHANGE

INCREASINGLY, Gayo reflect on their own practices with some ambivalence. Even within the short span of my visits to Isak between 1978 and 1989, I have seen close friends such as Abang Das and Abang Kerna agonize over and alter how they heal, worship, or bury the dead. In Takèngën, friends scornful of Isak's penchant for pre-Islamic practices nonetheless wonder at the power of the healers who live there. These and other Gayo men and women see themselves as negotiating between a multitude of local memories, powers, and customs on the one hand, and what they perceive to be the broader, universalistic Islamic tradition on the other.

How they accomplish this negotiating—the tenor, sites, and audiences for their reflections—differs markedly between village and town, and these differences signal larger-scale changes in the ways Gayo articulate older forms of knowledge and practice within broader political and religious cultural spheres.

CREATING PRIVATE AND PUBLIC SPHERES

In Isak direct confrontation over a religious matter is relatively rare. One can tackle an impressive range of practical problems—healing the sick, punishing the malevolent, saving the rice crop, easing the "torment of the grave" for one's father, offering a sacrifice for the afterlife—without ever having to publicly declare precisely what one is doing. Each person may construct a distinct theory of her or his practice without subjecting it to public scrutiny.

These local theories bring Islamic concepts to bear on immediate, practical problems. They do so by underscoring the power of correctly formed language: du'ā' addressed to God are interpreted as dowa that can be used to shape the world; inner knowledge through ma'rifat becomes the powerful imagination of maripët; God, the Light of Muhammad, and the spirits of the prophets (along with spirits of ancestors, hills, and seas) become regular sources of directable social power. Gayo firmly embed these sources of power in their local environment through the mediation of such objects as the afterbirth and the many symbolic forms of rice.

Isak ideas about language and power also give to each ritual practice a definite social shape. They do so, first of all, by specifying the community of people who engage in the ritual event. The theory of sacrifice, for example, highlights the kin ties among men and women who share a sacrificial victim (and who will ride together to the place of judgment). The theory of agricultural ritual posits that a successful crop depends on the state of social relations in the local community, and it identifies that community in terms of its precolonial rulers. The theory of mortuary chants places a value on attracting large numbers of chanters to the sessions in order to increase the merit generated for the benefit of the deceased, thus creating an obligation for all relatives, neighbors, and friends to attend. Each of these ideas about how ritual works thus generates specific moral obligations and social images (cf. Hubert and Mauss 1964).

These ideas also explain how people can harm one another. By postulating the power of inner speech and imagination, they allow people to attribute misfortune to others and to act on those attributions without making public accusations. And indeed people do ascribe misfortune mainly to the spite, greed, or lax morals of their own relatives and neighbors. If a jin causes illness it is probably a fellow villager who sent it; a poor rice crop may be due to a headman's peccadilloes or to cheating on the zakāt. Not that jin are incapable of acting on their own, but in contrast, say, to Malay communities where jin shoulder most of the blame (Laderman 1991), in Isak the responsibility for misfortune is allocated to nearby humans.

The means to counter such human failings and evil deeds involve no public confrontations, and thus provide personal satisfaction with relatively little risk of open conflict, fighting, or police intervention (unlike, again, the public assignment of responsibility in Malay rituals [Laderman 1991]). These relatively private forms of spells, exorcisms, and divinations provide buffers between personal hatreds and open conflicts in a society that historically has managed controversy by keeping it out of the public realm.

In rites of healing or harming, the private character of ritual action makes it possible to avoid making explicit interpretations in public. Most of the time, people need not come to any public agreement as to the meaning of a ritual (or of a narrative; recall the diverse stories about Cain and Abel in Isak, and each narrator's allusions to others' versions).

Insofar as there is a dominant public discourse about religion and ritual, it is that of the modernist religious teachers who monopolize sermons in the Isak mosque. But their sermons rarely touch directly on the funeral chanting, the child's initiation ritual, healing and sorcery, or the myriad spells of everyday life. Instead they concern the narrow domain of "religion" and leave to the offstage venues of the riverbank, the house, and the hills the still-vibrant and, in the eyes of their practitioners, morally essential set of practices aimed at maintaining the welfare of the community, its ancestors, and its descendants.

The Gayo case suggests that the recent emphasis on the psychological, cultural, and social importance of public confrontations (Brenneis and

Myers 1984; Watson-Gegeo and White 1990), apt though it is, ought not to lead us to ignore cases where much of this psychosocial work takes place in private settings: in exorcisms, at isolated ritual sites, or through personal prayer. To some degree the public ritual of Gayo society does indeed seek "the reconstruction of a collective vision of social reality through the mutual involvement of community members" (White and Watson-Gegeo 1990:8). Such is particularly the case for, say, events of public ritual-speaking, as I have emphasized elsewhere (Bowen 1991:139–68). But that collective vision is not an encompassing one; it conceals vast regions of disputed cultural territory.

When Isak people do talk publicly about a ritual, they rarely make explicit the controversial aspects of the event. Recall the case of the speech given during the Isak funeral chant, where the speaker explained that chanting "helps the spirit of the deceased." The explanation allows each individual to figure out just how this help reaches its destination. Some think that the food eaten and words recited travel straight to the spirit of the deceased, who enjoys their benefit. Others reject emphatically such an idea but believe that the words reach God, who then relieves the burdens on the deceased because he is pleased by the recitations. Still others participate in the recitations on the assumption that they are simply recitations for the glory of God and that it is entirely up to him, whose will is unfathomable, what he does about the deceased. Such, for example, is roughly the position held by Tengku Daud, a modernist who nonetheless attends samadiyahs. A few people, Tengku Asaluddin among them, find no possible interpretation acceptable and avoid these events.

These ambiguities of exegesis allow people to resist, or at least to deflect, demands that they turn away from older ritual practices. One way of doing so has been to privatize the more controversial segments of a ritual. In agricultural ritual, for example, the portion of the opening ritual that must be public (because it coordinates planting and because it represents the social order in morally powerful ways) has been separated from the portion that can be performed privately and which has drawn objections. Ritual specialists have gradually moved the appeals to the Ancestors and the exorcism of the pests away from public scrutiny, to a place where ulama could ignore it. In the 1950s villagers still exorcised pests by setting out offerings for the pests in each village. By the 1970s the offerings had disappeared, and the ritual specialist let adrift a raft with offerings on it; and by the late 1980s the ritual specialist had begun to hold the small gathering of village representatives in his house, and to then release offerings into the water by himself.

Here the controversial and ritually effective portion of the overall event is done "offstage," allowing the "public transcript" (Scott 1990) to show only that an (unobjectionable) meal was held and prayers recited. Those who participate in the meal can pretend that the earlier event did not take place, for rarely is it mentioned publicly. Nor do the ulama generally wish to point to the objectionable events, for their own way of living in the midst of such "backward" practices is to deny that they take place: recall the embarrassed Kuakek's protestations that the steps taken to introduce a child to the spirits of the waters "used to be done but they are not done anymore." Displacing unpleasant rituals into the past is one way of coping with their continued nonpublic presence, but it depends on a tacit agreement to keep them out of public space.

The resulting religion-and-ritual landscape in the Isak of the 1980s is a combination of generally acceptable or at least tolerable public events, and less observable, more controversial events—even extending to parallel Friday worship services in the older style held in a village prayer house. This differentiated ritual climate permits an economy of professed ignorance, where those who object to some current events can claim that they only happened in the past: in the pre-Islamic jāhilīya period of world history, in the distant "Hindu" past of the highlands, or in the almost-remembered past of the early twentieth century. The tacit compact that allows these conflicting claims to coexist is supported not by an interest in secrecy (as, for example, in some New Guinea ritual complexes [Wagner 1984]), but by a culturally constructed capacity to ignore the unpleasant and to allow disagreements to remain implicit (a capacity found in many Indonesian settings and commonly expressed in the Indonesian phrase *tidak mau tahu*, "to not wish to know").

It is the unsaid, the underinterpreted, the absence of exegesis at the event itself that permits ritual practitioners to reconstruct community on top of a wide diversity of individual opinions about what is ritually proper and practically possible.[1]

The development in the highlands of public scholarly debate over religion brought a new emphasis on Muslims' accountability for their actions, and it redefined religious actions to include intentions as well as observable behavior. To some degree this shift has been the joint product of modernist and traditionalist scholars. All Takèngën ulama today advocate modern education and scriptural study, and we must be careful not to project too far backward the division between modernist and traditionalist. It was, after all, a follower of the Shafi'i legal tradition in Mecca who first introduced the writings of Muhammad 'Abduh to West Sumatrans. Moreover, traditionalists, meaning adherents to the Shafi'i legal tradition, were active in developing

---

[1] The "underinterpreted" here is not to be confused with Bourdieu's concept of the *doxa* of everyday life that are "undiscussed" because taken for granted (1977:159–71). The multiple theories Gayo advance are already highly interpreted; what is at issue here is not a difference in consciousness but of publicness.

new schools, writing vernacular textbooks, and teaching Arabic in Sumatra as well as elsewhere in the Muslim world (cf. Metcalf 1982).

Yet the role of the traditionalist scholar has been qualitatively different from that of the modernist. The very category of "traditionalist" (kaum tua) was created as a residual category for scholars who did not join one or another self-styled modernist movement. Whereas modernists can represent themselves as operating outside of any particular cultural context (which, of course, is not to say that they do transcend culture), traditionalist scholars see their task as brokering between an array of village practices (only some of which they defend) and the requirements of scriptural fidelity.

In this regard one can view traditionalist scholars' theories of the opacity of intent as an effort to make into religious theory the local styles of "under-exegesis" and tacit knowledge. Recall that traditionalist scholars such as Ali Salwany argued that intent is not implied by or contained in a particular form of behavior. It follows that scholars must tolerate a wide range of ritual forms, as actors may hold in their minds a proper religious intent even if the practice (for example, the burning of incense) may appear to be non-Islamic. (It also follows that stating one's intent to worship, the controversial ushalli, is useful and proper.)

Modernists have sharply criticized the notion that ritual form is opaque to the associated intent; indeed, the modernist challenge has been as much on epistemological as on theological grounds (cf. Lambek 1990:31). We might summarize their objections to particular issues, considered in the preceding chapters, in terms of two propositions about knowledge: that religious and ritual forms are transparent to their originally intended meanings, and that scripture contains a set of exhaustive and unique norms for religious action. These two ideas have implications for human subjectivity as well as for the social context of religion.

The first proposition, on the transparency of meaning, underlies modernist positions on issues of translation, liturgy, and interpretive pluralism. Unlike many traditionalist scholars, modernists affirm the possibility and necessity of translation because of the importance of conveying to the widest possible audience the referential meaning of scripture. Translation (or, more properly, that combination of translation and interpretation known as tafsīr) is necessary so that Muslims will have direct access to scripture's universal truths. Translatability of truth also validates Indonesian as a language of religious communication, and thus validates association with other Indonesians in a local religious sphere as well.

The same conception allows the scholar to inspect a religious practice and impute to it a specific, original intent. To burn incense, modernists reason, is prima facie to make an appeal to a spirit. It thus implies polytheism, whatever those who burn the incense might say. Just as sacred words have definite, assignable referential meanings, so do gestures and objects. Herein lies the basis for the thoroughgoing critique of all religious and ritual events that might impinge on the realm of religion.

The close association of outer form with inner intent also has normative implications for the subjectivity of the worshiper. It is not enought that worshipers replicate the proper form of worship; they must also replicate the proper intent. Modernists reserve their harshest, often highly sarcastic criticism for those people who appear to fulfill their religious obligations but who fail to adopt the correct inner attitude toward God, merely mouthing the words or worshiping with worldly purpose in mind. "You only receive as you intend" is the refrain. (Thus modernists strongly oppose the practice of stating one's intent to worship, because intent should be always present as an inner state; the intent statement implies otherwise.) Modernist ideas of form and meaning thus reinforce a general emphasis on intent, attitude, and mental state—and thus on subjectivity—but always in connection with outer, observable actions (cf. Rosen 1984:49–56).

Religious actions and intentions are bounded, of course, by scripture. Yet a scholar's insistence on closely hewing to scripture does not in itself indicate how much variation in ritual he or she will accept. Modernism's founder, Muhammad 'Abduh, argued strongly for the exercise of individual reasoning (ijtihād) precisely because he found the Qur'ān and hadīth to be unclear in places (Hourani 1983:147). But the scholar who holds that scripture is transparent in its intent is more likely to argue that it yields a unique set of dictates. This view, generally held by Takèngën modernists, leads away from the celebration of individual reasoning toward the insistence on conformity to a single authoritative position. Recall how the modernist Alimin argued against the idea that people ought to choose for themselves what kind of funeral ritual they will follow. They may choose, he said, "only after they have been told what really is in the Qur'ān and hadīth." Indeed, at times Indonesian modernists have condemned the very existence of differing ritual practices as indicative of people's failure to read scripture correctly and their tendency to follow the misleading teachings of past ulama (Noer 1973:96–99).

Some Gayo people take rather self-assured stands in favor of one or the other of these positions, such as Alimin on the modernist side or many of those engaged in transactional rituals in Isak on the other. But many others try to tack between older ideas of language, power, and action, and their desire to adapt to what they see as modern religious knowledge.[2] Tengku Asaluddin illustrates this desire to combine the world of older learning and piety with a more recently acquired scriptural knowledge in his own mono-

---

[2] As is true, of course, of many Muslims elsewhere; for detailed, recent studies of these negotiations on the religious plane see, for South Asia, Ahmed (1988) and Metcalf (1990); for Iran, Fischer and Abedi (1990); and for the Sudanese Berti, Holy (1991).

logues and reflections. And in his growing doubts about the validity of his healing practices, Abang Kerna embodies the worry and ambivalence of people caught between alternative positions. Once a passionate transactor with spirits, he has begun to seek out alternative sources of healing power that would avoid catching him up in improper (and possibly Satan-inspired) uses of scripture. The historic shift in highlands religious thinking is not a once and for all change, but a process of reflection and rethinking of the old and the new.

Two Modes of Cultural Rationalization

Highlands religious change has many of the hallmarks of the religious "rationalization" described by Max Weber (1963). As Weber saw it, the development of religions, and more generally cultures, has been characterized by a process of "disenchantment of the world." Participants in many distinct cultural traditions have gradually moved away from a magical orientation toward the world, in which Weber included the belief in the efficacies of sacrament. They have come to embrace in its stead an "ethics of conviction" based on a set of ultimate values. This movement has been motivated by the need to develop general explanations for the presence of evil in the world. Weber understood this general process as the rationalization of religion, a process that included the adoption of universalistic beliefs and the embracing of an inescapable tension between the cares of the world and the demands of the beyond.

In many respects the development of a public sphere of Islam in Takèngën does fit Weber's model. The terms of the debate between modernists and traditionalists are indeed universal, in that scholars in both camps eschew cultural-specific defenses of current practices and, more important, advocate religious action based on its degree of fit with the universal set of norms provided by the Qur'ān and hadīth rather than on instrumentalist grounds—a change that Weber saw as basic to the process of rationalization. Modernist discourse appears as particularly "value-rational," using Weber's term, to the degree that it revolves around such moral-evaluative terms as ikhlās (sincere devotion), tauhīd (the unity of God), and niyya (intent).

But rationalization is not the smooth trajectory toward a single consistent worldview that the term may imply. For one, Weber's assumption that traditional, magic-bound religions lack reflection and systematic thought has by now been undermined by the ethnography of small-scale religious systems (of which Evans-Pritchard's study of Nuer religion [1956] is as close to a classic as one might find). In Chapter 4 we learned how Gayo wielders of spells situate their actions in broader logics of sacred history and spirit powers. Religious change appears today less as a matter of unreflective thinking becoming more reflective than a matter of increasing pressures on religious practitioners to articulate their beliefs vis-à-vis other sets of beliefs.[3]

Furthermore, there is no reason to think of rationalization as a clearly defined process. Weber himself used *rational* in myriad ways (Brubaker 1984), and introduced at least two distinct modes of cultural rationalization. One is a process of systematizing beliefs to make them more internally systematic or coherent (Weber 1958b:293–94). The other is a process of modernizing beliefs to rid them of magical content (Weber 1963:143–44; cf. Habermas 1984:174–78).

I would argue that the Gayo case illustrates the possibility that these two modes of rationalization—one favoring coherence, the other, modernity—describe a sphere of conflict rather than a uniform direction for religious change, and that the debates between modernists and traditionalists highlight tensions that are basic to the very idea of rationalization. (Furthermore, accounts of older village practices have their own rationalized forms, as when Tengku Asaluddin links the individual morality of farmers to the success of their crops.)

At first glance Takèngën modernists seem to be the more highly rationalizing of the two groups. After all, they stress the need to subordinate instrumental concerns to universal values and also the importance of direct, inner dialogue between humans and God. Moreover, modernists wage continual war against magic and sacramentalism (for example, in their opposition to transactional understandings of sacrifice and recitation). They seem to be worthy exemplars of Weber's modernizing mode of rationalization.

But the traditionalist scholars (and many villagers) are the main proponents of the other, "coherence," version of rationalization. Most scholars in Isak, for example, would insist that all elements of the worship ritual ought to be evaluated for consistency with the general principle of communication with God. One ought to enunciate the basmala aloud, for instance, because doing so enhances the clarity of communication. Traditionalist scholars make such arguments in terms of general principles of religious reasoning—for example, that any action that supports a required religious action is itself meritorious (used to defend the ushalli).

Modernists explicitly deny the validity of these arguments. Instead, they argue that one must above all conform to the historical example set by the prophet Muhammad, regardless of the degree of internal logical fit one achieves. In arguing points of correct ritual behavior, modernists often play up the apparently illogical nature of certain prescriptions—why should

---

[3] Wilfred Cantwell Smith (1963) provides an influential historical treatment of this process from a history-of-religions perspective; for a recent demonstration of this process in a Muslim society see Eickelman (1989b). Geertz's essay on "internal conversion" in Bali (1973:170–89) makes similar points, though it emphasizes more the internal Weberian processes than the external state-driven pressures.

morning worship be shorter than that done at noon, when in fact we have much more time in the morning?—in order to emphasize that one may not tinker with religious ritual but must accept it as it is.

Cutting across this difference in religious orientation is a difference in the context of discourse. Takèngën scholars of either orientation speak in quite distinct ways about religion in different discursive settings. Traditionalists and modernists alike stress the process of reasoning from scripture when engaged in exchanges with other scholars, but emphasize the cultural coherence of the Islamic worldview when delivering sermons or lessons. The same scholar thus may exemplify one or the other mode of rationalization depending on his audience.

The tension within Takèngën public religious discourse is in fact of long standing in the Muslim world (and not only in the Muslim world; see Zaret [1992]). It can be formulated as the tension between reason and revelation—between philosophy and theology—and it provides alternative pathways for religious reformers.[4] Gayo scholarly exchanges thus exemplify not a transition from "traditional" to "world religion" but rather the enduring contestations within the field of a world religion over its foundations (cf. Hodgson 1974, III:179–92).

The concept of reason also figures as a term *within* local religious discourses, where it takes on particular cultural associations. In particular, an emphasis on reason over passion is often linked to a valuing of men over women: local discussions of rationalization thus have implications for changing gender roles and values.

In societies as diverse as Iran, Morocco, and Aceh, the contrast between *'aqal* (reason, rationality) and *nafs* or *nafsu* (desire, passion) is central to the ways men, in particular, discuss human nature (Loeffler 1988:100–104; Rosen 1984:30–47; Siegel 1969:98–115). In Aceh the contrast became one of life in villages, where men felt themselves under women's control, versus life in towns or schools, where men could struggle for the mastery of passion by reason through work, worship, or religious study (Siegel 1969). Acehnese religious reform took on a strong gender coloring, partly because a broader Islamic discourse of reason and passion converged with a local social pattern of male migration for study and work.

Disputes over religious reform in the Gayo highlands did not articulate onto gender divisions as they did in Aceh, largely because men's and women's lives were not already separated by patterns of labor migration. Men lived their lives in villages, and even those men and women who mi-

---

[4] See Hodgson (1974, I:410–43) on the debate over philosophy and reasoned disputation in early Islam; Fischer and Abedi (1990:101–12) on the Qur'ān's warnings concerning the perils of reason; and Turner (1974:148–50) on the tensions within modernist discourse on this issue in the context of Weberian social science.

grated to Takèngën town retained strong ties to their nearby village relatives. Modernists in the highlands did not, therefore, seek to replace or transcend either kinship ties or the ties between men and women, but rather to reform the ways all persons carried out religious actions. For that reason they did not make use of the available and already highly gendered contrast of 'aqal and nafs, but highlighted instead the concepts of intent and the oneness of God, and the understanding of scripture. Highlands modernism makes a reformist discourse of subjectivity central to its platform, but it underscores fidelity to scripture rather than male self-fashioning.

Nor have modernists singled out specifically female roles for criticism. True, they have decried certain ritual practices in which women played a large role, such as ritually bathing infants or speaking to the spirit of the rice plant. Yet they have leveled most of their explicit criticism at male roles such as the Lord of the Fields, or at joint male-female practices such as funeral chanting.

Modernist institutions do incorporate a consistent asymmetry of men's and women's roles. In the public sphere of Islam, it is men who issue religious opinions, deliver sermons, and act as imāms for the Friday services, and these exclusions of women are found in most Muslim societies. But Takèngën modernism (and Indonesian scholarly Islam in general) has not excluded women from religious activities; rather, it has urged on them active but auxiliary roles. Starting in the mid-1930s, Takèngën ulama created women's Qur'ān study groups as well as women's associations in Muhammadiyah and al-Washliyah (both called Aisyiah), and in many villages women started religious poetry groups.[5]

Perhaps because highlands modernism focused less on "reason" ('aqal) and more on the proper following of scripture, its greatest social effects have come from its antisacramental, "disenchantment" side. Weber argued that because universalistic religions focus on issues of salvation and ethics rather than on immediate practical needs, they become divorced from worldly concerns, giving rise to "the mutual strangeness of religion and politics" (Weber 1958c:335) as well as religion vis-à-vis family, economics, and aesthetics (ibid.:331–57; cf. Habermas 1984:316–42). Religion continues to inform action in these spheres, of course—otherwise Weber could not have written his treatise on the implications of Calvinists' ideas and anx

---

[5] In at least one case a religious institution with a definite male bias has been created; namely, the Islamic court with its capacity to impose a two-to-one estate distribution to children. In fact judges often counsel informal distributions among the parties following a general principle of equal shares for sons and daughters (Bowen 1987). Here the offstage practices are as importance to an overall assessment of gender and religious change as are the public pronouncements. For a highly nuanced analysis of the topic in Sudanese society see Boddy (1989).

ieties for economic life (1958a). But rationalized religion's noninstrumental character, its refusal of magic and sacramental powers, leads actors to reconstitute other domains of social life on distinct, nonreligous grounds.[6]

Religious rationalization thus gives rise to new institutions that partake of religious values but eschew instrumental efficacy in the religious sphere. This part of Weber's theory does illuminate the Gayo case, where we can see such processes of societal differentiation in Takèngën. By defining religion by means of a rational-critical discourse centered on scriptural interpretation, Takèngën ulama have narrowed religion's legitimate connections to interests of individual, family, or community. Whereas Isak rituals of sacrifice, agriculture, and chanting describe a nested set of communities situated between the household and the whole of Isak, modernist forms of religious ritual do not single out subsets of the entire umma, the worldwide Muslim community. Interests and values of family and local community are therefore defined elsewhere, in nonreligious events that often parallel the explicitly religious ones.

Takèngën celebrations of the Feast of Sacrifice are a case in point: every effort is taken to deny any personal, private interest in killing or eating. Eating becomes a community affair, takbīrs are shouted throughout the town, and worship in a public place becomes the central social activity of the day. By contrast, the home becomes deritualized, the place for reaffirming "family" solidarity rather than engaging in a transaction with the divine. Family meals are pointedly not made into religious events; they (along with meals served at the prayer house) become explicit "unkenduris." In this and other instances, Takèngën modernists have created alternatives to the instrumentalist institutions of the village: neighborhood gatherings to "eat together" in place of the chanting sessions held after sacrifice, Qur'ān recitation and poetry in place of kenduris, donations to the bereaved in place of funeral meals.

PUBLIC DISCOURSE AND THE STATE

Changes in highlands religious thinking are part of broader transformations in ways of thinking and conversing, and in particular contribute to a public sphere of discourse that combines religious, social, and political messages. In this respect the Gayo case serves to indicate the limits of generalizing from European formulations of civil society (Taylor 1990). Gayo public discourse differs markedly from the "bourgeois public sphere" described by

---

[6] Here the literature is vast and growing. A collection from the heyday of modernization theory (and thus with a comparative, empirical bent) is that of Eisenstadt (1968); the more recent study by Lash and Whimster (1987) features non-Weberian critiques of the rationalization thesis. In both collections (as in Habermas [1984]) the issue of how rationalization relates to the differentiation of social spheres remains central.

Jürgen Habermas (1989) for Europe in the late eighteenth and early nineteenth centuries. The European ideal involved the free exchange of ideas outside the family and also outside the state, accomplished through letters (novels, newspapers, tracts) and in such places as coffee houses, meeting halls, and women's salons. The ideal rested on certain fictions (such as freedom from economic determination; Habermas [1989:43–56]) and exclusions (especially of bourgeois women; cf. Landes [1988]), but its voluntary and egalitarian ideology did underlie the democratic movements of the period (Baker 1992; Eley 1992).[7]

Absent from discussions of the West European case, and probably less important than in Islamic societies, is religion (cf. Zaret 1992), and here the experiences of Muslim societies (and, of course, others as well) may broaden our understanding of what a civil society is or can be. Islamic schools, whether classical or reform oriented, have provided relatively open-ended institutional and cultural frameworks for scrutinizing contemporary social arrangements and speculating on the desired forms of public life (Eickelman 1985; Fischer 1980; Metcalf 1982). As in Europe, letters and their electronic successors have cultivated religious spheres of discourse that extend far beyond local face-to-face communities; these include printed, popular religious literature (Mardin 1989; Metcalf 1990) and the media of television and videocassettes (Eickelman 1989b).

The Gayo civil society that developed in the decades of late colonial rule and early independence was religious, social, and political in varying mixes and degrees. Although the history of this process requires further study, it appears to have been largely through events designated as "religious" that Gayo began to engage in critical public discussions about society. The first public debates in Takèngën were those concerning scriptural disputes.[8] Moreover, because open political activity was prohibited during most of the colonial period, the most effective way to gather together townspeople was under the banner of religion. People of all political and religious leanings gathered to plan religious celebrations, to hear speakers for Muhammadiyah or al-Washliyah, or to discuss the need for new religious schools. Speakers at each type of gathering urged Gayo men and women to rationally rethink how they ordered their lives, from matters of dress and hygiene to what sort of music and literature they read.

---

[7] Habermas seems to shift his stance in the course of his book from an ironic analysis of bourgeois rhetoric to a nostalgic contemplation of a world that by the end of the nineteenth century was lost—or such is my own reading. For other views on this tension in the book see Baker (1992) and the excellent overall summary by Craig Calhoun (1992).

[8] Compare the late-nineteenth-century public debates in India described by Ahmed (1988) and Metcalf (1982:215–34); for early-twentieth-century debates see Freitag (1988). See also the role of religious elites in Malay nationalism analyzed by Roff (1967) and his study of a public debate in 1937 (Roff 1988).

The new religious schools, especially the Muhammadiyah and Islamic Education schools, taught students to be "modern" as well as religious—playing Western musical instruments and composing songs were part of both curricula. Muhammadiyah schools also mixed a strong dose of nationalism into their programs, choosing books about national liberation for Arabic language instruction, for example. Muhammadiyah taught "Indonesia Raya," the nationalist anthem, to its youth and, after the anthem was prohibited by the Dutch, taught them a Muhammadiyah song that used the anthem's melody to pass through Dutch censorship.

Residents of Takèngën (and students from elsewhere attending these schools) thus by and large learned about the ideas of Indonesia and modernity in contexts of religious education, and they learned to be part of a public, multiethnic sphere of rational discourse largely under religious auspices. The modernity that was enthusiastically adopted by these men and women was a religiously informed modernity, whose emblems could be modest clothing and Arabic literacy as well as a familiarity with Indonesian literature and the doings of Sukarno.

The new consciousness extended to other Indonesian Muslims as well, creating an intermediate level of identifications between the Gayo-cultural and the Indonesian-national. Some Gayo also made journeys to study elsewhere in Sumatra, or even to schools in Java—many more than made the civil servant's "administrative pilgrimage" to Jakarta that Benedict Anderson has argued strengthened a shared identity as East Indies "native" (1983:104–28). These educational pilgrimages left indelible impressions in the form of enduring networks for obtaining knowledge and prestige, and scholars retained the details of these journeys as central pieces in their narratives of personal development (as we saw in Chapter 3).

The emerging sense of a wider network of Muslims generally supported the idea of an Indonesian community, because the networks were in practice, though not in principle, Indonesian. Although the first Gayo book was printed in Cairo, it was sent there by way of an Islamic bookstore and school in Surbaya, East Java. And while a greater command of Arabic made it possible for Gayo scholars to read works written in the Middle East, they learned Arabic and obtained their knowledge of law, theology, and tafsīr from other Indonesians, with Indonesian as the medium of instruction. Although the major religious scholars in Takèngën base their professional opinions on quotations from Arabic hadīth collections (and from the Qur'ān), they also regularly consult multivolume Indonesian manuals on worship or law. Such is even more true of the second rank of local ulama, such as Tengku Asaluddin in Isak.

From these experiences some Gayo began to see themselves as sharing ideas, experiences, and language with their Muslim counterparts in, say, West Sumatra and East Java, and as not sharing these features with similarly educated men and women in, for example, Christian Batak areas or Bali. They also saw similarities, however socially and politically tenuous, between themselves and Muslims from Malaysia or Singapore, with whom they shared language and publishing networks as well as religion. Arabic, not Dutch, was the language they were concerned to master. The community of Indonesian Muslims (potentially extendable to their Malay counterparts) became an intermediate reference group between Gayo and Indonesia.

The Gayo society that eventually became part of an Indonesian nation and state was thus not a society constructed around "primordial sentiments," as a discourse of "old societies and new states" once had it (Geertz 1963b). Nor did it have only one possible supralocal community to imagine. Rather, Gayo (and other) societies already included associations of men and women with distinct ideas about modernity and political loyalties. The Darul Islam rebellion that racked Aceh in the 1950s was over conflicting ideas about *what kind* of Indonesia to build, not about whether there should be such a thing, and the same was true of most of the rebellions occurring throughout Indonesia between 1950 and 1964.

The dance of religion, nation, and state is an ever-shifting one. Since the 1970s Indonesian Muslims have, if anything, increasingly lodged their religion in an intermediate, nonpolitical sphere of discourse, in large part because of the state's efforts to reduce the effectiveness of Islamic political parties. In 1973 the state merged the existent Islamic parties into the United Development Party (Partai Persatuan Pembangunan, PPP). Party leaders were generally selected by the Suharto government, which at the same time forced civil servants and village leaders to support the state party, Golkar. The state also banned village-level political activity except when carried out by Golkar, which was defined as an umbrella organization of civil servants rather than as a party (Emmerson 1978). Then in 1982 President Suharto ordered all political organizations to affirm the state ideology of Pancasila as their sole principle, a command ratified by Parliament in 1985.

The general response of Islamic organizations to these events has not been withdrawal from public life, but rather a movement away from the "by now pointless arena of party politics" (McVey 1983:218) toward nonelectoral public activities. Rather than further dilute their religious identity, many Muslim activists and associations chose to leave political life for activity in nongovernmental organizations, religious schools, and the mosques and prayer houses of cities and towns. In 1984 Indonesia's largest Islamic organization, the Nahdlatul Ulama (NU), decided to withdraw from politics and concentrate on building religious cadres through its network of pesantren religious schools on Java (see Dhofier 1982). After its 1989 Congress, NU also began to create development banks (operating with normal interest rates) and to engage in efforts to obtain benefits from the state for its rank and file (van Bruinessen 1991).

Yet the government has followed ulama from politics into these nonpolitical spheres. Since the 1980s the Ministry of Education and Golkar have engaged in a wide variety of activities designed to spread a state-controlled form of Islam throughout Indonesia. In Java these activities have been designed to Islamize previously "nominal" Muslims through Qur'ān study groups, distribution of religious literature, and uniform, required religious-study classes in state schools (Hefner 1987); in Islamic areas of Sumatra and Sulawesi these endeavors have taken the form of government support for, and thus control of, new mosques and prayer houses in towns and rural areas. The state assumption of control over congregational worship in Takèngën is one manifestation of this effort, as is the intrusion of prodevelopment messages into sermons.[9]

In the political climate of the mid-1990s, it is only religious associations that continue to maintain some degree of independence from the state, and even their relative autonomy is continually eroded through the state's combination of support for religious institutions and discipline of those who refuse its offers. (In Aceh, including the Gayo highlands, the continued activities of the Aceh Merdeka rebels is used as a justification for detentions of "unruly" ulama.) What the ulama have left is their religious discourse, carried out in informal meetings, scripture study sessions, and religious schools.

But the schools, sermons, and print media that make up the public Islamic sphere in the highlands in turn exert pressure on other, less publicly exhibited ritual practices. Public discourse about religion as an exclusionary, scripture-based domain acts both to underwrite a local religious sphere vis-à-vis the state and to censor practices that ulama see as antithetical to religion. Religion is a gatekeeping category that threatens to distort any analysis that begins and ends on its terms (cf. Kipp and Rodgers 1987). In that respect it functions in Indonesia today as have the categories of "class" and "sexuality" in shaping modern European self-understanding (Foucault 1982; Jones 1983). None is a neutral category for social analysis; all are part of the restructuring of social forms around uniform, rationalized models for conduct; and all conceal alternative understandings.

In particular, Gayo notions of religion as a scripture-based set of practices have been developed against a set of discourses that gives social and

---

[9] Most recently the government has attempted to create a formal public sphere of Islamic scholars that would operate outside the state (and thus be different from the Council of Ulama) yet be susceptible to government control. In the late 1990s the Association of Indonesian Islamic Intellectuals (Ikatan Cendekiawan Muslim Indonesia, ICMI) was formed, with a director already informally designated by the government: the Minister of Research and Technology, B. J. Habibie (*Tempo*, 8 Dec. 1990, 26–36).

moral value to transactions with spirits. In perhaps all Islamic discourse there is an "other" against which a version of proper religion is figured—whether that other is conceived of as "village superstitutions," other schools of Islam, competing religions, or alternative cultural formulations of truth.[10] And, of course, Islam itself can become the other for a specific state project of legitimation.[11]

Anthropologists (along with many scholars in history and political science) have in recent years turned toward the study of implicit and unofficial discourses that serve as mediums for resistance to (or at least deflections of) dominant forms of knowledge. The critique of the public sphere has perhaps been most developed with regard to gender (Abu-Lughod 1990; Bourdieu 1977:30–71; Lamphere 1989); James Scott's recent work (1990) extends it into a general theory of concealed oppositional discourse. Religious discourse demands a similarly critical analysis, in its multiple degrees of publicness and internally diverse connections to sites of power and authority.

In Isak, even as some Gayo have pursued paths toward a public, univocal realm of religious representations, others have resisted this direction by manipulating space and discourse so as to delimit totalizing claims to power and truth. Here some Isak people draw on older ideas of internal power, lying outside the realm of the visible, to continue their history of transactions with powerful spirits. Excluded from the dominant discourse of religion, they maintain their own discursive linkages with the divine.

[10] On the tensions between Islamic formulations and alternative Persian ideas see Fischer and Abedi (1990) and the interviews collected in Loeffler (1988); on the corresponding Javanese case see Geertz (1960) and the opposed argument in Woodward (1989); on Malaysia see Laderman's (1991) account of the contrasting Islamic worldviews of healers and ulama.

[11] As in Turkey, where, under state suppression of certain public religious rituals, women's rituals have become central sites for reproducing religious forms of importance to both men and women (Tapper and Tapper 1987). The result is much the same as in the Gayo highlands: Muslims shift the expression of religious ideas and sentiments that are now out of favor into a less public realm.

GLOSSARY OF GAYO AND ARABIC TERMS

The glossary includes terms in Gayo, Indonesian, and Arabic that are frequently used in the book. All are used by Gayo people in discussions about religion and in this sense are Gayo terms. Yet most speakers would consider some of these terms, such as *'aqīqa* or *tajwīd*, to be part of a technical religious vocabulary that retains an Arabic flavor. Other terms, such as *aulië* or *azan*, have weaker-felt ties to their Arabic origins and are used as ordinary Gayo words. These distinctions are complex—a speaker using *'aqīqa* is choosing an Arabic term over a Gayo cognate (*kikah*) and thus indicating his or her concern with following religious norms, whereas *tajwīd* is less familiar to most speakers but has no Gayo equivalent and thus suggests familiarity with technical terms but not a special valuing of religious norms. Some terms, such as *azan* or *ulama*, are considered to be standard Indonesia-wide terms without distinctive Gayo forms.

I have attempted to indicate these distinctions in the Glossary in the following way. When most Isak speakers would consider an entry to be part of ordinary Gayo vocabulary it is unmarked; when it is considered to be an Indonesian term or name it is marked as (Ind.). In a few cases an Indonesian equivalent is given. Standard Indonesian conventions of orthography are used. Because Gayo may pronounce a term in different ways, depending on their intentions and religious education (a matter discussed in Chapter 4), I have had to decide which sound to represent in the Glossary (and in the book). In most cases I have chosen that form which is closest to Indonesian dictionary entries or to an Arabic cognate to make it easy for readers to see cognatic relations among the three languages. Often this decision regards the relatively trivial issue of long vowel markings (which I usually adopt). When the choice makes a semantic difference or indicates something about a speaker's identity, I have discussed the matter in the text and would refer readers to the Index.

When a term retains a strong Arabic flavor in Isak it is marked as (Ar.); Arabic derivation but with a weaker association with Arabic is indicated as (<Ar.). In a few cases where spelling is very different the Arabic form is given a separate entry. Glosses are for the entry, not for the source word unless otherwise indicated (the Arabic may have a wider or narrower range of meaning, or a different meaning entirely).

Aisyiah (Ind.): women's branches of Muhammadiyah and of al-Washliyah
'aqīqa (Ar.; = Gayo *kikah*): seventh-day naming ritual
arwah (<Ar. *arwāh*, pl. of *rūh*): spirit of the deceased
aulië (<Ar. pl. of *walī*): saints; pious ones
azan (<Ar. *adhān*): call to worship
basmala (Ar.): the invocation *bismillāh irrahmān irrahīm*, "In the name of God, the Merciful, the Compassionate"
batin (<Ar. *bātin*): inner; spiritual; esoteric
berkat (<Ar. *baraka*): blessing, power

bid'a (Ar.): innovation, illegitimate innovation

dalīl (<Ar.): proof, sign

doa (<Ar. *du'ā'*): prayer; spell; recitation

du'ā' (Ar.): prayer; recitation

ëdët (<Ar. *'āda*; = Ind. *adat*): culture-specific norms and traditions

al-Fātiha (Ar.): the opening chapter of the Qur'ān

hadīth (<Ar.): reports of deeds and statements of the prophet Muhammad

hadīth qudsī (Ar.): extra-Qur'ānic report of God's words to Muhammad

ibëdët (<Ar. *'ibādāt*): worship and service to God

idul adha (Ind.; <Ar. *'īd al-adhā*; = G. *reraya haji, reraya qurbën*): The Feast of Sacrifice

idul fitri (Ind.; <Ar. *'īd al-fitr*; = G. *reraya*): The Feast of Breaking the Ramadān Fast

ijtihād (Ar.): independent reasoning

ikhlās (<Ar.): sincere devotion

al-Ikhlās (Ar.): chapter 112 of the Qur'ān

ilët dengki: connive, hate

ilmu (<Ar. *'ilm*): knowledge; skill; science

ilmu ladani (<Ar. *'ilm ladunnī*): divinely inspired knowledge

īmān (<Ar.) faith

imëm (<Ar. *imām*): worship leader

isharat (<Ar. *ishāra*): sign

jāhilīya (<Ar.): pre-Islamic times (of ignorance)

jama'a (<Ar. *jamā'a*): congregation for worship

jin (<Ar. *jinn*): spirit

Kejurun Blang: Lord of the Fields, rice ritual specialist

kemèl: shame

kenduri (<Urdu-Persian): ritual meal

khatīb (<Ar.): preacher

khilāfīyah (Ar.): disputed questions

khutba (<Ar.): sermon

kiamat (<Ar. *al-qiyāma*): the day of judgment

kikah (<Ar. *'aqīqa*): seventh-day naming ritual

kitëb (<Ar. *kitāb*): writing; scripture

kun fa-yakūn (Ar.): Qur'ānic phrase meaning "'Be,' and it was"; used by Gayo to mean "absolute power."

lahir (<Ar. *zāhir*): outer; material; exoteric

luh mahful (<Ar. *lauh al-mahfūz*): preserved tablet (on which God wrote)

madhhab (Ar.): legal tradition or school

ma'rifat (Ar.): gnosis

maripët (<Ar. *ma'rifat*): powerful depictive imagination

ma'zizët (<Ar. *mu'jizāt*): miracles

Molut (<Ar. *maulid* [*al-Nabī*]): the prophet Muhammad's birthday and its celebration

Muhammadiyah (Ind.): modernist Islamic organization

nasir (<Ar. *'anāsir*): elements (of the physical world)

niët (<Ar. *niyya*): intent

nur Muhammad (<Ar.): the Light of Muhammad, existing before creation

nyawa: soul

pahla (<Ar. *falāh*, success): merit

qādī (<Ar.): religious official; judge

rajah (<Ar. *rijā'*, wish, desire): spell used to imbue an object with healing power

rak'a (<Ar.): cycles or units of the worship ritual

reraya: The Feast of Breaking the Ramadān Fast

reraya haji (= *reraya qurbën*): The Feast of Sacrifice

ruh (<Ar. *rūh*): spirit

salāt (Ar.): worship ritual

samadiyah (<Ar. *shamad*, eternal): postmortem chanted recitations

semangat: vital force

semiyang (= Ind. *sembahyang*; = Ar. *salāt*): worship ritual

Shafi'i (Ar.): legal tradition followed in Indonesia (after Imam Shāfi'ī, d. 819)

sharī'a (Ar.): Islamic law; lit., "path"

shirk (<Ar): idolatry, polytheism (adjectival form: *mushrik*)

sihir (<Ar. *sihr*): black magic

sunna (Ar.): way of the Prophet; recommended (as a legal term)

sūra (Ar.): chapter of the Qur'ān

tafsīr (Ar.): interpretation and commentary (of the Qur'ān)

tahlīl (Ar.): reciting *lā ilāha illā Allāh*, "there is no deity but God"

tajwīd (Ar.): Qur'ān cantillation and its study

takbīr (Ar.): proclaiming *Allāhu akbar*, "God is great"

taqlīd (Ar., lit., "imitation"): following a legal tradition

tasbīh (Ar.): repeating "subhān Allāh"

tauhīd (Ar.): the oneness of God

ta'zīya (Ar., lit., "condolences"): visiting a grave

telkin (<Ar. *talqīn*): funeral catechism

tulak bëlë: lit., "pushing back danger"; kenduri held to exorcise pests and spirits from the rice crop

turun mani: lit., "going down to bathe"; child's initiation ritual

ulama (<Ar. *'ulamā'*): religious teachers and scholars

umët (<Ar. *umma*): the community of Muslims

ushalli (Ar. *'usallī*): lit., "I pray"; beginning of statement of intent to worship

wājib (<Ar.): required

al-Washliyah (*al-Jammiyat al-Washliyah*) (Ind.): lit., "Society for Unification"; traditionalist organization of ulama

zakāt (Ar.): religious tithe

zikr (<Ar. *dhikr*): spiritual exercise; esp. chanting of the *tahlīl*

BIBLIOGRAPHY

Note: The journal *Bijdragen tot de Taal-, Land- en Volkenkunde* will be abbreviated as BKI throughout.

Abbas, K. H. Sirajuddin.
1976 40 masalah agama [Forty Religious Issues]. 4 vols. Jakarta: Pustaka Tarbiyah.

Abdullah, Mal An.
1979–80 "Upacara kematian di Dusun Meranjat dan Meranjat Ilir, Sumatera Selatan" [Death Ritual in Meranjat and Meranjat Ilir Villages, South Sumatra]. *In* Moeslim Abdurrahman, ed., Agama, Budaya, dan Masyarakat. Pp. 27–33. Jakarta: Departemen Agama.

Abdullah, Taufik.
1971 Schools and Politics: The Kaum Muda Movement in West Sumatra (1927–1933). Ithaca: Cornell University Modern Indonesia Project.

Abu-Lughod, Lila.
1990 "The Romance of Resistance: Tracing Transformations of Power through Bedouin Women." American Ethnologist 17:41–55.

Ahmed, Rafiuddin.
1988 "Conflict and Contradiction in Bengali Islam: Problems of Change and Adjustment." *In* Katherine P. Ewing, ed., *Sharī'at* and Ambiguity in South Asian Islam. Pp. 114–42. Berkeley and Los Angeles: University of California Press.

Alexander, Jeffrey C.
1983 Theoretical Logic in Sociology, Vol. 3: The Classical Attempt at Theoretical Synthesis: Max Weber. Berkeley and Los Angeles: University of California Press.

Anderson, Benedict R. O'G.
1972 "The Idea of Power in Javanese Culture." *In* Claire Holt, ed., Culture and Politics in Indonesia. Pp. 1–69. Ithaca: Cornell University Press.

Anon. [Lubis, Arsyad Thalib].
1969–70 Fatwa. Medan: Firma Islamyah.

Antoun, Richard T.
1976 "The Social Anthropologist and the Study of Islam." *In* Leonard Binder, ed., The Study of the Middle East: Research and Scholarship in the Humanities and the Social Sciences. Pp.137–213. New York: John Wiley & Sons.
1989 Muslim Preacher in the Modern World. Princeton: Princeton University Press.

Anwarmufied, S.
1981 Ritus tanah [Land Ritual]. Ujung Pandang, Indonesia: PLPIIS.

Asad, Talal.
1983 "Anthropological Conceptions of Religion: Reflections on Geertz." Man (n.s.) 18:237–59.
1986 The Idea of an Anthropology of Islam. Washington, D.C.: Georgetown University Center for Contemporary Arab Studies, Occasional Papers Series.

Asy'ari, Alfaqir A. Muzakki Muchtar.
N.d. Pasti ajal Datang: Tata cara memandikan jenazah; tahlil dan talkin; terjema-

han Yasin [One's End Is Certain: How to Bathe the Corpse; Litanies and the Teaching; Translation of Yā Sīn]. Jakarta: M. A. Jaya.

al-Attas, Syed Naguib.
1970 The Mysticism of Hamzah Fansuri. Kuala Lumpur: University of Malaya Press.

Ayoub, Mahmoud M.
1984 The Qur'an and Its Interpreters, Vol. 1. Albany: State University of New York Press.

Badone, Ellen, ed.
1990 Religious Orthodoxy and Popular Faith in European Society. Princeton: Princeton University Press.

Baker, Keith Michael.
1992 "Defining the Public Sphere in Eighteenth-Century France: Variations on a Theme by Habermas." *In* Craig Calhoun, ed., Habermas and the Public Sphere. Pp. 181–211. Cambridge: MIT Press.

Berque, Jacques.
1980 Langages Arabes du Présent. Paris: Editions Gallimard.

Bloch, Maurice.
1982 "Death, Women, and Power." *In* Maurice Bloch and Jonathan Parry, eds., Death and the Regeneration of Life. Pp. 211–30. Cambridge: Cambridge University Press.
1986 From Blessing to Violence: History and Ideology in the Circumcision Ritual of the Merina of Madagascar. Cambridge: Cambridge University Press.

Boddy, Janice.
1989 Wombs and Alien Spirits: Women, Men, and the *Zār* Cult in Northern Sudan. Madison: University of Wisconsin Press.

El-Bokhari [al-Bukhari].
1903 Les traditions islamiques. O. Houdas and W. Marcais, eds. 4 vols. Paris: Imprimerie Nationale.

Boland, B. J.
1982 The Struggle of Islam in Modern Indonesia. The Hague: Martinus Nijhoff.

Bourdieu, Pierre.
1977 [Orig. 1972] Outline of the Theory of Practice. Cambridge: Cambridge University Press.

Bousfield, John.
1983 "Islamic Philosophy in South-East Asia." *In* M. B. Hooker, ed., Islam in South-East Asia. Pp. 92–129. Leiden: E. J. Brill.

Bousquet, G. H.
1939 "Researches sur les deux sectes musulmanes (Waktou Telous et Waktou Lima) de Lombok." Revue des Etudes Islamiques 13:149–77.

Bowen, John R.
1984 "Death and the History of Islam in Highland Aceh." Indonesia 38:21–38.
1986 "On the Political Construction of Tradition: Gotong Royong in Indonesia." Journal of Asian Studies 45:545–61.
1987 "Islamic Transformations: From Sufi Poetry to Gayo Ritual." *In* Rita Smith Kipp and Susan Rodgers, eds., Indonesian Religions in Transition. Pp. 113–35. Tucson: University of Arizona Press.

1988 "The Transformation of an Indonesian Property System: Adat, Islam, and Social Change in the Gayo Highlands." American Ethnologist 15:274–93.

1989 "*Salat* in Indonesia: The Social Meanings of an Islamic Ritual." Man (n.s.) 24:299–318.

1991 Sumatran Politics and Poetics: Gayo History, 1900–1989. New Haven: Yale University Press.

1992 "Elaborating Scriptures: Cain and Abel in Gayo Society." Man (n.s.) 27:495–516.

Boyer, Paul, and Stephen Nissenbaum.

1974 Salem Possessed: The Social Origins of Witchcraft. Cambridge: Harvard University Press.

Brandes, Stanley.

1990 "Conclusion: Reflections on the Study of Religious Orthodoxy and Popular Faith in Europe." *In* Ellen Badone, ed., Religious Orthodoxy and Popular Faith in European Society. Pp. 185–200. Princeton: Princeton University Press.

Brenneis, Donald L., and Fred Myers.

1984 Dangerous Words: Language and Politics in the Pacific. New York: New York University Press.

Brown, Michael F.

1985 Tsewa's Gift: Magic and Meaning in an Amazonian Society. Washington, D.C.: Smithsonian Institution Press.

Brown, Peter.

1981 The Cult of the Saints. Chicago: University of Chicago Press.

Brubaker, Rogers.

1984 The Limits of Rationality. London: George Allen & Unwin.

Bruinessen, Martin van.

1990 "Kitab Kuning: Books in Arabic Script Used in the Pesantren Milieu." BKI 146:226–69.

1991 "The 28th Congress of the Nahdlatul Ulama: Power Struggle and Social Concerns." Archipel 41:185–200.

Burke, Edmund III.

1979 "Islamic History as World History: Marshall Hodgson, 'The Venture of Islam.' " International Journal of Middle East Studies 10:241–64.

Burke, Edmund III, and Ira M. Lapidus, eds.

1988 Islam, Politics, and Social Movements. Berkeley and Los Angeles: University of California Press.

Burkill, I. H.

1966 [Orig. 1935] A Dictionary of the Economic Products of the Malay Peninsula. 2 vols. Kuala Lumpur (Malaysia): Ministry of Agriculture and Co-operatives

Calhoun, Craig.

1992 "Introduction: Habermas and the Public Sphere." *In* Craig Calhoun, ed., Habermas and the Public Sphere. Pp. 1–48. Cambridge: MIT Press.

Chelhod, Joseph.

1955 Le sacrifice chez les Arabes. Paris: Presses Universitaires de France.

Collins, William.

1979 "Besemah Concepts." Ph.D. diss., University of California, Berkeley.

Combs-Schilling, M. E.
1989 Sacred Performances: Islam, Sexuality, and Sacrifice. New York: Columbia University Press.
Damsté, H. T.
1928 "Hikajat Prang Sabi." BKI 84:545–609.
1939 "De legende van de heilige zeven slapers in het Atjehsch." BKI 98:407–88.
Daudy, Abdurrahman.
1938 (ed.) al-Tafsīr al-Gayo. Cairo: Mustafa Bab.
1950 [untitled manuscript].
Delaney, Carol.
1991 The Seed and the Soil: Gender and Cosmology in Turkish Village Society. Berkeley and Los Angeles: University of California Press.
Denny, Frederick Mathewson.
1985a "Islamic Ritual: Perspectives and Theories." In Richard C. Martin, ed., Approaches to Islam in Religious Studies. Pp. 63–77. Tucson: University of Arizona Press.
1985b An Introduction to Islam. New York: Macmillan.
1988 "Qur'ān Recitation Training in Indonesia: A Survey of Contexts and Handbooks." In Andrew Rippin, ed., Approaches to the History of the Interpretation of the Qur'an. Pp. 288–306. Oxford: Clarendon Press.
Dhofier, Zamakhsyari.
1982 Tradisi pesantren. Studi tentang pandangan hidup kyai [Pesantren Tradition: Study of the Kyai's World View]. Jakarta: LP3ES.
Dijk, C. van.
1981 Rebellion Under the Banner of Islam. The Hague: Martinus Nijhoff.
Dobbin, Christine.
1983 Islamic Revivalism in a Changing Peasant Economy: Central Sumatra, 1784–1847. London: Curzon Press.
Donaldson, Bess Allen.
1937 "The Koran as Magic." The Muslim World 27:254–66.
Douglas, Mary.
1966 "The Abominations of Leviticus." In Purity and Danger. Pp. 41–57. London: Routledge & Kegan Paul.
Drewes, G.W.J.
1977 Directions for Travellers on the Mystic Path. The Hague: Martinus Nijhoff.
Drewes, G.W.J., and L. F. Brakel.
1986 The Poems of Hamzah Fansuri. Dordrecht: Foris.
Drewes, G.W.J., and R. Ng. Dr. Poerbatjaraka.
1938 De mirakelen van Abdoelkadir Djaelani. Bandoeng: Koninklijk Bataviaasch Genootschap van Kusten en Wetenschappen.
Duri, A. A.
1983 The Rise of Historical Writing among the Arabs. Princeton: Princeton University Press.
Durkheim, Emile.
1965 [Orig. 1912] The Elementary Forms of the Religious Life. Joseph Ward Swain, trans. New York: Free Press.

Eickelman, Dale F.

1976 Moroccan Islam. Austin: University of Texas Press.

1979 "The Political Economy of Meaning." American Ethnologist 6:386–93.

1982 "The Study of Islam in Local Contexts." Contributions to Asian Studies 17:1–16.

1985 Knowledge and Power in Morocco. Princeton: Princeton University Press.

1989a The Middle East: An Anthropological Approach. 2d ed. Englewood Cliffs, N.J.: Prentice Hall.

1989b "National Identity and Religious Discourse in Contemporary Oman." International Journal of Islamic and Arabic Studies 6:1–20.

Eisenstadt, S. N., ed.

1968 The Protestant Ethic and Modernization: A Comparative View. New York: Basic Books.

Eley, Geoff.

1992 "Nations, Publics, and Political Cultures: Placing Habermas in the Nineteenth Century." In Craig Calhoun, ed., Habermas and the Public Sphere. Pp. 289–339. Cambridge: MIT Press.

Emmerson, Donald K.

1978 "The Bureaucracy in Political Context: Weakness in Strength." In Karl D. Jackson and Lucien W. Pye, eds., Political Power and Communications in Indonesia. Pp. 82–136. Berkeley and Los Angeles: University of California Press.

Evans-Pritchard, E. E.

1929 "The Morphology and Function of Magic: A Comparative Study of Trobriand and Zande Ritual and Spells." American Anthropologist 31:619–41.

1937 Witchcraft, Oracles and Magic Among the Azande. Oxford: Oxford University Press.

1956 Nuer Religion. Oxford: Oxford University Press.

Federspiel, Howard M.

1970 Persatuan Islam: Islamic Reform in Twentieth Century Indonesia. Ithaca: Cornell University Modern Indonesia Project.

Fischer, Michael.

1980 Iran: From Religious Dispute to Revolution. Cambridge: Harvard University Press.

Fischer, Michael, and Mehdi Abedi.

1990 Debating Muslims: Cultural Dialogues in Tradition and Postmodernity. Madison: University of Wisconsin Press.

Fortune, R. F.

1932 Sorcerers of Dobu: The Social Anthropology of the Dobu Islanders of the Western Pacific. London: Routledge.

Foucault, Michel.

1972 [Orig. 1969] The Archaeology of Knowledge. New York: Pantheon.

1982 "The Subject and Power." In Hubert L. Dreyfus and Paul Rabinow, Michel Foucault: Beyond Structuralism and Hermeneutics. Pp. 208–26. Chicago: University of Chicago Press.

Frazer, James G.

1935 [Orig. 1911] The Golden Bough: A Study in Magic and Religion, Part I: The Magic Art and the Evolution of Kings. 3d ed. 2 vols. New York: Macmillan.

Freitag, Sandria B.

1988 "Ambiguous Public Arenas and Coherent Personal Practice: Kanpur Muslims 1913–1931." *In* Katherine P. Ewing, ed., *Sharī'at and Ambiguity in South Asian Islam.* Pp. 143–63. Berkeley and Los Angeles: University of California Press.

Gaffney, Patrick.

1987 "Authority and the Mosque in Upper Egypt: The Islamic Preacher as Image and Actor." *In* William R. Roff, ed., Islam and the Political Economy of Meaning. Pp. 199–225. Berkeley and Los Angeles: University of California Press.

Geertz, Clifford.

1959 "Religion and Social Change: A Javanese Example." American Anthropologist 59:32–54.

1960 The Religion of Java. Chicago: University of Chicago Press.

1963a Peddlers and Princes: Social Development and Economic Change in Two Indonesian Towns. Chicago: University of Chicago Press.

1963b "The Integrative Revolution: Primordial Sentiments and Civil Politics in the New States." *In* Clifford Geertz, ed., Old Societies and New States. Pp. 105–57. Glencoe, Ill.: Free Press.

1966 "Religion as a Cultural System." *In* Michael Banton, ed., Anthropological Approaches to the Study of Religion. Pp. 1–46. London: Tavistock.

1968 Islam Observed. New Haven: Yale University Press.

1973 The Interpretation of Cultures. New York: Basic Books.

Geertz, Clifford, Hildred Geertz, and Lawrence Rosen.

1979 Meaning and Order in Moroccan Society. Cambridge: Cambridge University Press.

Geertz, Hildred.

1975 "An Anthropology of Religion and Magic, I." Journal of Interdisciplinary History 6:71–89.

Giddens, Anthony.

1971 Capitalism and Modern Social Theory: An Analysis of the Writings of Marx, Durkheim and Max Weber. Cambridge: Cambridge University Press.

Gilsenan, Michael.

1973 Saint and Sufi in Modern Egypt: An Essay in the Sociology of Religion. Oxford: Clarendon Press.

1982 Recognizing Islam: Religion and Society in the Modern Arab World. New York: Pantheon.

Gladney, Dru C.

1991 Muslim Chinese: Ethnic Nationalism in the People's Republic. Cambridge: Council on East Asian Studies, Harvard University.

Goldziher, Ignaz.

1967 [Orig. 1889–90] Muslim Studies, Vol. 1. S. M. Stern, ed. London: George Allen & Unwin Ltd.

1981 [Orig. 1910] Introduction to Islamic Theology and Law. A. Hamori and R. Hamori, trans. Princeton: Princeton University Press.

Goody, Jack.
1968 "Introduction." *In* Jack Goody, ed., Literacy in Traditional Societies. Pp. 1–26. Cambridge: Cambridge University Press.

Graham, William A.
1977 Divine Word and Prophetic Word in Early Islam. The Hague: Mouton.
1983 "Islam in the Mirror of Ritual." *In* Richard G. Hovannisian and Speros Vryonis, Jr., eds., Islam's Understanding of Itself. Pp. 53–71. Malibu, Calif.: Undena.
1987 Beyond the Written Word: Oral Aspects of Scripture in the History of Religion. Cambridge: Cambridge University Press.

Habermas, Jürgen.
1984 [Orig. 1981] The Theory of Communicative Action, Vol. 1: Reason and the Rationalization of Society. Thomas McCarthy, trans. Boston: Beacon Press.
1989 [Orig. 1962] The Structural Transformation of the Public Sphere: An Inquiry into a Category of Bourgeois Society. Thomas Burger, trans. Cambridge: MIT Press.

Hallaq, Wael B.
1984 "Was the Gate of Ijtihad Closed?" International Journal of Middle Eastern Studies 16:3–41.

Hamka [Haji Abdulmalik bin Abdulkarim Amrullah].
1973 Tafsir al-Azhar: Juzu' 30. Surabaya: Yayasan Latimojong.

Hanafiah, Sulaiman.
1974 Perkembangan sistim pendidikan pesantren di Kabupaten Aceh Tengah [The Development of the Pesantren Educational System in Central Aceh District]. Darussalam, Aceh: Pusat Latihan Penelitian Ilmu-Ilmu Sosial.

Hasjmy, A.
1983 Kebudayaan Aceh dalam sejarah [Acehnese Culture in History]. Jakarta: Penerbit Beuna.

Hassan, Ahmad.
1968 Soal-Jawab tentang berbagai masalah agama [Questions and Answers on Various Religious Issues]. Bandung: Diponegoro.
1979 [Orig. 1930] Pengajaran shalat [Salat Manual]. Bandung: Diponegoro.

Hazeu, G.A.J.
1907 Gajosch-Nederlandsch woordenboek. Batavia: Landsdrukkerij.

Hefner, Robert W.
1985 Hindu Javanese: Tengger Tradition and Islam. Princeton: Princeton University Press.
1987 "Islamizing Java? Religion and Politics in Rural East Java." Journal of Asian Studies 46:533–54.

Heller, B.
1983 "Lukmān." *In* the Shorter Encyclopedia of Islam. Pp. 289–90. Ithaca: Cornell University Press.

Hertz, Robert.
1960 [Orig. 1907] Death and the Right Hand. Rodney Needham, trans. New York: Free Press.

Hodgson, Marshall G. S.
1974 The Venture of Islam: Conscience and History in a World Civilization. 3 vols. Chicago: University of Chicago Press.

Holmberg, David H.
1989 Order in Paradox: Myth, Ritual, and Exchange among Nepal's Tamang. Ithaca: Cornell University Press.

Holy, Ladislav.
1991 Religion and Custom in a Muslim Society: The Berti of Sudan. Cambridge: Cambridge University Press.

Hooykas, C.
1974 Cosmogony and Creation in Balinese Tradition. The Hague: Martinus Nijhoff.

Hoskins, Janet.
1989 "Burned Paddy and Lost Souls." BKI 145:430–44.

Hourani, Albert.
1983 Arabic Thought in the Liberal Age, 1798–1939. Reissue, with new preface, of 1962 ed. Cambridge: Cambridge University Press.

Hubert, Henri, and Marcel Mauss.
1964 [Orig. 1898] Sacrifice: Its Nature and Function. W. D. Halls, trans. Chicago: University of Chicago Press.

Jay, Robert R.
1963 Religion and Politics in Rural Central Java. Yale University, Southeast Asia Studies, Cultural Report Series No. 12.

Johns, Anthony H.
1955 "Dakaik al-Huruf by Abd Al-Rauf of Singkel." Journal of the Royal Asiatic Society, Parts 1&2: 55–73; Parts 3&4: 139–58.
1957 "Malay Sufism as Illustrated in an Anonymous Collection of 17th Century Tracts." Journal of the Malayan Branch of the Royal Asiatic Society 30 (2), no. 178.
1961 "Sufism as a Category in Indonesian Literature and History." Journal of Southeast Asian History 2:10–23.
1961–62 "Muslim Mystics and Historical Writing." In D.G.E. Hall, ed., Historians of South-East Asia. Pp. 37–49. London: Oxford University Press.
1965 The Gift Addressed to the Spirit of the Prophet. Canberra: The Australian National University.
1978 "Friends in Grace: Ibrāhīm al-Kūrānī and 'Abd al-Ra'uf al Singkeli. In S. Udin, ed., Spectrum. Pp. 469–85. Jakarta: Dian Rakyat.
1984 "Islam in the Malay World: An Exploratory Survey with Some Reference to Quranic Exegesis." In Raphael Israeli and Anthony H. Johns, eds., Islam in Asia, Vol. II: Southeast and East Asia. Pp. 115–61. Boulder, Colo.: Westview Press.

Jones, Gareth Stedman.
1983 Languages of Class: Studies in English Working Class History, 1832–1982. Cambridge: Cambridge University Press.

Josselin de Jong, P. E. de.
1965 "An Interpretation of Agricultural Rites in Southeast Asia, with a Demon-

stration of Use of Data from Both Continental and Insular Areas." Journal of Asian Studies 24:283–91.

Juynboll, G.H.A.
1983 Muslim Tradition: Studies in Chronology, Provenance, and Early Authorship of Early Hadīth. Cambridge: Cambridge University Press.

Juynboll, Th. W.
1930 Handleiding tot de kennis van de Mohammedaansche wet. Leiden: E. J. Brill.

Kepel, Gilles.
1985 Muslim Extremism in Egypt: The Prophet and the Pharaoh. Berkeley and Los Angeles: University of California Press.

Kipp, Rita Smith, and Susan Rodgers.
1987 "Introduction: Indonesian Religions in Transition." In Rita Smith Kipp and Susan Rodgers, eds., Indonesian Religions in Transition. Pp. 1–31. Tucson: University of Arizona Press.

al-Kisā'ī, M.
1978 Tales of the Prophets of al-Kisa'i. W. M. Thackston, Jr., ed. and trans. Boston: Twayne.

Kister, M. J.
1988 "Legends in Tafsīr and Hadīth literature: The Creation of Adam and Related Stories." In Andrew Rippin, ed., Approaches to the History of the Interpretation of the Qur'ān. Oxford: Clarendon Press.

Knappert, Jan.
1971 Swahili Islamic Poetry. 2 vols. Leiden: E. J. Brill.
1985 Islamic Legends. 2 vols. Leiden: E. J. Brill.

Kraus, Werner.
N.d. Some Notes on the Introduction of the Naqshbandiyya-Khalidiyya into Indonesia.

Kreemer, J.
1922–23 Atjeh. 2 vols. Leiden: E. J. Brill.

Kuipers, Joel.
1990 Power in Performance: The Creation of Textual Authority in Weyewa Ritual Speech. Philadelphia: University of Pennsylvania Press.

Kurin, Richard.
1984 "Morality, Personhood, and the Exemplary Life: Popular Conceptions of Muslims in Paradise." In B. D. Metcalf, ed., Moral Conduct and Authority: The Place of Adab in South Asian Islam. Pp. 196–220. Berkeley and Los Angeles: University of California Press.

Laderman, Carol.
1991 Taming the Wind of Desire: Psychology, Medicine, and Aesthetics in Malay Shamanistic Performance. Berkeley and Los Angeles: University of California Press.

Laitin, David D.
1986 Hegemony and Culture: Politics and Religious Change among the Yoruba. Chicago: University of Chicago Press.

Lambek, Michael.
1990 "Certain Knowledge, Contestable Authority: Power and Practice on the Islamic Periphery." American Ethnologist 17:23–40.
Lamphere, Louise.
1989 "Feminist Anthropology: The Legacy of Elsie Clews Parsons." American Ethnologist 16:518–33.
Landes, Joan.
1988 Women and the Public Sphere in the Age of the French Revolution. Ithaca: Cornell University Press.
Lane, Edward William.
1860 [Orig. 1836] An Account of the Manners and Customs of the Modern Egyptians. 5th ed. London: John Murray.
Lansing, J. Stephen.
1991 Priests and Programmers. Princeton: Princeton University Press.
Lapidus, Ira M.
1988 A History of Islamic Societies. Cambridge: Cambridge University Press.
Laroui, Abdallah.
1976 The Crisis of the Arab Intellectual: Traditionalism or Historicism? Diarmid Cammell, trans. Berkeley and Los Angeles: University of California Press.
Lash, Scott, and Sam Whimster, eds.
1987 Max Weber, Rationality and Modernity. London: George Allen & Unwin.
Leach, Edmund, and D. Alan Aycock.
1983 Structuralist Interpretations of Biblical Myth. Cambridge: Cambridge University Press.
Lev, Daniel S.
1972 Islamic Courts in Indonesia. A Study in the Political Bases of Legal Institutions. Berkeley and Los Angeles: University of California Press.
Lévi-Strauss, Claude.
1969 [Orig. 1949] The Elementary Structures of Kinship. Rodney Needham, ed. Boston: Beacon Press.
Lewis, Bernard.
1988 The Political Language of Islam. Chicago: University of Chicago Press.
Lieban, R. W.
1967 Cebuano Sorcery: Malign Magic in the Philippines. Berkeley and Los Angeles: University of California Press.
Loeffler, Reinhold.
1988 Islam in Practice: Religious Beliefs in a Persian Village. Albany: State University of New York Press.
Lombard, Denys.
1967 Le sultanat d'Atjeh au temps d'Iskandar Muda. Paris: Ecole Francaise d'Extreme-Orient.
1985 "Les tarekat en Insulinde." In A. Popovic and G. Veinstein, eds., Les ordres mystiques dans L'Islam. Pp. 139–63. Paris: Editions de l'Ecole des Hautes Etudes en Sciences Sociales.
McAllister, Carol.
1990 "Women and Feasting: Ritual Exchange, Capitalism, and Islamic Revival in Negeri Sembilan, Malaysia." Research in Economic Anthropology 12:23–51.

Macdonald, D. B.
1953 "Dhikr." *In* the Shorter Encyclopedia of Islam. P. 75. Ithaca: Cornell University Press.
McKinley, Robert.
1979 "Zaman dan Masa, Eras and Periods: Religious Evolution and the Permanence of Epistemological Ages in Malay Culture." *In* A. L. Becker and Aram Yengoyan, eds., The Imagination of Reality: Essays in Southeast Asian Coherence Systems. Pp. 303–24. Norwood, N.J.: Ablex.
1981 "Cain and Abel on the Malay Peninsula." *In* Mac Marshall, ed., Siblingship in Oceania. Pp. 335–418. Lanham, Md.: University Press of America.
McVey, Ruth.
1983 "Faith as the Outsider: Islam in Indonesian Politics." *In* James P. Piscatori, ed., Islam in the Political Process. Pp. 199–225. Cambridge: Cambridge University Press.
Malinowski, Bronislaw.
1935 Coral Gardens and Their Magic. London: George Allen & Unwin.
Malti-Douglas, Fedwa.
1991 Women's Body, Women's Word: Gender and Discourse in Arabo-Islamic Writing. Princeton: Princeton University Press.
Mardin, Serif.
1989 Religion and Social Change in Modern Turkey. Albany: State University of New York Press.
Martin, Richard C., ed.
1985 Approaches to Islam in Religious Studies. Tucson: University of Arizona Press.
Mauss, Marcel.
1950 [Orig. 1936] "Les techniques du corps." *In* Sociologie et Anthropologie. Pp. 365–86. Paris: Presses Universitaires de France.
Mernissi, Fatima.
1991 The Veil and the Male Elite: A Feminist Interpretation of Women's Rights in Islam. Mary Jo Lakeland, trans. Reading, Mass.: Addison-Wesley.
Messick, Brinkley.
1986 "The Mufti, the Text and the World: Legal Interpretation in Yemen." Man (n.s.) 21:102–19.
1989 "Just Writing: Paradox and Political Economy in Yemeni Legal Documents." Cultural Anthropology 4:26–50.
Metcalf, Barbara Daly.
1982 Islamic Revival in British India: Deoband, 1860–1900. Princeton: Princeton University Press.
1990 Perfecting Women: Maulana Ashraf 'Ali Thanawi's *Bihishti Zewar*. Berkeley and Los Angeles: University of California Press.
Metcalf, Peter.
1982 A Borneo Journey into Death: Berawan Eschatology from Its Rituals. Philadelphia: University of Pennsylvania Press.
1991 "Introduction to the Second Edition." *In* Peter Metcalf and Richard Huntington, Celebrations of Death: The Anthropology of Mortuary Ritual. Pp. 1–23. Cambridge: Cambridge University Press.

Mitchell, Timothy.
    1988 Colonising Egypt. Berkeley and Los Angeles: University of California
    Press.
Momen, Moojan.
    1985 An Introduction to Shi'i Islam. New Haven: Yale University Press.
Myers, Fred R., and Donald Lawrence Brenneis.
    1984 "Introduction: Language and Politics in the Pacific." In Brenneis and
    Myers, Dangerous Words. Pp. 1–29.
Nagata, Judith.
    1984 The Reflowering of Malaysian Islam: Modern Religious Radicals and Their
    Roots. Vancouver: University of British Columbia Press.
Nakamura, Mitsuo.
    1983 The Crescent Arises over the Banyan Tree. Jogjakarta: Gajah Mada Univer-
    sity Press.
Nelson, Kristina.
    1985 The Art of Reciting the Qur'an. Austin: University of Texas Press.
Noer, Deliar.
    1973 The Modernist Muslim Movement in Indonesia, 1900–1942. Kuala Lum-
    pur: Oxford University Press.
Nor bin Ngah, Mohd.
    1982 Kitab Jawi: Islamic Thought of the Malay Muslim Scholars. Singapore:
    Institute of Southeast Asian Studies, Research Notes and Discussions Paper
    No. 33.
Ortner, Sherry B.
    1978 Sherpas through Their Rituals. Cambridge: Cambridge University Press.
Osman el-Tom, Abdullahi.
    1985 "Drinking the Koran: The Meaning of Koranic Verses in Berti Erasure."
    Africa 55:414–31.
Ossenbruggen, F.D.E. van.
    1977 [Orig. 1916] "Java's monca-pat: Origins of a Primitive Classification Sys-
    tem." In P. E. de Josselin de Jong, ed., Structural Anthropology in the Nether-
    lands. Pp. 32–60. The Hague: Martinus Nijhoff.
Padwick, Constance E.
    1961 Muslim Devotions. A Study of Prayer-Manuals in Common Use. London:
    S.P.C.K.
Peacock, James L.
    1975 Consciousness and Change: Symbolic Anthropology in Evolutionary Per-
    spective. Oxford: Basil Blackwell.
    1978a Purifying the Faith: The Muhammadijah Movement in Indonesian Islam.
    Menlo Park, Calif.: Benjamin/Cummings.
    1978b Muslim Puritans: Reformist Psychology in Southeast Asian Islam. Berke-
    ley and Los Angeles: University of California Press.
Peletz, Michael G.
    1988 "Poisoning, Sorcery, and Healing Rituals in Negeri Sembilan." BKI 144:
    132–64.
Polo, Marco.
    1958 The Travels. R. Latham, trans. Middlesex: Penguin Books.

Qishashul.
N.d. Qishashul anbiya [Tales of the Prophets]. Bandung: P. T. Alma'arif.
Qusyairi, Ahmad.
N.d. Mujarrobat Lengkap [The Complete Effective Remedies]. Jakarta: Bintang
Terang.
Redfield, Robert.
1956 Peasant Society and Culture. Chicago: University of Chicago Press.
Reid, Anthony.
1988 Southeast Asia in the Age of Commerce, 1450–1680, Vol. 1: The Lands
Below the Winds. New Haven: Yale University Press.
Ricklefs, M. C.
1981 A History of Modern Indonesia. Bloomington: Indiana University Press.
Riddell, Peter.
1990 Transferring a Tradition: 'Abd Al-Ra'ūf Al-Singkilī's Rendering into
Malay of the Jalālayn Commentary. Berkeley: Centers for South and Southeast
Asia Studies, Monograph No. 31.
Rippin, Andrew.
1988 "Introduction." In Andrew Rippin, ed., Approaches to the History of the
Interpretation of the Qur'ān. Pp. 1–9.
Rippin, Andrew, ed.
1988 Approaches to the History and Interpretation of the Qur'ān. Oxford: Claren-
don Press.
Robertson Smith, W.
1972 [Orig. 1894] The Religion of the Semites. New York: Schocken.
Robson, James, ed.
1963–65 Mishkāt al Masābīh [Niche of the Lamps]. 4 vols. Recension by Walī
al-Dīn al-Tibrīzī of Baghawī's 12th century C.E. Masābīh al-sunna. Lahore:
Sh. Muhammad Ashraf.
Rodgers Siregar, Susan.
1981 Adat, Islam and Christianity in a Batak Homeland. Papers in International
Studies, Southeast Asia Series, No. 57. Athens: Ohio University Center for International Studies.
Roff, William R.
1967 The Origins of Malay Nationalism. New Haven: Yale University Press.
1985 "Islam Obscured? Some Reflections on Studies of Islam and Society in
Southeast Asia." Archipel 29, I:7–34.
1987 "Islamic Movements: One or Many?" In William R. Roff, ed., Islam and
the Political Economy of Meaning. Pp. 31–52. Berkeley and Los Angeles: University of California Press.
1988 "Whence Cometh the Law? Dog Saliva in Kelantan, 1937." In Katherine
P. Ewing, ed., Sharī'at and Ambiguity in South Asian Islam. Pp. 25–42.
Berkeley and Los Angeles: University of California Press.
Rosaldo, Michelle.
1984 "Words That Are Moving: The Social Meanings of Ilongot Verbal Art." In
Brenneis and Myers, Dangerous Words. Pp. 131–60.
Rosaldo, Renato.
1984 "Grief and the Headhunter's Rage: On the Cultural Force of Emotions." In

Edward Bruner, ed., Text, Play, and Story: The Construction and Reconstruction of Self and Society. Pp. 178–95. Washington, D.C.: American Ethnological Society.

Rosen, Lawrence.

1988 Bargaining for Reality: The Construction of Social Relations in a Muslim Community. Chicago: University of Chicago Press.

Rosenthal, F.

1989 "General Introduction." *In* al-Tabarī, The History of al-Tabarī, Vol. 1.

Sa'd Ibn.

1962 "Kitāb at-tabaqāt al-kabīr" [Great Book of Classes]. *In* A. Jeffery, ed., A Reader on Islam. Pp. 189–96. 's-Gravenhage: Mouton.

Said, M.

1977 Kitab tauhid (sifat dua puluh): Awwaludin Marifatullah [Book of Tauhid (The Twenty Attributes): Basics of Religion, Knowledge of God]. Bandung: P. T. Alma'arif.

Schacht, Joseph.

1964 An Introduction to Islamic Law. Oxford: Clarendon Press.

Schimmel, Annemarie.

1975 Mystical Dimensions of Islam. Chapel Hill: University of North Carolina Press.

1985 And Muhammad Is His Messenger. Chapel Hill: University of North Carolina Press.

Scott, James C.

1990 Domination and the Arts of Resistance: Hidden Transcripts. New Haven: Yale University Press.

Sherzer, Joel.

1990 Verbal Art in San Blas: Kuna Culture through Its Discourse. Cambridge: Cambridge University Press.

ash-Shiddieqy, T. M. Hasbi.

1950 Tuntutan Qurban [The Demand of Sacrifice]. Jakarta: Bulan Bintang.

1952 Al-Islam. 2 vols. Jakarta: Bulan Bintang.

Shiddiqi, H. Nourouzzaman.

1987 Muhammad Hasbi Ash Shiddieqy dalam perspektif sejarah pemikiran Islam di Indonesia [Muhammad Hasbi Ash Shiddieqy from the Perspective of the History of Islamic Thought in Indonesia]. Yogyakarta: IAIN Sunan Kalijaga.

Shinar, P.

1977 "Traditional and Reformist Mawlid Celebrations in the Maghrib." *In* M. Rosen-Ayalon, ed., Studies in Memory of Gaston Wiet. Pp. 371–413. Jerusalem: Institute of Asian and African Studies, Hebrew University.

Sibeth, Achim.

1991 The Batak. London: Thames and Hudson.

Siegel, James T.

1969 The Rope of God. Berkeley and Los Angeles: University of California Press.

1979 Shadow and Sound: The Historical Thought of a Sumatran People. Chicago: University of Chicago Press.

Singer, Milton.

1964 "The Social Organization of Indian Civilization." Diogène 45:84–119.

Skeat, Walter W.
1967 [Orig. 1900] Malay Magic. New York: Dover.

Slaats, Herman, and Karen Portier.
1993 "Sorcery and the Law in Modern Indonesia." In Roy Ellen and C. W. Watson, eds., Understanding Witchcraft and Sorcery in South-East Asia. Honolulu: University of Hawaii Press.

Smith, Jane Idleman, and Yvonne Yazbeck Haddad.
1981 The Islamic Understanding of Death and Resurrection. Albany: State University of New York Press.

Smith, Wilfred Cantwell.
1963 The Meaning and End of Religion. New York: Macmillan.

Snouck Hurgronje, C.
1903 Het Gayoland en Zijne Bewoners. Batavia: Landsdrukkerij.
1906 [Orig. 1893–94] The Achehnese. 2 vols. A.W.S. O'Sullivan, trans. Leiden: E. J. Brill
1931 [Orig. 1888–89] Mekka in the Latter Part of the 19th Century. I. H. Monahan, trans. Leiden: E. J. Brill.

Soeratno, Siti Chamamah.
1978 "Khidlir est Proche, Dieu est Loin." Archipel 15:85–94.

Steedly, Mary M.
1988 "Severing the Bonds of Love: A Case Study in Soul Loss." Social Science and Medicine 27 (8): 841–56.

Steenbrink, Karel A.
1974 Pesantren, madrasah, sekolah: Pendidikan Islam dalam kurun moderen [Pesantren, Madrasah, School: Islamic Education in the Modern Period]. Jakarta: LP3ES.

Stocking, George W., Jr.
1989 "The Ethnographic Sensibility of the 1920s and the Dualism of the Anthropological Tradition." In George W. Stocking, Jr., ed., Romantic Motives: Essays on Anthropological Sensibility. Pp. 208–76. Madison: University of Wisconsin Press.

Suhaimi, Masrap.
N.d. Terjemah Majmu' Syarif [Translation of the "Holy Collection"]. Surabaya: Karya Utama.

Sukanda-Tessier, V.
1977 Le triomphe de Sri en pays Soundanais. Paris: Ecole Francaise d'Extreme-Orient.

Sweeney, Amin.
1987 A Full Hearing: Orality and Literacy in the Malay World. Berkeley and Los Angeles: University of California Press.

Syihab, Drs. Tgk. Z. A.
1986 Terjemah Aqidatul 'Awam [Translation of the Creed for the Uninitiated] [in Jawi]. Jakarta: Dian Intan Nusantara.

al-Tabarī, Abū Ja'far Muhammad b. Jarīr.
1987 The Commentary on the Qur'ān, Vol. 1. J. Cooper, ed. Oxford: Oxford University Press.
1989 The History of al-Tabarī, Vol. 1. F. Rosenthal, ed. Albany: State University of New York Press.

Tambiah, S. J.
1970 Buddhism and the Spirit Cults in North-East Thailand. Cambridge: Cambridge University Press.
1990 Magic, Science, Religion, and the Scope of Rationality. Cambridge: Cambridge University Press.

Tapper, Nancy, and Richard Tapper.
1987 "The Birth of the Prophet: Ritual and Gender in Turkish Islam." Man 22: 69–92.

Taylor, Charles.
1990 Invoking Civil Society. Working Papers and Proceedings, No. 31. Chicago: Center for Psychosocial Studies.

Thackston, W. M., Jr.
1978 "Introduction." In al-Kisā'ī, Tales of the Prophets of al-Kisa'i.

al-Thaʿlabī, A.
N.d. Qisas al-anbiyāʿ [Tales of the Prophets]. Cairo: ʿIsā al-Bābī al-Halabī.

Turner, Bryan S.
1974 Weber and Islam. London: Routledge & Kegan Paul.

Urban, Greg.
1991 A Discourse-Centered Approach to Culture. Austin: University of Texas Press.

Valeri, Valerio.
1985 Kingship and Sacrifice: Ritual and Society in Ancient Hawaii. Chicago: University of Chicago Press.

Volkman, Toby Alice.
1985 Feasts of Honor: Ritual and Change in the Toraja Highlands. Urbana: University of Illinois Press.

Waardenburg, J.J.C.H. van.
1936 De invloed van den landbouw op de zeden, de taal en letterkunde der Atjehers. Leiden: Dubbeldman.

Wagner, Roy.
1984 "Ritual as Communication: Order, Meaning, and Secrecy in Melanesian Initiation Rites." Annual Review of Anthropology 13:143–55.

Watson-Gegeo, Karen Ann, and Geoffrey M. White, eds.
1990 Disentangling: Conflict Discourse in Pacific Societies. Stanford: Stanford University Press.

Weber, Max.
1958a [Orig. 1904–5] The Protestant Ethic and the Spirit of Capitalism. Talcott Parsons, trans. New York: Charles Scribner's Sons.
1958b [Orig. 1922–23] "The Social Psychology of the World Religions." In H. H. Gerth and C. Wright Mills, eds., From Max Weber: Essays in Sociology. Pp. 267–301. New York: Oxford University Press.
1958c [Orig. 1915] "Religious Rejections of the World and Their Directions." In H. H. Gerth and C. Wright Mills, eds., From Max Weber: Essays in Sociology. Pp. 323–59. New York: Oxford University Press.
1963 [Orig. 1922] The Sociology of Religion. Ephraim Fischoff, trans. Boston: Beacon Press.

Wensinck, A. J.

1953a "Ashāb al-Kahf." *In* the Shorter Encyclopedia of Islam. Pp. 45–46. Ithaca: Cornell University Press.

1953b "al-Khadir." *In* the Shorter Encyclopedia of Islam. Pp. 232–35. Ithaca: Cornell University Press.

1953c "Salat." *In* the Shorter Encyclopedia of Islam. Pp. 491–99. Ithaca: Cornell University Press.

Werbner, Pnina.

1990 The Migration Process: Capital, Gifts and Offerings among British Pakistanis. New York: Berg.

Westermarck, Edward Alexander.

1926 Ritual and Belief in Morocco. 2 vols. London: Macmillan.

White, Geoffrey M., and Karen Ann Watson-Gegeo.

1990 "Disentangling Discourse." *In* Watson-Gegeo and White, eds., Disentangling. Pp. 3–49.

Woodward, Mark R.

1988 "The Slametan: Textual Knowledge and Ritual Performance in Central Javanese Islam." History of Religions 28:54–89.

1989 Islam in Java: Normative Piety and Mysticism in the Sultanate of Yogyakarta. Tucson: University of Arizona Press.

Ya'cub, H. Abubakar.

1977 Tauhid (sifat duapuluh) [Tauhid (the Twenty Attributes)]. Medan: Islamyah.

1978 Cara sembahyang praktis [Practical Guide to Worship]. Medan, Indonesia: Saiful.

N.d. Takhtim tahlil dan do'a [Recitations, Litanies, and Prayers]. Medan: Damai.

Yakub, Tk. H. Ismail.

1980 "Gambaran pendidikan di Aceh sesudah perang Aceh-Belanda sampai sekarang" [Sketch of Education in Aceh from the End of the Aceh-Dutch War until Now]. *In* Ismail Suny, ed., Bunga rampai tentang Aceh [Selections on Aceh]. Pp. 318–72. Jakarta: Bhratara.

Yunus, H. Mahmud.

1979 Sejarah Pendidikan Islam di Indonesia [The History of Islamic Education in Indonesia]. Jakarta: Mutiara.

Zaret, David.

1992 "Religion, Science, and Printing in the Public Spheres in Seventeenth-Century England." *In* Craig Calhoun, ed., Habermas and the Public Sphere. Pp. 212–35. Cambridge: MIT Press.

el-Zein, Abd el-Hamid.

1977 "Beyond Ideology and Theology: The Search for an Anthropology of Islam." Annual Review of Anthropology 6:227–54.

Zulfa, Drs. Abu.

1988 Yasin tahtim dan tahlil [Yā Sīn, Recitations, and Litanies]. Medan: Su'udiyah.

INDEX

Abbas, Kiyai Sirajuddin, 53, 302, 304n
'Abduh, Muhammad, 20, 23n, 61, 318, 320
'Abdurra'ūf of Singkel, 111, 113–14, 124–27
Aceh, 33n, 58; education in, 43nn.6, 7, 48–
52, 56, 62, 72, 95n; history of, 15–16, 20,
44, 72, 110–14, 124–27, 247, 204n.2; reli-
gion in, 5n.2, 37, 110–14, 255, 268, 275n,
278n.8, 279n, 299, 323–24; religious au-
thorities in, 19, 27, 65, 69–70, 72, 303
Acehnese, 33, 37, 42
Acehnese language, 42, 46–47, 198
Adam, 30, 91–93, 110, 114–16, 237n, 240;
and Eve, 152, 202–19, 224–25
al-Afghānī, Jamāl al-Dīn, 20
Afterbirth, 118–22, 218–23
A'isa ('A'isha), 205, 207–8, 210
Aisyiah (organization), 57
'Ali (son-in-law of Muhammad), 78, 89, 141,
203–4, 207, 265, 292
Ali Jaidun, Tengku, 54–56, 240, 304–6
Ali Salwany, Tengku, 39, 48–55, 60, 69–71,
256–58, 264–67, 301–8, 319
Alimin, 18–21, 25–27, 30, 284
Allāh. See God
Ancestors, 30–31, 127; Datu Béwang, 174–
77, 195–96; Datu Gergung, 132–33; in
healing, 169; Merah Mëgë, 181–86, 195–
96, 234–37; and rice farming, 173–86,
194–200
Anderson, Benedict, 166
Angel of Death. See Izra'il
'Aqīqa. See Child's initiation ritual
al-'Arabī, Ibn, 110–11, 113
Arabic, 95, 327–28; instruction in, 24, 39–69
passim; use in spells and prayer, 77, 85–87.
See also Jawi; Language; Letter symbolism
Arabs, in Indonesia, 61–62
Archangels, 102, 117, 139–42, 155–56, 203.
See also Izra'il; Jibra'il
Arwah. See Spirit
Asad, Talal, 10
Asaluddin, Tengku: education of, 39–42, 44–
47, 57–60; on religion, 71–73, 100, 114–
15, 123, 140n, 167–68; on ritual, 183, 189,
194, 233–34, 269–70, 280, 289; on spells,

80–81, 86–88, 103–6; as worship leader,
291–93, 299, 304, 310–11
Asyin (Muhammad Yassin), 18–21, 25–27,
30, 68, 293–94
Aulië. *See* Saints

Bali, 118n.12, 128n
Bani, Aman, 184, 231, 263, 267, 276, 279,
293
Basmala, 18, 26, 31, 125–27, 135, 147, 238,
276, 285, 306–9, 313
Batin, 106–23
Berkat. *See* Blessing
Bid'a. *See* Innovation
Birth, 145–46, 241
Blessing, 178, 206–8
Bloch, Maurice, 201, 252
Books, religious, 28–29, 40–52, 61–64, 66,
68, 70, 215, 255, 290n.3, 302–4, 327; used
in healing, 134
Bourdieu, Pierre, 9, 11, 318n
Bukit domain, 35–37, 63–64, 287

Cain, 121; and Abel, 209–26
Cairo. *See* Egypt
Calhoun, Craig, 326n.7
Catechism after death (*telkin*), 4, 18–19, 26–
27, 30–31, 54, 60–61, 254–59
Children of pious deeds, 260, 269–70
Child's initiation ritual, 222, 240–50, 278
Ciq domain, 35–36, 63
Circumcision, 126, 246–47
Citrus (*mungkur*), 115n, 152–58, 168–71;
used in divination, 186–90
Clever Chief, 59–60, 183–85
Clothing, 57, 283
Colonial rule, 28, 32–37, 39–45, 57–58, 66–
67, 326–28; imposition of, 15–16; resis-
tance to, 42, 48, 50, 53
Combs-Schilling, Elaine, 7, 273n
Commerce: and religion, 33–37, 63, 65, 70,
323–25; in Takèngën, 32–37, 56
Communication with spirits, 30–32, 38, 82–
84, 90–94, 106–7, 116–23, 145–50, 152–
71, 229–37, Chap. 11 *passim*